The Lost Imperialist

Also by Andrew Gailey

Ireland and the Death of Kindness: The Experience of
Constructive Unionism, 1890–1905

Crying in the Wilderness, Jack Sayers: A Liberal Editor in
Ulster, 1939–69

The Lost Imperialist

*Lord Dufferin, Memory and Mythmaking
in an Age of Celebrity*

ANDREW GAILEY

JOHN MURRAY

First published in Great Britain in 2015 by John Murray (Publishers)
An Hachette UK Company

1

© The Dufferin Foundation and Andrew Gailey 2015

A CIP catalogue record for this title is available from the British Library

ISBN 978-1-444-79243-0
Ebook ISBN 978-1-444-79244-7

Typeset in Bembo MT by Hewer Text UK Ltd, Edinburgh

Printed and bound by Clays Ltd, St Ives plc

John Murray policy is to use papers that are natural, renewable and recyclable
products and made from wood grown in sustainable forests. The logging and
manufacturing processes are expected to conform to the environmental regulations
of the country of origin.

John Murray (Publishers)
338 Euston Road
London NW1 3BH

www.johnmurray.co.uk

To Lindy

and

To Shauna and Emily

Contents

PART III: Kipling's Viceroy: Dufferin in India, 1884–8

PART IV: Making it Up, 1889–1902

The bronze portrait statue of the Marquess of Dufferin and Ava, Governor General and Viceroy of India from 1884 to 1888, originally stood facing the east approach to Fort William on Red Road in Calcutta. The statue, by the eminent sculptor Joseph Edgar Boehm, RA, was completed in 1890 and exhibited at the Summer Exhibition of the Royal Academy before being shipped to the subcontinent . . . Today the statue [is] untraced.

Mary Ann Steggles, *Statues of the Raj* (2000), p.76

Prologue

Indeed my whole life has been a series of surprises.
Dufferin to his daughter, Nelly, 29 January 1894

I T WAS TO be a journey as rich in symbolism as in memory. In the summer of 1890, perhaps one of the most glamorous of the Victorian proconsuls set out from Florence, heading for the Apennine hills and the castle of Barberino di Mugello. Once Viceroy of India, he was a striking figure. With his high forehead and flowing white hair, he still looked every inch the patrician. And yet, if his dress was distinctly English, the waxed moustache, carefully trimmed beard and dark complexion gave him a continental, even Latin air. As such he looked at one with his surroundings as his open carriage meandered in the still heat of the Tuscan countryside. For this was not for him a foreign land. Now, staring up at the half-castle and half-house, with its ruined towers, portcullis, courtyard and little chapel, he could conceive his mother in 1826 'still a girl, looking out of the windows, pacing the garden or walking the steep ascent, so proud and so happy with her baby in her arms'.[1] Sixty-four years later, Frederick Temple Hamilton-Temple-Blackwood, 1st Marquess of Dufferin and Ava had returned to his roots.

Such sentimental pursuits are commonplace. Yet this pilgrimage revealed the very essence of the pilgrim. His obsession with his mother since her death in 1867 simply reflected the intensity of their love when she was alive. To Dufferin, his mother was the overwhelming force guiding, invigorating, inspiring, always protecting him and to whose service he had dedicated his life. Such chivalric devotion pointed to other influences. Behind his admiration for this medieval ruin of a home lay the appeal of Romanticism and the reassurance to be found in the permanence of the past in an age of seemingly incessant upheaval.

The Barberino di Mugello held its secrets too. At the very heart of the idyll lay irresponsibility and disapproval; the irresponsibility of a love match on only £500 a year and the disapproval of his grandparents for his mother's Sheridan descent. Hence Dufferin was to be born in virtual exile and it was no accident that for the rest of his life he was acutely attuned to the demands of propriety and reputation. For one held to be so admirable in so many ways, he could, nevertheless, astound contemporaries with his concern for popularity. They could never understand his anxieties over his place in society and the little humiliations that could lie in wait.

So it was perhaps fitting that the housekeeper at the Barberino di Mugello, resolutely barring all strangers, refused to let him inside.[2]

PART I
The Ascendancy of Helen, 1826–72

You may remember, when I am gone, how much I loved you . . .
But you can repay me a thousand fold for the agony of your
birth . . . by proving that you remember what I have tried to
teach you.   Helen to her son, 21 June 1832

My heart aches for her, [for] nobody will ever love her like me.
                    Dufferin's Diary, 5 February 1856

I

A Conflict of Traditions

THE HOME FREDERICK had been barred from at birth was Ballyleidy near the shores of Belfast Lough. Newly restored and somewhat lost in the surrounding trees, this bleak grey mansion heralded the arrival of a family on the make. The Blackwoods were settlers from Scotland who had fled to Ulster in 1586 after becoming too closely associated with the cause of Mary, Queen of Scots.[1] Nevertheless, by the late eighteenth century, through the profits of agriculture and economic management and the even greater profits of marriage, they had emerged as a prominent force in Co. Down, with large estates both to the west of Strangford Lough and on the Ards peninsula near Ballywalter as well as the family seat at Ballyleidy outside Bangor. By 1800 these produced a rental of £10,000 a year, which was respectable enough in contemporary terms, even if it was dwarfed by the incomes of the two leading families in the county – the Downshires and the Londonderrys.

By comparison with these families, with their English connections and national influence, the Blackwoods were parochial indeed. Nevertheless with control of two Irish parliamentary seats they could begin to aspire to the Irish peerage. And, as fate would have it, in the aftermath of the United Irish rebellion of 1798, there would be no greater opportunity for social advancement. Determined to rule Ireland from Westminster, the British government attempted through extensive bribery to force an Act of Union through the Irish Parliament. Family myth decreed that the head of the Blackwood family, Sir John Blackwood, had died, incorruptible to the last, tying up his boots before setting out to vote against the Union. His death however proved timely, for it enabled his son, James, a Union supporter, to accept a barony on behalf of his mother, the Hamilton heiress, Dorcas Stevenson, whose wealth had transformed the Blackwoods' standing.[2] In spite of such advances the Blackwood tradition remained one of sturdy country squires, worldly clerics and the military professions. Only Sir Henry Blackwood, Nelson's confidant and comrade in arms at Trafalgar, achieved national pre-eminence. Most were perfectly content to indulge in Tory politics and the bucolic pleasures of hunting, shooting and drinking copious bottles of claret.

Such a lifestyle and a wide range of dependants inevitably drained family resources, compelling the heir to the title to seek an advantageous marriage. Sir James Blackwood, 2nd Baron Dufferin, having inherited the title from his mother, had done just that in marrying Anna, the daughter of Baron Oriel; only for the marriage to prove childless, making his brother Hans (1758–1839) heir. He too had married well, but lost his wife's considerable fortune in a speculative venture, building one side of Dublin's prestigious St Stephen's Green. After paying off his debts, he retreated to the outskirts of the city to wait nearly twenty years for his brother's death and his own salvation. Four children came from his first marriage and another seven from his second. Of his three sons, the eldest, Robert, was a dashing officer in 'the 52nd'. Recuperating from his wounds when news reached Ballyleidy of Napoleon's escape from Elba, he finally caught up with his regiment at Waterloo just as the battle commenced. One of the last to arrive, he had been one of the first to die – cut in two by a round shot. Hans's second son died soon after, having been sent abroad to Naples to avoid a love marriage to an impecunious but determined Miss Stannus.

The revival of the family fortunes consequently came to rest on the third son, Price, the future father of the 1st Marquess. Frank, open and kind to a fault, he was a man of action, unburdened by mere cleverness. Largely uneducated, except 'by the navy', he held his principles with the vigour and occasional naivety of a man of honour. Never expecting to inherit, he felt little need to temporise and frequently came to blows with his father, not least over his 'womanising'. This rarely amounted to more than a grand flirtation and many an affair died with the return to sea. After one close shave too many, he was made to sign an assurance never to marry without his father's consent. It was with this in mind that he was eventually recalled in 1825 and sent to his uncle, Lord Dufferin, in Cavendish Square, for the season. With no experience of

London society and little in the way of 'conversation', Price set out to find the 'good, sensible girl with a well-regulated mind, good family and some money' that his family demanded of him. Helen Sheridan was not what they had in mind.

'The Sheridans are much admired but are strange girls, swear and say all sorts of things to make men laugh', declared Lady Cowper to Frederick Lamb. 'I am surprised so sensible a woman as Mrs. Sheridan should let them go on so. I suppose she cannot stop the old blood coming out.' It was precisely such 'cleverness' that made the Blackwoods fear the worst and to them the very public decline of Helen's illustrious grandfather (after a lifetime of elopements, duels and debauchery) was a most fitting end. By contrast, resentment had long festered in the Sheridan family over the lack of recognition shown to Richard Brinsley Sheridan in his last years. The comic genius who at the age of only twenty-eight had conquered the London stage and with his beautiful wife, Elizabeth Linley, had overcome the obstacles of wealth and birth to win entry into the highest circles of Whig society. Thereafter he produced memorable parliamentary performances, the equal of anything heard at Westminster in an age of great orators. And yet he was denied major office. Condemned to the anonymity of perpetual opposition, he drank himself relentlessly towards the grave, until, in the week he died in 1816, the bailiffs were at the door. Not even the magnificence of his funeral in Westminster Abbey could erase such humiliations. No man, after all, was ever made by a wake. Since then the Sheridans had struggled. When in 1817 his son Tom Sheridan died of consumption at the Cape of Good Hope, he left his wife virtually destitute with seven children. To Helen aged nine, the eldest child and the only one with him when he died, the ignominies of the previous years would have a lasting impact. Denied by her sex the opportunity to restore the family name, she was to ensure that any son of hers would never be distracted from this appointed task.[3]

Granted a grace and favour apartment in Hampton Court, Helen's mother could maintain a lifestyle of genteel poverty, proudly display-ing her daughters and declaring that 'all these girls will be beautiful', almost as if their lives depended on it (which of course they did).[4] Of the three Helen's looks were the least classical. Scarcely seventeen when she came out, she was a slim, graceful figure with delicate hands and tiny feet. Her face, with its high forehead and small mouth, was lit by eyes that radiated an enquiring, childlike innocence. Set off against a backdrop of delicate modesty, was a quick-witted gaiety that could be quite sharp, however flirtatious and light-hearted the delivery. It was a combination that many found alluring. But without any money she wasn't a catch. However, to Price Blackwood, flattered at 'passing muster' and rather out of his depth among the smart set of London, she seemed irresistible. The same could hardly be said of him. With his reddish hair already turning to grey, he had a long, protruding jaw with a nose to match. His expression was by nature stern and his eyes burned as if he was in a permanent state of agitation. And all this on very short legs. It is hardly surprising that Helen initially looked elsewhere.

It was her mother who persuaded her to take Blackwood seriously, warning that the 'handsome and agreeable men of the world like a more extensive theatre than their own fireside'. Helen herself recognised the value of Price whose 'only pleasure is in pleasing me'; while her pragmatism reflected a desire for control as much as for property or emotional satisfaction. She may have found his 'fussing over trifles' irritating and was quite startled at the strength of his prejudices. Yet she could not help admiring his 'true heartedness and firmness of spirit'. And hence eventually she accepted his offer of marriage.[5]

On 11 June 1825 Price wrote of his news to his father, who presuming it to be a request for permission to propose, rejected it on the grounds of there being no fortune and rank, considering his son 'bound' to seek both. The fact that her father and grandfather were 'play actors' – a 'wicked profession' – really rankled. Even Hans's second wife, who was well read and had all Sheridan's plays at her fingertips, viewed the fashionable world in which he had made his name as essentially immoral. To her, virtue could only flourish in the countryside and, as for 'genius', to all Blackwoods it was 'a very dangerous possession, leading to the breaking of the whole Decalogue'. Still nothing shocked them more than Price's decision to 'keep his word with Miss S'. After an increasingly acrimonious correspondence, all of his family refused to attend his wedding. Consequently on 4 July 1825, after a service at St George's, Hanover Square, Price and Helen Blackwood left for Italy – all they could afford on the half-pay of an out-of-work naval captain.[6]

★

8

'Its eyes and mouth are like Helen's and its nose (alas!) like Price's', relayed Helen's younger sister, Georgiana (often shortened to 'Georgia' or 'Georgy' by the family), to their brother, Brinsley, then languishing in India on colonial service. 'But it does not signify so much for a boy, as a man may be good looking even with a nose some yards long.' To one destined for grandeur, it was a rather inauspicious entrance. For his mother on the other hand the arrival of Frederick Blackwood was nothing short of traumatic. By 21 June 1826 he was so long overdue that her doctors warned her as she entered labour that it would be impossible to save both mother and child. As they resorted to 'instruments', she begged them to save the child. Gripping the hand of her friend, a Mrs Balfour, she said with extraordinary presence of mind, 'now I shall look into your face and then I shall know whether they kill my baby or no'. Throughout the suffering, she clung to her companion, staring desperately for any flicker of betrayal. When at last it was over and she had given birth to a boy, the doctors were astonished to find that it weighed 15 lbs. Or so reported Georgia, who could be a great stickler for truth but rarely for precision. Nonetheless, it was to be another two weeks before Helen was out of danger and thereafter her health would never be robust.[7] Thus it was that she found herself convalescing seventeen miles outside Florence at the Barberino di Mugello, besotted by her son, nicknamed Ghigo by their Italian maids. Hence too the return of the child over six decades later in search of the origins of a bond that would shape so much of what was to come.[8]

It would be another year before Helen and son could return to England. By then her two sisters were hailed the greatest beauties in London, invited to every ball and courted voraciously.[9] Significantly, when in 1830 Georgia became engaged to Lord Seymour, the heir of the wealthy Duke of Somerset, it was a family triumph that Helen celebrated. '"Poor, dear Frances [Lady] Londonderry" has not yet recovered [from] the shock of hearing that Georgia is to be a Duchess, and moreover, the first duchess in the kingdom, as her husband comes next to the Duke of Norfolk, who has no spouse, so you may conceive her state of mind on the occasion, "poor, dear thing"!' Equally shocked were Seymour's family at whose request the wedding party was kept small, with only the duke supporting his son. Such snubs were not going to stop the Sheridans in full cry and that evening they threw a party for 200. For all her anxiety to attend, 'poor dear Frances' was not invited.[10]

Anna, Lady Dufferin, on the other hand, was. Helen had been in exile too long to want to snub Lady Dufferin. Only the previous winter a reconciliation had been effected, and distinctly fragile it remained. 'Ballyleidy is a very beautiful place . . . though not intended so by nature' was Helen's first impression; that and the fact that they must have 'spent thousands' to create it. But such prattle could not disguise the daunting prospect that confronted her. After all the harsh words, the men caused little difficulty.[11] They were easily captivated by her winning charm and by the sentimental songs she composed, most famously the 'Irish Emigrant', that after dinner would reduce the inebriated to tears.

Made of rather sterner stuff was Anna.[12] A beauty in her youth, now in her late fifties, with a sour, turned down mouth, prominent nose and sharp, vindictive eyes, she looked as she was, 'naturally tyrannical'. Helen's flippant wit irritated her; and, along with the display of frailty, was dismissed as an affectation to win over 'her' menfolk. Worse, Helen's arrival with a young heir only served to emphasise Anna's barrenness. The only congenial spirit in this repressive atmosphere was Lizzie Blackwood [later Ward], Price's half-sister. Although no beauty, she was bright-eyed, vibrant and often laughed, heaving her shoulders in silent, secretive chuckles – Lady Anna having declared laughter to be unladylike. Still at least she laughed and Helen clung to her friendship. 'Everybody here is kind . . . *in the main*,' she reassured her mother during one of her early visits. 'Yet there are a thousand little things that make one feel uncomfortable.' Among these was her hosts' full-blooded Toryism. When the children entered the dining room for dessert, Lord Dufferin used to summon little Frederick onto the polished mahogany table to drink great Tory oaths. Powerless in the face of what she saw as the Blackwoods attempting to take possession of her Sheridan son, Helen became profoundly depressed and talked morosely of 'giving up the point'.[13]

But at least at Ballyleidy they had saved money. With the advent of peace after the Napoleonic Wars, the British navy had suffered substantial cuts leaving the vast majority of captains on half pay. Eight years of virtual unemployment had left Price 'mad to get a ship'. The appointment of Helen's uncle, Sir James Graham, to the Admiralty in 1830 led within a year to Price being given the command of a twenty-eight-gun frigate, HMS *Imogene*, destined to patrol the South Seas and the pirate-infested Indian Ocean. Inevitably excited talk followed of imminent wars and the capture of great 'prizes', three eighths of whose booty went to the successful captain. All this proved hopelessly optimistic. As it was, any additional income was already committed under their marriage agreement (drawn up largely in Helen's interest by Sir James Graham) to an insurance policy on Price's life. The premiums for this soon reduced Price to borrowing from his half-brother William. Reconciliation with his family had at least resulted in Uncle Dufferin paying off most of his debts. However, before departing for the southern hemisphere, Price was obliged to negotiate a £3,000 loan from his uncle to be guaranteed by further insurance policies.

Thus solvency came to depend on the mortality of his relations. In this respect, affairs took a turn for the better the following year when three uncles and another relation died all in the space of one month. 'I hardly ever heard of such a mortality in one family', commiserated Mrs Sheridan in a tone almost of reproach. These included the admiral, Sir Henry Blackwood, who caught typhus while tending his son and daughter (both of whom survived). He died in the mezzanine room at Ballyleidy and such were the fears of infection that they knocked a hole in the wall and lowered his coffin down rather than bring it through the house. In time the hole became a window and remains so to this day. Convinced that these deaths would at last provide financial stability, Price was furious on discovering that his name was not on the deed and that much of the additional funds went to the children of his father's second marriage. As a consequence, all he could provide for his wife to live on was £50 a quarter; his embarrassment compounded by the fact that she had just sold three of her songs for £56. Even so, standing on the quay at Portsmouth to bid farewell as Price left 'swaggering away to the Downs . . . like the *Flying Dutchman*', Helen and young Frederick measured their loss in other terms. For they were not to see him again for another four years.[14]

2

The Triumph of the Sheridans

PONDERING IN 1854 on Reynolds's painting of St Cecilia which
had immortalised the exquisite loveliness of Sheridan's wife,
Elizabeth Linley, the historian Thomas Macaulay declared that she
was the 'beautiful mother of a beautiful race', whose granddaughters
in their turn were 'three of the most beautiful women of my time'.[1]
Hailed in London as 'the three graces', by 1834 their reputation had
spread to Paris where they were feted by all 'from the royal family
downwards'. Balls, concerts and levees were arranged as French society competed to honour 'La Belle Trinité'. 'You never saw such a fuss
as the dear folks made about us', wrote Helen to Lizzie (facing a
desultory Christmas at Ballyleidy). 'We were obliged to give ourselves
up, body and soul, to our mantua makers and milliners!' 'In short', as
Helen once asserted only slightly tongue in cheek, 'the world owns
that we are the best looking family in England and we are pretty well
disposed to agree.'[2]

In the case of Georgia, the attraction was almost wholly visual.
'Anything so splendid I never gazed upon [before] . . . clusters of the
darkest hair, the most brilliant complexion [and] a contour of a face
perfectly ideal,' reported Disraeli. Her sister Caroline seemed to the
painter Benjamin Haydon, 'like a Greek sculpture just breaking into
life'. Vivacious, impulsive, even dangerous, to those who adored her
the appeal was unashamedly sensual; which was why, to Helen's innocent amazement, Caroline was 'admired by men even more than
Georgia'.[3] A sparkling conversationalist, she had that teasing wit that
both beguiled and intimidated. It particularly intimidated those of her
own sex, who had to look on as their gentlemen fluttered round what
their wives held to be irredeemably vulgar. 'Mrs Norton is so nice',
exclaimed Harriet Granville. 'It is a pity that she is not quite nice, for

if she was quite nice, she would be so very nice.' And she was to prove a friend! Such snubs hinted at a change in the air, with the nineteenth century soon to assume the drab mantle of Victorian respectability. But, as on the eve of a storm when the sun shines at its brightest, Caroline continued to enthral society by living defiantly on the frontiers of convention. For the present, as Lady Dover confided to a friend, with the 'great deal that is in bad taste about her . . . one wonders at feeling not more shocked on recollection'.[4]

The spell of the third grace was altogether different. 'Nelly's vanity', observed Caroline, is to have all the room claim: "What a pretty woman!" Mine is that the two or three persons I care about should turn around and cry "Here she comes!"'[5] Not that Helen was without her admirers. 'Georgia's the beauty and Carrie's the wit, and I ought to be the good one, but then I am not,' she quipped to Disraeli, who was immediately entranced declaring her 'very handsome and very Sheridanic'.[6] They met in February 1833 just as Disraeli was finishing the proofs of his novel *Alroy*, an absurd historical romance set in Arabia in which the heroine was the Caliph's highly erotic daughter, Schirene. Helen did not like this character, but when Disraeli protested of her similarity to the heroine, she began to sign her letters 'Schirene'. What followed was a playful correspondence in which Helen acted the submissive lover to Disraeli's despot. The trouble for Disraeli was that it was all too virginal, for Helen was quite happy just to dream. 'Dreams, dreams, dreams,' muttered Disraeli when discovered at the end of his life by a friend staring into the fire, apparently lost in a reverie of Helen Blackwood and what could never have been.[7]

Yet he had a point for it was not for respectability that the Sheridans were renowned. With their good looks, wild affairs and crippling debts, they had entertained and scandalised for three generations. Above all, they were reckless. Here lay their true appeal and the latest generation were not to disappoint. Most spectacularly, in 1835, Helen's brother Brinsley stunned London society by eloping to Gretna Green with Miss Marcia Grant, her father, Sir Colquhoun Grant, in pursuit. She, though no beauty, was much sought after, being of sweet disposition and the heiress to a fortune. That she should cast in her lot with the Sheridans who were penniless and barely respectable infuriated many a titled mother of a spendthrift son. At a ball, given by

Lord Hertford, Helen and Lizzie found 'people in tiers of benches around the room' eagerly awaiting the return of the couple. Their entrance, as they walked up the room was a triumph. To Helen, with Brin displaying all the insouciant modesty of the victor, it could have been the reincarnation of her grandfather.

Others also made the same connection. At a dinner party replete with Richmonds, Stanleys and Sutherlands, Creevey found 'a flock of admirers surround[ing] the three neat'uns – the sisters Norton, Blackwood and Seymour. I am afraid it is too good fun to be true that old Colquhoun Grant is to prosecute these sisters for a conspiracy in robbing him of his daughter for the benefit of their brother, but they say that it is true. I am glad the young gentleman's name is really *Brinsley*; it keeps alive the talent of the family name.'[8] The frivolity itself was kept alive by Uncle James, Lord Dufferin, who failing to see the humour in the accusation, felt honour bound in the absence of his nephew to defend Helen's name and, despite being nearly eighty, called Grant out. Sense prevailed and indeed, in time, so enamoured did Grant become of his son-in-law that he eventually left him all his estates.[9] As for the young couple, they lived a respectable, God-fearing life of conjugal bliss. For Creevey's indulgent fondness for the Sheridans and their stylish notoriety (licensed as it was by irresistible charm) had already too much the ring of nostalgia. Within a year, the Sheridans were to discover the perils that came with a reputation of living dangerously.

By now Caroline's marriage at the age of nineteen to the barrister and brother of Lord Grantley, George Norton, was rapidly disintegrating. Almost from the start it had been a disastrous alliance. Virtually monosyllabic and at ease only with his drinking companions, Norton soon became violent; and increasingly so as his parliamentary career disintegrated and her literary star rose sufficiently to support them both. When she began her affair with the prime minister, Lord Melbourne, relations had become such that Norton was only too willing to acquiesce, particularly as she persuaded Melbourne to appoint him to a £1,000 a year position in the magistrates' court.[10]

However, in 1836, whether out of pique or at the urgings of his Tory confrères, Norton sued for divorce and named Melbourne, thus provoking a public scandal with the press attending the trial in droves. Included among their number was Charles Dickens reporting for the *Morning Chronicle* and who would satirise the event when writing *The Pickwick Papers*. Sensationally, amid scenes of pure farce, Norton's case collapsed on the first day for want of evidence. Yet the fact remained that many, including her mother, were willing to believe almost anything of Caroline. While in all probability the affair was never consummated physically, Caroline so flaunted their alliance that even the charitable were forced to take notice. It was as if the more respectable the age grew the more she savoured the outrageous or courted catastrophe. Yet when it came she was so distraught that Helen could only feel sorry for her. The 'calumnies' may be 'cruel', she admitted in an effort to rally Caroline's spirits, 'but what a million times worse it would be if they were true'.[11] Gossip though could be borne but not public defamation. Caroline lost everything in the separation that followed: her children, all her property including her income from her writing and above all her reputation. It says something for her that she survived, that she won her way back into society while helping to stir opinion into changing the iniquitous laws of which she had been a victim.[12]

For the rest of her family there was renewed humiliation as in every court case over custody the affair was 'continually raked up before the public'.[13] Frederick was ten years old at the time of the first trial and it would prove formative. In later life he never came to terms with the injustice meted out to his aunt and the acute embarrassment that her outrageous behaviour aroused.[14] In the light of the latter, the more he became the model of Victorian rectitude the more preoccupied he was with his Sheridan inheritance, in which genius lay alongside more sybaritic traits of character. Indeed for most of his life he was forever on guard against the 'flaws of the blood'.

So too was Helen and at the first signs of it in her son she sent him off to the firm discipline of the schoolmaster at Hampton, a Mr Walton. Initially it had not been her intention to send him to school at all. With his mother always quick to assert that her son's educational and 'manly development' were not 'in the least damaged by the society of us women', Frederick was brought up in a world peopled almost entirely by the opposite sex. Not surprisingly as the only child he was much adored and a little spoilt. At times this cosseting went too far. Memories of his first nurse, Foley, 'a horrible Irish woman . . .

who always took me to bed with her which I hated', could still even in his sixties stir his anger. Her successor, a Miss Plume, proved a kindly figure supported by 'Fair Marg'ret'. Needless to say Margaret was anything but and to young Frederick was memorable mainly for her curious habit each morning of slipping 'her nightshift down to her waist' in order to 'go through the extension motions at the foot of my bed'.[15] Nevertheless, cocooned in this essentially female world, it is not hard to see how Frederick came to prefer female company and to develop a femininity of manner that would later disconcert heartier contemporaries.

Soon he was displaying a 'most amusing rattle of conversation, talking incessantly and in a manner far superior to his age'. Consequently he was always treated as an adult (and chastised when he proved a child). The little vanities that ensued were indulged because they were entertaining but also because they hinted at 'Sheridanic' qualities from which his family expected so much.[16] Restraining such precociousness fell to Helen. Taking charge of his education, she chided him on his reading and spelling and taught him his catechism. For discipline, however, she resorted to emotional blackmail, exploiting his vulnerability as an only child by withdrawing her love.[17] If he unwittingly erred from her path, the tone would become icy, distant, parental, pulling her son up short like a dog on a lead (and so contributing to his insecurity in adult life over his popularity). Nor did she lose any opportunity to inculcate him with an awareness of guilt and of a God who judgeth the earth. More positively she also gave him a goal – a sense of his own destiny in which he would inherit the mantle of his great-grandfather and achieve the greatness denied to him. All these themes were brought together in a letter to cover for her absence on his sixth birthday; a letter extraordinary for its nakedly possessive tone and written so,

> that you may remember, when I am gone, how much I loved you . . .
> But you can repay me a thousand fold for the agony of your birth . . .
> by proving that you remember what I have tried to teach you and by
> being a good and just and honourable man, not only for my sake and
> also for the sake of your character in men's eyes but for the love of Jesus
> who died for you and who left you his example to follow. I feel my

dear child that . . . I am still too anxious about things of less importance, that I wish too ardently that you should be clever and celebrated
in the world, forgetting that it is better to be unknown to men and
beloved of God. You will hardly believe or understand now what I am
saying to you but hereafter, at the end of your life, you will wish you
had been born a fool, rather than have to answer to your Creator for
the sin of wasting your talents. Keep this letter, my dear child, and read
it every birthday and think when you read it that it is your mother
speaking to you, so whether I am dead or distant from you, my love
will still be with you.[18]

Plainly her son's bounden duty would lie as much to his mother as to
his Maker.

Mr Walton quickly revealed himself to be a firm disciple of 'energetic flogging . . . and copious dosing with brimstone and treacle'.
Under his care Frederick hunted, fished, was left virtually blinded in
his left eye by a 'cork bung' while playing hockey, and almost drowned
in the Thames. As to what he learned there is no record and possibly
little to record. Nevertheless, in later life Frederick's verdict was
generous, fondly remembering Walton as a 'good school master' who
was 'both severe and passionate'. Passionate was not how Helen's
letters to her son could be described. These were crisp and business-
like, enclosing Bibles and strictures on the need for moral courage
against ridicule in his preparation for 'greatness'. 'You were sadly
cheated at Easter' was all she managed after leaving him at school over
the holidays. In her absence it was perhaps typical that her son should
overcome any loneliness by making friends with the only girl in the
school – Walton's youngest daughter whose photograph hung in
Frederick's study for the rest of his life.[19]

Such respites were not to be found at his next school. Eton in the
1830s was no place for the sensitive and retiring. Discipline was lax and
the school from time to time verged on the rebellious. For all the
tradition of Keate (who was infamous for once beating the whole
school in one day), Frederick was only flogged twice in his whole
career, both of them 'child's play compared to Hampton'. He was
placed in Corner House with, as his tutor, the Rev. W. G. Cookesley.
Cookesley was scholarly and his house quite sought after, but he

proved a master 'whom his pupils liked much more than they respected . . . [one] who could make himself popular but could not make them work'.[20] Or stop them bullying. 'Have you been under the necessity of fighting yet', asked his mother rather tremulously, or '"milling" as you rather elegantly term it.' Amidst the mayhem Frederick did win a 'prize' for mathematics and a reputation for writing clever essays. Helen rejoiced at these minor triumphs, but, fearful lest her son become idle, she never slackened the pressure: 'always bear in mind that you are half a Sheridan and that I expect you to do honour to that parentage'. Within three years he was able to assume the privilege of wing collars (or 'stick ups'). Frederick 'greatly grown', reported Price on visiting his son in 1841: 'instead of stooping as he used, he now holds himself quite erect and looks uncommonly well in his stick ups'.[21] Notably Frederick used his influence to protect the vulnerable Lord Robert Cecil, frail and too sensitive for his own good. Cecil was later, on his promotion to College, to be scarred for life by his experiences. But, as the 3rd Marquess of Salisbury and Tory prime minister, he would never forget his gratitude to the future Whig peer.[22]

Eton provided other connections that were to prove useful in time, including the future Lord Kimberley. 'One of the cleverest boys at Eton', Cookesley had called him when Frederick met them both at breakfast on his first day. Cookesley rather cultivated the able including William Johnston, the eminent scholar and teacher. Frederick was included in this circle and with Johnston would walk either side of their tutor trying to impress – Frederick earning the sobriquet of 'the Orator' for his pains.[23] This may not, it has to be said, have been wholly flattering, for from early on it was clear that his standing would be based as much on his charm as his academic achievements, along with a useful reputation for throwing the best parties.

By now Price had inherited from his father. Hans, having waited decades to succeed his brother, only held the title of Lord Dufferin for three years. But this was long enough for him to make generous provisions for the five surviving children from his second marriage, and £700 a year for Price's half-brother, William Blackwood. Such arrangements saddled Price with crippling charges and only left him feeling 'neglected and ill-used . . . fancy[ing] that his father almost disliked him'. Helen 'quelled' her family in uproar over his inability once again to provide her with the long expected fortune. But her fierce assertion to Lizzie in 1838 of 'the necessity of vindicating a wife's claim to a proper degree of authority in her own house' hints at the difficulties of readjusting to her husband's return from sea.[24]

Such tensions were rarely expressed save in the reappearance of 'a nervous irritability' and frequent pain. This left her a willing victim to leeches and a whole succession of quack doctors, one of whom – a Dr Locock – recommended 'a nice dose of arsenic, the only poison I had not tried'. Her preferred poison was opium. This in the form of laudanum drops was very freely available and was used quite liberally as a painkiller and a relaxant. While few took it purely for pleasure, many of the sickly took great pleasure in their addiction. Helen always denied to Price that she was addicted to 'your enemy, opium' but she was never short of an excuse for a 'dose' and this soon became a point of gruff contention.[25] Others followed and such frictions raised the issue of incompatibility. Helen's mother had never disguised her 'contempt' for the 'priggish, provincial Blackwoods', while her daughter felt little in common with Price's 'mahogany coloured brother fishes' at Portsmouth. Not surprisingly, she viewed her impending incarceration in Ireland with some dread.[26]

It is easy to make too much of this. To Helen Price remained unfailingly devoted and there was no danger of a rift as between Caroline and Norton. Nor did he lack a rapport with his son. In fact Price and Frederick shared much more in common than the Sheridans allowed, including an imagination fired by the great events of history and the novels of Walter Scott. 'You must be prepared to draw much upon your poetic fancy when you come', he wrote to his son on the eve of a visit to Kenilworth Castle where, despite the ravages of Cromwell's cannon, 'enough is left to show the magnificence of Leicester and the generosity of Good Queen Bess'.[27] Their historical interests figured too on a trip to the Rhine in 1839. At Waterloo Frederick surveyed the plain, 'immense, gently undulating, as if it was just intended for a field of battles' and left with an armful of swords and bullets as souvenirs. In Aix-la-Chapelle, he would sit on Charlemagne's throne, while at Cologne he was transfixed by the sight of the skulls in the tomb of the 'three kings of Cologne'. The next day he celebrated his thirteenth birthday. 'But neither papa nor mamma found it out till the evening when I told them.'[28]

The following summer the holidays were spent at Ballyleidy, though Helen, pleading illness, didn't go.[29] Despite this, father and son had an idyllic time, hunting, fishing and travelling around the estate. 'Frederick is the most perfect companion to me', wrote Price to his wife, who now complained that she never saw her son. In contrast, since returning from sea Price had regularly visited Frederick at Eton where his son would row him on the Thames – once nearly drowning them both at a lock. Having viewed his father as a rather alarming figure, Frederick now recognised a warmer, more affection-ate parent, one with whom he could laugh as well as admire.[30]

Also to admire at Ballyleidy was Harry Piper. An African with a 'magnificent' physique and the 'manners of a prince', he had served as warrant officer under Sir Henry Blackwood and had followed him back to Co. Down, staying on after his master's death. While building a flat-bottomed boat for the river, he would regale the young heir with his ancestor's heroic victory in the frigate *Penelope* over the eighty-gun *Guillaume Tell* in the aftermath of the Battle of Aboukir Bay (1798).[31] Nelson himself had been effusive, writing famously: 'is there a sympathy which ties men together in the bonds of friendship without having a personal knowledge of each other? If so, I was your friend and acquaintance before I saw you.' On the morning of Trafalgar, Sir Henry had witnessed Nelson's will amid much bravado of twenty prizes by nightfall. 'God bless you, Blackwood', said the admiral as he left to take up his station, 'I shall never speak to you again.'[32] These were the titans and the tales that so thrilled the young Frederick. For all his mother's incantation of the Sheridan myth, it was the Blackwoods who provided his early heroes. And it was this heroic tradition that Price maintained when he led the attack in September 1834 against the Chinese Bogue Forts, so forcing a passage through the Bocca Tigris. While his son was not to join the navy, he became renowned as a sailor and the naming of his boats after the vessels of his forebears was testament to their influence.

By the autumn Price and Helen were in Italy in pursuit of yet another cure for her illness. When Irish business finally compelled him to Ballyleidy, her progress was sufficiently encouraging for her to remain behind. Given the frustrations of an Irish estate, it was only natural that Price should look also to a career in politics, particularly with the value placed on parliamentary achievement by his wife and her family. Unfortunately his efforts were dogged by failure. In 1837 he had lost badly a by-election at Plymouth. Three years later negotiations to secure his election to the Irish representative peerage in the House of Lords broke down. Each rebuff only served to diminish his stock still further.

On arriving back in England in June 1841, Price went the next day to the Carlton Club and offered to stand in the general election. His decision was undoubtedly impulsive. Fired up by the excitement of the election and talk of a Conservative victory, and by assurances, all too easily given, of Wellington's future support of his claim to the representative peerage, Price put his name forward for the naval constituency of Chatham. After a 'sharp two day canvas' and a show of hands he felt quite confident. Yet this was a government borough. What was humiliating was not just his defeat but that on polling day Price was not only out-bribed but also essentially out-voted. In retrospect, it had been a foolhardy escapade which only looked more so with each victory in the Conservatives' spectacular triumph. With it went any further hope of Parliament upon which the Sheridans set such store. Facing now a dull lifetime of retreat at Ballyleidy – a prospect that held little attraction for his wife – he wrote to Helen on 4 July, some days after his defeat, bravely making much of his determination 'not to run my purse'; as if he could have done so. He had not heard from her for a month but he would have known the depth of her disappointment on hearing of his news.[33] The post to Castellammare, near Naples, took on average seventeen days from London. On 21 July, Helen was sitting after lunch painting when a letter arrived for her. Standing to study it, she had been reading for a few moments when she suddenly screamed and fell to the floor. After being revived by smelling salts, she came round and, though obviously still distraught, she sought to reassure her assembled friends that they must not think she had received any bad news. About the same time in Eton, her son, his cases packed, was idling away the last day of the half. Watching the willows waving in the wind as he stood on a little bridge overlooking Barnes Pool, he turned to a friend and said,

'It is very odd, I have every reason to be happy; tonight we have the Boats, and tomorrow the holidays begin, and I am going over to my father in Ireland, and yet I feel quite wretched!' Unknown to mother and son, earlier that morning, as the steam packet SS *Reindeer* docked in Belfast harbour after sailing overnight from Liverpool, Price had been found dead in his cabin.[34]

His death certificate recorded an accidental overdose of morphine, which 'appeared' to have been administered by the ship's steward. In time a picture emerged of an elaborate course of events with Price arriving agitated by the effects of 'fever' and sending the unfortunate steward out to a chemist on the quay for a sleeping draught. As this was being concocted, the ship's bell rang and in the rush the steward was handed the lethal dose. No one, however, seems to have been taken to task for this. It was Frederick's official biographer who first conjectured on the importance of Price being 'worried and greatly fatigued' by the Chatham election. This point had been emphasised by Frederick himself writing in the 1890s when he described how Price had left straight after the Chatham result no doubt 'upset by the excitement of the election'. Exhausted, his failure to check the dose was only too understandable.[35] Except that he had left for Liverpool nearly three weeks after his defeat. As for his 'fever', this he had suffered in India in 1832. Although it could reoccur from time to time, he had since then, as his son admitted, become 'accustomed' to taking his morphine pills 'when feeling out of sorts'. In his earnestness to prove that it was not suicide Frederick in effect acknowledged that it might have been. None of which escapes the realm of conjecture. What is certain is that at one o'clock in the morning of 28 July 1841, Frederick, two of his uncles, two agents, an old butler and a groom set out in the pitch-black to ride to Killyleagh. There at 6 a.m. Price, 4th Baron Dufferin, was buried with only seven in attendance.

Almost immediately the new Lord Dufferin, aged only fifteen, set out for Castellammare and his mother. The loss of her husband at last left Helen free to shape the destiny of their child. Showing quiet purpose, she made sure that his horizons would be Whiggish, English, literary and wealthy. He would become a Sheridan. So successful was she in this that in time Frederick's father would barely survive in his memory.

3

The Birth of 'Authentic' Dufferin

ETURNING EVENTUALLY TO Eton, the young Lord Dufferin
soon became insufferably grand. Dressed in a colourful
swallow-tailed coat, high collar and silk top hat, he cultivated a
foppish Regency air, replete with 'dogskin gloves', haircuts at Truefitts
and mildly risqué humour ('a chair please, in whose arms I have
thought of spending the night'). It was all too much for his mother.
As Tory Eton celebrated the anniversary of Charles II's restoration,
she organised her brother to take him to the Royal Apartments to see
a portrait of his illustrious Whig ancestor, R. B. Sheridan. Then in
April of the following year when Dufferin suffered a bout of illness,
she seized her chance and withdrew him from the school.

Helen now hired a private tutor to inject a little seriousness and
educate him for his future responsibilities. Mr Cartmell was 'a short,
ugly' don from Cambridge whose lessons Dufferin found intermin-
ably 'dull' and initially led only to a mastery of the art of 'look[ing]
very industrious, maps, books, manuscripts scattered in every direction'. Other than the reading of Maria Edgeworth's *Castle Rackrent*,
to serve, no doubt, as a warning of the moral ruin brought about
through profligacy on a great estate and a family name (a lesson that
would be wholly ignored), the focus was on preparation for Oxford.
Somewhat unusually Helen viewed this as an essentially intellectual
training, necessary for any scholar-statesman. With this in mind,
attention was paid to the Classics and especially to History and the
study of great men and heroic events, shifting, as Dufferin became
more engrossed, from the feats of Horatio (via Hume's *England* and
Macaulay's *Essays*) to the controversies of the English Civil War – still
the touchstone of dinner-table politics.

Yet his true historical mentor, as he was for many of Dufferin's generation, was Sir Walter Scott. His vivid descriptions of violent battles and blood feuds, often set against the towering backdrop of the Highlands or within the walls of ruined castles complete with moat and drawbridge, fired Dufferin's youthful imagination. So too did the Eglinton Tournament of 1839 at which high society, inspired by Scott, indulged itself in a medieval re-enactment with his aunt Georgia heralded as the Queen of the Tournament. Scott's influence was stamped on beliefs Dufferin would hold for the rest of his life on matters as diverse as the role of the gentleman, the nature of women, even his artistic and architectural preferences. 'I love Sir Walter Scott', he was to write in his seventies, 'with all my heart; and my mother excepted, I think he has done more to form my character than any other influence; for he is the soul of purity, chivalry, respect for women and healthy religious feeling.'[1]

Exactly what constituted a 'healthy, religious feeling' depended entirely on the believer. Helen, for all her Sheridanic ancestry, had been impressed, as were so many, by the spread of evangelical ideas, which in the wake of the revolutionary wars and the rise of Dissent had led many, through Wilberforce and the Clapham Sect, to adopt a set of values to counter the inertia of the Established faith. These included the primacy of duty and sober living; an active faith – 'vital Christianity' – in which religious morality underpinned one's daily work; and, above all, a seriousness which insisted on the need to account for one's time on earth in preparation for the Day of Judgement. Nevertheless Helen's faith remained essentially Broad Church. By contrast Dufferin's uncle and guardian, Sir James Graham, made no secret of his belief in the arbitrary authority of a stern God, who occasionally displayed His Providence in the world.[2]

For all their differences these were creeds that encouraged intro-spection and bred anxiety. And Dufferin, 'separated [from 'the world'] since I left Eton', would have plenty of time for both. Soon he was reading Arnold's *Sermons*, biographies of Wilberforce and Ignatius Loyola and spiritual guides such as Bishop Taylor's *Holy Living* and its sequel *Holy Dying*. By the end of the year he had embarked on a trawl through the Gospels to collect material for a biography of Christ. In this, he was encouraged by his mother who saw such a scheme primarily as a discipline, training him to read the Bible attentively: 'the only book that can never lose its interest till the latest hour of your life'. But enthusiasm unchecked quickly gave way to obsession and a preoccupation with guilt. Soon he found himself forever apologising to her for 'being so sulky' and owned up to a 'great dread of being bearish and being hated by everyone'. By now he was finding that 'the least thing makes me cry. Pleasure, pain, excitement, an angry word, a start and sometimes nothing at all.' Pleading that the temptations and noise of London prevented him from praying earnestly, he fled to Ireland. There with little to distract him he hounded himself relentlessly: physically with Dinneford's horsehair strap, spiritually by a rigorous daily self-examination of his soul; both serving only to convince him of his imminent damnation. Complaints of 'melancholic humours' foretold of what was actually imminent and by the autumn Dufferin was in the throes of a nervous breakdown.[3]

Looking back two years later on the crisis of autumn 1844, Dufferin obliquely touched on its fundamental cause. After describing it as 'a dreadfully black scene to look back upon', he confided to his mother that 'if it had not been the cause of so much torment to you, there is nothing for which I am more grateful than that healthful sickness of mine'. At first glance this seems extraordinary. Until one remembers that his parting plea to his mother on leaving London for Ireland was that she should not see it as rejection. Since as he went on to state that there was no point in staying in London as he only saw her for at most twenty minutes in the day, clearly it was he who had felt rejected.[4]

Such sentiments were perhaps the product of his mother's unexpected attachment to a man barely three years older than her son, the Earl of Gifford, who was the heir of the Marquess of Tweeddale. Gifford was learned, a young man more of letters than the sword, and for that had been despised by his brute of a father. Never sent to school and starved of friendship, over the years he had withdrawn into a morbid, diffident shell, when Helen first met him at Castellammare. His plight undoubtedly aroused her maternal instincts. But more than this, she admired his scholarly intelligence, shared his interests in music and literature and appreciated his gentleness and sensitivity. Indeed his company offered her all that her husband's never could and her son was still too young to comprehend. Disguising her 'interest' in Gifford as that of a mother or even a 'granny', she was by December 1841 playing the role of the aggrieved lover, 'vexed' over Gifford's absence. Under her protective wing he was transformed, growing in confidence and with it increasingly devoted to Helen. That she talked the language of Romance simply reflected the novels she read and a courtly ritual that required nothing of her but that she remain chaste. But the fact that their friendship did not wither over time suggested a deeper affection. By 1843 in her letters to her confidantes she was referring to 'Giff', partly in jest, as 'the object of my guilty passion'.[5]

As a child Dufferin had revelled in his mother's adoration and the 'hourly proofs of his affection' for her it required. His father's death had only intensified this, leaving him both more dependent on her and at the same time keen to take over the role as her 'protector' (with all its possessive overtones). Instead he had a competitor. The pursuit of his mother's favour now only demonstrated to him his unfitness for the task. His enthusiasm for shooting and fishing with his Blackwood cousins and his driving the tandem 'to Jericho and back' no longer seemed to impress. Instead it was to Giff that Helen wrote (on Dufferin's seventeenth birthday) in praise of his wisdom and steadiness in giving up 'these years of your life to your books'. Her letters to her son, however, were sharply critical of his 'pretty, flattering speeches' for lacking any 'openness of heart'.[6] In the face of his mother's expectations Dufferin felt compelled to seek the seriousness that she so admired in others. But without even his tutor Cartmell's prejudices as his guide, he drifted over the abyss.

If his breakdown took Helen by surprise, her response was swift enough as she braved the Irish Sea for Ballyleidy.[7] Over the next three months she nursed him back to health, reading and talking to him as she had to Giff at Castellammare, 'her very laughter a caress'. Not for the last time would sickness enable Dufferin to reclaim her and hence this time was 'heartfelt' in his memory. But it also meant that his adolescence never quite developed the emotional independence of adulthood. From this moment one can begin to date a style of intimacy that was to shape profoundly his personality and (to his contemporaries) went beyond the normal bonds of mother and son. In an age when parental relations with their children were frequently detached, formal and overly preoccupied with discipline, the Dufferins' relationship came to be viewed as peculiarly affectionate. 'You see, my mother and I were young together in the reign of George IV. We shared our youth', was how Dufferin later explained it to an envious acquaintance. And it had been this sense of shared youth that had echoed at the Barberino di Mugello where he had envisaged himself in her arms, 'she being herself almost a child'.[8]

What made them more than friends was 'the passionate ecstasy of [her] affection', expressed in a manner not only protective but also playful, teasing, even openly flirtatious. It was this blurring of the boundaries, of the child being treated as an intimate and contemporary and in private almost as a lover, that really established Dufferin's emotional reliance on his mother. 'I am not going to be married dear,' she in turn wrote to a friend. 'I have not the slightest intention of marrying again. Ghigo is husband enough for me.'[9]

In early January 1845, Oxford was cold and bleak when Dufferin, escorted by Sir James Graham (now Home Secretary in Peel's government), drew up outside the Mitre. Yet his first night in Christ Church found him 'desperately sick from sheer excitement' and not even the discovery that his rooms 'instead of having medieval windows were pure George III' could dampen his joy.[10] What did rather was the company. One night in particular, when conversation ran beyond sexual innuendo to 'the deriding of the Lord's Supper', a very raw nerve was exposed. 'Never argue on religious subjects,' warned his mother. 'A true heart is but a bad match for a mocking tongue.'[11] Taking her advice, Dufferin was soon to be seen in the corner of the room with his latest purchase, two volumes of Froissart's *Chronicles*, while his contemporaries spent the night gambling for huge sums. That such pretentious display did not land Dufferin in the fountain in Tom Quad can only have been due to the fact that eight of the company were sent down before the term was out.

Soon he found his own society; but not among the charmed, privileged circle of the tufts – the sons of nobility with their servants, horses and high table – many of whom were rarely expected to open a book. Nor did he strike up a rapport with those of his status who were scholarly or destined like Fortescue (later Lord Carlingford), Wodehouse (Lord Kimberley), and Baring (the future Lord Northbrook) for high political office.[12] In fact he despised the college privileges that came his way as a peer – 'the unjust and misplaced respect that is paid to rank in this place'. Instead he settled among the undergraduates from the lesser nobility and professional classes, emerging with a loyal group of friends, none hugely talented and all bound invariably by religion. Prime among these were Francis Hepburn, who was destined for a Sussex parish; and George Boyle, the unprepossessing younger brother of the Earl of Glasgow. 'Very Scotch looking and speaks with a horrible accent, his looks are very boobyish', was Dufferin's first impression. Yet, while others sniggered at this uncouth arrival, Dufferin was quick to appreciate beneath the awkwardness his integrity and breadth of scholarship. All in all, this was a circle Dufferin could move in with confidence, safe in the gratitude with which his friendship was received.[13]

Barely a month after his arrival Dufferin found himself outside the Sheldonian trying to gain admittance to one of Oxford's great set pieces, 'the degradation of Mr. Ward'. W. G. Ward faced this fate on account of his pamphlet *The Ideal of a Christian Church*, which had sensationally declared that the Thirty-Nine Articles were compatible with Roman Catholicism. Ward's pamphlet had been the culmination of a series of such tracts, published over the previous decade by, among others, Newman, Keble and Pusey – all leading Anglo-Catholic, Oxford dons.[14] 'I had no idea until I came to Oxford', Dufferin reported to an old schoolfriend, 'how far Tractarian principles had spread.'[15] One of the leading lights of the movement was a canon of Christ Church, Dr Edward Bouverie Pusey. A High Churchman keen to revitalise the Catholic and apostolic tradition in Anglicanism, his chosen pursuit of a life of ascetic saintliness through fasting and meditation drew on the austere example of the early saints. So it was perhaps predictable that Dufferin should be 'deeply affected by Puseyism'.[16] However, by far the greatest influence on him came from his friends, especially Boyle.

Boyle had arrived in Oxford already in thrall to High Anglicanism. Soon Dufferin was riding out with him to take communion at

Littlemore, Newman's contemplative community. In the pretty chapel with its raised chancel and stone altar – giving a fresh prominence to the sacraments – together with its choir, elaborate altar cloth, stained-glass windows and abundant flowers, was an openness to beauty in worship not seen in many a Protestant church since the Reformation.[17] Here Dufferin could find the haven that he had longed for during his tortuous obsession with his own sinfulness. It was to be a brief respite.

On 12 October 1845, not long after their return for the new term, Boyle and Dufferin set off for Littlemore. To their surprise they discovered the chapel closed. At dinner with the Antrims the next night Dufferin heard of 'Mr. Newman's secession to the Church of Rome' five days previously. 'This will make a great noise all over England and indeed Europe', he confided to his mother; 'Dr. Pusey is horrified.' So too was Dufferin who found himself 'so unsettled' at the news. And no wonder, for converts to Rome in Victorian England risked becoming social outcasts. Inexorably he sought resolution again in meditation on the works of 'sound divines' and encouraged by Boyle, he took up fasting. On one occasion after a heavy frost he spent two freezing hours in his tutor's garden declaiming the Bible. All of which foretold the return of 'my old melancholy'.[18]

This time Helen saw the warning signs. Persuading her son to abandon self-examination and place greater faith instead in the eating of a hearty breakfast, she summoned the level-headed Bishop of Ely to guide Dufferin back into the fold.[19] She then provided him with some feverish excitement of her own in the form of Christmas in Paris. There while his mother 'flirted immensely – principally [with] octogenarians',[20] her son danced with Louise Nugent at Foucher's Rooms, dined on Christmas Day at the embassy, attended the opening of the Chamber of Deputies and visited again the Louvre – being 'mobbed' in the Tuileries for his pains. At the Rothschilds' ball, he saw the historian and former foreign minister Adolphe Thiers and later was presented to King Louis-Philippe. 'Fils de Lady Dufferin?' asked the Queen to which Dufferin answered with a low bow: 'Oh, il a les traits de sa mère.' Helen was delighted and left the embryonic courtier to the embassy ball, where he danced until five in the morning, his night of triumph being only slightly marred by his being 'shoved through a glass door'.[21] For all Boyle's letters and Mme Sainte Aulaire's desire to talk 'a little religion', Dufferin was now admitting privately that 'nothing gives me greater pleasure than conversation and society'. Having made him promise not to study theology any more, Helen let him return to Oxford until he came of age, even offering to send him French novels to keep him distracted.[22]

Not that he needed much distraction. Dining at his Aunt Caroline's, Thackeray had asked him 'if I was going over to Rome'. A 'very pretty Miss Hogg' had been just as blunt before asking Dufferin to her ball. It did not require the antennae to be acutely tuned to pick up these signals. More significant was his emerging perception of God. 'Truly no one has ever been so blessed as I am', he recorded in his journal in July 1846; and 'All crowned and enlightened by the sense of God being my merciful father, Jesus my Redeemer and my Shepherd, the Holy Ghost my comforter and guide.' With the disappearance of the Tyrannical Judge went also his insidious self-criticism. Indeed by December he was 'almost disposed to worship my creation'.[23]

It is striking how easily he was distracted from these debates. He would be the first to admit to lacking intellectual stamina. 'Ever since I came up to Oxford my mind has not been able to stretch his legs or stand upright beneath the tons of compressed learning thrown down at it,' he once protested to his mother. 'I am positively out of breath.' Undoubtedly (and only maybe as a result), he was 'very unpersevering'. Just as enervating was the weight of maternal expectation: 'you know I judge you severely as I love you greatly', she once declared. In response he assured her he was 'continually' making plans for displays of 'future affection' and that he was determined 'to become good and great *for your sake*'. But with little faith in future success as he pleaded that 'the present is very different from your dreams'.[24]

'I wish yet more', given 'the great end you have in view', she would still write. 'I wish you to be a good and great man, a philosopher and a Christian.'[25] What was different was that Dufferin could engage with this now, never missing an opportunity to tease her in turn about her 'fogeys' in Paris. Hearing reports that Helen had been seen in London with Landseer, Dufferin pounced joyously: 'Mother, mother, so marked! Anything but an artist!' She too gave as good as she got: 'I was told at the Embassy that you were going to be married'

(after Dufferin had danced twice with a Miss Lambton at a ball). 'Am
I asked to the wedding?'[26]

Liberated from religious anxiety, Dufferin was free to immerse
himself at Oxford in what Tennyson dubbed 'the thoughts that shake
mankind'. In particular, he shared the excitement in the opportunities science offered the age – from youthful chemistry experiments
that nearly blinded his aunt and an attempt at mesmerism that left a
maid trapped in hysterics for a week, to a mature understanding of
engineering and the application of steam power especially in ships.
Like many contemporaries, he too would be fascinated by the dis-
coveries of geology without being disturbed by the evolutionary
implications. But for all the thrill of the new, there was no denying
that such inventions and ideas threatened the settled order of things.
It was Tennyson's genius to capture the angst this aroused and to
evoke an overriding humanity in an apparently reductionist industrial
world. 'I never cared for Byron,' Dufferin remarked fifty years later;
'but the moment I opened a volume of Tennyson as a young man at
Oxford, I felt he was my poet.'[27] In the face of encircling doubt, he
created a redoubt for the soul. For all Dufferin's declared allegiance to
Scott, it was Tennyson, with his *In Memoriam, Idylls of the King* and
'Maud', who would shape his belief in a humane God, in the values
of dedication, faithful service and nobility of spirit (not least in his
relationship with women), all within a moral vision still rooted in the
'certainties' of the past.[28]

'Everybody is astonished', he declared to his mother, 'at the luxury
and taste which prevails in my room and really I am myself beginning
to tremble at it . . . Granny would be quite aghast.' So presumably was
Landseer when he was reminded of a casual promise to paint the
undergraduate's rooms.[29] Such display enhanced his reputation as a
party host. Even at the height of his depression he would rise from his
sickbed to give a 'large wine' in the evening. Despite the much-
vaunted teetotalism that was to come in later life, in his student days
Dufferin could drink with the best; and revelling in his popularity, he
'banished dull care from my brow'. With Christ Church appearing
'every day . . . merrier and brighter', there was, 'except for . . . home',
'no place I love so much as Oxford'.[30]

That Dufferin found himself popular owed more to his personality than his abilities and perhaps most of all to his manner. 'Nobody can cultivate that quality ['to appreciate grace in little as well as great things'] too much if one does but consider of what importance manner is', advised his mother; because 'all the good a man can do in this world will depend much on the influence he attains over the minds of others'. It was a lesson that Dufferin never forgot. As a result his many friends were captivated by an urbane and generous spirit that quickly set them at their ease and by the courtesies so delicately delivered and yet already strangely cosmopolitan. These virtues combined to create what one contemporary called 'his singular winning power' and what later his nephew, Harold Nicolson, was to dub the 'authentic Dufferin'.[31] Of course, much of this was cultivated but it remained sufficiently instinctive to convince the many who wished to bask in the glamour.

For a few inevitably the attraction went further. Morant 'has taken a fancy to me', he noted with more irritation than frisson. In spite of his more precious mannerisms – the affected lisp, the flamboyant gesture – that confirmed his 'effeminacy' for the more aggressive of the species, the only physical descriptions in his diary at this time were of women. Of which that of Miss Proctor, whom he sat next to at Thackeray's, was perhaps typical: 'a nice, unaffected, little body'. In male Oxford there were few opportunities and one of the more hilarious sights to greet him at Christ Church were the 'polka parties' where upwards of forty men were to be found in a stuffy room all dancing the male lead and crying out for the ladies. Dufferin was not immune to such sport.[32]

Writing after Dufferin's death to Sir Alfred Lyall (Dufferin's biographer), his contemporary Herbert Fisher urged that Dufferin himself would have wished for some recognition of his friendship for Francis Hepburn – what Fisher remembered as 'an intense love'. As usual Dufferin kept little from his mother. 'You need not fear that I dread loving anyone too much . . . I envy the qualities which are possessed by one of my friends here, whom I hope some day that you will know.' How, if at all, physical their relationship was is impossible to determine. Dufferin had failed to keep up (or lost?) his diary for the first six months of 1847. In letters from Hepburn written just after they left Oxford, the clergyman 'confess[es]' to having 'too great a love' for his friend: 'it may be a weakness but I can't help it'. Whatever the temptations that may have been repressed, such friendships were intense usually because they were chaste. Indeed, Dufferin's love of Hepburn was a worship of innocence. Writing to Fisher in 1893 after visiting the dying Hepburn for the last time, Dufferin blurted out, 'Poor Hepburn! He was already an angel when he was at Oxford. I never knew such an innocent nature, and innocent is the only term to be applied to his entire life.' The repetition of the word highlighted a concept that was to lie at the heart of all Dufferin's important relationships. His love for Hepburn, who arrived at Oxford with the guileless air of one 'preordained for holy orders', and his later adoration of women and little children, were rooted in his perceptions of them as being essentially sinless; symbols of purity in an evil world – to be worshipped but not defiled.[33]

If this was the stuff of dreams, so were his early politics. That he should be interested in politics was an inevitable consequence of what his mother had decreed to be his Whig ancestry. Yet it was the Peelites who first attracted his sympathies, primarily no doubt because of the prominence his uncle and guardian, Sir James Graham, enjoyed as Home Secretary in Peel's government. At the height of the parliamentary controversy over the repeal of the Corn Laws, it was Peel's 'endurance', sitting quietly 'while such a wasp [as Disraeli] abuses him', that most impressed Dufferin.

However, the deliberations of the Pythic Club – a small circle of his friends who met regularly to discuss an essay and to enjoy the pleasures of exclusivity and riotous debate ('Great disorder, seditious placards, Blackett finis') – were more revealing of his political instincts. Subjects ranged widely from Milton (Dufferin in favour) to hunting (Dufferin rather surprisingly speaking against, with his mother in full support of his attack on the 'Fowl sex').[34] In this Tory company, Dufferin often found himself arguing for the verities of Whig history, if not always with great conviction. Perhaps not surprisingly: for if debates on the desirability of factories or the Poor Laws uncovered quite a Young England camp in Boyle and Hunt (Disraeli's future chancellor), these ideas were not new or indeed alien to Dufferin. His Eton housemaster, Cookesley, was 'one of the godfathers of the

Young England movement' in whose house Disraeli penned the first Young England novel and among whose boys would be counted one of the acolytes of the movement and the model for Coningsby, George Smythe.[35] None of this suggests any serious ideological commitment. In fact the only time Dufferin nearly came to blows over politics was when Boyle challenged his proposal that voting need no longer be compulsory at meetings – so denying Dufferin the comforts of ambiguity. Typically, a week after this ruling in defence of what Dufferin called 'private judgement', he presented to the club two silver cups for the ballot balls.[36]

In May 1846 Dufferin was attending a debate in the Oxford Union on Polish independence when 'to the astonishment of myself and friends, I found myself on my legs. Though I had not thought of speaking two minutes before I found no difficulty . . . and . . . upon the whole made a pretty good speech.' What made him 'excessively delighted at this' was that he had overcome a stammer that he acquired since leaving Eton. Deciding to 'practise pretty often', he was to develop into a polished public speaker, capping his Oxford career with the presidency of the Union in 1847.[37]

Such rapid promotion was a direct consequence of the Irish Famine, which like nothing else politicised the young Irish peer. Horrified at reports coming out of Ireland, in February 1847 he went with Boyle to Skibbereen in Co. Cork to see the tragedy first hand: 'the fighting, the screaming, the swaying to and fro of the human mass as it rushed in the direction of some morsel'. In the wake of the publicity aroused by his publishing a 'Narrative of a Journey from Oxford to Skibbereen', Dufferin established a Famine fund in Oxford, opening the donations anonymously with a cheque for £1,000 (it would now roughly equal £100,000). Such extravagance appalled his guardians but there was no stopping him. It was, as Helen recognised, his 'first act of independence' and however 'quixotic' was irreversible. Restraining herself, she merely enquired if he planned to show similar extravagance towards the poor of Jerusalem or Cracow.[38]

In another way too the Irish Famine marked a turning point in his life. With the pamphlet providing 'the first proof that we are making a noise in the world', there emerged a marked divergence of opinion among his student friends over their 'mission'. To Boyle, the events of the Famine screwed up still tighter the intensity of his faith, seeing in the catastrophe both God's anger at man's avarice and the imminence of the Day of Judgement. Consequently he developed a practice of near incessant prayer, going down on his knees whenever the spirit moved him, whether in the street or in a drawing room; fasting was for him 'a Christian privilege'. But not now for Dufferin. Within two years Boyle would have built his Littlemore on the bleak Scottish Isle of Great Cumbrae, complete with a school, church, four choristers and a chaplain from Cambridge. For Dufferin, the road led elsewhere: to Ireland, to Parliament, to the public life expected of him. When Boyle and his other friends returned to Oxford in the autumn to take their degrees, Dufferin was not with them. That summer, with his coming of age, he had entered into his inheritance.

'What real connection can there have been', mused Harold Nicolson in his biography of his uncle, 'between this astute Pro-Consul and the small, swarthy, betasselled and perturbed anchorite of his Christ Church period?' For all that Dufferin later reminisced on Oxford providing the 'happiest days of his (unmarried) existence', his closest of university friends very quickly became only 'sentimental responsibilities', rarely to be seen again throughout his life. Yet it was in these years that what Nicolson himself had called the 'authentic Dufferin' was born: the suave, effortless charm and aesthetic instincts so finely honed, which combined to give an impression of imminent greatness.[39] Beneath the polished grandeur, however, romantic sensibility had yet to acquire the sense it would need to survive in public life. It was this, the measured judgement bred during years of a life held taut by self-restraint, that would separate the student and the proconsul.

4

'The one great purpose and interest of my life'

I will think of your deep, deep love for me and your desire that I
should do my duty, and I will do my duty, darling Mother, even for
your sake . . . and I will be brave and honourable towards men for
your sake, that you may see me honoured and loved, and respected,
and I will do my best that you may be proud of me, and think of what
your firmness and self-command, as well as your love and devotion,
has done for your son.[1]

S O WROTE DUFFERIN to his mother on his twenty-first birthday,
21 June 1847. That he should then leave her to return to Ballyleidy
to celebrate his coming of age struck Helen as decidedly perverse. So
was his declaration that 'the improvement of Ireland [was] the one
great purpose and interest of my life'.[2] Yet, if any place had come to
represent home for Dufferin, it was Ballyleidy. Along with the freedom to be himself,[3] there was the ready companionship of his many
Blackwood cousins and his friends and neighbours, Dick and Harry
Kerr. With the latter especially, he led a rollicking lifestyle, hunting
and drinking, returning to enact plays or cavort with the ladies at
local dances.[4] In quieter moments he and the Kerrs would ride over
to stare at the ruins of Portavoe, the Kerr house renowned for its huge
water tanks in the roof built as a precaution against fire but which in
1846 had burnt down nonetheless; as a precaution against the cold the
maids having earlier emptied the tanks to secrete their turf.[5] Such
frivolity aside, for Dufferin the appeal of Ireland was the far more
serious and supremely moral challenge posed by the Irish Famine of
1845–9 in which 800,000 (or 10 per cent of the total population)
were to die.

Nothing had prepared him for horror on such an incomprehensible scale as he had witnessed at Skibbereen. Appalled at the degradation of his fellow man, he too bridled at the 'exports [of corn by the larger farmers], which astonish everyone'.[6] If the catastrophe highlighted the moral responsibility of the landlord for his tenants, it was a challenge that the new landlord of Ballyleidy was glad to take up. It goes without saying that Dufferin's view of his new role was shaped as much by his imagination as by circumstance. If he was scathing of 'those Irish landlords who [in the face of typhus] are running away', it was because in his eyes the Famine gave them the opportunity to revive those traditional bonds of faithful deference and generous leadership that he believed should regulate landlord and tenant relations.

As a statement of intent he set out to visit all his 6,819 tenants in person over the winter of 1847–8. It was dreary work, with the lanes often rendered impassable by the weather. Yet touring his estates in a phaeton, his new agent, Howe, beside him, Dufferin came to recognise, seemingly for the first time, that his was a 'bleak, bare country, studded thickly with the gables of ruined houses and blotted over with low, black cabins, without a hedge or a tree but intersected with rugged blue stone walls and flooded black bogs'. With their 'half-cultivated fields' and cottages 'green outside with damp and dark inside with smoke', he witnessed the pathetic efforts of his tenants to 'scrape together his Lordship's rent' and endured a daily diet of excuse and complaint. By February a little iron had begun to enter the soul. Much of the destitution among 'Our people', he reported back to his mother, was 'mainly owing to their own perverseness and mismanagement'. For all that, his faith remained undimmed: 'time, good management, education, nothing [can] resist'.[7]

However, by now other forces were on the move. At a dinner for his tenants to introduce his new agent, Dufferin had described an Irish landlord as 'a well-dressed gentleman who ['does not get rent' and] is shot with impunity'; a quip that went down very well with his audience and very badly with his powerful landed neighbours. And not without reason, for along with the fear of local jacqueries seeking food and retribution was added the prospect that Daniel O'Connell's Repeal of the Union campaign in the hands of Young Ireland would descend into revolution and the 'abolition of landlordism'. By April Dufferin was fearfully consulting Howe on how 'much blood [will have to be] spilt' if they were, 'for ever, to crush the idea of this Repeal'.[8]

Admittedly they were living through times for which his old tutor, Cartmell, could only find explanation in the Book of Revelations.[9] The year 1848 had seen revolutions in Vienna, Paris, Rome, Berlin and Budapest. Titans of the European stage such as Metternich had suddenly fallen and in the vacuum another Napoleon had come to power in France, while in Italy the Pope had had to flee from the Vatican. Closer to home the Duc de Montebello, a minister in France's government, had escaped in disguise to England where Helen harboured her now penniless friend. Thus visions of destitution and exile could appear only too real. All but 1,000 of Dufferin's 6,819 tenants were Dissenters, men who in Co. Down in 1798 had rallied to the rebels' cause. 'If it comes to a real struggle how far can Ulster be counted on?' he asked anxiously of his agent. A private petition of loyalty suggested not, with only 1,300 signatures raised from among his tenants.[10]

'What an excellent trouncing the representatives of Brian Borrrrrooooo [have] received', wrote Pakington, an Oxford friend, a month later, revelling in accounts from Boyle of how Dufferin had 'bolted across the channel with your pockets full of balls, your hat full of powder and muskets . . . let into the seams of your trousers'.[11] In fact he spoke too soon as the government's pre-emptive attempt to arrest the leaders of Young Ireland on treason charges ended in legal disarray. The revolt when it came proved equally shambolic, amounting to little more than a brief altercation in Tipperary between the police and forty rebels on Widow McCormack's cabbage patch. For all this, the events of 1848 had marred the romantic ideal, which not even a royal visit a year later could alleviate. It may have been 'a beautiful historical picture' which Dufferin witnessed, as the crowds ('frantic with loyalty and enthusiasm . . . shouting "When will you come back to us, darling?"') bid an emotive farewell to their Queen as she stood on the quarter-deck of the *Victoria and Albert*, dressed in a pelisse of Irish poplin, emerald green in colour and embroidered with gold shamrocks. But what struck him most was 'the fickleness of the populace'.[12] With famine returning in 1849 Dufferin came now to believe that Ireland required surgery as much as sympathy and quickly, too, sentiments that were reinforced on a tour of the north-west with the Marquess of Abercorn.

Baronscourt, Abercorn's estate in Fermanagh, was, for Dufferin, 'a perfect territory', representing the harmony that came with the tempering of nature by civilisation and good order. What they were to witness in the coming weeks was nature free and untrammelled, seemingly irresistible in its destructiveness. Inspecting the Abercorn estates in Donegal, Dufferin found himself in a landscape, at once terrifying and extraordinarily beautiful ('The wildest and most magnificent scenery I have ever seen.'). Yet there could be no denying that this 'mournful . . . county' produced 'nothing but water, bog and stones'. With the Famine taking hold they were confronting a society on the very edge of the abyss.

> The people in appearance, language and manner of living are completely barbarous and even their faces have been degraded below the ordinary type of humanity, the projecting jaws and low foreheads giving them an air more of monkeys than of men. But the saddest sights of all are the little children. There is an unnatural look about them, which without exaggeration makes one shudder to see them. Their eyes are so bright and eager, their faces are so pale and wan and their limbs are so thin and emaciated, so unlike youth, that one can scarcely conceive of them to be mere ordinary children. Their manner too is more like old men . . . as they stand looking at you . . . gravely exchanging observations in whispers to one another, as if they were planning your murder and half-expected you to hear them.

Such scenes affected Dufferin enormously. By now he was convinced that, as he recorded in his diary, 'the only way to save Ireland is to send off immense numbers to the Colonies. The half-ruined propri-etor must be got rid of . . . and replaced by "real farmers", who would have the drive and means to create an efficient Irish economy – if one sustained by a regular emigration of the "superabundant population".' Indeed one million had already emigrated from Ireland in the thirty years before the Famine first struck.[13]

Significantly though, it was the 'upper classes' that Dufferin chose to indict for this state of affairs. Crucially, for him, the irresponsibility of some landlords amounted to abdication of a task that was God given – with consequences as great as any suffered by Sodom and Gomorrah.[14] However, the moral-force paternalism that Dufferin was now advocating had a distinctly unsentimental edge. Thus, he argued, Palmerston 'behaved most humanely' in funding the emigration of nearly 2,000 of his tenants (although conditions aboard the ships provoked a scandal).[15] Yet few landlords could afford Palmerston's expenditure. Faced with declining rent rolls, many were confronted by bankruptcy – or as Lord Sligo bluntly declared 'the necessity of ejecting or being ejected' – with consequences that were to tarnish landlordism irredeemably in the decades ahead. Dufferin may have had little sympathy for such men, though by their actions they contributed to the rationalisation of Irish landholding that he insisted was both necessary and inevitable. Nearly 50,000 families were dispossessed (or 250,000 people) between 1849 and 1854 and 3,000 estates sold in the bankruptcy courts. This, together with the increasing adoption of primogeniture, which eliminated the fatal grip of subdivision, encouraged the consolidation of holdings into more economic units. With emigration taking hold, a further million left for America and elsewhere in the 1850s and by 1900 the population of Ireland had halved to just 4 million. What had not really changed were the 10,000-strong body of landlords. For all the land sales of the Encumbered Estates Court, all but 300 of the 7,200 buyers were Irish as was the vast majority of the capital expended, none of which suggested there had been the infusion of entrepreneurial new blood that Dufferin had presumed.

Not that he was proving much more successful on his own estates where, despite reducing rents, his 'proprietorial revolution' had run up against the Ulster Custom.[16] Rather than tenants being recompensed by the landlord for any improvements they made to their holding, under the Ulster Custom these improvements were 'bought' by the incoming tenant. The consequence of this was that, while progressive landlords like Dufferin sought to keep rents below the market price to ensure that the tenant had income to spend on improvements, in practice this surplus was quickly absorbed in the charge the incoming tenant paid to the existing tenant. As it was, Dufferin's tenants were often in hock to loan sharks. These arrangements made nonsense of his proprietory rights. It made it virtually impossible for him to determine who should be his own tenants since no one could take up the tenancy without paying the inflated interest of the outgoing tenant or suffer the inevitable reprisals of boycott and violent outrage. Above all it acted as a block on economic progress, leaving the initiative over improvements with the tenant and not with the landlord. No wonder Dufferin despaired of the Ulster Custom: 'A man with an estate', he fumed to his mother, 'feels like a person who is compelled to keep servants he knows to be perpetually robbing him. If I had the land entirely in my own possession I could double my income.'[17]

Such grievances coloured his sense of Irishness too. As late as September 1846 he could be found in animated conversation with Harry Piper, drawing comparisons between Young Ireland, with their insistence on the right to resort to physical force, and the sixteenth-century Swiss freedom fighter, William Tell.[18] Once again the Famine changed everything. As he saw it, Ireland had almost wantonly stumbled into this human catastrophe and this shaped his view of his nation and its inhabitants for the rest of his life. The images were now all of decay. To his tenants in December 1847 he described Ireland as 'an unsightly wreck upon the waters . . . a monument of national listlessness – a blot on the face of Europe'.[19] The crucial lesson he drew from this was that the Irish were incapable of governing themselves. While Irish nationalists then and since were to hold up the inadequate response of Westminster to the crisis as proof of British unfitness to rule Ireland, Dufferin came to believe the exact opposite. With a starving, savage peasantry and an irresponsible elite (whether landlord or rentier), the necessity for disinterested British leadership seemed to him irrefutable. Paradoxically, therefore, the Famine had made him a unionist. Like Scott's Edward Waverley, he had come to view the Union as the only effective guarantor of civilised progress and stability 'sixty years hence'.

This did not lessen his love for Ireland but it became increasingly an affection for the place rather than for its inhabitants. The latter were now seen in pre-Darwinian terms or as fond stereotypical, stage Irishmen with heavy brogues and a feckless charm to match.[20] Behind such perceptions lay assumptions of cultural superiority;

assumptions that had been powerfully enforced on a young Dufferin by the characteristic disdain of his mother's family who weren't above poking fun at the locals. Like their grandfather, they wore their Irishness very lightly.

From now on so did Dufferin. Romantic Ireland was no longer to be sought amongst its people but from its landscape, particularly from that most deserted of landscapes – a great demesne. It was here that he would seek the fulfilment of his vision. Symbolically, on attaining his majority, he changed the name of his family seat from Ballyleidy to 'Clandeboye'. Claneboye was the anglicised version of lands that had once belonged to the Gaelic clans of O'Neill but in the wake of the Elizabethan conquest had eventually come into Blackwood hands through the heiress Dorcas Stevenson. In a country without Rob Roy its ancient chieftains were the next best thing. Lest anyone failed to appreciate his purpose, Dufferin added a 'd' to create Clandeboye, as Walter Scott had called the lost O'Neill lands in his epic poem 'Rokeby'.[21]

Unfortunately it would take more than a change of name before Clandeboye would begin to inspire the imagination. 'I dare say Clandeboye does look rather desolate just now', his mother commiserated in the autumn of 1849.[22] Her son had recently returned from Scotland where he had been thrilled by the sight of Inverary Castle, the seat of the Dukes of Argyll, and even more so by Dunrobin – the Sutherland retreat and 'a beautiful Brabant castle such as I would love to have'.[23] What he did have was an unprepossessing, late-Georgian country house, which was perfectly comfortable (it had been substantially rebuilt as recently as 1800) but was in no way grand – an example of an Irish vernacular architecture, which its new owner derided as 'debased Hibernic'. Inside, the proximity of the trees cut out most of the light while the nearby hall ensured sufficient draught to chill the Gallery. There were no pictures ('except for some dilapidated ancestors stowed away in the housekeeper's room') and no ornaments. There were almost 800 books but they were safely lodged in the recesses of the Saloon. Outside, apart from the inauspiciously named Anna's Ditch, there were no rivers or lakes and the walled garden was cut off from the park by the main road from Craigantlet to Bangor which passed within a hundred yards of the house.[24] It was hardly surprising that it should seem such a dismal prospect to a young man who would soon find himself at Castle Howard, 'full [as he described it] of all sorts of magnificence' and reminding him 'of the state kept by the ancient nobles of feudal times'. Or that the land of Walter Scott came to have an irresistible appeal; so much so that Dufferin briefly considered selling Clandeboye and settling on a small baronial estate in Scotland.[25] In the end he settled on bringing Scotland to Clandeboye.

'Clandeboye looking quite beautiful' under 'cloudless skies', Helen reported back to her sister, Caroline, 'and Fred is doing 40,000 things to it.'[26] Prime among these was Helen's Tower, a gothic folly built on the top of a hill with panoramic views over the countryside and Belfast Lough, even as far as the Scottish coast on a clear day. Designed in 1848 by William Burn, in the manner of a sixteenth-century Ulster-Scots fortified tower of the kind that figured in the Waverley novels, its grey stone walls wound around a spiral staircase that culminated in a gabled turret. Although 'christened' (by Mrs [Rowan] Hamilton, 'the champagne went all over her') in November 1850, the interiors took another ten years and included a sitting room with Gothic panelling and a ribbed ceiling, also of wood, richly emblazoned with heraldry. But this was a tribute not only to a style but also, as the fashion dictated, to his liege lady. Built originally as a gamekeeper's house, possibly as a means of providing employment during the Famine, it quickly became a symbol of a son's filial devotion to his mother.[27] This Tennyson immortalised in his lines written at Dufferin's request to mark the completion of the tower in October 1861:

Helen's Tower, here I stand,
Dominant over sea and land.
Son's love built me and I hold
Mother's love in letter'd gold.
Love is in and out of time,
I am mortal stone and lime.
Would my granite girth were strong
As either love, to last as long!
I should wear my crown entire
To and thro' the Doomsday fire,

And be found of angel eyes
In earth's recurring Paradise.

In the same chivalric vein, coronets and coats of arms were scattered throughout Clandeboye; while in their new London house in Grosvenor Place, Dufferin had Benjamin Ferrey decorate a back room in the 'style of Edward IV'. Nothing gave him more pleasure than the way he reconciled an ancient feud with his Hamilton cousins over the ownership of the Gate House at Killyleagh Castle. His acceptance of an annual tribute, alternately of a golden rose and a spur, was pure Scott. So was his generosity in renovating (at his expense) the entrance as if 'out of a page of romance'.[28] Captain Archibald Rowan Hamilton, was delirious over the great medieval battlement that Dufferin planned to erect at his gate, although his request for a clock must have sent a shudder through his benefactor.

The 1850s also saw Dufferin build a railway station at Greypoint (later renamed Helen's Bay) with a private entrance designed by Benjamin Ferrey. This passed under the track through an arch resplendent with elaborately carved coats of arms, replete with supporters and flanked by turrets. Linking this with the house, he planted an avenue of trees more than three miles long with further, though less imposing, arches. But for the most part it meandered through fields, enlivened by the careful plantation of clumps of trees to create a variety of views. The inspiration behind this was James Fraser, the leading exponent of picturesque landscaping in Ireland.[29] Rejecting the grand sweep of classical landscape, he sought to catch the atmospheric and unpredictable nature of Romanticism by creating pools of dark suddenly broken by shafts of light or unexpected, often spectacular vistas (or 'peeps') that would draw the fascinated observer into the mystery. Plantations of largely deciduous trees were established to screen the estate. Similar plantations were used to enhance the hills around the house, leaving the open pastures undulating below to provide movement with only the occasional tree to sharpen the perspective. Drives and walks were cut through the woods and in the 1860s the land by the main house (and the nearby main road)[30] was flooded to make two large connected lakes. Dotted with wooded islands and little coves, their elusive outline

44

led the eye through an ever-changing landscape. And so the gloomy countryside of bog and small fields and run-down cottages that had greeted Helen on her arrival in 1826 was transformed into a landscape which trumpeted nature as a creative force. But it was a force that, however much it champed at the bit, was not to be allowed the freedom of the reins.

Out of his efforts emerged a spectacular setting and one that to this day continues to enchant and thrill; and stands as a monument to his artistic flair, insight, courage and sensitivity. But the fact remains it was only within his demesne walls that Dufferin could realise his romantic vision of Ireland.

5

In Search of Favour

Avoid Mrs Lambton [and] pray make yourself charming to the
Grosvenor girls.   Helen Dufferin to her son[1]

B Y NOW, FOR Dufferin, England pointed the way ahead. 'I want
you', Helen wrote plainly, 'to see what is called the best of
London Society' – the families of her grandfather's Whig friends
among whom she now sought to launch her son.[2] Cosmopolitan and
metropolitan, defined as much by birth as wealth or politics, this was
intimidating company with its own salons, moral codes and even
accents to emphasise their distinction from ordinary mortals. If truth
be told, Richard Brinsley Sheridan, for his talents and wit, had been
patronised by his friends, never accepted. Likewise his granddaughter
could effect an entrée for her son without much difficulty but he, like
his illustrious forebear, would never, for all his popularity, experience
the security of truly belonging.

Where he could always feel secure was trailing in the shadow of his
vivacious mother. Not that this was dull for in London she kept an
eclectic set of friends. A contemporary sketch of 'Tea time at Lower
Brook Street' portrayed Helen entertaining the likes of the Granvilles
and the Shelbournes, Lady Ailesbury and the Comte de Flahaut as
her son lounged on a distant sofa in the background. Here one might
meet writers of the calibre of Macaulay, Thackeray and Dickens or
the painters Landseer and Swinton. By the summer of 1849 Dufferin
would set off for Hyde Park in the olive-green cabriolet, specially
commissioned from Thrupp & Maberly, or ride in Richmond Park
with Lord Jocelyn to pick up the latest gossip on politics and Peel.
Later in the afternoon visits would be made to the drawing rooms of

the powerful – Lady Palmerston, the Duchess of Bedford or the Duke of Devonshire at Chiswick. In such company Dufferin reverted to the fop that had left Oxford two years before, if not more so:

> His long hair was brushed forward above the ears and scented with bear's grease or Macassar oil. He could still, in 1849, wear a sky-blue tail coat without attracting criticism. His trousers were fastened in equestrian fashion by a strap beneath his instep. His waistcoat was cut low across the stomach and enriched with buttons of enamel. Above it billowed a vast kerchief of black satin secured by two separate pins connected to each other by a thin gold chain. In his yellow silk gloves he would carry a light cane and an enormous hat. The seals at his fob jingled together as he slowly walked.[3]

This was more pastiche than Regency and plainly something of an act. As it was, in Ireland he had made quite a name for himself as an actor, revelling in the bustle of country-house theatricals. On hearing that Lady Castlereagh was seeking a maid, Helen couldn't resist sending her son, duly disguised and armed with a letter of recommendation. Her joy was unconfined when the mistress of the house – failing to recognise Dufferin – declared that she 'would be very glad to take me into her service'. In similar mood he travelled '2nd class' with Dick Kerr to Slough and from there to Ascot where, dressed as gypsies, they entered the course. Attracting some genuine gypsies to add credibility (including 'a very pretty girl', whose name was 'Goneril [and who] insisted on giving me a kiss on parting'), they strolled the enclosures 'eventually overtaking [their friend] Augustus Paget with two ladies in a carriage. We chaffed him unmercifully, he telling us to go away, and we calling him by his Christian name, to the astonishment of his lady companions – "What, Mr. Paget, do you know the creatures?" "No, certainly not!" "Oh! Augustus", I cried, "don't you remember?" and so on, very amusing.'[4] But rather less so when at the end of July he went with Grevilles, Granvilles, Cowpers, Sandwichs and Jocelyns for three days' racing and to his horror caught the eye of 'my Ascot gypsy'.[5]

A week later, in Dublin for the Queen's visit, he heard from Lady Jocelyn how the Queen 'had been laughing at my long hair'. So too did the 'mob' outside who hooted with mirth as the police blocked his attempt to join the royal 'platform'. His protestations of being 'a very great man' proved to no avail, with the result that he had to spend the night sleeping in a dining room with a friend who 'snored with a brogue'.[6] The fact was that the affected flamboyance of dress and manner, while it entertained the ladies, only made him ridiculous in the eyes of their husbands.

Invited by Abercorn to his shooting estate at Laggan in 'North Britain', Dufferin found himself in a party which included Grevilles, Granvilles, Bagot, Landseer (with whom Dufferin shared a room and would later join in a 'prize fight'), Jocelyns, Malmesburys and their hosts.[7] It was soon apparent he had been invited not to shoot but to entertain Abercorn's four young daughters. They passed the days rowing him around the lake, while he in turn attempted to 'make them laugh a good deal by playing some of the old Clandeboye tricks, dancing a jig as a ghost, and finally appearing as a woman and kissing the ghillie'. Such frivolity only confirmed to hardened sportsmen like Malmesbury that Dufferin was 'rather a muff'. Against the butt of male ridicule, self-mockery provided a defence of sorts but left him pondering 'the great inconvenience' in his rejection of shooting 'as [it] is the chief occupation of English gentlemen'. His change of heart convinced few, with even supporters such as Lady John Russell doubting 'your being quite worthy of the "Land of the mountain and the flood"'. It was two weeks before Dufferin was given the chance to show them 'I was as much a man as anybody.'

After stalking all day it was not until dusk that they came across the herd. Abercorn let Dufferin have the first shot. Taking aim, he fired. 'For the [first] few seconds of suspense I felt sick with disappointment.' Until the ghillie yelled, 'He's got it.' The stag still got away and with night falling they thought they had lost it. Then hearing 'his almost demoniacal bay', they ran for two miles and found him eventually 'standing in a waterfall' and looking 'so grand'. Any student doubts on the immorality of hunting were now long gone, as the ghillie cut the beast's throat and laid it on the bank for Dufferin to 'gloat over' in triumph.

'Ghigo shot a deer?' exclaimed his Sheridan grandmother. 'He must have hit it by accident.' All this Helen gleefully relayed to her son. Yet for all the playfulness the rebuke was not long in coming. 'Surely it is hardly worthwhile to take up a pursuit merely to please other people. You and I both desire too much to be loved.' She had hit on a truth. 'Perhaps it is foolish being so anxious that people should like me', Dufferin would admit a little forlornly. But it was a vulnerability he would never completely master.

From Laggan Dufferin progressed to Inverary – the seat of the Argylls. 'The little red Duke does not keep any great state in his northern castle,' he reported back to his mother, but his host he declared 'a fine manly little man' and 'the Duchess the happiest of women'. Leaving Inverary he sailed down the Caledonian Canal on the yacht of the Earl of Stafford (the heir to the Duke of Sutherland), whose wife, the young heiress Anne Hay-Mackenzie, Dufferin deemed 'very pretty', not least for her habit 'when at sea [of] always wear[ing] her long hair hanging down over her shoulders like a mermaid'. Together his recent companions would become lifelong friends and his greatest supporters.[8]

In November 1849 Dufferin's appointment as a courtier to the young Queen surprised few – her protestations that he was 'much too good looking and captivating' fooling nobody. From the moment he was shown to his rooms ('decorated with glowing pictures of heathen goddesses and furnished in an ancient and gorgeous style') the rigid formality was inescapable. Such duties as came his way were hardly riveting ('to church with the Queen to return thanks for the abatement of the cholera. Put a chair between her and the fire'). No wonder he was to be found when time hung heavy strolling down across the Thames to Eton where he watched with some envy 'the boys playing football': 'did so long to kick it'. Nevertheless he quickly developed a rapport with the Duchess of Kent and once at his ease he was soon 'flirting' and dancing (until 5.30 a.m. at the Guards Ball) with the ladies – the role for which presumably he had been chosen. He was just as capable of listening reverently as the old Duke of Wellington recounted how one of his aides-de-camp had once asked him if he had ever seen Elizabeth I; or when the Duke of Devonshire arrived with a gigantic leaf of a waterlily 'which we duly admired'.[9]

Helen meanwhile had her eyes on a distinctly tougher theatre

– Parliament. This raised the question of which party? Dufferin's instinctive 'sympathy' lay with Peel whose moral stand over the Corn Laws at the cost of his career and party had, in Dufferin's eyes, re-asserted the nobility of politics. Many of his Irish friends – Abercorn and Jocelyn – and county neighbours were Tories. However, his guardian (and Peelite) Sir James Graham determined that with the Conservative Party fundamentally split, his charge's future should lie with the Whigs. In particular, he urged Dufferin to seek an English peerage. This would dramatically enhance his standing locally and give him some political weight in England; and without any costly elections. Peerages were rarely given in the 1850s and not to 'out-siders' of the governing party and especially to those like Dufferin who at twenty-three had little claim. However, in the political climate of 1849, with the government of Lord John Russell in some disarray and the prime minister dependent on Peelite support, Graham saw a brief opportunity to launch an audacious coup. Negotiations began in June 1849 and lasted five months with Russell reluctant to pay Graham's price. 'Quite fat with joy', Helen wrote on hearing the news of Dufferin's eventual elevation as 1st Baron Dufferin and Clandeboye in the English peerage: 'Oh! I am in a hurry to grasp the bauble.' For in a sense it was hers – as was her parting shot: that this 'very nearly [fulfilled] my wish'.[10]

In the meantime her son set about sealing his triumph – as later in his public life he always would do – by shaping the record after his own fashion. Clothed in the ermine and deep red robes of the baron-age for a portrait commissioned from Ary Schaffer to celebrate his elevation, Dufferin looked dignified and aristocratic but also purpose-ful and with the confident air of one on the edge of greatness. It was also fashionably medieval. Two generations later, Harold Nicolson presumed it a picture not of his uncle but of Sir Galahad or a Crusader, 'so marked was the impression of self-dedication, of young knight-hood, of virile virginity'.[11] Whether reality would live up to the glamorous image only time would tell.

I dared to ask Miss H. to waltz or rather she offered herself to me . . . Trrrr goes her gown. 'Never mind,' says she. 'I beg your pardon a thousand times,' says I. 'Let us go into the other room by ourselves,'

says she; we go again, another tear. You cannot think how good
natured she was about it and good humoured and looked so pretty you
cannot think.[12]

As befitting his portrait, Dufferin indulged in the rituals of classical
romance, so beloved by his generation. These portrayed women as
vessels of modesty and gentle saintliness, and in marriage dutiful and
supportive. Often passionate, their feelings remained nonetheless
immaculate, valuing the spiritual over the physical in relationships.
Purity was the key. Hence lovers, in the fashionable code of letter
writers, were 'pearls'. The denial of sex was seen as cleansing, a purging of motives. Those who, like Lancelot or Tristram, succumbed
to temptation ultimately brought on only ruin and destruction. The
young knights, who courted 'M'Lady', were more guardians of her
honour than genuine suitors. Dufferin was one of many young men
who partook of this medieval charade, pledging themselves in service
to the young wives of often considerably older husbands in a dance of
secret assignations, intimacies and occasional hurts that were the price
of discretion, but where the thrill of the dance replaced the triumph
of consummation. Thus when Lady Stafford presented her knight
with 'Eilan Dhu' – an island that proved wildly romantic in the imagination and a barren rock off Ullapool in reality – Dufferin responded
by commissioning a present for her (from the ever-willing Carlo
Marochetti) of a statuette, portraying himself as 'The Hermit Knight'.

The chief object of his affections was Lady Jocelyn, Palmerston's
stepdaughter and lady-in-waiting to the Queen. Married into the
Roden family who had strong interests in Co. Down, she had visited
Clandeboye in January 1849 en route for the viceregal levee in Dublin.
There followed the ritual of chivalrous romance. He would ride down
almost daily to see her at Kew, 'leaving a drawing of my disappointment' if she was not at home. By the time of the Queen's visit to
Ireland in August, the game was in full swing. Sighting her on the
royal yacht through a telescope, Dufferin gatecrashed the proceedings
and once on board 'threw myself at [her] feet', she looking 'so well
and tidy in her little barège that I could hardly help kissing her'.
When another of her admirers likened her to 'a morning star',
Dufferin rather ungallantly repeated this to his rival's wife.[13]

Not that the relationship was entirely one-sided: it was she who persuaded the Queen to appoint him to court and it was she who later 'fought like a tiger' on his behalf at Laggan. There too, while staying overnight in a bothie on the shores of Loch Ericht, she had, symbolically, made his bed. Soon they were regularly placed beside each other at dinner or invited to the same house parties, where after the men had retired Dufferin would join her in her bedroom ('she look[ing] so pretty in her dressing gown'). Such intimacies were in all probability just occasions for sharing of confidences. This escapism was rife at court and none indulged more in this than the high-spirited Queen. Calling late at night on Lady Jocelyn in her rooms at Windsor, she discovered Dufferin there. Immediately she dropped into an elaborate curtsy, greeting him as if he were her lord.[14]

It was Helen who first raised the alarm. 'I cannot help sometimes fearing for you when I think how charming and good natured a certain lovely lady is! Such friendships are dangerous', she warned, 'for they may engross too much of your thoughts . . . and perhaps end by making you discontented and unhappy.' Almost erased in his diary lies his anguished protest over his mother's warning 'not to fall in love with Lady J . . . I know my heart is [weak?] and that though I love her, it is all in truth and purity'.[15] None of this would secure the match on which Helen's ambitions depended.

By now Dufferin was something of a catch. Good looks, wealth and status inevitably meant that rumours abounded of an imminent match. And yet the rumours came and went with the seasons. To Hepburn the answer lay in Dufferin's mother – 'she has spoilt you for a wife'. And yet in truth it was not just Helen. As he confessed to her, 'I have a weakness for old women and feel comfortable in their presence.'[16] Describing him as 'the spoilt darling of our home', Argyll's daughter Frances remembered how 'no one could take such daring liberties with my mother, no one made his adoration of her more felt . . . He would put up his eye glass and look round the full luncheon table, including us all in one general endearment of "Darlings". He would then proceed to tell some adventure . . . not usually quite on the side of the proprieties, but which my parents became too helpless with laughter to in any way quell.' Much happier wooing the mothers, Dufferin would flirt madly with elderly duchesses such as

Harriet, Duchess of Sutherland.[17] Or, in the case of Lady Waldegrave, fall in love with them, so unwittingly foiling her elaborate match-making on his behalf. Equally unobtainable but much feted were the young wives of his close friends such as Elizabeth, Duchess of Argyll, and Anne, Countess of Stafford.

And then there was what Nicolson called his 'hidden streak of femininity' which, truth be told, was not particularly hidden at this time. He was ever ready to give himself over to his hostesses to be dressed, powdered and bejewelled for their entertainment. But to woo their daughters was the manner not a little too camp?[18] Even Dufferin wondered so. The plaintive 'I wish I could be like him' (which Dufferin much later attempted to obliterate from his diary) referred to his friend Argyll because he was 'so manly'.[19] Other uncertainties also hindered his progress. For all his recent elevation to the English peerage, he was sensitive of being something of a parvenu in the company of his more exalted friends. When he tried to drop Dufferin from his new title to become Lord Clandeboye (something on which 'I had so long set my heart'), the Granvilles 'laughed and joked a great deal about my changing my name' which left him 'very vexed'. To make matters worse, not only did Lady Jocelyn join in the chorus of disapproval but more decisively so did the Queen. For the new Lord Dufferin *and* Clandeboye the episode proved highly embarrassing.[20] These insecurities encouraged him to love chastely from a distance with inevitable consequences.

The extent of his inexperience was demonstrated by his courtship of the Duchess of Sutherland's daughter, Constance Leveson-Gower. They first met when Dufferin and the Sutherlands were guests at Castle Howard for the Queen's visit in August 1850. The younger sister of Elizabeth, Duchess of Argyll, Constance had become a considerable beauty with an aquiline profile and light golden hair. Nevertheless her charm lay less in her looks than in her irrepressible gaiety and Dufferin danced with her until 4 a.m. 'Duchess most kind, like a mother to her son', Dufferin noted with pleasure on his departure. Yet for the next six months he did nothing. In the end it took 'a remarkable conversation with Lady Waldegrave' before he realised that Constance was expecting something more. Within weeks he was regularly placed next to Constance at dinner and escorting her to dances at Devonshire House or at Windsor. At Ascot he 'walked' with the duchess and her daughter and later that week, when the Queen attended Speeches at Eton, he sat beside Constance almost as a matter of course. Then on 8 June 1851, calling on Lady Jocelyn, he found her 'greatly puzzled. Talked to me of Lady Chesterfield.'[21]

Lady Chesterfield was the mother of Evelyn Stanhope, with whom he had been briefly infatuated (Lady Evelyn 'acted divinely, so graceful, so charming'). Clearly, more had been read into Dufferin's attentiveness to her daughter than was intended and he would later 'bitterly reproach myself for not having been more guarded in letting her see how much she enchanted me when I was at Bretby'. Yet this was not the first time he had stumbled into such confusion. His protest after the Laggan trip that he had 'avoided any too cordial advances' on Rachel Russell was belied by her mother's too cordial manner. While at least one of his Graham cousins, Hermione, was to misconstrue his intentions.[22] Matters went from bad to worse the next day when the death of his Sheridan grandmother saw Helen rather melodramatically overdose on laudanum ('her heart and pulse quite motionless'). With his guardian summoning him to discuss his apparently simultaneous wooing of Lady Evelyn and Lady Constance – a prospect too mortifying to contemplate – Dufferin chose (in the interests of his mother's recovery) to escape abroad.[23]

There some months later he heard of Constance's engagement to Hugh Lupus Grosvenor, the future Duke of Westminster.[24] He was utterly taken by surprise and surprised too by the hurt. Yet he had only himself to blame,[25] as his aunt, Georgia, made plain ('Long talk with Georgy about young ladies'). Having lost one grand match the Sheridans were not prepared to lose another. Evelyn Stanhope, for 'all her flighty faults', was affectionate, capable and crucially very rich. More to the point she was still infatuated with Dufferin. His continued intimacy with Constance caused a furious row with his aunts ('Ghigo, Ghigo. Your letter [to the Duchess of Sutherland] is that of a thorough Blackwood')[26] and again with his mother ('Fie, Mother!'), after she had shared his confidences with her sisters.[27] But in truth he worried 'lest I should find the illusion vanished on my side'. And so it proved. By June every reference to their courtship in his diary was later expunged, except on 30 June when they spent the dance at Lady

Wilton's talking on the staircase. Thereafter whole pages were cut until 6 July when he landed at Bangor. 'The people came to meet me with guns and cheering. So happy. Clandeboye looking so well.'[28] As for 'Lady Evelyn – poor child', he confessed to his mother, 'I hope whatever happens may be for her own good, for evidently it is a most fragile, tender, able heart.' And broken too, he might have added, for it would be years before she would get over his apparent desertion.[29] All this was a far cry from the knightly gallantry that romantic legend had decreed. In commissioning Marochetti to sculpt him as 'The Hermit Knight' Nicolson's 'virile virgin' was proving to be too virginal for his own good.

6

The Politics of Romance

Something I will be, for the honour of the five generations of
distinguished creatures that have gone before me.[1]

JUST TO BELONG to the House of Lords gave Dufferin a thrill, as
when in 1852 after the defeat of Disraeli's budget, 'we and half a
dozen Whig magnificoes were chatting on the railway platform [and]
Lord Derby bounced in among us, to his evident disgust, on his way
to Osborne to resign'.[2] Yet politics was a serious business requiring
considerable commitment. And after barely six months he was receiving curt reprimands from Lady John Russell, presuming his failure to
attend regularly to support the government was 'at best . . . carelessness'. Two weeks later he was on his feet making his maiden speech,
on a topic designed to appeal to his patron – the extension of the
vote. With Sir James Graham in the gallery and 'chilled' by the silence
of the chamber, he was relieved to hear from the Queen that night
that the reports of his speech were 'very good'.[3]

Not that many more followed. He did speak in favour of continuing the Maynooth Grant and when he left (in August 1851) for
seven months in Italy with his mother, he was careful to become the
'good Italian patriot' Lady John requested, sending back gloomy
accounts of the oppressive Austrian military presence, with the streets
of Milan 'absolutely overflow[ing] with foreign soldiery . . . and
white coated little officers in tight stays – unwholesomely tight'.[4]
Nevertheless exposure to the tyranny of autocratic rule did little to
fire his political ambitions. When in February 1854, he actually
introduced a bill of his own (on Tenant Right in Ireland) his self-
interest was all too evident. The bill, while it had no prospect of

success, was still an impressive construct and helped to establish a reputation in the Lords as a Whig expert on Ireland.[5] Or it might have if Dufferin had made any effort to build on this. Admittedly it cannot have been much fun defending the Whig cause in a profoundly Tory House. Furthermore a career founded on being an Irish expert flew in the face of the Whig insensitivity to Ireland. This took many forms – from the mismanagement of the Famine to Argyll's dreadful warning of his impending arrival at Clandeboye in August 1853: 'So we come to Paddyland, only just fancy; leave some well boiled potatoes for us – praties I ought to say.'[6]

The Peelites were more appreciative and Lord Aberdeen's congratulation after the Maynooth speech left Helen 'very conceited'; hence she was miffed to see a duel between Disraeli and Gladstone in 'the other house' take the headlines. And there lay the rub. It was possible to make a successful career from the Lords, but usually after winning one's spurs in the Commons. As it was, Dufferin did not relish this cut and thrust and hated the occasional viciousness of competitive debate, preferring instead the formality of the great speech. Family myth had prepared him to view politics as a field for heroic artistry in which power lay in sparkling oratory in the grand manner. Instead, to his disgust, he learnt that 'the whole business is got through [with] everybody talking, yawning, lying or walking about'.[7] As for stands of principle, he felt at a loss trying to understand how Palmerston could suddenly defeat Russell when palpably in the wrong or how Disraeli could so breezily reject protectionism on which he had just made his name and destroyed Dufferin's hero, Sir Robert Peel, into the bargain.

The disillusionment of youthful idealism is a rite of passage in a parliamentary career but it did not see a sharpening of Dufferin's political instincts. Instead politics came to bore him. While in the early days he could be seen bearding Disraeli in Grosvenor Square to 'jaw' on recent elections, by late 1852 he found a dinner party at the Ellices with seven cabinet ministers 'very dull'. He pleaded with his mother that he lacked the stamina for a 'life of great drudgery and constant application' necessary to become the distinguished statesman she desired.[8] In time he would resolve the dilemma by reinventing rather than re-establishing Sheridan. But, for now, he remained lashed to the wheel of family aspiration: 'a poor figure', judged 2nd Earl Granville, the Whig leader in the Lords, 'who does not require a bribe'.[9]

As it was, his family were providing distractions a plenty. By August 1853 Norton's debts had brought him to court again. Caroline's fierce defence of her cause so stirred the court that, with the crowd roaring her on, mayhem ensued as Norton rushed at his wife in a blazing temper with fists flying. 'God knows, I think the applause was about as great a disgrace as the censure', Helen complained. Caroline, however, was unstoppable, entering into a vitriolic correspondence in *The Times* with her husband, trading insults with revelations. The following May she produced a pamphlet (*English Laws for Women in the Nineteenth Century*), dismissing Dufferin's fears over 'publicity'. Her work, she assured him at the outset of the Crimean War, would be remembered as much as an officer 'who is gone to serve England in the Baltic or Black Sea'. Such audacity was astounding until one remembers her application to Peel to be made Poet Laureate — Peel chose Wordsworth.[10]

As ever with Aunt Caroline events soon were careering wildly out of control. 'It is not true', wrote Elizabeth Argyll in disbelief, 'that young Brinsley Norton has made an Italian marriage?' It was only too true. In time Dufferin would come to appreciate the virtues and decency of Maria Federigo as being more than Caroline's feckless son deserved but in October 1853 the talk was of trying to prevent this marriage to 'the donkey girl at Capri!!'. In the same month Caroline retreated to Clandeboye, despite having fallen out with the rest of her family over, in Helen's eyes, 'that hateful annuity from the Melbourne family'. Helen simply couldn't 'credit that she was receiving it'. After all, Caroline had always denied its existence to her family; indeed she had denied being Melbourne's mistress. Norton's revelation of this in court caused Helen acute embarrassment.[11]

The young peer and courtier felt the shame of these improprieties as keenly as his mother.[12] Once again escape appeared the only option. In October 1853 he hired Lord Templetown's yacht and sailed to his Highland friends in the Western Isles — with Lady Jocelyn as 'my fair freight'. After this he briefly contemplated the ultimate escape, the life of a poet, provoking his anxious mother to counter that 'the only true and enduring poetry is in "action"'. Yet she could never have imagined that he would take her at her word and sail off into battle.

'Have a mind to see a shot fired over you?' Admiral Napier had barked out from the deck of his flagship.[13] Only too eager, in the summer of 1854, Dufferin joined the *Penelope* (a frigate with the same name as that commanded by his Uncle Henry at Trafalgar nearly fifty years before) as she set out to engage the enemy. Her objective was to test the firepower of a Russian garrison, cooped up in the Baltic fort at Bomarsund in the disputed Åland Islands. However, in trying to coax a response from the Russian guns, the ship suddenly found herself in range, and then made matters worse by becoming grounded on a rock. For two hours they were pounded by shot as the ship struggled to break free. More than once Dufferin was showered in a hail of splinters with shot crashing around him on the deck. Another cannon ball came through a porthole and 'ploughed up' three sailors, one of whom Dufferin saw had 'his skull cut off just above the eyes'. Such awful scenes would frighten most ordinary mortals; as they did a 'poor little middy, a mere child of 13', who had only left his mother five weeks previously and was now by Dufferin standing behind the mast, plainly terrified but 'determined to behave like a man'. So too Dufferin. For one so intimidated in Parliament, Dufferin never lacked physical courage: exulting amid the crash of battle at being 'in my very heart an English gentleman, scorning to feel nervous or afraid'. Only at the expressed (and at Dufferin's insistence *written*) command of the captain was he finally persuaded to leave the stranded ship.

This was but a trivial incident in a major conflict. Although an unnecessary war fought to little immediate effect, the Crimean War (1854–6) proved in time to have enormous consequences. With Britain joining France to halt the spread of Russian influence in the East, there began the process that would lead ultimately towards the creation of a united Germany in 1870 and the undermining of the balance of power in Europe that had ensured four decades of peace on the continent. It was also a war that would become a byword for chaos and suffering, primarily as a result of staggering maladministration and pigheadedness shown by military commanders on all sides. But to Dufferin and his contemporaries, war was still inhabited by heroes, whose valour had become glamorised into the embodiment of manliness. Here stalked the memory of his dead generations: of his uncle with Nelson at Trafalgar or later of his father storming the Bocra Forts. So Dufferin and his friends had set sail in part for the excitement but also to test themselves and feel the sensation of being under fire. And, of course, alongside such rites of passage was the desire to have a lark.

On board the *Foam*, anything less like a fighting ship could hardly be imagined. It was lined with chintz throughout, while on the walls were pictures of Elizabeth, Duchess of Argyll, and Louisa, Marchioness of Abercorn. The inner sanctum found Watts's drawing of Helen and Dufferin's sketch of Annie Stafford, while against the doors hung curtains of red cloth studded with silken Maltese crosses. Lest any should question the military credentials of the *Foam*, there was a brass four-pounder on deck (alongside the hutch for 'my dog "Sailor"') and a case of twelve rifles and revolvers, 'intended [with poor sense of geography] to protect us from the attack of Mediterranean pirates'.

Once off Bomarsund, Dufferin was quick to savour the thrilling spectacle: a scene 'full of noise, music, piping, and hoarse boatswains' voices; while every now and then, "boom" would go the report of some huge gun practising her men at target' (and on one occasion only just missing his yacht). That night, sitting on the sofa with the 'old admiral' the young aristocrats pleaded to join the action. The next day, after the troops had laid siege, Dufferin and his friends followed. Almost in the mode of tourists, they climbed up through slopes of rock and heather, with 'wild flowers, butterflies, the hum of bees, and the odour of the sweet-scented shrubs' until they stumbled into the field of battle.

Soon they were running a gauntlet of fire as they scuttled from battery to battery. Then Dufferin spotted a white flag hoisted above the fort. With considerable brio, he and his companions leapt from cover and sauntered up to the main gate to accept the surrender. Their presumption proved premature. Just as they were close enough to see 'the muskets and the dirty faces of the fellows inside' a Russian officer darted out: 'Mais messieurs, Retirez vous! Retirez vous! Nous ne sommes pas encore rendus. [We are not yet lost.]' 'Expecting with every minute to hear a dozen rifle shots singing over [their] heads', they beat as hasty a retreat as the necessary sangfroid would allow. This was a battle straight out of the pages of Scott, with 'shot, shell and grape whizzing every now and then over our heads, and everyone laughing beneath.'

The battle won, Dufferin climbed through the rubble to discover in an oval courtyard 1,600 Russian soldiers with closely shaven heads, looking more like convicts than combatants. Ironically, among the dead was the gallant officer who had earlier sent them back. Lost somewhere amongst the crowd of onlookers [were] the three English admirals – 'forgotten, trodden upon, disregarded' – when to a flourish of trumpets, the gates were thrown open and General Baraguay d'Hilliers (the French commander, who had 'left behind [an arm] in 1812') entered on his charger, his generals and aides-de-camp riding alongside. 'I never saw anything so theatrical!' was Dufferin's dismissive verdict but it was a lesson in the power of display that he would come to appreciate. Less impressive were the 'horrid scenes' as drunken troops began looting the citadel. Even so, Dufferin then tried to carry off two beautiful wall pieces from the chapel with the help of some British troops, only to be confronted by a furious d'Hilliers who publicly accused him of being 'un voleur'. His French friends interceded on his behalf and the pieces were promised 'in good time' but it was a tawdry end to the enterprise.

Nevertheless the escapade at Bomarsund proved one of the most formative of his early life. In vigorous action and danger he discovered the release to be found for energies enervated by contemplation and doubt. Abroad too was the excitement of different cultures and the remnants of an aristocratic order fast losing sway in industrial England. Outside England he found the confidence to act. Not surprisingly, he was soon planning a new voyage, this time to the East.

In the meantime, with his Uncle Graham questioning such frivolity 'when death and anguish and suffering and want are the lot of thousands', he agreed to accompany his 'liege lord', Lord John Russell, as his private secretary at a peace conference in Vienna – for which he got very little thanks from Russell who found Dufferin's feudal affectations profoundly irritating.[14] Having picked up a 'magnificent bearskin coat', he set off with Lord John on 20 February, his reluctant host wearing wrappings like 'boxing gloves on his feet' to counteract the cold. It became apparent that the will was not yet there for a settlement and that Russell's eccentric approach wouldn't fashion one either. With Russell departing within the month, Dufferin was left to the clerical drudgery of writing and copying despatches.[15]

Somewhat to his surprise, he began to enjoy himself. These negotiations were a useful diplomatic initiation as well as offering the chance to make some early contacts. He impressed in particular the influential Austrian foreign minister, Esterházy, with his knowledge of fine art. What made Vienna though was Henrietta Todesco, the future Princess Bathyani. 'Come here if you have nothing better to do,' was her laconic invitation and for the next few weeks Dufferin rarely left her side. Just how intense this relationship was can only be surmised from the heavy cuts made to Dufferin's diary and from his irritation at his sudden recall to Palace duties ('upset all my arrangements'). So, barely two months after his arrival, he recrossed the Danube, reaching London five days later. And there he 'found a little "Faust" from Mme T., like Benjamin's cup in the mouth of my sack'. 'My Dame Blanche', he had called her and perhaps that was all she ever was.[16]

'Get me any nice little wife you choose,' he had instructed his mother from Vienna. 'I must marry somebody soon.' There was a solution, obvious to many including Janey Ellice who cheerfully reported in January 1856 that 'your marriage to Lady J[ocelyn] is the news contained in the P.S.s of everybody's letters to everybody'. Her husband had died of cholera. But, rather than look to Dufferin, she immersed herself in deep mourning, a condition she was fated to endure as over the next two decades all her children died one after the other. Not surprisingly, Dufferin looked elsewhere.[17]

'Not pretty but odd looking, [and] like her mother graceful as a fawn' was Dufferin's first impression of Louisa ('Tiny') Abercorn. They had first met at Laggan in 1849 when she was still a child. While he was away in Vienna, Helen took up the cause, dining with 'your Abercorn friends', protesting that it meant playing 'charades and riddles all through the first course and riddles and charades all through the second'. For someone who thrived on intellectual company, and once described a dinner in Paris as 'like sitting with four or five pleasant books and reading them all at once', it can only have been wearing. But there was no denying the benefits of such a match and soon no denying the need.[18]

Through the summer of 1855 Dufferin's courtship of Tiny progressed happily with plans laid for their families to gather at Clandeboye, only for matters to come to a shuddering halt in late August. Pressganged into action, Janey Ellice wrote plainly enough: 'Though she [Lady Abercorn] sees the Splendour of it ... she [asserts?] *most positively* that Tiny could not return his affections ... that Tiny's heart is not her own to give.'[19] It could not be other than a humiliating blow. By now Lady Abercorn's real motives were clear. It was not her daughter but the family's Irish estates that she sought to offer Dufferin, for close on £1 million with 'Baronscourt thrown in for nothing'. Luckily Abercorn had second thoughts on selling because in an attempt to prove his worth Dufferin was only too eager to buy.

7

The Thrill of Escape

The Blackwoods had in fact for long been a seafaring race and
from his earliest childhood to his extreme old age Lord Dufferin
entertained a passion for the sea.

Harold Nicolson, *Helen's Tower*, p.100

TO EMBARK ON a round trip of almost 6,000 miles, travelling far
into the Arctic Circle in the *Foam*, a small wooden eighty-ton
schooner powered only by sail, without back-up or communication,
seems even now utterly foolhardy. No wonder Dufferin's friends in
London bade him farewell half expecting never to see him again,
while the day before he took the sacrament at St James's with his
mother. 'My heart aches for her', he confessed after taking his leave
the next morning; 'nobody will ever love her like me'.[1]

Not that such concern was going to stop him. He revelled in the
refreshing, carefree simplicity of the conflict with the elements.
Writing from Reykjavik to 'my poor little pit-a-pat hearted mother',
he declared that he was 'enjoying myself – heart, body and soul –
more than I could tell you . . . Life is almost too exciting'.[2] Yet the
pleasure of the moment lay also in the traces of the past. In a lecture
entitled 'Northman', given in Belfast after his return, he made a
passionate plea on behalf of the Vikings as a people invigorating an
enfeebled Saxon culture and a decadent Latin world.[3] When Dufferin
sailed north it would be in the tradition of a Viking explorer. And
symbolising this fantasy, rising high from the prow of his own ship
was a bronze figure of his liege lady (this time the Duchess of Argyll)
cast at considerable expense once more by Marochetti ('Dear Lord
Dufferin. You are my Providence'). 'Tell her she looks too beautiful,'

Dufferin instructed his mother. 'If only she could have seen how the passionate waves of the Atlantic flung themselves up towards her lips vainly striving to enchain her in their watery arms, as she proudly burst through their embraces and left them moaning and lamenting far behind!'[4]

With the *Foam* tumbling amidst huge Atlantic rollers, Dufferin's crew were quickly put to the test. They were certainly an exotic collection. The ship's Master was Ebenezer Wise who, with his silk tartan waistcoat, 'seemed [more] a cross between a German student and a commercial gent' than a captain of roughs. Also in the party was Sigurdr, 'my Icelander' and interpreter, whose attractions were many. 'So gentlemanly, such pretty manners and, as all women would think, too lovely to look upon', he teased his mother, '[with] his piercing eyes, dark auburn beard . . . and the complexion of Lady Stafford.'[5] Very different was Dufferin's valet, Wilson, who approached life 'with the air of one advancing to his execution'.

Nearing Iceland the storm finally abated and in warm sunshine they were escorted by whales spouting jets of air, porpoises, seals and geese, as they played chess on deck at midnight in broad daylight; all to the consternation of their cockerel who, denied the dawn, eventually sought oblivion in the sea. And then on 18 June 'a silver pyramid of snow' heralded their arrival in Iceland and 'a bright aureole shot upwards from behind the hard edge of the blue sea'.[6]

If Reykjavik proved a disappointment, a dreary collection of wooden sheds on the edge of a desolate lava plain, the islanders made amends the next day with a spectacular dinner at the Danish governor's house.[7] Dufferin was fully prepared for the traditional 'bumpering' and the governor had 'beamed with approval' when Dufferin, rising to the challenge, downed his glass in one and turned it to his host bottom upwards 'with the orthodox twist'. After twelve toasts in a row, however, Dufferin feared that he might not get through to the second course. Wisdom suggested a tactical withdrawal. Honour, however, prevailed and disaster ensued. Overcome by a 'horrid, wicked' desire to 'floor' the governor ('Was not I my great-grandfather's great-grandson, and an Irish peer to boot? Were there not traditions, too, on the other side of the house, of casks of claret brought up into the dining-room, the door locked, and the key thrown out the window?'), he 'winked defiance to right and left' and the drink flowed for another forty-five minutes. 'At last their fire slackened', leaving the governor 'partially quelled' and Dufferin distinctly frail. Hence his horror at the sight of twenty guests, descending on him to try their turn with this redoubtable champion from foreign shores. With retreat unthinkable, 'the true family blood, I suppose, began to show itself, and with a calmness almost frightful, I received them one by one. After this began the public toasts . . .' And after that the evening became a 'dreamy mystery':

> I can perfectly recall the look of the sheaf of glasses that stood before me; I remember feeling a lazy wonder they should always be so full, though I did nothing but empty them . . . Suddenly I felt as if I were disembodied – a distant spectator . . . of the feast at which my person remained seated. The voices of my host[s] . . . became thin and low, as though they reached me through a whispering tube; and when I rose to speak . . . cheers, faint as the roar of waters on a far-off strand, floated towards me.[8]

What then followed was a triumph of an Etonian education, a speech of perfect nonsense in flowing Latin, received with tumultuous applause by his hosts. Considerable longeurs followed, culminating some hours later in sailing to a nearby island for a hunt (it being still daylight). The 'day' only drew at last to a close when Dufferin attempted to track a 'rabbit', which promptly spread its wings and flew off; as puffins do when approached by the inebriated.

Such dissolution behind them, some days later Dufferin and his friends set out for Jan Mayen Island, lying in the far deadlier interior of the Arctic Circle. He had first heard of it in the Shetlands from a whaling captain. 'Imagine a spike of igneous rock shooting straight up out of the sea to a height of 6870', not broad based like a pyramid nor round topped like a sugar loaf but needle shaped, pointed like a spire of a church.' Since its discovery in 1614, climatic change had left it often inaccessible, imprisoned by 'eternal fields of ice' and impenetrable, near permanent fog. The last French man-o'-war to attempt the journey never returned.[9] By coincidence Dufferin discovered the

French were embarking on their latest attempt. The *Reine Hortense*, a screw corvette of 1,100 tons belonging to HIH Prince Napoleon,[10] represented the height of French technology. Rapidly accepting her generous offer of a tow, the *Foam* soon crossed into the Arctic Circle.

After 300 miles skirting around for a passage through the ice and still 120 miles from their destination, the French abandoned the challenge. Doubtful of success and anxious over his coal supplies, the French captain was not going to take risks with his imperial cargo. Naturally he expected Dufferin to follow. After all the temperature was rapidly falling (they had not seen the sun for two days) and visibility was deteriorating by the hour. The danger was not icebergs necessarily but ice floes threatening to entrap the *Foam*, slowly crushing her wooden sides, which at only two inches' thickness offered little protection. Moreover they would now be reliant on sail power alone. That Dufferin should choose to go on was unquestionably reckless. But stirring his crew to put one over on the French, he dipped the ensign three times in farewell and 'the little schooner glided off like a phantom into the North'.[11]

Retreating out of the ice field, they sailed far to the east in search of a fresh passage. Eventually they did find a break only to become entombed in fog so dense that it 'hung in solid festoons from masts and spurs'. Unable to see in front of them let alone the island they had come to see, the crew became restless lest the ice should claim them. Taking the last watch before they would have to turn back, Dufferin stared hopelessly into the mist. When 'as if by magic a sudden vent was made in the blanket of mist and thousands of feet above its lower folds stood out clear and distinct, the rugged purple top of the mountain of Beerenberg.' Almost before he had realised it, the moment was gone 'like an enchantment'. By the early morning the fog finally lifted and as the mountain reappeared, standing out as if perched on the fog, seven great glaciers rolled into the sea: 'tumbling and raging in a thousand foaming billows, and then frozen into a stillness and silence so sudden, that even the spray has become rigid'.[12]

Despite the encroaching ice, Dufferin was still determined to effect a landing. Rowing ashore, he planted the white ensign of St George and left his beloved figurehead on a ledge, overlooking the hastily renamed Clandeboye Creek – a stretch of sand barely fifteen yards long beneath sheer cliffs nearly 1,000 feet high that formed the base of the mountain. Less than two hours later he was on his way back, struggling initially to reach the ship through the endlessly reforming floes of ice. By now the ice was drifting so fast that it seemed to surround them as far as the eye could see. Realising that they had to keep moving at all costs, they were often trapped in a cul-de-sac of ice as the ice began to concentrate into an impenetrable maze. And each time they had to retrace their course, their chances of survival diminished. Under this strain Wilson was a predictable 'Cassandra'. Yet even Dufferin began to waver, inexplicably hearing English church bells ringing out over the fiercely cold wind. Still it was this same wind that was to prove their saviour. Swinging abruptly around to the east, it whipped up the ice packs and before they could resettle the *Foam* dashed for the open sea, nearly twelve hours after Dufferin had risked all to leave his mark on Clandeboye Creek.

The escape from the perils of Jan Mayen left him raring to set sail again. His new destination was Spitzbergen, a rocky outcrop of an island deep in the Arctic Circle, 630 miles from the pole and almost as far north as any ship had ever managed. He calculated that three weeks of largely good weather with temperatures often in the 80s, along with the warmth of the Gulf Stream, might just expose the north-west tip of Spitzbergen. For eleven days they circumnavigated the ice fields to no avail and then, with even Dufferin admitting the 'sheer folly' of pressing on, they suddenly spotted a narrow strip of open sea to their east and under warm skies they drifted into the safety of English Bay.

The exhilaration of such inspired seamanship quickly evaporated as they took in the 'outlandish scenery' that surrounded them:

> Its most striking feature was the stillness of this new world . . . not a sound of any kind interrupted the silence; the sea did not break upon the shore; no bird nor living thing was visible; the midnight sun, by this time muffled in a transparent mist shed an awful, mysterious lustre; no atom of vegetation; an universal numbness . . . seemed to pervade the solitude . . . a deadness [in a landscape of] Primeval rocks and eternal ice.

This funereal aspect was reinforced as they wandered around the island by the driftwood and debris washed up from sunken vessels; particularly the macabre sight of a Dutch whaler who had died almost a hundred years before and whose bleached skeleton lay primly in its deal coffin on the frozen shore. Soon Dufferin was exploring the glaciers in the mountainous interior, experimenting with an early camera and stopping the crew from a 'senseless slaughter of seals'. However, having arrived too late to prevent the killing of a polar bear, he decided it would make a 'respectable trophy' – as it still does, stretched out before the fire in the outer hall at Clandeboye.[13]

By September Dufferin was back and settled into Dufferin Lodge, his new home in Highgate. Deemed to be 'five miles outside of London' with panoramic views over 'hill and dale', it provided a haven to write the book that would first make his name. Based on his letters to his mother, *Letters From High Latitudes* overcame the reviewers' disapproval of his 'irreverence' and 'taste' to record huge sales. Published in July 1857, it was on its third edition by the end of the year, having sold 4,000 copies; and it has rarely been out of print ever since, with its eighteenth edition appearing in 1915 and the latest reprint coming out as recently as 2006 – 150 years after it first appeared.

That it should prove so popular reflects its appeal on many levels: from a learned travel record – one of the earliest examples of the genre – that was later much beloved by W. H. Auden and Louis MacNeice, to a yachting saga that enthrals sailing enthusiasts to this day.[14] Crucially, while it displayed much erudition on Norse legend and custom, this was a serious travel book that wore its scholarship lightly. Indeed too lightly for some of his critics. On the other hand much of its contemporary popularity lay in his revelling in the superiority of British pluck over the spineless French, shamelessly pandering to populist sentiments in a tract for Palmerstonian times. 'When I think of what you did and the French did not do, [this is] a simple tale of old Viking daring and doughtiness', enthused his close adviser and friend, G. W. Dasent, who had no difficulty in picking up the message.[15] Needless to say, if it had been a race the French would never have offered Dufferin a tow.

As any good storyteller Dufferin had a fine eye for character and especially that of the richly comic Wilson. Fabulously melancholic and relentless in prophesying catastrophe, the valet was the perfect foil to Dufferin's irrepressible optimism. Yet much as Dufferin relished mocking his servant (whose 'upside down' face was only ever seen to brighten with the prospect of the cook's death), it remained a compassionate portrait; sufficiently so for Wilson to take pride in being recognised as 'The Wilson'. In any case, the victim was really Dufferin himself and his intimate, almost confessional style of gentle irony and self-parody endeared him to the reader. For *High Latitudes* was indiscreet, often extremely funny, and with just a hint of impropriety to excite the sales.[16]

At the same time the exhilaration he describes of being at sea has a timeless appeal, recognisable to sailors down the ages. Even the most determined landlubber could not help being stirred as the *Foam* races for the narrow channel at Spitzbergen:

> 'Turn the hands up, Mr Wyse!' ''Bout ship!' 'Down with the helm!' 'Helm a-lee!' Up comes the schooner's head to the wind, the sails flapping with the noise of thunder – blocks rattling against the deck, as if they wanted to knock their brains out – ropes dancing about in galvanised coils like mad serpents – and everything to an inexperienced eye in inextricable confusion; till gradually she pays off onto the other tack – the sails stiffen into deal-boards – the staysail sheet is let go – and heeling over on the opposite side again she darts forward over the sea like an arrow from a bow. 'Stand by to make sail!' 'Out all reefs!' I could have carried sail to sink a man-of-war! – and away the little ship went playing leapfrog over the heavy seas, and staggering under her canvas, as if giddy with the same joyful excitement which made my own heart thump so loud.[17]

Such language might seem overblown to modern tastes but was in accord with a style of romance – and in Dufferin's hands more akin to the Gothic novel – so popular in the nineteenth century.[18]

However, Dufferin was not about to let the realm of imagination take over the world of action. Unlike the present day, his was a world of explorers with places still to explore. Men like Livingstone (whom Dufferin, after meeting at Campden Hill in March 1857, described as the man 'who has walked up and down the interior of Africa as familiarly as we stroll Bond Street') were heroes whose expeditions were largely funded by a public interested in the world beyond their shores. Such was the popular interest in the Arctic that as Dufferin published *High Latitudes*, Charles Dickens and Wilkie Collins were writing a play, *The Frozen Deep*, on an earlier, ill-fated expedition. Therefore it is just an exaggeration of scale to place Dufferin's sketches and accounts of Spitzbergen on a par with the first photographs from space, and goes some way to explain the symbolism in Dufferin presenting the Queen with a copy of *High Latitudes* bound in drift-wood from Spitzbergen.[19]

With *High Latitudes* Dufferin became a public name. Decades later at the height of his diplomatic career, it was to meet the author of this book that Bismarck granted the diplomat a private audience. It would be impossible to read it without appreciating his seamanship, his courage in the face of physical danger and his coolness under pressure. Nor do you have to be Harold Nicolson to recapture 'in those printed lines . . . the slow and silken cadences of his lisping voice', the chivalric modesty and the subtle charm of a fashionable man. This was the author as companion, wooing his readership in much the same way he flirted with his mother. For all the breadth of interests, *High Latitudes* remained profoundly autobiographical. And the Dufferin that emerged was undoubtedly someone the author aspired to be. It was not so much a desire to be seen as a hero and adventurer (although to make his mark undoubtedly appealed). Just as the Ary Schaffer portrait in 1850 was commissioned to give him lineage, so *High Latitudes* was designed to portray him to a wider public as more than the fop his aristocratic friends knew. It was an attempt at reconstruction, to show what he could be, and as such declared his emergence into public life.

8

'Any pearl?'[1]

WITHIN A MONTH the court at Windsor had reclaimed him.[2] Nor did Westminster offer any excitement. When in July 1858 he found himself speaking on Irish education with 'only three peers on my side [and] seven starving ministerialists on the other', the parliamentary life seemed very 'miserable [and] dreary'.[3] Yet in other respects these were happy years, not least because, with the acclamation of *High Latitudes*, he was now a man of some literary repute and widely sought after. 'My dear Lord Dufferin', beseeched Tennyson, 'come whenever – real Havanas if you are a smoker.' At a ball in 1857 one onlooker reported that Dufferin was 'the crack beau of the room'.[4] Henrietta Bathyani, not too long married but already regaining as she put it her 'carnal spirits', caught something of his attractiveness when she wrote longing for 'a chat with you, so kind, so good, so strangely conscious of other people's feelings'.[5]

As it turned out, in April Dufferin had come face to face with carnality in a traditional guise when he was solicited by a young girl in the Haymarket. Such degradation of a child appalled him and he hired a private investigator to track down the girl and have her institutionalised for the good of her soul. Such rescue work risked ridicule. Given Dufferin's acute sensitivity on this score, the arrival at Dufferin Lodge in June 1857 of a 'Miss Jones' ('keen to give up her present way of life') was both an embarrassment as well as a challenge.[6] Nor does there seem to have been the visceral thrill in the proximity of the forbidden that partly accounted for Gladstone's interest. Instead it was the preservation of innocence that was paramount to him, as in all his dealings with the opposite sex.

That said, the unexpected arrival of Mrs Anna Thomas – 'my dear Lady of Avenal' – whom he had met on his way back from Spitzbergen, stirred deeper feelings. She was passing through London in November 1857 en route to 'Chili' (sic) to join her husband in his new posting. Her departure before Christmas, with the wind blowing a gale in the Channel, left him distraught, writing long passages in his diary (which were vigorously excised much later) and pouring out his feelings to Elizabeth Argyll. She let him down lightly, giving him the gentle reassurance that 'the person concerned knows that there has been something and perhaps that is enough'. And perhaps it was for Dufferin too. 'The more I see of other women, now that the first illusions of youth have gone', he wrote to his mother, 'the more I love and appreciate you.'[7]

By the mid-1850s, however, he realised that he no longer had a monopoly over his mother's affections. Her relationship with Gifford became increasingly overt with her successful campaign in 1855 to get him elected to the House of Commons. She had become inordinately fond of her young friend, ever anxious about his health and keen for his company, and giving him his own apartment in Dufferin Lodge. And with 'Fred' so often away, there were fewer restraints.[8]

Not that outsiders ever noticed. Dining at Lansdowne House, J. L. Motley was most struck by her son: 'a very handsome youth of nearly thirty [who] sat near her looking like her brother'. The local minister mistook her for Dufferin's wife at a reeling party in Scotland that same year. Helen could still look like a young girl and at dinner parties she sparkled, playing the ingénue, ever so delicate yet steely.[9] Disraeli's 'capricious Bird of Paradise' still, she kept her two young men competitive, chiding and flirting with them as if they were equals.

By now Dufferin had his own plans. Keen to combine the latest technology of the steam engine with the traditional power of sail, in September he had bought (at the prohibitive cost of £3,000) the *Erminia*, a 220-ton yacht. Free at last from Palace duties, he planned to sail the eastern Mediterranean and settled in Portsmouth to oversee the reconstruction of the *Erminia*.[10]

'Any pearl?' quizzed Elizabeth Argyll, having not heard from Dufferin for three months. 'Tell me if there is a pearl in sight – this year was to be the final one, you thought.' Nelly Graham, his guardian's daughter, was never intended to be a pearl. Hers was the intimacy of a close cousin ready to support his cause. With her father, she

joined Dufferin on the *Erminia* to sail to Cherbourg for the unveiling
of a statue of Napoleon I. After the ball the following day Dufferin
had a 'long talk with Nelly at night on deck'. Two days later when
they docked again at Portsmouth his diary was referring to 'my ador-
able Nelly' only for this and much else besides later to be furiously
erased. What was actually said on deck that night may only be deduced
from subsequent evidence, suggesting an exchange of rings and his
commissioning of Sant to paint her portrait.[11] The same day he
recorded that he had 'called the bay at Greypoint [by Clandeboye]
Helen's Bay after her'; the last word still just visible despite its later
replacement with 'my mother'.[12]

There is reason to suggest that Helen Dufferin was taken by surprise
at the turn of events. Whole pages were cut out of her son's diary at
this point and many of the passages that survived, heavily blacked out,
began with 'a long talk with my mother'. While it might have been
natural for Helen to be upset by the prospect of sharing her son, jealousy was not like her. Nelly was in fact very like the wife Dufferin
would eventually marry – pretty rather than beautiful, utterly devoted
and loyal, unfailingly cheerful – but too affectionate and trusting for
Helen to resent. What aroused Helen's anger was a new will Dufferin
had drawn up after the Cherbourg trip. Such was her anger that she
forced a codicil on Dufferin (presumably to protect her income),
who then had to raise further life insurance. The will has not survived,
but perhaps the naming of Helen's Bay was symbolic of intention.
Equally symbolic perhaps was Nelly's sister Cossy's poignant farewell,
assuring him that she and Nelly couldn't love him more 'if you were
our brother'.[13]

Helen did not win all her battles. Petrified of the sea, this cruise was
the last thing she wanted and as Sir James reminded Dufferin 'she
only wishes to go because she cannot bear long separation from
you'.[14] That said, she insisted on inviting Giff. Dufferin agreed, determined that nothing was going to stop him.[15] And nothing did; not
even 'Mrs Stukeley's sister'.

Mrs Stukeley's sister was Annie Gilbert, whom Dufferin first met
in June when the Earl of Stafford came to sail for a week and brought
his mistress; for so she was. Whatever turmoil Dufferin may have felt

at being a party to the betrayal of one of his first 'liege ladies', he was soon won over by Miss Gilbert, showering her with gifts of money. She in return wrote to him on his birthday the following week – a letter that along with most of her correspondence was later cut out of his bound letter-books. Why he should have been so emboldened is not known, although it has to be said that few men are so generous as to subsidise the mistresses of their richer friends. With Stafford away they would ride out every day (resulting later in much expunging from his diary).[16] Until 14 October when Helen arrived, together with a cousin, John Hamilton. The *Erminia* departed England the next evening. Six months later with Dufferin still in the Mediterranean, Elizabeth Argyll wrote to him a little tetchily: 'What an odd life you are leading considering that you pretend to want a pearl.'[17] Indeed.

'It is too late for the Bay of Biscay for the ladies,' advised Argyll; and indeed within two days they almost came to grief in a gale off Cape Finisterre. Amid 'thick rainy weather' and 'heavy seas', and with smoke pouring into Dufferin's cabin, Helen became hysterical in the darkness as a collapsing table sent a lamp crashing to the wooden floor.[18] However, the storm passed and soon they were landing at Alexandria, where they toured the sights with all the insensitivity of those who are mentally still at home. 'Very much amused', Dufferin wrote, 'by the novelty of the scene, camels, blackamoors, turbans . . . Very hot, hotter than summer in England.' The sight of a young girl, 'surrounded by a crowd of shrieking friends' as she waited timidly outside the door of her bridegroom, struck them as faintly barbaric only to find the wedding party in their turn 'greatly scandalised [by] my mother taking my arm'.[19]

By the end of the week Dufferin had an audience with the ruler of Egypt, Said Pasha: 'a large coarse red man in full white Egyptian trousers and white jacket, with a tarboosh in his hand'. Pipes were brought and they discoursed in French, with Dufferin (in a scene that presaged much of his life to come) flattering his host shamelessly. Learning that the Pasha's 'sole delight' was his army, the young traveller complimented their uniform, drawing chuckles of delight from the ruler. And amid the bonhomie Dufferin saw for the first time the contradiction of the Ottoman Empire. Here was 'a good natured, irascible, bustling, childish man', much given 'they say' to 'the most infamous of practices', with a huge army of decorative soldiers but who only survived in power by 'allow[ing] everyone to cheat him'.[20]

Outside, as it approached midday, Dufferin found himself by a small mosque where worshippers were sitting around an imam, chanting 'Allah il Allah' in a steady monotone. Gradually the tempo increased and the worshippers began to sway and shake their heads building up to a crescendo, so violent and frenzied and then just as suddenly stilled. Disturbed by this display Dufferin quickly put it down to 'mesmeric influences'. But in reality it was he who was hypnotised. Later with the fierce sunlight creating deep shadows, he wandered happily, amid the bustle and noise and dazzling colour, in and out of the stalls and past conjurers, dancers and hawkers plying their delicacies. Only then to stumble across 'a brute of a man dressed (or rather undressed) as a woman, dancing in a tent'. Equally jarring to the senses, the next day, he came across a gang of youths beating up a drunken old man. Having 'whipped off the crowd', he had to resort to brandy to restore his equilibrium.[21]

By now, Giff had joined them in Cairo, only to fall ill. Nevertheless Dufferin pressed on. In January 1859, Dufferin, Hamilton and Helen hired the *Arrow* for £150 and set sail up the Nile for Aswan. On either side of the river lay vast temples, almost entirely preserved, the last 'vestiges of the first race that was ever civilised'. Fascinated by all he saw Dufferin made a determined effort to master the hieroglyphics. After reaching Philae, they drifted back, stopping off to visit temples and read more inscriptions. And inevitably to excavate: a block of stone with the cartouche of Tirhakah upon it, found in the remains of a Roman wall, proved so intractable that Dufferin's valet, Wilson, had to mobilise the locals to aid its removal (for which Dufferin gave 'all my Nubian friends' £5 and a knife). Further visits were made to Silsileh, now Gebel-es-Silsileh ('wonderful Grosvenor Squares dug out of the heart of the mountain'), the temple of Karnak at Thebes and afterwards to Luxor, where excavations were more organised, producing further artefacts (including a vast granite altar, remnants of ancient columns, and most spectacular of all, a statue of the god Amun) – all destined for the hall at Clandeboye. Only in his desire to bring back the head of Rameses II was he foiled, having to be satisfied with the great toe from the granite statue. And while the present looted the past, Wilson recorded it all on an invention with a future, the camera.[22]

The outbreak of the Franco-Austrian War in April 1859 provided a convenient excuse to delay his return, so they sailed north to Greece and Constantinople where the heat would be more bearable for his mother. En route they visited the Acropolis; and at the site of the mausoleum at Halicarnassus, one of the Seven Wonders of the World and birthplace of Herodotus, Dufferin discovered the carved names of later Crusaders.[23] For Helen, after a month of steaming into bays in search of yet more ancient remains to plunder, the thrill began to pall. Constantinople initially raised her spirits, 'with the sparkling Bosphorous, dashing and splashing under my windows'. But not for long. A visit to the harem of the Turkish prime minister did little to improve her mood, describing her hostess as a 'ball of fat with fine eyes in it'. With Giff already recuperating in London, the death of her dog, Gypsy, from a scorpion bite left her crying silently for 'our smoky, fussy, safer England'.[24]

Her son on the other hand felt at ease in the flurry of diplomatic dinners and receptions, and flattered to be lionised by ambassadors. Such was his impact that both the prime minister and the grand vizier would pay their respects on his departure. In turn, he was fascinated by the diplomatic chatter and the challenge of operating in such an ornate culture. Travelling to Seraglio Point, Dufferin was struck by the opulence of the Sultan's procession and the frenzied cheering that greeted it. But what really impressed him was the Sultan's 'supreme indifference to everyone's homage'; and the attention paid to the details of hierarchy and ritual, down to the 'two strips of cloth pinned to the Sultan's sofa to represent "the hem of his garment" beyond which none could advance'.[25] Like many Victorians Dufferin was entranced by the Orient: enthralled by a world of colours, of romance, and where savagery seemed but the veneer of civilisation away. For all his mother's pining for home, Dufferin was in no mood to leave. Seizing the opportunity to carry out a minor diplomatic mission, Dufferin set off for the Holy Land. As it turned out, it was a decision that was to determine the future course of his life. En route he dropped anchor off the site of Troy where, according to Homeric legend, King Priam had held Helen captive. Determined 'that my first glimpse of Troy might be from the invaders' point of view', he landed and from the top of Ajax's tomb he watched for two hours 'the procession of the dawn' over this ancient setting.[26]

By October he was in Beirut[27] and preparing to embark on a pilgrimage to the Holy Land. There he met up with Cyril Graham, who was to act as his guide. Only twenty-five, he was already a renowned traveller in the Middle East ('having found eighty-three pre-Greek stone cities'), and the two young men fast became friends as they set off for Damascus.[28] Throughout Graham talked of the Arabs. He was a fervent advocate for the cause of the Druze, a small sub-Shiite sect, who had broken away from Ismaili Shiite Islam in the eleventh century and as a consequence were regarded as heretics by much of the Muslim world. Their survival was conceivably only possible where Shiites were not outnumbered by Sunnis: Mount Lebanon. A complication was added by the conversion late in the eighteenth century of Sunni rulers into Maronite Christians. Where many Westerners would have seen the Druze as barbaric tribesmen defending an archaic way of life, Graham saw the miraculous survival of an ancient civilisation with a rich culture. He looked beyond the violence to the inherent nobility of the savage, endeavouring to find in their leaders what he wanted to find: men of honour, civility and integrity.[29]

Once in Damascus, they threaded their way through the gardens and orchards to the British consulate with its pretty courtyard and walls of coloured marble. There Dufferin met with Mr Brant and discussed the row simmering between Druze and Maronite, which had alarmed Sir Henry Bulwer in Constantinople and prompted Dufferin's mission. The next day they rode out to Ah'med Pasha, the Governor General of the province, finding him 'a very gentlemanly Turk in the prime of life'. A former ambassador in Vienna, this was a meeting of cosmopolitans whose conversation was almost wholly concerned with the fate not of the Druze but of the *Great Eastern*, Brunel's steamship (then the largest in the world), which had run aground. Yet away from such civilities, Dufferin was beginning to agree with those he met who argued that 'if they chose, the Turks could keep the peace in Lebanon without difficulty'.[30]

Damascus itself appeared calm, if riveting: 'the only city on this side of the Euphrates which retains in all its purity the Oriental character', he informed his Aunt Anna (reassuring her that the only Europeans found outside the consulate were Protestant missionaries from Bangor). Entertained by a flourishing Jewish community, Dufferin was 'much struck' by the ladies with their shaved eyebrows lined in black kohl, their long black hair intertwined with strings of diamonds and pearls, their silk trousers and jackets – blue, red or pink, and all trimmed with silver and gold, and above all by 'their bosoms which were left quite bare'. But it was a visit to a Christian household that left a lasting memory. His host was a rich Syrian merchant and his young wife, who

> lived in the street, which is still called 'Straight', just as it was in St Paul's time. To my surprise, however, instead of finding myself at the gates of an imposing mansion, we entered through a mean door in a clay wall. Going along a narrow passage built with sun-dried bricks, we came to another door, and so on to a third; and then I suddenly found myself standing at the threshold of Paradise. Before us lay a large courtyard paved with marble, with a living river running through it, and interspersed with palm trees and a variety of scented shrubs. On all four sides there rose lofty structures of the most beautiful Arabic architecture, with highly decorated porches, doors and windows in the style of the Alhambra, with gilded lattices framed in lovely Arabesque lace work, and interspersed with intricate marble pillars, colonnades and friezes, while every sign and symptom of the existence of the dust, tumult and toil of the outer world was shut out.

They whiled away the afternoon with this attractive couple; he highly intelligent and soon deep in scholarly discussion with Graham, while his wife ('looked quite a girl') with her two small children was 'full of gaiety and merriment'. It made 'a profound impression on me', Dufferin was to write almost forty years later, 'contrasting as its sweet tranquillity and peace did with the semi-barbarous' world beyond its walls.[13]

His mission completed, the remaining weeks were dedicated to pilgrimage. It was only when back on board *Erminia* that he learned of his cousin Fletcher Norton's death. Ever the consumptive,

Caroline's glamorous, favourite son had succumbed finally in Paris.[32] At this news, Helen, holed up in Athens 'lonely and sad . . . and longing to be in England again', panicked over her only son's safety. Having not heard from him for two months she continually imagined the worst. To the last, Dufferin delayed his return, desiring to enter Piraeus at sunrise 'with the plain of Attica shimmering in the mist [and] the Acropolis . . . rising up like an island out of it'. By the time he eventually docked, Helen had rushed on board to reclaim her son, leaving a trail of quarantine regulations and officialdom in her wake. And in so doing she brought his year of adventuring to a close.[33] Was this all it had been? Those with genuine public ambition would not have left to sail in Mediterranean backwaters. Yet in doing so, Dufferin had stumbled on ground that he would walk for the rest of his life.

First, however, he had to confront the perils awaiting him at home. It was John Hamilton who first warned Dufferin of the breaking scandal that 'Stafford and Miss Gilbert have been for some time past too intimate'. Dufferin felt keenly the social humiliation of his friend. Stafford on the other hand was more complacent. 'The world has been very good-natured as it always is about us', the heir to a dukedom reassured his friend.[34] However, with his wife playing the wronged woman for all that it was worth and threatening separation, Stafford had no alternative but to drop his lover. Hence within two months of his return Dufferin found himself sheltering a pregnant Annie Gilbert in Dufferin Lodge.[35] Was the child his or Stafford's? Certainly he made all the arrangements for her to retreat to Southsea, near her sister, where she eventually gave birth to a boy.[36] If scandal was avoided, suspicion was not. Obliquely referring to 'the Riddle', which she instinctively disapproved of, Elizabeth Argyll questioned his involvement 'unless you make the woman your country woman'.[37]

There is no evidence that Dufferin did, or at least any longer. But it is suggestive of some relationship that, just before the crisis broke, he should arrange for the two of them to be photographed together by the society phototgrapher Camille Silvy.[38] And there was an intriguing sequel to these events. Thirty-five years later when ambassador in Paris, Dufferin received a letter asking for his help in securing a position in the colonial police for the correspondent's son. Such correspondence filled the postbags of aristocratic England. In this case the supplicant was a doctor at the West London Hospital called Richard J. Gilbert – the nephew of Annie Gilbert and her sister, Emma Stukeley Buck. Not only did Dufferin respond promptly but the favours Gilbert requested for this son and a later one were not slight, requiring Dufferin to intervene with a cabinet minister (Lord Spencer),[39] a future Chancellor of the Exchequer (C. T. Ritchie) and Gladstone's former secretary (Sir Algernon West). Why he put himself out in this way for so tenuous a connection is curious.

But it is even possible that Dufferin initiated the correspondence, for it appears he was searching for a particular drawing of Annie Gilbert which by implication he had drawn of her. Gilbert recognised the sketch as one inherited by his Aunt Buck on her sister's death. However, she refused to part with it; and continued to do so even when Dufferin sent another portrait to replace it, which Gilbert acknowledged as 'wonderfully correct and skilfully drawn'. Keen not to offend his patron, he sent a miniature of his Aunt Annie 'taken' in late 1861, which Dufferin returned six months later (presumably after making a copy). Also sent at Dufferin's request was a photograph of Gilbert's daughter, with her father pleading its 'marked indications of an eventual resemblance to my affectionately remembered Aunt'.[40] As for the aunt herself, it would seem that she had died in the 1880s. If he had written to her, she had never replied. And yet her memory apparently stayed with him to the end.

Another who had failed to write was Nelly Graham. Whatever agreement they had made on the deck of the *Erminia* did not survive his absence and she was to marry a Colonel Baring, amid crying aunts and torrents of rain. The bride was 'very pleased with her military bargain' reported his uncle Brinsley. Nevertheless at the church she had taken 'the little opal ring that you gave her', her sister, Cossy, assured Dufferin, and 'put it on over the wedding ring of which it is destined to be the Guard as long as she lives'.[41]

Not that he appeared frustrated by these events. Any sexual uncertainty aside, marriage was always going to be a problem for one who viewed it as the physical sacrifice of a woman for a higher purpose. Hence his preference for the company of women who were already spoken for, like Madame Todesco and 'My Lady of Avenal'. Of no one was this more true than his mother, to whom he renewed his vow of fidelity.

> My own darling, you are the only person I have ever really loved since I was born. And I have loved you better than life or happiness or anything else, and I know well that in this world I shall never find anyone to love like you do ... We are, thank Heaven, almost like brother and sister in years, and in the course of nature cannot live very long the one beyond the other ... [when] ... the real love, which now can but imperfectly make itself felt, is known.
>
> Your affectionate son, my own, own darling mother.[42]

If genuinely felt, this was still an expression of emotional convenience, a fantasy of mother love that precluded action. Other actions spoke louder than these words. As Helen watched Nelly Graham walk up the aisle clutching her son's ring, Dufferin had actually returned to Syria but this time as the representative of the British government.

9

Dangers Abroad

EARLY JUNE 1860 saw Cyril Graham in the Lebanon, guiding another party of English travellers when, looking back, they noticed the valley of the Lebanon enveloped in a dusky blue haze. Only at their destination did they discover that this was no khamsin wind blowing up dust from the desert. Rather, the vast cornfields and brushwood in the valley had been set ablaze, with some thirty villages in flames. The tribal conflict between Druze and Maronite had finally broken out. Soon tales were coming out of unbelievable carnage. Up to 15,000 dead and 200 Maronite villages razed to the ground leaving 100,000 refugees. In Damascus, the Christian quarter was destroyed, with 5,000 out of 20,000 of its inhabitants killed, another 400 raped, and 1,500 to 2,000 homes and businesses torched.[1]

Graham was soon witnessing ethnic cleansing with the massacre of 1,200 Maronites at Zahleh, where the Druze were abetted by some Turkish troops caught up in the tide of religious fanaticism. Later at Hasbeya he endured a local Druze leader proudly taking him through the houses of the murdered Christians, naming each and every mutilated corpse, before moving on to the great court where hundreds more lay on bloodstained pavements. It was the 'diabolical expression of delight' on his face that Graham would never forget. In blind fury he now denounced the Druze as 'a set of butchers and cowards', only for his guide to turn on him menacingly. 'Look here', the Druze said slowly drawing out his pistols. After a brief pause, he turned one round. There on its handle, Graham could see that the ornamental steel setting, which these warriors took such pride over, was missing. 'I spoiled this beautiful pistol against their cursed skulls.' Graham held his tongue. However, six months later he would remember the name of Beshir el-Awaj.[2]

Almost as suddenly as it had started, the wave of massacres died away. Yet for all its spontaneity, this was a conflict that had been long expected. A tribal society overlaid with religious enmity between Christian and Muslim and complicated by the separate existence in the mountains of the Druze, the Lebanon had become especially unstable of late. What made this situation dangerous was the Islâhat Fermâni (Ottoman Reform Edict) in 1856 – a legal insistence from the Porte, the Ottoman government, on the equality of Muslim and Christian. This had been forced on the Sultan by the Western powers after the Crimean War. Such a policy had little appeal for Ah'med Pasha, the Governor General in Damascus who sought only a quiet life and a comfortable income. Moreover he knew that the notables in the town were incensed at the prospect of equality. Just as vehement were the Maronites who, fired up by the demagogic Bishop Touma, had become intolerant of any delay in obtaining their new rights. By 1860 the Lebanon was a tinderbox. As it turned out, it was the Maronites who provided the spark, forcing some Muslim youths in Damascus to sweep the Christian quarter after they had hurled insults at passing Maronites. This proved an insult too far and the Muslim community rose up. Later, there would be much debate over how far the retaliation had been planned and of the role of Said Bey, the Druze leader, and of the Turkish authorities. But in truth, once stirred, mobs move at the behest of their instincts.[3]

Resuming her self-appointed role as defender of Christendom in the East, France called for an international commission to sit in judgement and proposed sending an army to restore order. The British under Palmerston sensed the danger in this (fearing that, once there, this army may never leave). Also, such a commission, by definition, undermined the credibility of Turkish rule. An independent Ottoman Empire was essential for the balance of power in the continent and for keeping the Russians out of the Mediterranean – a key British interest. However, as the extent of the massacre became clear, popular outcry in Britain made it impossible to block the French proposal.[4]

'Syria?' squealed Janey Ellice on hearing of Dufferin's appointment as the British commissioner. 'People are murdered there.' But with Graham writing gruesome accounts from Damascus, the challenge (as well as the chance to win 'some glory') in a land that had caught his imagination was irresistible. With Elizabeth Argyll bestowing her blessing on her 'pilgrim and crusader', it would prove, as she said, 'a very interesting beginning'.[5] More surprising was the choice of Dufferin as commissioner. Speed, though, was of the essence, with the British keen to get their representative to Syria before the French arrived with an army. Dufferin's recent fact-finding mission to the area and his willingness to leave at a moment's notice appealed to Lord John Russell, who as Foreign Secretary felt he could rely on his protégé to do as he was told.[6]

By the end of July Dufferin had left, accompanied by a Foreign Office official, Robert Meade. Off the Straits of Messina they witnessed one of the great revolutionary moments of the nineteenth century, as they picked out the red shirts of Garibaldi's Mille bivouacking on a shingle shore in the baking heat. Opportunists and the merely curious were soon scurrying hotfoot to witness the Risorgimento. Among them, Dufferin discovered the novelist Alexandre Dumas, who had sailed down accompanied by 'a girl of 18 in a man's clothing' and 30,000 rifles (for which he hoped to drive a hard bargain with Garibaldi).[7] Still what was amusing for an author was embarrassing for a government minister. Dufferin had long gone by the time the papers broke the story that his Uncle Somerset's son had also appeared with his mistress similarly disguised. But at least Ferdy St Maur was there for the fight.[8]

In Constantinople he heard word that the Turkish authorities had already begun to execute the Druze in droves. Commandeering a boat, Dufferin met up with Graham at Beirut from where they rode through the day to arrive at Damascus by nightfall on 4 September 1860. No amount of briefings could prepare him for the inhumanity that confronted him there. The vibrant Christian quarter was now a mass of destruction: 2,000 houses reduced to smouldering ruins, burnt rafters and the debris of private possessions scattered in the looting; its inhabitants barely buried beneath the rubble as gangs of dogs sniffed through the devastation. 'Such a monument of human wickedness and sorrow I have never beheld', he would write almost forty years later. Desperately he began to search for the young merchant's house where only a year before he had found himself 'on the threshold of Paradise'. All that remained now was 'a labyrinth of burnt walls' within which he attempted despairingly to place the memory of 'the happy little family group – the young merchant, his pretty wife and two little children – that had welcomed us so kindly'. All 'brutally murdered by the Turkish soldiery and the fanatical rabble'.

The juxtaposition was not accidental. For all that the Druze had carried out most of the murders, both Graham and Dufferin saw the ethnic violence as wholly preventable if the Turks had chosen to exercise their authority. Instead they had stood aside and even on occasion let their troops participate, apparently happy in an outcome that would leave the population more manageable. Such impressions were reinforced by the distressing sight of 'poor old Consul Brant'. Four times Brant had braved the murderous crowds to remonstrate with the local pasha and all to no avail. His family had survived but his nerves were shot and he was now to be found wandering aimlessly, mumbling to himself.[9]

With the other commissioners and the French troops still to arrive, Dufferin seized his chance and by midnight was being received in the castle above Damascus by Fuad Pasha. One of the great reformers and now Foreign Minister of the Ottoman Empire, Fuad Pasha was also, as Dufferin recognised, 'one of the most remarkable men in Europe' and highly experienced in continental diplomacy. By now middle-aged he was impressively 'tall and handsome', speaking French 'to perfection' and with an amiable, disarming manner. With a brief to defend Turkish sovereignty and honour, Fuad had sought to re-establish law and order and so demonstrate the authority of Turkish government – in effect seeking to remove the problem before the commission arrived. Central to his strategy was appeasing the French by making the Druze the scapegoats, so pleasing the local Maronites at the cost of Syrians and Arabs who Dufferin noted were 'of little account' to the Turks. But Fuad recognised that it would take British support to defeat French ambitions once they had an army in the area. Even so, what followed he had not expected.

Once pipes and coffee had been left and they were alone, Fuad 'began enumerating the extraordinary severity' he had imposed: 'on such a day he hanged so many, on the next day so many, on the third so many and tomorrow so many had been ordered for execution'. Dufferin waited until Fuad paused and then quietly asked after the fate of the leading Turkish officials and army officers who had let these massacres happen unchecked, mentioning by name five or six including Ah'med Pasha. Fuad began to equivocate, exploring to what extent Britain's representative would allow him to save his friends and the Turkish reputation. Cutting in, Dufferin was 'perfectly frank'. Such reputation as the Turks had, depended 'from a political point of view' on the executions of these officials being carried out and at the initiative of the Turks. With the commission already gathering in Beirut, time was now very short. Fuad was shrewd enough to grasp the position, even agreeing to release the forty Druze due to be executed in the morning. But to execute the officials would be to accept some Turkish culpability, and, for him, would complicate matters significantly.

Up before dawn Dufferin and Graham were on the road to Beirut when they were overtaken by a Turkish aide, who informed them of the judgement on the 'five great officers'. Ah'med Pasha had not realised what was about to happen when he was led at daybreak into the privacy of the cavalry barrack yard. There he saw the small square crowded with over 300 soldiers, standing silently in ranks. Turkish honour determined that no civilian would witness this humiliation. The sentence was read, the shots rang out and Ah'med fell dead – in the castle where barely a year before he had spent a pleasant afternoon with a young Anglo-Irish aristocrat drinking tea and discussing the fate of the *Great Eastern*.[10]

'Dear Duffy, you blood thirsty monster!' wrote Argyll, as he gleefully reported back the British press's admiration of Dufferin's 'firmness'.[11] No doubt his fellow commissioners noted it too, smarting a little at the young man's presumption. As experienced diplomats they knew that Dufferin's early initiative would not prove decisive. In Beirut Dufferin took a house close to Fuad Pasha and set himself up for the long haul. After days filled with meetings and receptions, he worked to 4 a.m. writing despatches for London, which the others would copy up for the morning mail. It was a punishing routine especially as, one by one, they went down with fever, Dufferin succumbing on 11 October.[12] By then the negotiations were drifting away from him. For, with nearly 40,000 refugees in Damascus alone and disease breaking out, the immediate humanitarian crisis had left the commission dependent on the French army. Lonely ('no friends here and few acquaintances') and fearing failure, a strain of melancholy set in to the letters home.[13]

Into this gloom, unannounced and unexpected, appeared his mother, falling 'like a bomb among them'. In a sense she had always been there, as Dufferin's staff had noted the need to pay homage to her photograph on their master's desk. Still, it was an astonishing act, given her dislike of travelling by boat and the fact that she travelled alone. Her opinion of the East had not changed: 'Beirut perfectly lovely from the sea', she reported back to her sister, 'but like all these Eastern cities the charm vanishes when you enter it.' Her arrival was a strikingly impulsive, maternal gesture, reflective of an emotional bond reaffirmed in the aftermath of Fletcher Norton's death. Mother and son, friend and lover – theirs was a blurring of instincts in an intense relationship that remained happily undefined until thrown unexpectedly into sharp relief. They were never to be as close again, except in the memory; but, for now, morale restored, a rejuvenated Dufferin rose again to the diplomatic challenge.[14]

Immediately pressing were the politics of punishment. For all their expression of humanitarian outrage, the French wanted primarily to expand their 'Empire' by establishing a Maronite state in Syria under French protection. Standing in the way of this were the Druze and the Turks. To Western eyes the Druze already stood condemned by the massacres. However, Fuad's pre-emptive executions had left Turkish guilt falling on local officials and, as Dufferin had intended, not on Turkish rule in general. Privately he had no doubt that Turkish officials and the Druze had 'connived' in the 'extermination' of the Maronites and thus Turkish government had failed. But to extrapolate from this, as Cyril Graham did with characteristic vehemence, 'Turkey must fail, Turkey will fail', was not an option open to Dufferin. British interests depended on the continuation of the Ottoman Empire, irrespective of its corruption and brutality (a fact unappreciated by liberal opinion back in Britain). Dufferin's brief was to get the French out and keep the Turks in. With the French military itching, at the behest of the Maronites and with the authority of the commission, to attack the Druze on Mount Lebanon, Dufferin recognised the danger of an ethnic cleansing that would leave the Maronites dominant and the French position strengthened immeasurably. So he determined to take matters into his own hands.[15]

The hijacking of the eighth session of the commission with an 'interpellation' (literally an interruption of the agreed agenda) caught the other commissioners unawares. If Dufferin's insistence that justice did not affect Turkish sovereignty was predictable, his defence of the Druze was not. He made no attempt to deny their responsibility for 'unimaginable butcheries [and] criminality'. But it had been the Maronites who had struck the first blow – thus provoking the Druze 'against their will'. Portraying it as a civil war, Dufferin held both sides to be responsible for reprisals even if, as he laconically remarked to Carnarvon, 'the Druze seem to have been the most successful'. He argued that not only must all criminal verdicts be based on hard evidence, but they must also take into account the 'inveterate tradition' in this 'country of vendettas'. Thus the massacres were portrayed as a 'blood feud' with its own rules, a situation whose 'historical parallels', as he rather graphically put it in a later lecture (in Dublin in 1864), 'can be found in the book of Moses . . . [a time when] the book of the Law was lost and contending tribes smote each other hip and thigh, sparing no male child'. In contrast to a dynamic, modernising West, the East was 'changeless . . . Time there almost seems shorn of its wings and all things remain as they ever have been.'[16]

Dufferin's recognition of 'primitive innocence' tore asunder the prevailing consensus over the guilt of the Druze. In so doing he had bought time and negotiating space. Yet he had done so at considerable risk, for he was now vulnerable to the accusation of defending the murderers of Christians, including many missionaries – one of whom, the Rev. William Graham, came from his local town, Bangor. A decade later Disraeli's government would be overwhelmed by the outcry over the Turkish massacre of 12,000 Christians in Bulgaria. Hence the importance, with Palmerston working the editors in London and Dufferin wooing their local correspondents, of keeping the British press in line. Hence too his call to Fuad Pasha to protect the small Protestant community in Nazareth 'or he will have all the Protestants in England about his ears'.[17] For the next two months it was Maronite complaints that filled his ears as the original list of 4,600

Druze criminals was whittled down by forensic investigation to 1,200. Of these Dufferin expected only 50 to be executed – 'the cold blood murderers' (such as Beshir el-Awaj). All this represented a major climbdown by the French.

'We are at this moment puzzled how to get the French out of Syria', Prince Albert confided to his ancient mentor, Baron Stockmar.[18] As for Helen, by now missing Giff ('my lonely owl, how I long to see your face again'), she was furious on hearing of the two-month extension to the French military presence in Syria. Clearly feeling that she had fulfilled her maternal side of the bargain, she insisted Dufferin resign and take her home. His refusal unleashed a furious row between them – words spoken 'overlooking the Bosphorous' for which forgiveness would only be sought some years later as she lay dying. Certainly she was uncharacteristically vicious as she reported of Dufferin returning '"back to his vomit", Beyrout'. Within a month she would work herself up into quite an illness.[19]

Admittedly even Dufferin now viewed Syria as 'my penal servitude'. Actually languishing in jail was Said Bey Jumblatt, the Druze chief. Now under sentence of death after a travesty of a trial, he remained an iconic figure to his people. For the Maronites, who had seen their list of Druze criminals whittled down to double figures, his head had become an absolute minimum. Even Dufferin came to have 'doubts' over Said Bey's innocence.[20] But his execution would only provoke another Druze rebellion and give the French an excuse to occupy the region.

With time no longer on Dufferin's side, nature intervened. By May 1861 it was clear that Said Bey was dying from consumption. So Dufferin ensured that the Druze chief was released to die among his own people. Free from the diplomatic stalemate, Dufferin then seized the opportunity to strike a deal on a new constitution for the region. (An early proposal of an autonomous Syria under a largely independent governor general had come to nothing.[21]) In this second initiative some historians have accused him of selling out to the French.[22] By agreeing to Lebanon being ruled by a Christian governor he had enabled the establishment of a French client state. That this never materialised was because his proposal was far subtler than first appeared. For a start, the Christian governor could not be chosen from within Syria; thus at a stroke denying France's Maronite allies power. Moreover the appointment remained with the Porte – so maintaining Turkish sovereignty. Such fleetness of foot was more than matched by the serious thought Dufferin had put in regarding the internal government of Syria and which made up the greater part of the Règlement Organique. Key to this was a consultative assembly to advise the governor, which had considerable administrative influence, from budgets and taxation to the movement of Turkish troops. This council (and the local versions it spawned) was representative but on tribal rather than democratic grounds. In effect the governor had to rule through the council, so ensuring less arbitrary and more stable government. As a mechanism for the regulation of sectarian societies it would prove sufficiently successful to last until the fall of the Ottoman Empire in 1918; to be then replaced by a similar arrangement that kept the Lebanon stable until the 1970s. The old tribal structures would remain, renewed and resilient against Western nationalism. And in that lay Dufferin's greatest satisfaction.[23]

Dufferin had achieved all he had set out to do. Of course, his success owed much to others. Diplomatic fatigue and increasing problems at home and abroad made the French more amenable. Recent historians also attribute the outcome to the experienced diplomacy of Fuad.[24] He was a smooth operator and Dufferin admired how he played a weak hand to great effect. Yet it was Dufferin who forced the execution of the Turkish officials, protected the Druze leaders, persuaded Fuad to return Turkish troops to the Mountain and so remove the need for the French army; and later he determined the constitutional settlement and exploited Fuad's common interest with Britain in expelling the French – which was ultimately realised amid much fanfare in June 1861.

'Let the West rejoice in anthem', acclaimed Lord Shaftesbury on hearing of Dufferin's triumph. Russell especially praised his protégé's 'zeal [in pursuit] of public justice . . . and the claims of humanity'; and public honours in the form of a KCB duly followed. In diplomatic circles, what caught the eye, as the French Foreign Minister, Thouvenel, admitted to Cowley, the British ambassador in Paris, was Dufferin's capacity 'to disarm even those who may not agree with you by your frankness and conciliatory disposition'. 'You are a heaven born diplomat', his uncle, Sir James Graham, had reassured him as Dufferin left for Syria and nine months later it appeared to most observers that the young peer had at last found his vocation.[25]

Reflecting his new standing, Dufferin was asked to move the Royal Address at the opening of Parliament, the first formal opportunity for the expression of public remorse over the death of Prince Albert in December. With the Queen 'sublime in her anguish', this would be a delicate task and all the more so for being carried out under the critical gaze of the press and society. At 5 p.m. on 6 February 1862 with the House crowded and with the galleries packed with ladies in black, the Lord Chancellor read out the Queen's speech and then Dufferin rose to reply. 'There was a dead silence, and for a second, the roof and benches seemed to me all confounded together in one mass of whirling confusion.' Quickly recovering, he spoke through the silence: 'no cheering, no expression of either dissent or approval, but one long agony of solitary exertion'. And in silence he concluded. He would not have to wait long for a reaction. With a 'good many' ladies in the galleries in tears, he sensed that the speech had been 'pretty successful'. The Queen soon let it be known how much it had 'moved' her. And where she led others quickly followed with private plaudits mirrored in public praise in the press, including *The Times*, which printed the speech in full. In one of those unexpected and indulgent outpourings of national grief that barely survive in the memory, Dufferin had captured the transient mood with 'uncommon pluck and nerve'. Among those 'quite taken . . . with Dufferin's show speech' was William Cory, now an Eton beak and tutor to the future Liberal prime minister, the Earl of Rosebery. 'Do you remember Dufferin', he wrote to a friend, 'how Cookesley called him the orator?'[26]

In the wake of this triumph, the next day Sir Charles Wood at the India Office made Dufferin an offer: the Governorship of Bombay and £12,000 a year and 'outfit', together with the prospect of being viceroy 'by forty'. Here at last was the breakthrough he had long awaited. Yet three days later he turned it down.

10

Family Politics

'Banishment' was how Helen described his posting to India. She could not countenance exile from the 'political stage where I hope he may yet play a part'.[1] Sheridans after all had made their name prosecuting Indian administrators, not becoming them! Events too conspired to make leaving England inconceivable.

In early September 1861, Giff had been supervising some workmen on the family estates at Yester as they dismantled masonry near Gifford Castle. Surveying the scene from the top of a wall, he suddenly noticed that the men had inadvertently disturbed an enormous stone above them. He had rushed forward and just managed to hold it up until they made their escape. At which point his strength had given way. The stone fell safely out of harm's way but he had severely ruptured his bowels and stomach. Helen was at Clandeboye when she heard of the accident. Gifford reassured her that his injuries were little more than badly torn muscles. And so she had stayed at Clandeboye, 'thinking of you' she wrote, 'most hours of the day'.

It was not until mid-December that they met in London. By now a 'wasting illness' had set in and with Helen railing at the neglect of his parents ('he will have been as certainly murdered . . . as if they had taken a knife to him'), doctors were summoned. Dufferin had been shooting on 16 January when he heard of the diagnosis of a tumour. Cancelling dinner, he raced to London to comfort his mother and was there too when the surgeons came on the 26th. As it turned out Gifford would linger on in their Highgate home ('one week better, one week worse') for the best part of a year during which time Helen nursed him with what her son later described as the 'tenderest solicitude'.[2]

'Don't think that I can go on account of my Mother', he had confided in his diary after the Bombay offer.[3] 'Had I been alone in the

93

world, I would have accepted at once,' he protested to Elizabeth Argyll. 'But if I had gone, my mother would have come after me and . . . the climate would have killed her . . . Am I not a dutiful son? For I am very ambitious and would risk anything myself in order to do something.'⁴ To politicians and Indian administrators this smacked of anything but ambition.⁵ More to the point, if he had gone, would she have followed him? After all, such was her all-consuming concern for her patient that it was only on the day Dufferin was due to speak that she finally agreed to hear her son's eulogy on the Prince Consort. Plainly she would never go to India for him. Yet nor was he quite ready to walk out on her.

'What do you think of all these marriages – Miss Seymour, Lord Bath, Lady Evelyn Stanhope. Does it make you think it is time for you to shake yourself?' teased Janey Ellice. 'Suggest Hermione Graham.'⁶ Nothing would have made his old guardian happier but nothing was further from his mind. Instead his eye came to rest on his 'pretty cousin' Hariot Hamilton ('Lal') of Killyleagh. The sudden death the previous Christmas of her father left him assuming many of the responsibilities of a guardian and he duly gave a coming out ball for her at Clandeboye. In truth, he had known her all her life without ever being really aware of her. Hence she was compelled to return a present of a dress on her thirteenth birthday because her family deemed it 'too beautiful and too old for me . . . Don't be angry'. Now eighteen, she had to remind him that she was no longer a little girl when thanking him for the present of a doll (that had arrived with so few clothes on she assumed it was 'Lady Godiva'). A playful correspondence ensued in which she discussed the merits of spurious suitors, because 'you said that I may look at you as an elder brother', with whom perhaps she was becoming a little infatuated.⁷

In January 1862 Hariot was brought to London for six weeks, ostensibly as a companion for Helen. As such, she was a great success: 'a very superior girl, so sensible and sober minded, and so honest and natural'. Taken out into society by Lady Jocelyn, both she and Helen approved that, in contrast to the flighty fashionable ladies, 'her head was not in the least turned by it'. Nor did it appear that Dufferin's was turned by her. For all that he showered her with dresses and gifts (including her first watch, which by August she still 'had not got into the way of going yet . . . not from the want of winding'), he spent much of the time she was at Highgate away with old friends, to whom he showed little inclination of introducing his Irish cousin.[8]

And yet, while her leaving promise 'to become all that you would wish' was that of a child to her guardian, arranging for her photograph to be taken without (at Dufferin's insistence) her mother's knowledge was not.[9] More overt was his spending much of his next visit to Clandeboye in April supervising the rebuilding of the gatehouse at Killyleagh Castle. By now he was dining with the Hamiltons regularly ('Hariot great fun') and joining them at communion on Good Friday.[10] Nevertheless this remained a very private courtship. Although his engagement in August left him 'a little mad, I think, with happiness', he had delayed its announcement until his friends had scattered to the provinces. Even the Argylls – among his oldest companions and confidants – only heard on the grapevine over a month later. Others like Lady Jocelyn, who after all had approved of Hariot, were hurt by Dufferin's denials in the summer: 'why did you go out of your way to do this? Why? Why? Why?'

The answer lay in what Elizabeth Argyll left out. 'What a beautiful story it is', she assured him: 'The giving of the old castle, the friend of the father, the companion of the widow becoming the beloved husband . . . of the child?' Her husband was less tactful. Joshing his friend for 'diving in home waters for your pearl', he congratulated Dufferin on marrying 'one to whom you sent a doll at [the age of] 6'.[11] At nineteen Hariot was hardly in Victorian terms a child bride. But at nearly twice her age and as her self-appointed guardian, Dufferin undoubtedly felt vulnerable to ribaldry and gossip. But then this was inevitable for, as Lady St Helier recorded decades later in her memoirs, 'to women he was exceedingly attractive' and one whose marriage was always going to cause 'great excitement'. And all the more so for this being not the grand Whig match everyone had expected. Helen foresaw some of this disappointment and defiantly wrote to her Blackwood cousins that she 'wouldn't exchange Hariot for Miss Coutts or Princess Mary', only then to hint at worse when claiming that they would come to love her 'in spite of her undemonstrative manner'.[12] Given all this, why did Dufferin marry her?

For all his experience of society, Dufferin had remained remarkably inexperienced in his relationships with women. Whether as a consequence of the abuse he had suffered as a child in the hands of Miss Foley or the fiercely exclusive affection between mother and son, he had rarely, if ever, been physically intimate with the opposite sex. True he was an accomplished flirt and could converse with sensitivity and understanding rare in most Victorian men, and it was this, together with his looks, that made him so appealing to women. Part of that appeal was also that he remained elusive. As a consequence his concept of love had progressed little beyond the mantras of nineteenth-century chivalric literature. Here the heroines combined beauty with quiet morality and openness of feeling; angelic virtues he had only really found in young girls – where the innocence of youth, he held, had yet to be defiled by the carnality of marriage. In sending that dress to Hariot he was indulging (as he used to do earlier with Lady Jocelyn's daughter, Alice) in the creation of images of purity. Transcending this would require a sea change in perception and perhaps at thirty-six would not have been possible without Hariot's summons to Highgate. Proximity under one roof allowed him to get to know her as he had not known any other woman.

Also important was Helen choosing to encourage the relationship – surprising given her longstanding ambitions. Perhaps she was too absorbed with Giff to care. Whether Dufferin noticed this is impossible to say but his nephew, Harold Nicolson, would later speculate on whether Dufferin was substituting 'the girl-mother of 1826 for the girl-wife of 1862'; both nineteen, eager and fresh, and then boundless in their adoration of him. Such fantasies aside, even Helen noted with approval that 'my new daughter . . . loves him as he deserves to be loved'. Over the next five years Helen more or less openly groomed her to take on the mission of making a Sheridan out of Dufferin. 'My dearly loved Lal', she once wrote, 'our hearts understand each other and I love you as fervently as if I had given you birth.'[13] No wonder many years later Hariot would be a willing collaborator in the mythologising of Helen. But this marriage was no rebranding of an old order. With time she became more the counsellor and less the disciple, but she was 'never the critic'. Instead she would give him the self-reliance that his mother's strictures had ultimately denied him.[14]

Meanwhile October saw Dufferin full of plans. First there were the alterations to a dowager house adjoining Clandeboye at Craigdarragh, the thought of which Helen found so odious that in the end she never found a convenient time to move in. In contrast to such subtle resistance, there was a classic set-piece squabble with Aunt Anna over the transfer of the family diamonds to the new Lady Dufferin. Nor did his wedding go quite to order. The intention was to get married at nightfall and not invite 'a single soul'. Hariot was to forego brides-maids. Her brothers and sisters would suffice. John Hamilton would be his best man; otherwise, he would only be accompanied by his mother. 'I have always had the greatest horror of public weddings', he explained to his aunt, 'and it must be one thing or another.'[15]

In his position such privacy was never realistic. As he 'dashed up' in a closed carriage to Killyleagh Castle at 3.30 p.m. on 23 October 1862 there were large crowds to greet his arrival. Passing under the new gatehouse, with its high Gothic tower and battlements, he found tenants there ready to cheer him as he then laid the final stone. After a family dinner the Rev. Dr Hincks, 'the celebrated Egyptologist', married them in the drawing room in Killyleagh and a single firework announced the event to the villagers beyond the walls. It was past eight o'clock when the Dufferins left, but the crowds had stayed on to release the horses and drag their carriage through the streets. Eventually the couple drove the twelve miles to Clandeboye in a barouche with postilions and outriders through villages brightly lit with bonfires in their honour.[16] Arriving at Clandeboye, with Dufferin still resplendent with the green ribbon of St Patrick across his waistcoat and the star on his breast, they were astounded to be greeted with bonfires and fireworks; and then to find the gallery brimming with local school children all dressed in white, who greeted them with great cheering and the declaiming of an ode. Such a charming scene utterly disarmed him.[17] All that was missing was his mother. But then she had not come.

Ten days before and without warning, on 13 October 1862, she married her son's friend the Earl of Gifford. Fifteen years her junior and heir to the Marquess of Tweeddale, by marrying Giff Helen knew exactly what she had stirred up. Without awaiting events she let it be known that her marriage was a 'sacrifice'. Within days others had picked up the theme and diarists like Henry Greville were recording the gossip 'at Lady Tankerville's' that Helen 'has yielded to his dying request to be allowed to call her wife in return for the devotion of his whole life'.[18] But Helen was never that cold. She affected amusement for his youthful adoration because she presumed that what she felt was, in the times, impossible and hence inexpressible. Outwardly he was another 'son', although even Dufferin later acknowledged that she acted more like 'the clever older sister towards a younger brother'. Slim, elegant and looking anything but fifty-five, she retained a youthful, carefree manner and an easy rapport with the young.[19] But with Giff she had come to adore the creative, sensitive spirit she had unlocked at Castellammare. Here was someone with the interests and affection to be a genuine soulmate – in a way her husband and later her son could not.

Decades later Dufferin would explain his mother's marriage as a 'most heroic act' springing from a 'passion of pity', an impulsive decision made as the doctors left, having pronounced Giff to be beyond recovery. Yet for all its suddenness it was something she had long desired. Later letters would reflect her regret at having denied herself for years. Tellingly, just hours after the ceremony, she wrote to her unsuspecting father-in-law of her desire 'to mourn [Gifford] openly'. Nor had their differences in age been the obstacle. As she admitted to Tweeddale, she had already given, some seven months previously, 'a half promise' to marry Gifford 'if Fred did' (i.e. marry). Significantly there was no talk of sacrifice for at the time Giff was ill 'but not hopelessly so'. Equally her insistence on subjecting him to a gruesome operation in the pursuit of 'a very precarious chance of life' was a measure of how much she wanted him to live. Later to a French acquaintance she would express her 'remorse' that she heeded the sensitivities of her son and had not married Giff earlier.[20] In the light of this, her avid support of Hariot that spring was perhaps only to be expected. Having waited so long she feared she could not risk waiting any longer. What really terrified her was not simply that Giff was dying but that he might die the agnostic he had always been. This had become an obsession for her and there is just a hint of a deal struck between them, as hours after their marriage they took the sacrament together for the first time.[21]

Her marriage she insisted defiantly to a friend would 'affect no one's happiness but mine', only for her to decide at the last minute not to go to her son's wedding.[22] With doctors apparently predicting Giff's death within '48 hours', her duty, she had written a little archly, lay now with her new husband; adding a typically matriarchic postscript ('I earnestly hope that no smell of paint [at Clandeboye] remains' before the wedding). There is no surviving record of Dufferin's reaction. Huge disappointment presumably, laced with a trace of resentment – possibly. After all, the imminence of Giff's death had been much heralded and in the end he survived for another two months. Her letter was awash with blessings and prayers, in an emotional torrent that reflected her state and no doubt a little of her guilt: 'my best and dearest of sons . . . my darling one, my only one, my dear, dear Ghigo. May no cloud ever come between us again.'[23] For there can be little doubt that one had. Indeed so hurt was he that thirty years later he still felt the need to set the record straight, only to do anything but, in a long introduction to a collection of his mother's poems and songs. Among the distortions of memory, the placing of his mother's marriage after his is arresting. So too was his decision to use her original title, Lady Dufferin, in the book title when she had insisted on taking the name of her second husband.[24] Even more defiantly, she renamed Dufferin Lodge, which her son had bought for her, Gifford Lodge. In marrying Giff when she did, she had made explicit the primacy of a relationship that all previously had felt safe in denying.[25] In fact such pretence had already begun to crumble and this realisation might have come sooner with the completion in September 1861 of the tower at Clandeboye. Built as a monument to the love of mother and son, she had already offered it to Giff for his study and observatory.[26]

To the pain of revelation could be added his instinctive dread of scandal. The Sheridans, after all, had previous. Not only had her brother eloped with an heiress, but Dufferin's mother had had to go into exile after her first marriage. Her second marriage at fifty-five to a forty-year-old as he lay on his deathbed was always going to be too fascinating for the salacious to ignore. Soon Caroline was reporting back 'lots of gossip' and Elizabeth Argyll was speaking out against the 'rumour mongers'. Much of the source of this was Tweeddale himself.

Still Helen had brought much of this on herself by insisting that Gifford did not invite any of his family to the wedding. Instead they were married with just her brother, Brinsley, and a witness present. Convinced that his son had been seduced for his inheritance, Tweeddale refused to pay for any of his son's debts, including £1,200 of doctors' fees. Desperate, Helen was forced to sell off Giff's valuable library, further fuelling the rumours that the Sheridans were cashing in. With his mother beginning to sound like his aunt, Dufferin stepped in to pay the debts in full.[27]

'Giff with God', she finally reported to Dufferin on 22 December 1862, begging him to come over to her; only then to spoil it in her characteristic way by insisting that he come 'only for a day'. Dufferin didn't go at all. Lady Jocelyn wrote of her surprise and Georgia begged him to quell the gossip by representing the family at the funeral.[28] But as Giff was buried in the churchyard at Friern Barnet, that honour fell instead to Dufferin's uncle, the Duke of Somerset. With Helen, in her grief, blaming her son for denying her the opportunity of marrying Giff sooner, it was with some irony Dufferin pleaded the cause of his now pregnant wife, although she was not to give birth for another six months (when of course Dufferin was nowhere to be seen). That summer Helen chose not to catch a glimpse of this, her first grandchild, preferring instead the quieter company of her new sister-in-law, Emily Peel, and her villa on the edge of 'a soft, glassy lake' with its views of Mont Blanc. While into Craigdarragh moved 'Mr Jaffé', a leading Belfast merchant; Helen would have thought it quite appropriate.

'How Irish of you to manage to be away but Lady D had no business to get over the first time with such velocity', wrote Elizabeth Argyll in congratulation at this first child.[29] For Hariot the triumph lay less in the ease of the labour as the fact that she had produced an heir, giving birth to Archie on 31 July 1863.[30] However, her first full London season proved an ordeal for one so painfully shy and inexperienced. Nothing had prepared her for the 'sharp gusto of the Palmerstonian circle or the tremendous solemnities of Windsor'.[31] If she knew few in London, it was infinitely worse when the French Emperor, Napoleon III, invited them to Compiègne, outside Paris. Compiègne was a hunting lodge on a lavish scale: with electricity in china globes lighting its long passages, armies of servants, and a never-ending stream of feasts, entertainments and drives in the forest. The Emperor was at his most seductive, mesmerising Dufferin with a glimpse of statecraft on a grand scale: from French designs in Italy to the latest Polish Revolt or the future of the Rhineland. In less than a decade such dreams were destined to be shattered at the battle of Sadowa.[32] Such intimacies reflected that they had met before. By contrast, Hariot was very much on her own in a world of high fashion at its most intimidating. Here, aristocratic establishment confronted the spectacular wealth of the self-made Napoleonic order with its extravagance, hedonism and unabashed display, characterised by the décolleté of the trophy wives such as Mme de Persigny. 'The wonder is that she takes the trouble to cover anything', Helen confided, before warning of such 'mauvaise tongues' and the 'lynx eyes of the French ladies'. As it turned out, only the very British Lady Cremorne, was positively rude.[33]

Back in London, with her husband keen to get into government, Hariot soon came to resent Dufferin's endless departures ('Ghigo gone to horrid breakfast')[34] and the distractions that came in their wake – the wedding anniversaries forgotten, her twenty-fifth birthday that saw Dufferin dining with a local editor, leaving his young wife 'very lonely . . . sitting by myself'. Oddly worse were the lulls between office – Dufferin in January 1868 taking refuge in silence or playing billiards all day with political cronies such as Sir John Hay. Or escaping to London where he could, as her mother-in-law unhelpfully put it, 'plunge into the pool of iniquity'.[35] Such unintended cruelties were rare and seldom more than thoughtlessness – the inevitable product perhaps of a marriage unequal in age and social experience. But they still sapped morale. When in May 1867 Dufferin delayed his return from the Paris Exhibition, Hariot found herself 'crying nervously when I went to bed'; only then to be 'wild with delight' at his return, putting on her best violet dress to greet him. That evening, however, she suddenly went into labour and at 8 a.m. produced a little boy. 'So full of life at the start', he soon developed breathing difficulties and Hariot watched in horror as her child turned 'so blue and unnatural'. After five hours he gave up the struggle. Later

Dufferin brought him up in a little white coffin and 'let me kiss the little cold cheeks and touch the son who should never know me'. Naming him Sidney Temple, they had the baby photographed and later buried beside Giff, which pleased Helen. For Hariot his loss was a devastating blow leaving her for a time ricocheting between incomprehension, resentment and guilt. ('He lived such a short time', she wrote in her diary, 'and yet has left so great a blank behind.')[36]

With her husband immersing himself in politics again, she felt on her own once more. By now she had three children (Archie 1863, Helen 1865, Terence 1866) and another on the way. On 6 August 1868, Ian was born, only surviving for four hours. 'Lost him too' was all she could bring herself to write. Soon she was profoundly depressed again, even to the point of being only able to face her children briefly in the evenings. By now, even Dufferin appreciated that not all was well.[37] In an attempt to lift her melancholy, he took Hariot on a cruise of the Western Isles. 'My darling hub, I do love you so much and do enjoy this quiet life with you', she declared, if only to her diary. This was to be a constant refrain. She was at her happiest when they had Clandeboye to themselves and could plan gardens and cut paths through the 'wilderness', or walk out on top of Helen's Tower and gaze at the distant Scottish hills. In the evening they would draw up architectural schemes or she would simply listen to him as he read to her.[38]

But all the while London beckoned him back. With Hariot too shaken to go out, Dufferin was on his own in society, taking refuge in a certain recklessness: be it taking rides in hot air balloons or more dangerously meeting up twice in July 1869 with 'Mrs Stukeley' (Annie Gilbert). Among his literary friends he was to be found toasting Dickens's health at banquets in Liverpool and Belfast (and later finding his son, Frank, a post in the Canadian police force); receiving numerous pleas whether from Holman Hunt to vote against 'The Street Music Bill' as the artist couldn't think over the noise; or from William Carleton in support of his pension.[39] This period would also see him elected a Fellow of the Royal Society. With politics again claiming their wedding anniversary, Hariot lapsed back into despondency.[40] It took Nelly Baring to come to the rescue, taking her off in the new year to Cannes. Rejuvenated at last, Hariot survived a stay at

Osborne and was soon back at Westminster watching the debates. Entering a reception at Lady Cowper's in March 1871, it was Hariot, assured and elegantly dressed ('a lovely sight' in 'a gown of old chocolate and gold brocade over a blue waistcoat'), who caught Lady Cavendish's eye. But by then she had successfully given birth to another daughter (Hermione) and on 4 November 1870, Basil had been born: 'all well'.[41]

It is hard to gauge just how blind Dufferin had been to his wife's post-natal depression. He remained strikingly naive (and, no doubt, felt helpless in this matter). But then he was also distracted by the showdown with his mother. Inevitably Giff's passing had in time opened the way for a reconciliation of sorts. Neither anyway had the stomach for a fight. As Helen's spirits revived, the gay frivolity returned that soon had old friends beating a path to her Highgate exile.[42] However, by June 1866, she was diagnosed with breast cancer. With her illness taking hold, Dufferin finally wrote his mother 'a little love letter', begging forgiveness for 'the harsh words and the love never fully returned'. Inevitably he sought comfort in his childhood: 'You have been my guardian angel, my wisest counsellor, my friend and dear companion and play fellow; and when I remember all this, I feel . . . as though I were again your own Ghigo as he was in those early days when all his little life was spent within the circuit of his mother's love.' It was a fantasy to which Helen now also returned, declaring that 'the affection . . . which we two feel for each other cannot be a faculty meant for Time alone'. After a brutal mastectomy[43] she made it over to Clandeboye to marvel at its transformation as he rowed her around the lakes and to visit for the last time old haunts and 'look long at the Tower, the monument of your love'. Nevertheless 'next to you' she reminded him she had loved Giff and thus in June 1867 he respected her wish to be buried by her husband in the 'quiet churchyard' at Friern Barnet where only weeks before he had laid his son, Sidney.[44]

Harold Nicolson called Helen's death 'the first and perhaps the greatest tragedy of his life'. One only has to consider the loss of his father while so young or indeed the gaunt figure at the graveside of his guardian to realise he had not been quite so immune.[45] That

Tennyson could write in 1868 of Dufferin that 'You are not like so many of your countrymen – semi-mad on their mothers', suggested also that something had been lost before her death.[46] In fact her death would prove distinctly liberating – not least in leaving him free to embalm her in myth, recapturing her past on his terms. As he began to collect her letters and to edit her works – a process that would occupy him over the next three decades – he patiently reassembled his bond with 'my love, my own most dear and saint-like mother'. Her memory, he once told Elizabeth Argyll, was for him 'a precious and eternal possession'; his, of course, to do with as he pleased. Moreover in the aftermath of her death, he threw himself into political life with a determination and conviction he had rarely displayed before. It was as if all her love and expectation had only left him dependent and inadequate, forever in fear of failing her. Now she was gone – though he would never have acknowledged this – he was free to be himself: free to replace the burden of expectation with the challenge of ambition.

II

Missionary Politics

L ITTLE MORE THAN the 'illegitimate daughter of a divorced
woman'. The target of Helen's withering verdict was Lady
Wodehouse; her crime that her husband, an Eton and Oxford
contemporary of Dufferin's, had in August 1864 pipped her son to
the Lord Lieutenancy of Ireland and a seat in the cabinet.[1] Having
convinced herself that Dufferin's appointment was a virtual certainty,
she took his rejection very hard. And all the more so as he eventually
only managed to scrape into the government as Under-Secretary of
State at the India Office. He was again passed over when the post
became available four years later and a sideways move to the War
Office and a later appointment to the Chancellorship of the Duchy of
Lancaster represented, as his nephew kindly put it, a career 'becalmed'.

To explain this, Nicolson and later historians have mainly echoed
the contemporary opinion that Dufferin was temperamentally
unsuited to political life and that the 1860s represented an unhappy
interlude before returning to the diplomacy which was to make his
name. 'Though clever', wrote one observer, Dufferin seemed to lack
the 'combative qualities' required to break into the 'leading rank of
English politicians'. Even John Thadeus Delane – the feisty editor of
The Times – worried privately about his protégé 'never giv[ing] out
the idea of being able to walk alone'. To the leading Liberals, Dufferin
lacked 'backbone'.[2] Small wonder then that most historians have
followed suit.

But in doing so they have missed the point. By interpreting the
later 1860s in terms of the early years of the decade, they have failed
to appreciate the emergence of Dufferin as a national figure after
1867. Instinctively he could be highly political. The diplomatic career
would have been unsustainable if he had not been. The calculations

of political networking would become almost second nature to him, whether of the press or senior figures of the party. His loyalties were not especially tribal, and he would prove astute enough when the opportunities for personal and party advantage arose. However, it was not until his mother died that his politics became energised with a sense of personal mission.

Urged on by Delane, Dufferin consciously set out to become the leading Irish expert for the Whigs. In the winter of 1866–7 he published a series of letters in *The Times* tackling the renewed agricultural depression in the Irish countryside.[3] In his advocacy of Malthusian arguments in favour of further emigration from a country whose population had apparently outstripped its resources, he impressed many with his mastery of detail and clarity of argument. And enraged others from Bishop Moriarty to Karl Marx, the latter denouncing this 'new bloodletting' as intended purely to create 'an English sheep-walk' for 'hard magnates [such as] Lord Dufferin'.[4] In the circumstances, these were useful enemies to have. Nevertheless, he would have to win his spurs in the dogfight of politics and that would take him into some very murky, local waters.

After the fervent Orangeman William Johnston of Ballykilbeg led an illegal march to Bangor across the Clandeboye estates on 12 July 1867, Dufferin attended the petty sessions the following September to ensure that Johnston and twenty-two others were sent to the Assizes for trial. In a major public speech in Belfast twelve days later, he was merciless in denouncing sectarian 'fanaticism', provoking riots with his call for a state-funded Catholic university and the disestablishment of the Church of Ireland.[5] That within two months he would be defending the Orange Order in the House of Lords seems incomprehensible.

But Johnston's stand as an independent in protest over the Tories continued support of the Processions Act and the Party Emblems Act[6] split the natural Conservative vote in Belfast and paved the way for an unholy alliance between Johnston and the Liberals. As a result, in the November 1868 general election widespread tactical voting saw them oust the Tories from both seats in Ulster's 'capital'. The architect of this strategy had been a local editor and leading Belfast Liberal, Thomas MacKnight. But Dufferin too played a surprising and crucial role. A founder member, with MacKnight, of the Ulster Liberal Society, Dufferin not only funded this organisation but apparently also contributed to Johnston's campaign costs. Then on 3 December 1867 in the Lords he defended the Orange Order in traditionally Tory language as 'loyal, orderly and respectable'. Lest the point was missed, Johnston was invited to Clandeboye in January. Dufferin's motives were not entirely tactical. With the outbreak of a Fenian terror campaign in which policemen were murdered and Clerkenwell Jail bombed, there was no point alienating loyalist opinion in the North if the Union was under threat. The threat was in fact minimal but the party gain spectacular; and with MacKnight he would celebrate 'shattering the [Tory party in Belfast] to atoms'.[7]

Success in Ulster was more than matched by sweeping Liberal victories across Britain and gave Gladstone a majority of 110. In the circumstances Dufferin had every reason to expect significant office. Successfully established as the party's Irish expert, as early as February 1868 he had long conversations with Gladstone on Irish affairs as the two men walked across the park from Westminster: 'he is going to follow all Dufferin's suggestions', Hariot wrote gleefully in her diary. With Gladstone's melodramatic declaration in December that his 'mission was to pacify Ireland', Dufferin could barely disguise his anticipation of the Lord Lieutenancy with a seat in the cabinet and his appointment was again widely canvassed in the press (and not just by Delane). So his eventual appointment as Chancellor of the Duchy of Lancaster was a devastating blow.

'Mortified' . . . 'humiliating' – this was the language of real anger and not the fatalism that had beset him in the past.[8] Equally angry was Delane 'and very angry too with yourself', he told Dufferin, believing the post would have been Dufferin's had he bothered to go to London when Disraeli's government had fallen.[9] In this he was almost certainly mistaken. But with Dufferin incapable of talking publicly of Hariot's depression, the impression of being a political dilettante had to go unanswered. What particularly rankled was that no Irishman was thought worthy of the post. But, as Argyll gently explained, how could Gladstone expect a fair hearing for his policy if it was fronted in Dublin by a publicly declared champion of the landlord cause with 18,000 acres in Ulster? Most important of all, as Dufferin would soon come to appreciate, he was not the only one who felt himself an expert in Irish affairs.

For none of these explanations take into account the extraordinary personality and ambition of the new prime minister. Formidably learned and serious ('Gladstone's jokes are no laughing matter', Derby famously quipped), he was not an easy companion, often 'eviscerat[ing]' subjects in lieu of conversation. With the apparent innocence of a genuinely spiritual man, he remained a jumble of paradoxes: the declared defender of aristocratic rule ('I am an out and out inequalitarian') whose radical rhetoric had made him the 'People's William'; the High Church Anglican who indulged in late night 'rescue' work among London's army of prostitutes; and the subtle political operator who claimed that he was the disciple of moral principle.[10] To his critics such contradictions bespoke of a charlatan in pursuit of power.[11]

There is no doubt that Gladstone did like power – as a true Peelite minister, he was never cut out to be a mere parliamentary foot soldier.[12] Yet for all its visceral thrill, political power remained for the most part a means, not an end, a force to be harnessed to the cause. For Gladstone that cause was God's will.[13] Convinced that 'The Almighty seems to sustain me . . . for some purpose of His own', he exhibited a certainty that knew few bounds.[14] Policy formation thereafter assumed the characteristics of its originator – mesmerising in the cool mastery of detail and yet also frenetic, highly charged, even impulsive. Above all, it was breathtakingly single-minded. 'Swimming for his life, a man does not see much of the country through which the river winds', Gladstone once explained. As with many conviction politicians, ideas would be the servant of the mission and their adaptation part of the creative dynamic that Gladstone found so exhilarating. Equally he could be unexpectedly violent in the relish with which he cut down the enemies of the cause.[15]

The real surprise was that his cabinet colleagues, let alone his MPs, put up with it. Yet few could match his financial insight or administrative zeal or fail to admire his willingness to take on a heroic challenge. Or match his extraordinary rapport with the new electorates amassing 'out of doors'. Herein lay the foundation of his authority. In huge numbers they would gather to hear him speak in tones more akin to an evangelical missionary; which in many ways he saw himself as. 'What power he has! What influence over public opinion and action!' wrote one cabinet colleague in admiration. With revolution but a Channel away, most were in awe at his moral energy and achievement. Not least Dufferin who, fully imbibing the religious imagery of the day, also believed in 'God's Providence' and the need to ask 'how more effectively [can we] fulfil our Master's bidding?'. In this, Britain's last great religious age, the nation had found its champion: as Argyll remarked to Dufferin, 'the elections are wonderfully Gladstonian'.[16]

It is in this light that the task facing Dufferin has to be judged. While he had established himself as an Irish spokesman, such expertise could pose a threat too. For Dufferin came with an agenda and Gladstone was astute enough (especially after Argyll had misguidedly forwarded on an intemperate letter from Dufferin) to foresee differences ahead over land reform. However, over Irish disestablishment they were largely in agreement. By June 1868, Dufferin was winning his spurs defending Gladstone's preference for complete disendowment and did so again a year later against his uncle, the Duke of Somerset, and a Whig revolt in the Lords. From his leader he had even picked up the language of atonement, declaring to his fellow peers that the Anglican establishment in Ireland was 'a mortification to me as a fellow citizen of my Roman Catholic fellow countryman'.[17] Such loyalty brought continued friendship and a little consultation over parliamentary tactics. He would need more than this if Gladstone determined that Irish victimhood stretched to the land question.

By late 1868 parts of Ireland were in the throes of agitation against landlordism. While there was not any significant resort to violence, leading articles in the Irish press would openly assert that 'the history of landlordism in Ireland was "steeped in blood"'. And they talked freely about bringing the 'alien possessor . . . face to face . . . with those who ought to be the true owners of the soil'. 'Naked communism' was how Dufferin described this to Edward Ellice.[18] Yet while the rhetoric may have been of expropriation, the specific nationalist demand was for 'fixity of tenure' for the tenant. With 77 per cent of Ireland held 'at will', there was certainly a case for providing greater legal security. However, the tenant protest aspired to more. Under the guise of what later became known as the three Fs, they demanded the right to 'free sale' of the tenant's interest as well as compensation for any improvements and a 'fair rent'. Or the Ulster Custom writ very large – to which Dufferin had been implacably opposed since the 1850s. For, in effect, such concessions would mean that the tenant would become a joint proprietor of the land with the landlord acting as his 'unsecured mortgagee'. In other words, this was expropriation by stealth.[19]

None of this would have mattered if English opinion had remained sound on the rights of property. Much to Dufferin's disgust in the 1860s 'transcendental moralists and philosophers' (including John Stuart Mill) were 'complacently' propounding arguments 'about the inherent rights of the Celtic race to the soil of Ireland'. These arguments, fuelled by tenant propagandists (who were drawing wild comparisons with the emancipation of the Russian serfs), began to strike chords with Liberal sentiment in England.[20] Dufferin fumed at the sentimental fashion for sackcloth. And he had a point. The spectre of the absentee English plutocrat with vast estates exploiting the Irish peasant before evicting them onto the roadside was largely a myth. Around 80 per cent of landed estates were barely economic at 2,000 acres or less and only 13 per cent were absentee. As for rents, these rose by 20 per cent in the three decades after the Famine, considerably less than agricultural profits which increased by 78 per cent. Hence evictions were low (1.36 per 1,000 holdings 1854–1880) and 99 per cent of all rents were collected without recourse to the law. How else can the huge sums paid by the incoming tenant to his predecessor in terms of tenant right (£565 on one small Donegal farm on the Abercorn estates when it only attracted £15 p.a. in rent) be explained other than to say that tenant right was 'partially a capitalisation [by the tenant] of uncollected rent [by the landlord]'? Such a practice, once well entrenched, made it vital for the tenant that rents were 'fair' (i.e. low) if he was to protect his investment.[21] Bluntly, for this level of oppression Russian serfs would have given their eye teeth.

And yet, such statistics were no match for other 'realities'. Local diversity meant that the profit margins were far less for both landlord and tenant in the west. Evictions may have been few but they never failed to cause a sensation. Brutal, arbitrary clearances as at Derryveagh in Donegal in 1861 only served to stoke up ancient resentment. Above all, there could be no escaping the 'reality' of the Famine, barely two decades before, and the depopulation that had followed in its wake and which would always mean that landlord and tenant relations in Ireland would involve much more than mutual economic advantage or legal rights.

Nevertheless, feeling sure of his ground, Dufferin moved quickly to ensure that his leader was onside. As early as May 1866 he was sending Gladstone a pamphlet on Irish land issues. Books, more pamphlets and sheaves of statistics followed through 1867, while in March 1868 his critique of Mill landed on Gladstone's desk. Faced with such a barrage, its recipient could not be other than flattering, acknowledging that in his ignorance he could 'repair to no higher source'. Even more reassuring was his declaration in 1867 that 'we cannot stand altogether well on this most important question until we are at one with you'.[22] Yet after the election, not only had Dufferin been excluded from Gladstone's Irish team but nor was he invited to advise a small cabinet committee set up by Gladstone on the Irish Land Bill in the autumn of 1869. Keen to make a gesture of atonement for the centuries of injustice that sprang from British expropriation, Gladstone instructed Fortescue, the chief secretary in Dublin, to consider fixity of tenure and an extension of the Ulster Custom.[23]

Distracted by the Irish Church debates, not until November 1869 did Dufferin catch wind of these developments. To assuage his anxiety, Gladstone invited him to produce a memorandum for the cabinet. Characteristically he produced three. The first of these, vitriolic in its rejection of Fortescue's scheme, verged on the offensive. In the others, warnings over Irish legislation providing British precedents were lost amid hyperbole. All of which enabled Gladstone to sail out the storm, breezily taking refuge in the comfort that: 'those who walk as far in the company as you and Fortescue are not likely to part for the rest of the road'.[24]

Desperately Dufferin sought to regain ground, warning that the extension of the Ulster Custom or rent fixing would force him to resign. A similar threat followed days later unless he was given access to cabinet papers – to enable him as 'the landlord's representative' to keep 'watch over' the bill.[25] Surprisingly Gladstone acceded to this petulance, seeking then to distract Dufferin further by urging him to produce an alternative bill – apparently so that his ideas could be compared with Fortescue's. This would, of course, take him the best part of a month. By then his cause had suffered two further blows. On 9 December, Spencer, the Lord Lieutenant, weighed in with a scheme for rent courts. Much worse, on the same day Elizabeth Argyll suffered a devastating stroke. Fearing it to be fatal, Dufferin raced to Inverary to comfort his friend and closest confidante. Only on 13 December did he finally send off his draft bill, but with Argyll in Scotland for the rest of the year, it had lost its key advocate in cabinet.

It is difficult to assess just how influential Dufferin's bill proved to be. On 4 December Argyll had led a withering assault on Gladstone's 'sackcloth and ashes' politics, provoking a furious exchange. Flushed out at last, the prime minister sought to scare his opponents by intimations of impending revolution, which would only demand more extreme measures if not nipped in the bud.[26] In this context Dufferin's bill offered a route out of the impasse. For Dufferin was more sympathetic to reform than his vehement defence of landlordism implied. Even in November he had been ready to consider the legalising of the Ulster Custom where it existed and provision of compensation for improvements and for eviction other than for non-payment of rent. In addition to exempting all leaseholders (and thus Dufferin's own tenants) from the act, Dufferin encouraged Bright's proposal for state-aided land purchase. It was these ideas, admittedly repackaged for Gladstone's conscience, which had comprised his draft bill. And it was these ideas, to Dufferin's 'relief', that appeared in the government's bill in the new year.[27] It was a measure of Dufferin's new importance that Gladstone briefed him twice privately as well as consulting him regularly during the last dash of redrafting (all on terms of 'absolute, impenetrable secrecy'). Not that all consultations were particularly significant: summoned from Ireland by Gladstone at very short notice to a private dinner to discuss the land bill, Dufferin arrived decrying the horrors of the sea crossing. This conversational opening developed bizarrely into an obsessive monologue from Gladstone on the perils of seasickness and travel, to the complete exclusion of any other subject. After which Dufferin caught the night boat train unaware of why he had been summoned.[28]

Nevertheless, Dufferin had played a significant part in ensuring that Irish landlordism would be able to survive this assault largely unscathed. To a degree Gladstone had sacrificed substance for form: a clause allowing the courts to adjudicate on local custom and rents (if 'exorbitant') offered scope to establish tenant right in all but name. Yet this was soon neutralised by the landlords rapidly adopting lease-holding – as Dufferin had always argued they should. Additionally Gladstone had had to accept a coercion bill to tackle the disorder and adopt Bright's purchase scheme (although on terms that then rendered it unattractive). In the end, this was not the heroic measure that Gladstone had hoped for: an act that would right the wrongs of centuries and recapture the Celtic imagination. Still 'at the altar this [Easter] day, it was the Irish land question that I presented before God more than aught else, living or dead'.[29]

Thus to attribute Dufferin's disappointing political career to personal failings – the 'wanting of some of those combative qual-ities'[30] – is to miss his development after 1867. If anything, he suffered from being too combative. Tactically inexperienced at the outset, he displayed an astute eye for resolution as negotiations approached their climax. Considering he was operating from a position of institutional weakness and often in opposition to the most formidable politician of the century, that he achieved what he did was highly creditable. Also the fact that he was so courted by January 1870 suggests that he had learnt to make 'trouble' effectively as his mother had advocated. By then he had become able to threaten resignation with impunity. When eventually he insisted, Gladstone kept his impending departure secret for nearly six months until March 1872 when he could offer Dufferin the office of Governor General of Canada. Equally symbolic was that the earldom, which Palmerston had rejected so easily, was now granted with alacrity.[31]

The problem for Dufferin was not that he lacked the competitive ruthlessness of the careerist politician but that the political world offered little of interest to him. Ireland had attracted his passionate concern in a way that selecting JPs for the Lancaster bench would never do. Ultimately he would prove to be as careerist as any but would choose a different field.[32] In escaping to the empire Dufferin was not alone. In the same year Northbrook became Viceroy of India and the empire figured strongly in the careers of Dufferin's other Whig contemporaries, Wodehouse (now 1st Earl Kimberley) and de Grey (recently elevated to Marquess of Ripon).[33] All had served under Sir Charles Wood at the India Office and from him had picked up a sense of 'Britain's duty as a progressive imperial power'. For them, the empire in the late nineteenth century was no backwater and represented the civilising mission on a global scale. Moreover there was the attraction of having great responsibilities and being liberated from the pettiness and compromises of parliamentary life. For Dufferin though there were more prosaic reasons for accepting the Canadian post.

12

Family Debts

IT WOULD BE Dufferin's creditors rather than his political rivals who would force him from political life. Inheriting Clandeboye and estates of 18,000 acres placed him just among the top 500 wealthiest landowners in the UK with a rental income of almost £21,000.[1] Yet barely twenty-five years on, with his rents largely unchanged, his surplus income had in effect been reduced to just over £3,000. Having assumed liabilities on the estate of £29,261, this debt doubled over the first six years of his majority and doubled again over the next five. Five years of married life added another £114,000 by 1867. As he sailed for Canada his debts had grown to a princely total of £299,171 – a tenfold increase over twenty-three years and more-than sufficient to get Blackwoods muttering darkly over the Sheridan blood. Actually, thanks to the annuities that his grandfather had placed on the estate, since his minority Dufferin's relations had drawn off up to £116,678. A flurry of deaths had by 1862 reduced this to an annual charge of £4,115 (£2,500 of which went to his mother). To this drain on resources should be added some poor investments: £2,200 on railways, an Irish–Scottish ferry scheme, the development of Helen's Bay as a dormitory town for Belfast (nearly a hundred years ahead of demand), and the £102,000 spent by 1874 on agricultural improvements. These produced a rent increase of barely £500 over the same period and came after he had reduced his rents by £2,000 p.a. in the aftermath of the Famine and let arrears of £21,000 build up. That he should then become the target of hostility from an ungrateful tenantry left him understandably bitter.[2]

Nevertheless the Blackwood territories could never have sustained the additional expenditure Dufferin would thrust on them. 'How economical we are building lakes', quipped Elizabeth Argyll in 1862.[3]

Almost £100,000 was spent on Clandeboye (66 per cent on landscaping alone) as well as houses kept in Grosvenor Place and Highgate, yachts crammed with the latest technology, and the social expenditure expected in the grandest society. All ensured that Dufferin was spending as fast as he could borrow. His biggest lender was a local Belfast linen manufacturer, John Mulholland, then making a fortune as the US Civil War disrupted the cotton industry. It had been his candidature for the Tories in the 1868 Belfast elections that Dufferin and the Liberals had scuppered. Such pleasures were short-lived. By now Mulholland owned 40 per cent of Dufferin's debt on short term leases at 5.5 per cent – and many of these loans were due to fall in the mid-1870s. With loans of £306,371 by 1875 sucking in £14,421 p.a. Dufferin was facing insolvency or the folly of remortgaging simply to pay the interest. Financially he had come to the end of the road.

'An Irish estate is like a sponge and an Irish landlord is never so rich as when he is rid his property', he confided with some bravura to Argyll.[4] Certainly the land sales he instigated, 1874–80, of up to 11,000 acres cleared his debts and produced a surplus of £54,850. But an income of only £6,000 from his remaining acres around Clandeboye threatened social extinction. Symbolically no one bid for Clandeboye itself with its 'English' demesne. Mulholland certainly had no need, absorbing Dufferin's Ards estates adjacent to his seat at Ballywalter Park.[5] Elevated to Baron Dunleath in 1892, he died in 1895 sixfold wealthier than the noble lord he had once facilitated. A new order had moved in.

What made this bearable for Dufferin was that he got a chance to escape. Whatever else, his appointment to Canada was a financial godsend. One of the most lucrative public offices, its salary of £10,000 p.a. was twice that of the prime minister and untaxed. In addition all basic living expenses, staff, removals, luxurious quarters were paid for. Admittedly the lavish entertainment expected meant that it would be easy to overspend the salary by £2,000–5,000. But this was more than made up by the savings at home – closing down London and country houses, laying off staff, cutting local subscriptions (£800 p.a. alone for Dufferin in the 1850s). In addition to maintaining his lifestyle, it also sustained his entré in the grandest circles.[6]

True to form, his family provided their own incentive to go west.

In 1863 his Aunt Caroline published possibly her best novel, *Lost and Saved*, a powerful tale of social ruin and eventual redemption that was quite savage on the snobbery of society. But its prospects were undermined by being deemed 'immoral' by the reviewers, a verdict unintentionally reinforced by her letter to *The Times* in which she justified subjects such as seduction, elopement and incest as regular themes in popular operas and thus part of the 'understandings of the higher classes of Great Britain'. As ever Caroline had gone down with all guns blazing.[7] In such circumstances her family offered little succour. With her favourite son, Fletcher, dead, her remaining son, Brinsley, had turned into a vicious drunk.[8]

Such embarrassments were not confined to Caroline's children. Georgia's eldest son, Ferdy St Maur, shunned academic study, travelling the world literally in search of a fight ('His love of soldiering is almost a madness') to the despair of his mother. Reckless to the point of folly, he would seek out conflicts, most notably serving at Lucknow during the Indian Mutiny and later joining Garibaldi's army in Italy. By contrast his brother Lord Edward was everything his father had hoped for in a son – scholarly, congenial, and industrious. By the age of nineteen he had already been an attaché in Vienna and Madrid. In 1865 he set out for India to track down his wayward brother. Out hunting in the jungle on 18 December, Edward was attacked by a wounded bear, which tore at his leg. Desperately grappling with the beast, they rolled over and over before he could get a telling blow in with his sword. That day doctors were forced to amputate the leg in an effort to save his life. But to no avail. Delirious with pain, he died the next day.[9] 'Poor Duke', Helen wrote to Dufferin, 'I think I never saw anything so painful and unnatural as his efforts to be perfectly calm and unmoved under a blow that really strikes to his heart.'[10] Four years later Ferdy was dead too (of a heart attack). With Georgia hysterical, in October 1869 Elizabeth Argyll urged Dufferin to go to his aunt's aid, for 'she will go mad or *will drink*'.[11] After this, there was to be no way back for his uncle. Some years later he was discovered by Dufferin padding the streets of London late into the night in silent grief.

Throughout all of this sadness Georgia and Caroline fell out quite spectacularly. The cause is not certain but may have been because

Caroline had embarked on one court case too many. Even Helen, who never fell out with either, couldn't contain her exasperation: 'Do Car open your eyes (and shut your mouth) and see that this is not our old world when we were all young handsome women, much observed and talked of, and that you are no longer an ideal of *Vanity Fair*. Do you imagine that the present generation even think or care about "the trial"?'[12] Dufferin was mortified to receive from Delane of *The Times* a warning that 'Mrs Norton was in imminent danger of becoming a "bore".'[13] Weary of his family, whose shameless displays only confirmed all the prejudices towards the Sheridan 'blood', Dufferin sought a brief respite in Paris – itself melancholic and 'desperate' in May 1872 after the Commune. With his old world disintegrating around him, he was more than ready to embrace the New World.

PART II

Troubleshooting, 1872–84

13

Canada

The Imperial Frontier

Ugh! Ugh! Horrid! Very rough; everybody ill except the wretched baby Basil, who is perfectly well, but can get no one to dress him and is handed about unwashed to engineers, waiters, to anyone who can stand.

SO BEGAN HARIOT'S daily journal of their Canadian adventure, whose glamour had quickly evaporated amid the pitch and swell of the Atlantic. Not so much victims of what Dufferin laconically dismissed as a 'stiff breeze', but of a heavy cargo of railway iron that meant the vessel 'rolled like a pendulum' and condemned them to four days of 'splashing, dashing and falling about'. With her sister ship lost off the Donegal coast the year before, many on the SS *Prussian* feared for their lives, not least among its other cargo: emigrants (including 107 'street Arabs' – orphans 'rescued by a saint of a woman', declared Hariot, and now destined for 'happy' Canadian families).[1] People and railways: these were the currency of the frontier and as they lost sight of the 'green grey headlands of Ireland' the Dufferins were not alone in pondering 'the immensity . . . of the plunge we are taking'.[2]

That immensity was not to be measured solely in oceans. Entering the Gulf of St Lawrence on 25 June 1872 they first sensed the enormity of the country as they stared over the hills at Gaspé and the 'primeval woods' stretching deep into the interior. From the Citadel high on a promontory above Quebec, they marvelled at the prospect before them: from the broad expanse of the St Lawrence below with hundreds of large three-masted ships, over a 'rich undulating plain, decorated with hundreds of white glistening vales, woods, lawns and cornfields, intermingled with many a church spire, and onto the far distant range of the Lawrentian Hills'.[3] It was a sight of which they would never tire.

By contrast the capital, Ottawa, was a great disappointment. After the historic elegance of Quebec, Ottawa was a town under construction – a ramshackle collection of half-built houses and shops, where the streets were of mud and only passable along wooden sidewalks with street light so ineffective that, according to the *Ottawa Citizen*, it only served to make the darkness visible. Paradoxically, at the heart of the city lay a spanking new Parliament and government buildings, all in the latest Gothic design and in rather better taste, Dufferin conceded, than their model at Westminster. The Governor General's residence on the other hand was simply 'hideous'. A dull grey building, Rideau Hall was tired and cold inside and on the outside overwhelmed by trees that blocked out the light and denied any views. Not surprisingly the Dufferins escaped to the Saguenay River and the prospect of some salmon fishing before the summer was over.

There they discovered Tadoussac, which had a quiet sandy bay with a good anchorage, and in subsequent years was a bolt hole where they could relax 'with no one between us and the North Pole'. On the edge of a cliff they built a wooden house on the lines of 'the old Cowes clubhouse' with a platform overlooking the meeting of the Saguenay and the St Lawrence.[4] And here they would embrace the wholesome outdoor life: camping, swimming in the sea (Hariot 'very striking' in 'waterproofs . . . of the brightest orange'), and especially fishing, both at Gaspé and off the Maritimes coast in his new yacht, *Dauntless*. Such expeditions were not without their dangers and occasionally the macabre. As in 1876, when they were being guided by a young boy whose father had been lost twenty miles upstream two months earlier. The body had never been recovered until inevitably the Governor General cast forth. Here also Dufferin could resurrect another of his passions – painting. And in one evocative picture from inside his small wooden hut, complete with carpets and mosquito nets, and with the painter's feet draped on a balcony rail overlooking the river, he caught the Canadian dream to which they all too happily succumbed.

Still largely unconnected by road or rail, Canada was an attempt at nation building in defiance of geography. For there was little to connect the eastern seaboard provinces of Nova Scotia, New Brunswick and Prince Edward Island with their focus on the Atlantic and the British fishing markets, to Quebec and Ontario and the economy of the Great Lakes. Or further west with the prairies and tundra where lay Manitoba and the Northwest Territories, peopled for the most part by Native Americans and the Métis – part French, part Native American. Further still, cut off by the Rocky Mountains, were the fertile valleys and mineral wealth of British Columbia. While to the north Inuit attempted to carve out an existence in the frozen wastelands. For all but the intrepid trader or explorer, these were separate worlds.

Economically Canada made little sense either. Its boundaries were the product of diplomatic accident in the form of the concessions of Minnesota (1818) and Oregon (1846), resulting in a straight line on the map that cut across the prairies to the west coast. In effect this border restricted development to an east–west progression when economic opportunity and communications naturally ran north–south. The outcome was, in Gladstone's withering assessment, 'a long and comparatively thin strip of occupied territory between the States on one side and the sterility of pinching winter on the other'.[5] With a population of only 3.7 million (1871) and a mainly agricultural economy of wheat and timber, Canada looked too vulnerable to resist absorption into the United States, free now from the distraction of the Civil War and at the beginning of its emergence as a world industrial power. Already most Canadian banks held their reserves in the United States. 'Before long your kingdom must become part of the Great Republic', wrote a friend to Dufferin, 'but hopefully not in your time.' Robert Lowe, Gladstone's Chancellor, was more impatient, urging Dufferin as he prepared to depart, 'to make it your business to get rid of the Dominion'.[6] With imperialism regarded in Britain as parvenu, French and immoral (and with Canada providing only 13 per cent of Britain's exports), the Dominion was not worth a conflict with the United States, especially after Prussia's startling victories over Austria (1866) and France (1870) realigned Britain's priorities nearer to home.

Facing such pressures was a society far from ethnically or racially homogeneous; let alone speaking one language. Religious divisions ran deep with Orange and Catholic violence as much a feature of Quebec and Ontario as in Ireland and Scotland from where such rivalries had been imported. The incorporation of the Northwestern Territories in 1869–70 had provoked an uprising by the Métis led by Louis Riel. Sympathetic to these rebels was a province that lay right at the heart of the country, Quebec. Profoundly French, this was a proud community, still resentful of its defeat by the British on the Heights of Abraham a century before and fiercely protective of its distinctiveness.

It was from such contradictory material that Britain had tried to forge a state over many years culminating finally in a Confederation in 1867 – a marriage of convenience that allowed Ontario and Quebec to separate, and won over the other provinces through coercion in the case of Nova Scotia and bribery in the case of the rest; failing miserably on both counts in the case of Newfoundland which stayed aloof. The constitution was thoroughly British with two houses of parliament and a Governor General, representing the Queen, and who remained responsible to the Colonial Office in London. But constitutions do not make nations or win hearts and minds.

Hence in 1871 Hamilton Fish, the US Secretary of State, could ask the British if there would be any objection to certain areas of Canada seceding to the United States on a free vote.[7] In practice most Canadians who sought the American way of life simply went there – up to one million of them by 1900.[8] Nevertheless the threat from Canada's acquisitive neighbour never lost its potency. The prime motive behind the Confederation was a perceived need to preserve Canadians' independence following the failure of the Southern States in the United States to safeguard their culture and, in 1867, an invasion from the United States by Irish Fenians. Hostility towards the United States in Canada was not solely the outcome of a border skirmish too many. Ideologically the democratic republicanism of the US challenged the spirit of the ancien régime in Quebec and the hierarchical social structures in Ontario where many royalists had fled in 1776.

By contrast the British connection brought a degree of security, access to global markets as well as membership of the most powerful and technologically advanced empire in the world. At the same time, 1867 offered local autonomy under the Crown rather than political subservience at Congress – a monarchical veneer rather than a democratic tyranny. Nor was Canada's Britishness just from fear of the United States. Instead it had laid roots for over a century and culturally, from the novels read to the goods bought, Britishness was omnipresent: 'who reads a Canadian book?' queried D'Arcy McGee[9] a little bluntly in an age when Walter Scott and Dickens dominated in the way that American film-makers would in the twentieth century. Its flag was the Union Jack, its anthem was 'God Save the Queen', and its celebrations were of Shakespeare's birthday, of Waterloo and Trafalgar, of Burns nights and of the 12th of July.

The sinews of the relationship with Britain were economic and technological: the shipping lines decreased journey times across the Atlantic, a transatlantic cable was laid during Dufferin's first year of office, 70 per cent of the capital that funded the three great railway schemes – the Grand Trunk, the Canadian National Railway, and the Canadian Pacific Railway – was British. To a degree the survival of Canada was the achievement of the City and banks such as Barings; and those Canadians who saw that only by amalgamating would they attract the financial capital of the world. By 1900 Britain would be providing up to 85 per cent of all the major capital investment and taking 50 per cent of Canada's exports.[10]

Hence the determination of the early nation builders, with Canadian loyalties in their infancy, to build the foundations on Britishness – a surrogate identity for the new transcontinental state.[11] At the same time, they resented interference and bristled at affectations of metropolitan superiority. Even strong imperialists like the Canadian prime minister, Sir John A. Macdonald, could smart over the opinions of 'an over-washed Englishman, utterly ignorant of the country . . . as all Englishmen are'.[12] Canada in the 1870s was very far from the society that would send its young to die on Vimy Ridge in 1917 for the British Empire. For now, its relationship to Britain was at times almost contractual in tone, its Britishness the most effective strategy for achieving the greatest possible freedom for Canadians in a hostile world. For it to become more than this, Britishness would need to be 'made in Canada'.[13] Yet for all the eye-catching rhetoric of the Canada First movement, it was provincial loyalty, not Canadian identity that was instinctive and immediate. The Confederation was still a novelty and by 1872 unproven; 'only yet in the gristle', as Macdonald explained to a friend, 'and it will require five more years before it hardens into bone'.

Dufferin was quick to appreciate both the opportunity for the Crown and the need for urgency. The onset of depression in Europe would see capital from Britain to Canada cut by a third (1876–80) and bring major development projects such as the Canadian Pacific Railway (CPR) to a halt. With the initial euphoria of the Confederation already evaporating in the economic gloom,[14] the political initiative began to ebb back to the provinces. Determined not 'to be handed down to History as the Governor General who had lost Canada' he may have been, but making Canada British was by no means a certainty as he sailed up the St Lawrence to take office.[15]

14

Frontier Politics

A T FIRST GLANCE the task was far beyond the office that Dufferin was taking up. Yet the Governor General represented, according to *The Times* on Dufferin's appointment, 'something of a constitutional King, something of a Prime Minister, something of a Home Secretary and last, not least, something of a hospitable country gentleman'. His predecessors had mostly kept a low profile. On the other hand the new Confederation was unknown territory and potentially offered the opportunity to define the role afresh and make it 'a personage again'.[1]

Fundamentally Dufferin saw his position as monarchical: 'a representative of all that is august, stable and sedate in the country; incapable of partisanship, and lifted far above the atmosphere of faction'.[2] Determined to avoid being just a functionary wheeled out for state occasions, he took his lead from Queen Victoria. The outcome was a style that was unashamedly regal. Asserting the dignity of his office, he did not hesitate to refer to 'our' Canada or 'my government', exploiting his constitutional duty to advise and warn by actively questioning 'his' ministers at every turn.

On first impression the Governor General was rather taken with his prime minister. With 'his pale complexion and blue eyes contrasting with the dark curls', Macdonald appeared 'the image of Dissy [Disraeli]', recorded Hariot, who became a devoted follower thereafter. Dufferin drew particular 'comfort' from his being 'a thorough gentleman' – a class ally among the natives – as much as for his breadth of vision and what Dufferin rather euphemistically referred to as his 'adroitness'. For Macdonald was an elemental force in Canadian politics: part fixer, part visionary who, through calculation, resilience and political acumen, could make things happen. Behind such creative energy was a mercurial character: for the most part quick-witted, sardonic, supremely confident; but prone on occasion to take refuge in the bottle.[3] Still, as he greeted Dufferin on the quay he was ready for action; ready, too, to bite his lip at the rhetorical self-importance of the new Governor General, for he was only too aware that he would need every ally he could get.

Macdonald had been the driving force behind the Confederation, and capitalised on the momentum of 1867 to win a landslide for the Conservative Party – an awkward alliance of property (in the form of big business, railway owners, and the banks), the Catholic Church (who brought in Quebec), and the states in the West with hopes of the railway. With the initial euphoria evaporating, in 1872 he had scraped back in. At the heart of Macdonald's vision for Canada was the building of the Canadian Pacific Railway, which would link eastern Canada with British Columbia. As in the US, so also in Canada, it was the railroad that was shaping the political map and binding distant communities into a nation. But the CPR was a huge project not simply in terms of distance but also of technical difficulty – not least the crossing of the Rockies. Consequently it was very expensive and with the economy slowing down the government would find it very hard to raise the capital without bankrupting the fledgling state; and all for the benefit of 1 per cent of the national population. Yet not to build it would break the commitment that brought British Columbia into the Confederation. With the US transcontinental railway already in place, without the CPR there would be every chance of a north–south connection to British Columbia and ultimately of its secession. Indeed the recent elections had required Macdonald to reaffirm that no railway would be funded by US investment. With the prime minister now dependent for his parliamentary majority on the deputies from the new provinces including British Columbia, his political future came to focus on a desperate race to make the original deadline of July 1873 for starting the CPR – now less than a year away.

The problem for Macdonald lay in finding the money. Keen to avoid raising taxes, he wanted to rely on local private finance, eventually awarding the contract to Sir Hugh Allen. With the London capital markets unsympathetic,[4] Allen had entered into an agreement for a joint venture to build the CPR with an American consortium headed by G. W. McMullan, who was a major shareholder in the US-owned North Pacific Railways. Fearful of the popular reaction, Macdonald forced Allen to break off this agreement – so making an enemy out of McMullan. Keeping this secret would be challenging enough but it would be a disaster should another secret come out – namely that Allen had privately bankrolled Macdonald's electoral campaign to the tune of at least $350,000. Together these secrets made a toxic mix, leaving Macdonald vulnerable to the charge of selling a national lifeline to the Americans in return for electoral funding. Inevitably rumours spread, accusations were made and commissions of inquiry set up, but without proof they came to nothing. So with the parliamentary session dwindling to a close, Dufferin agreed in May to Macdonald's request to prorogue Parliament on 13 August 1873.

Only then for the Liberal opposition to leak, through a series of interviews (4 and 17 July 1873) given to the *Globe* by McMullan, letters and telegrams that had been stolen from the office of Allen's solicitors.[5] These proved to be deeply incriminating and their publication provoked a sensation. 'I must have another ten thousand', ran one telegram from Macdonald to Allen at the height of the election. 'Will be my last time of asking. Don't fail me.' On their release, Macdonald went into hiding, fleeing to Levis, a small settlement on the St Lawrence, where until early August he sank into an alcoholic stupor. Not even his wife, let alone the Governor General, knew where he was.[6]

With Canada in a 'violent state of excitement [and] the press perfectly rabid', Dufferin had to assert publicly his 'impartiality'.[7] For the Liberal strategy now depended on breaking Dufferin as much as Macdonald. Having gambled all their evidence to discredit Macdonald, they were hell-bent on forcing a parliamentary vote of confidence. However, the earlier grant of prorogation would enable the prime minister to block any further business once Parliament reconvened on 13 August. Assuming this, many of Macdonald's supporters from the west had already left for the summer. On the other hand, if Dufferin could be pressured, on account of the strength of public opinion, to rescind the permission to prorogue, the Liberals, sure now of winning a vote of confidence, would have an opportunity to force an election and win on the back of the public uproar over the telegrams. Hence the campaign to question Dufferin's impartiality in the Canadian press. Upping the stakes further, George Brown, a leading Liberal politician and press magnate, led a delegation in early August to the Colonial Secretary Lord Kimberley in London, to protest over Dufferin's favouritism. As it was, Kimberley had twice already reminded Dufferin privately of the importance of being 'quite impartial'.[8]

There was no doubting the Dufferins' fondness for Macdonald. After all they had just made the 'debauchee' a godparent (along with Queen Victoria) to Dufferin's latest child.[9] If the accusation of partiality could be made to stick, it would be the end of Dufferin's career. Remarkably he chose to stick by his beleaguered, drunken prime minister. Constitutionally, of course, he could not do otherwise.[10] To retract prorogation would be to accept the opposition's accusations. Since he felt that all parties were up to 'vile dodges', the McMullan revelations did not have the impact on Dufferin that perhaps they should have had; while the press attacks against himself only hardened his resolve. All 'very provoking', it may have been, but he was not now going to throw over Canada's 'only statesman'.[11]

It was already 90° and mosquito-ridden when the parties gathered on 13 August. Inside the parliamentary buildings the sweltering heat mixed with raw anger, stoked up over four months of waiting, to create a malevolent atmosphere, itching to explode. With the failure that morning of a last-ditch attempt by 92 Liberals to petition Dufferin to delay prorogation, the procedural advantage lay with Macdonald. For the Liberals, their last hope lay in exploiting any lull between the end of official business and the sound of Black Rod summoning them to hear the prorogation. As soon as the Speaker had settled, Alexander Mackenzie, the Liberal leader, was on his feet. But he had broken too soon; the doors of the Chamber had not been closed. Once they had shut, he was up again. But as he rose the dull knocking of Black Rod sounded the death knell of the Liberals' hopes. For a few Liberals it all proved too galling and they grappled with the official as he worked his way to the Speaker. The deed done, with considerable elan Macdonald sloped off with his few followers to hear the Governor General end the session – the Liberals too furious even to attend.[12]

By the time Parliament reconvened in the autumn Macdonald had regained all his bravado. Buoyed up by the lack of further revelations and with all the worst details now well muddied, here was the 'glorious reaction' Dufferin had long predicted.[13] Yet not all were so optimistic. 'Tell me if all your government are scoundrels, or only a select lot of them', teased Argyll; but Dufferin was acutely aware of the danger amidst the jest.[14] On 5 September he held back the steamer until 4 a.m. to get off 'a monster dispatch' on the topic and later that month he admitted to Kimberley that whether guilty or not Macdonald would have to go: 'turn the matter as we may, it has a very bad appearance'.[15] Kimberley appeared to concur. 'In this country such conduct would undoubtedly ruin any government.'[16]

Under the pressure of such expectation and with the commissioners' draft report reinforcing his suspicions, Dufferin summoned Macdonald and advised him to resign.[17] Admittedly none of the evidence amounted to hard proof. However, for Dufferin, the last thing the new parliamentary system needed was a technical victory for corruption. As he would later confess privately, Macdonald's 'fall [was] almost a necessity in the interest of the public morality of the country'.[18] 'Why now?' Macdonald plaintively asked.[19] Dufferin's intervention threw the cabinet into turmoil, only for a letter from Kimberley to arrive insisting on leaving the decision to the Canadian Parliament.[20] Summoning Macdonald again, an embarrassed Governor General withdrew his request.

'Very cock-a-hoop', noted Dufferin of Macdonald at the opening of the session on 23 October.[21] With his party at full strength, he was outwardly invigorated by the prospect of battle. Privately though, he had been rattled by Dufferin's brief defection and, fearful that the Liberals might produce fresh evidence, he chose to hold back in the debate. If he had gone for the opposition from the start, he probably would have won with a majority of 'double figures'.[22] Instead he left the Liberals with the field for over a week. By the time he realised they had nothing new on him his majority was down to two and he was drinking heavily.[23] That night, shedding all uncertainty, he returned to the House at 9 p.m. and over the next five hours delivered a tour de force.

'It is most marvellous how the man can pull himself together', mused Dufferin; 'pale and haggard', he spoke with the 'greatest vigour and animation' and 'electrified the House'.[24] As Governor General, Dufferin had not been able to witness it.[25] Hariot was in the gallery and,

131

returning to stir Dufferin at 2.30 a.m., proceeded to spend the next two hours in a dramatic re-enactment of her hero's defiant stand. Nevertheless, by the next day, as the Liberals returned to the attack, even Macdonald recognised that his position was hopeless. Only the naive such as Hariot still kept the faith. Startled to hear of the government's fall, she still attended his resignation speech, enduring the smirks of the Liberal deputies as she passed by. With much to ponder, it was no wonder she later took refuge in vigorous exercise – skating on the clear smooth ice of the Ottawa for over a mile travelling as fast as possible on the outer edge.[26] As indeed she had been.

Dufferin's immediate response was to reconfigure the past few months for the record. With the establishment of constitutional practice as the overriding theme, he came to see himself courageously defending due process in August and stage-managing the removal of a prime minister in November. Much of this was for British consumption. Fully aware of the briefings against him in London, he moved his position closer towards that of the colonial secretary, whose promise of support had been tempered by the rider: 'unless you made some egregious error'. Thus Macdonald, whom he had defended against all advice only weeks before, had now become an 'intolerable embarrassment' who had to go.[27] Squaring this circle required two long letters to Delane.[28]

He also sent copies of a despatch – ostensibly for Kimberley reviewing the affair – to numerous friends and politicians in England, including the Queen, Argyll ('as complete a defence as ever I read'),[29] Lord Spencer and Delane.[30] The last recognising the potential value of his source printed the despatch in full for which Dufferin was intensely grateful.[31] The value of such friends was also demonstrated when the Queen intervened twice, insisting that her full approval of Dufferin's actions should be entered into the report.[32] As a result Dufferin survived with his standing in Britain intact. 'I heard Gladstone praise vehemently a letter from you giving an account of your late crisis', reported Argyll; 'Gladstone said it was a "notable" letter and showed great political faculty.'[33] Such shreds of gossip came as a relief; but paradoxically only served to convince Dufferin of his own propaganda and of the importance of his office. Fresh lessons would lie ahead.

★

Declaring that the new Liberal government were 'simply nonentities', Dufferin was determined to be friendly (unlike his wife) towards the new prime minister, Alexander Mackenzie, partly to belie the partiality slur but also because he saw an opening to guide a raw cabinet through the challenges ahead.[34] Within weeks he had his first opportunity with the capture of the rebel Ambrose Lepine. Lepine had been Louis Riel's lieutenant in the 1870 Métis rising in the Red River district of Manitoba. The rebellion was short-lived with its leaders escaping to the United States. But during the uprising they ordered the execution of Thomas Scott, an Orangeman from Ontario. His murder had polarised Canadian society along religious lines. Lepine's capture in turn threatened to stir up the controversy anew. By 1875, with Protestants calling for a death sentence and Quebec Catholics calling for an amnesty for all rebels, the government found itself struggling to avoid a decision. At which point, confident in the backing of the new colonial secretary (his old friend Carnarvon),[35] Dufferin commuted Lepine's death sentence to two years in prison, entirely on his own initiative. What made this remarkable was not just the lightness of the sentence – especially considering that Scott was the son of one of Dufferin's former tenants in Co. Down. Privately Dufferin thought Lepine should hang, but he was always highly sensitive to Quebec. Rather, it was the constitutional audacity of the act. True to form, he quickly despatched lengthy justifications to all his friends and secured the retrospective support of Kimberley and Carnarvon. And of course he had saved both the local parties.[36] But it did set the tone of a very distinctive relationship, perfectly captured in all its condescension by a cartoon in the *Canadian Illustrated News* in April 1875.[37] Dufferin is portrayed as a building site 'overseer' and Mackenzie predictably is the mason setting stones on which are inscribed various governmental policies. 'A very good Job, Mac, and you will be kept on', says Dufferin, 'though a few of these stones may perhaps be condemned by the Boss [i.e. the Colonial Office]'.

His next initiative would prove even more provocative. With the Liberals keen to renege on Macdonald's ruinous commitments to British Columbia, Dufferin was adamant that there should be no let-up on the CPR programme. So he was furious when the government effectively put the project on hold.[38] And even more so when his proposal to embark on a peacemaking journey to British Columbia – involving considerable hardship – was met with outright hostility.[39]

THE MASON AND THE OVERSEER.

OVERSEER. (LORD DUFFERIN.) A very good Job, Mac, and you will be kept on ; though a few of these stones may perhaps be condemned by the Boss.

Illustration from *Canadian Illustrated News*, April 1875

The presence in British Columbia of the formal representative of the Crown as a gesture to allay separatist sentiments had much to commend it (especially as very few national politicians or officials had ever made the arduous journey by rail – symbolically only accessible through the USA and then by ship). But the Liberals suspected that, once there, Dufferin would not resist the opportunity to commit 'his' government to what they were determined to resist. As it turned out, despite considerable provocation, Dufferin behaved very responsibly. Confronted on his entry into Victoria with an arch bearing the slogan 'Our Railway or Separation', he refused to pass under it unless the S was replaced by an R. A horse covered by a blanket inscribed 'Good but not iron' brought only a wry smile. Such sangfroid was hallmark Dufferin and he would need it all as he experienced the full depth of anger aroused by the postponement of the railway.

For five days he faced wave after wave of delegations, with Hariot left to carry out their formal itinerary on her own. In such an atmosphere it would have been inconceivable to have ignored the issue. Nor did he. In a detailed review of the question of the railway he went out of his way to be fair to the government – putting their case better than any minister had put it themselves, according to one historian. But to speak on the matter at all was to become political. Especially as he acknowledged that the Dominion government had broken its commitment (how could one do otherwise?). Worse was to follow with his hints at a future settlement having to involve London as well as Ottawa. And he ended with a ringing cry of encouragement to the province: 'Most earnestly do I desire the accomplishment of all your aspirations, and if ever I do have the good fortune to come to British Columbia again, I hope it may be by . . . rail.' Within hours this rallying call would be on every front page – as Dufferin knew it would.[40]

By 9 October he had returned to Ottawa full of the West and its possibilities, only to find Mackenzie closing off all room for manoeuvre: there would be no improved offer for British Columbia and certainly no conference in London. At which point Dufferin overstepped the mark. He wrote an 180-page report on the question broadly sympathetic to British Columbia's case and the Carnarvon terms. This was destined for the Colonial Office and only forwarded to Mackenzie on 14 November with a request to learn 'the course you are disposed to take'. The result was a major row, for which all apologised on the 17th, only to renew hostilities spectacularly on the 18th. In a historic exchange the prime minister reminded the Governor General that the Dominion was no longer a crown colony to which the latter retorted 'but neither are you a republic'. Considerably riled, he gave full rein to his viceregal presumption in a letter to Carnarvon: 'Within the walls of the Privy Council I have as much right to contend for my opinion as any of my Ministers, and in matters of the moment, they must not expect me to accept their advice merely because they give it but must approve it to my understanding and conscience.'

As it was he had already sent his memo circuitously to Carnarvon's secretary and accompanied it with a set of proposals; which Carnarvon had simply endorsed as his own and forwarded on to the Dominion government. Even more dubious were his secret negotiations with J. Trutch, British Columbia's prime minister, to whom he confided that he was 'fighting your battle tooth and nail'. This was very dangerous country for a constitutional head of state. And futile too; for if the Dominion government held their nerve, then there was little likelihood of their being coerced over a primarily Canadian matter. By late November even Dufferin recognised the danger and, professing himself now to be 'quite sick of the business', withdrew to await the return of the Conservatives.[41]

And yet the debacle over the CPR had established much of the political landscape for the rest of the century, from the limits on the 'political' role of the Governor General to the structure of the two-party system. Similarly, the arguments devised by the Liberal lawyer and politician Edward Blake, in his memoranda of April and September 1876 to modernise the constitutional position, in the end bore fruit in London. Not only was a Supreme Court established but so too were Letters Patent and Instructions for Dufferin's successors. These effectively removed many of the obsolete monarchical powers attached to the office and left others to be exercised by the Privy Council in its own right, while at the same time protecting the provincial legislatures from disallowance. In rewriting the constitutional position of the Governor General, Blake had closed off Dufferin's viceregal ambitions.[42] Not that all of this was immediately obvious – and Dufferin remained as regal as ever – but increasingly he would have to look outside politics to achieve his goals.

15

Reinventing British Canada

You may depend upon my doing my best to weld this Dominion into an Imperium solid enough to defy all attraction from its powerful neighbour across the Line, and to perpetuate its innate loyalty to the Mother Country.

Dufferin to Carnarvon, 1874

WHAT THE DUFFERINS came to appreciate was the potential for a power base that was social and cultural rather than political and economic.[1] Hariot spoke for them both in August 1872 when she declared that, 'Society is at present my business in life'.[2] And particularly so at the emergence of a nation, yet to acquire the loyalties that would bind it. With the politicians preoccupied by administration, as the social figurehead Dufferin sought to enshrine Britishness within any emerging Canadian identity.

First they had to make a splash. The decision to create a summer residence in Quebec was an early statement of intent. Converting the old officers' mess in the Citadel was in its own way provocative, with the Union Jack fluttering among the black cannon that still dominated the skyline. But with the creation of a long drawing room opening onto 'an immense platform big enough to give a ball on'[3] with breathtaking views over the old town and the expanse of the St Lawrence hundreds of feet below, they had a setting spectacular enough for their needs. 'Lady D and I are trying our best to waken up the old place', confided Dufferin to Elizabeth Argyll. 'The people seemed very pleased with the "little season" we have made for them.'[4] A series of large dinners and receptions – including the occasional 'drum' with military bands – followed, fuelled by much champagne. But not apparently allegiance: their first major event ended in embarrassment as the Québecois fled at the playing of the national anthem. Hariot simply redoubled her efforts. Only the Sabbath was spared as over the next two weeks they gave numerous large dinners, threw two huge balls and daily carried out a programme of visits – to convents, schools, asylums – as well as attending a major sports festival which attracted large crowds. They had their reward the next day. 'The whole population', Dufferin reported home, 'lined the streets, the sky was darkened with flags, we ourselves were deluged with bouquets and half a dozen steamers, crammed full of society, escorted us twelve miles up river.' 'No wonder we like Quebec!' wrote Hariot in her journal.[5] But the wonder was that Quebec had come to like a British Governor General so quickly.

There was to be no let-up. Within a week they were in Toronto, capital of the other major province, Ontario. By now the Dufferins were news, popular for being popular. Such was the interest in their progress that on occasion they were forced back by the crush of the crowds. Everywhere they went they were greeted by flags, arches and long processions of carriages.[6] Before departing five days later, they commandeered the state Parliament building and laid on a reception for 1,300 guests, 'who drank the Queen's health in a thousand bottles of champagne'[7] – all of which, not surprisingly, went off 'without a hitch'. Events like these became something of a signature. Eye-catching in their lavishness and scale, they opened up the thrill of exclusivity and fashion to a broader range of aspirants and the provincial elites.

Just as striking was the level of professionalism going into the organisation of these occasions. No detail was too small. When a servant mistakenly turned away visitors to an at-home in Toronto, Hariot had 104 personally written letters of apology in the post before nightfall. Similarly Dufferin, much to his eldest daughter's dismay, sent home the two cooks they had brought from Clandeboye because keeping the best table had become 'a matter of duty and conscience'.[8] Equally important they both had the physical energy and good health to live at this relentless pace. Hariot was indefatigable and only complained after one reception when she had to return 1,500 curt-sies. Most important of all, the Dufferins were natural hosts and made no secret of their enjoyment of Canadian society. 'The young ladies of Montreal . . . pronounced' Dufferin 'a brick', noted Hariot with some amusement after he danced with them until 4 a.m. Often she had to order the playing of the national anthem just to get him to leave. She too was no slouch, joining in the square dancing with some gusto. This was monarchy as the Canadians (or indeed anyone else) had never seen it before: affable, accessible and in tune with the frankness which the Dufferins so admired in the Canadians they met.

Returning to Ottawa for the winter and the forthcoming parliamentary session the Dufferins went to work on a strategy that would in effect place Rideau Hall at the heart of Canadian society. First it had to be made fit for purpose. Trees were cut back to open up the views and to lighten the gloom inside. The doors and corridors were painted white and crimson red carpet laid. Together with a new heating system and the eventual arrival of a few of their possessions from England, it became 'a very comfortable home'. In the public rooms a drawing room was created out of the original ballroom and a purpose-built ballroom added with a stage at one end for plays. Also included was an indoor tennis court. On major social occasions it served as a supper room: a red and white tent was lowered from its roof, a carpet laid and on the walls were positioned large white and gold standards bearing the arms of the different provinces. Overall they had the capacity to entertain up to 1,500 guests. As in Quebec they looked to invent the tradition of a season but at a time when winter was at its height and most inhospitable. The solution lay in turning necessity into a virtue and imaginatively grafting their social ambition onto an omnipresent culture of snow.

By November the snow was thick on the ground. 'There are over-stockings, over boots, over etcs of all descriptions to be put on', recorded Hariot, 'but once out, it is delightful and most exhilarating.' The children soon discovered a hill at the back for tobogganing: 'oh this is really cold; two ears, two faces, two knees and one finger frozen in our family . . . 22° below zero . . . in spite of this we skate'. Skating in fact became an obsession for the whole family and especially with the highly competitive Governor General who established a rink in the grounds and was soon going backwards and doing figures of eight.[9] Inevitably by December they had given their first skating party and it proved so successful they made it the cornerstone of the social regime – particularly as Lent put paid to balls and plays. Guests would arrive in the early afternoon. There would be curling and figure skating on the lake, while on the hill behind a 'groove' had been cut turning tobogganing into something more akin to bobsleigh with corners where bodies would be sent hurtling into the snow. Dufferin would be in the forefront of these activities; practising hard his skating 'aided by all the young ladies', Hariot noted wryly, 'who give him lessons in turn'.[10]

In time they would change for tea. And once inside guests could marvel at a style that journalists deemed English but was as much Old World and European: great majolica vases filled with begonias and geraniums and heliotrope in bloom would stand next to china – some of which once belonged to Empress Eugénie and bought at the sale of Napoleon III's effects – and a sculpture by Princess Louise. At 5.45 p.m. a cotillion would be struck up and the dancing would start in the ballroom. On the dais at the back were the two thrones but the Dufferins would soon mingle with their guests – conversing and dancing with what one journalist described as 'an easy splendour'.[11] The evening might then conclude with a short 'play' with various members of the household supporting Dufferin's children who would enthusiastically take the leads.

The focus of this Ottawa 'season' was primarily the parliamentary session. As if to emphasise this, the Dufferins would invite the full cabinet to dinner – all 'in uniform'. In addition to the usual receptions and dinners, Hariot (by now heavily pregnant with Freddie) would entertain parties drawn from across Canada, including all 280 MPs. Such occasions were not without political purpose, although the intention was not to influence policy as much as to introduce a British perspective. As ever, this was clearer to its critics than most contemporaries. Hence Goldwin Smith's electrifying denunciation of Dufferin's 'reign' as 'a perpetual effort by the use of all the social influence, flummery and champagne at his command to propagate aristocratic sentiment'.[12] To the Dufferins this was as much instinctive as it was planned. But there can be little doubt that the formalisation of seasons or events such as Drawing Rooms were importing the rituals of hierarchical society into an ostensibly egalitarian colony. And, of course, they could not have got away with this if the colony had been anything like as egalitarian as Smith presumed.[13]

In a way that seemed to them entirely natural, the Dufferins sought to fill the vacuum at the top of society with the value system of the most successful nation on earth. Thus they introduced an elaborate set of protocols, with Hariot producing a pamphlet on social etiquette for the unsure. To open up this world to greater numbers of 'new people',[14] they attempted to create a court whose impact might inculcate British values through the class structures emanating from the Crown. Hence, for all their winning informality of manner, they took pains to ensure that there was no presumption of equality; insisting, even on the most casual of occasions, that all stood on their entrance and every dance began with a regal procession to the two thrones on the dais. Yet the Dufferins were not snobs. Rather they took their role representing monarchy seriously, holding that by their actions they reinforced the lesser hierarchies that, for them, bound society together. Symbolism mattered. Hence Dufferin's solemnity when he carried out his ceremonial duties at events such as the State Opening of Parliament. Arriving in a sleigh to a 21-gun salute, and dressed in a uniform 'like that of the Queen's Household, collar of St Patrick and cocked hat kept on at all times', he processed to the Senate with Black Rod walking backwards in front of him.[15] This was more a case of imported than invented tradition, but it gave the ceremony a pronounced Britishness.

However, importing this tradition beyond Ottawa would require more than theatricals in Parliament. And thus the summers would see the Dufferins embark on pioneering two-month-long tours of Ontario and the Lakes, Manitoba and the prairies, and even circumventing the Rockies to reach British Columbia.[16] Despite all the discomforts of camping rough, the smudge fires to keep off the midges, the drenching rain that would (out of nowhere) ambush them, they would remember only the big skies and sunsets, descending rapids and expeditions through unmarked terrain to discover spectacular waterfalls, the exhilaration of being in a virgin land.[17] There they would see their first Native Americans. Unlike Sitting Bull (whom Dufferin had once met in Omaha: 'only one eye and nose of brilliant hue'), these they found mostly comatose on alcohol and 'vicious'. Still for all his marketing of Canada as a White Dominion, Dufferin deplored the brutal disregard of Indian title rights.[18] All this was to no effect as the Indian Act of 1876 would leave the aboriginal population at the whim of the racism of the settlers. Actually Ireland and presumptions of class did more to shape Dufferin's attitudes than race. In his view the fecklessness of most Native Americans differed little from that of his Irish tenants – neither able to forge a modern (as opposed to a romantic) nation – and so it was fitting that the red-coated Mounties, established in 1873 and the symbol of the British Empire in the west, should be modelled on the Royal Irish Constabulary.

These expeditions across the continent were extremely hard work. At every station, let alone every town, they would have to stop and long eighteen-hour days would be filled with openings, receptions, visits, dances, concerts, addresses – each requiring costume changes and polished little speeches in response, of which Dufferin became very fond. Attracting large crowds wherever they went, there would be little respite as they smiled through the periods of boredom, illness and exhaustion.[19] 'We work our passage', he remarked once and, sure enough, the next day he found himself giving nine speeches. On the 1874 tour alone he delivered 120. Although most went unrecorded, they were crucial to Dufferin's task of nurturing national conscious-ness within a loyalty to the British Empire among the small isolated communities of the West for whom the evidence of Canada, let alone Britain, had been scarce.[20]

For such local events to have any national impact required the press.[21] Dufferin recognised the importance of the media to publi-cise his message across a land of isolated homesteads where one visit to one small town would be read about in countless others. So they were accompanied by a team of journalists (four out of their party of fourteen in 1876). When the boat carrying the journalists was two days late arriving in Victoria, the Dufferins endured further seasickness rather than enter the port before their press were there to record the scene. They went out of their way to look after them. In 1874, after six weeks on the road, Hariot (by now three months pregnant) wrote of her delight on returning to Ottawa and some rest. And yet that night they were throwing a private dinner party for their 'faithful reporters'.

Exploiting these relationships, Dufferin sought to exercise consid-erable influence on what was written. On the eve of his highly controversial speech in Victoria on the CPR, he not only called in the journalists to give them a preview, he also edited their reports and insisted on numerous redrafts. Most journalists were compliant; such access, after all, was remarkable for the times. More to the point Dufferin invariably gave good copy. They in turn kept him front page news, wrote of the crowds and the spectacle that followed them, and continually reiterated his theme of Canada in the empire.[22]

The message was unchanging – a message of congratulation for a nation being built, of partnership in the dynamism and achievement of empire, of opportunity for all.[23] In essence this was Canada's manifest 'destiny' – one more than a match for her younger 'big, boisterous, hobbledehoy cousin' to the south:

> A dream of ever-broadening harvests, multiplying towns and villages, and expanding pastures, of constitutional self-government, and a confederated Empire; of page after page of honourable history, added as her contribution to the annals of the Mother Country and to the glories of the British race.[24]

What concerned him was the weakness of any specific Canadian identity at all.[25] 'The feeling here is British but anti-Canadian', Hariot had noted in Vancouver. The fledgling state was always going to struggle against the ready appeal of provincial and local loyalties. But it was in the cultural threat of the United States that, for Dufferin, the real danger lay. 'Already the social, political and intellectual monotony which pervades America is very oppressive', Dufferin warned his friend Carnarvon:

> And one shudders to think of this gigantic area becoming possessed by an enormous population of units, as indistinguishable from one another as peas in their habits of thought and conduct, and subject consequently to an instantaneous impulse from any sudden paroxysm or wave of hysterical sentiment. From this evil Canada will deliver them, if only she gets the chance of developing her individuality.[26]

By contrast, Canada's lack of homogeneity under the umbrella of the British Empire became, for Dufferin, a national strength, bringing 'into our existence a freshness, a variety, a colour, an electric impulse which otherwise would have been wanting'. Hence his campaign to preserve the ancient walls of Quebec from destruction by local administrators seeking to 'square up' the old city in the modern American style of numbered quadrangular blocks. Dufferin's initial plans for the restoration of Quebec included turning the city into 'a Canadian Carcasonne'.[27] Sense and cash (lack of, despite Dufferin compelling funds from everyone from the town council up to the Queen) prevailed. In a smaller project, the walls and gateways were restored and the dramatic Dufferin Terrace constructed along the ramparts with panoramic views over the St Lawrence. This spectacular surviving trace of his rule would be recognised in the 1980s as a World Heritage Site by UNESCO. Dufferin's sensitivity to French Quebec sprang not from a duty to a minority but because in this cultural struggle he believed that Quebec had a major role to play, producing a 'wonderful good effect' on 'the brutality of the John Bull element and the vulgarity of the emigrant classes . . . It has in great measure saved the English population from Yankification.'[28] In similar vein was his intervention to ensure that the Canadian side of Niagara Falls did not fall victim to the casual commercialisation that so disfigured the American side.[29]

By his estimate it would take a generation (or thirty years) before the new state would develop the depth of national identity to be resilient enough to resist Americanisation.[30] Hence the constant elaboration in speech after speech of the Canadian virtues. Hence also his call for a National Gallery and a Canadian Academy of Fine Arts, which was eventually realised in 1880 as the Royal Canadian Academy of Artists.[31] He also backed national games enthusiastically. The 1870s would see an explosion of sport in Canada, all avidly covered in the press. Success was not confined to home territory with Canadian marksmen winning at Bisley in 1872. Furthermore in Ned Hanlan, 'the boy in blue', they had a genuine hero: the first world champion oarsman, he dominated rowing throughout the empire winning all but 6 of his 350 races. Such achievements generated considerable national pride. And with thousands attending some regattas, Dufferin was quick to associate himself with this new phenomenon, donating cups, creating competitions and distributing medals. He also promoted Canadian sport abroad, organising in 1876 for a lacrosse ('practically the national sport here') match between 'Canadians and Indians' to play before the Queen at Windsor.[32] In the field of education he inaugurated the Governor General Academic Medals, among the most prestigious awards for school pupils across Canada to this day, with over 50,000 awarded since he initiated the scheme.

Just as Dufferin sought to sell Canada to Canadians, so he actively promoted its interests abroad, and nowhere more vigorously than in the cause of migration from Britain. Emigration had always been the lifeblood of the new country but especially so after 1871 when it would help to double the national population in just forty years. Not all of this was British but British predominance was inescapable.[33] In this most literal of ways of making Canada more British, Dufferin led the way. Not only were speeches and articles forwarded to the English press, national figures, such as Tennyson, were mobilised to further the cause and newspaper editors berated if they published any criticism of Canada or questioned her loyalty.[34]

Vital to the success of the whole enterprise was the portrayal of Canada not only as an aspirational society but also as an extension of life in Britain, but better. One measure of Dufferin's success is in the dramatic increase in the numbers coming from Britain during his reign – over 152,000, up 66 per cent on the previous decade. 'Lord Dufferin', reminisced the Principal of Queen's University in 1880, 'as a wonderful advertising agent, was worth more to Canada than all her emigration agencies.'[35] By putting himself at the forefront of the campaign, Dufferin sought to place Britain (and indeed the Governor General) at the heart of a process shaping the imagined community that was becoming Canada.

16

The Making of a Celebrity

O N 24 MAY 1878, at a military review to celebrate the Queen's birthday, such was the mass of spectators that some climbed the trees for a view and the surrounding hillsides were packed. There, outside the city, Dufferin and his staff rode through the ranks of three thousand troops. Bands played, cannon fired in salute, and the event culminated in mock re-enactments of famous British triumphs. For all the carnival mood ('Derby-like', Hariot described it), this was a carefully stage-managed affair providing early echoes of the legendary durbars of the Indian pro-consuls. What is remarkable is that this political theatre should attract such large numbers in Montreal in Lower Quebec where traditionally the British presence represented a historic defeat.[1]

This was some measure of Dufferin's achievement. 'A singularly effective Governor General' in the verdict of one recent historian, Dufferin had 'brought an energy and a style that transformed the institution; . . . [being] shrewd enough to appreciate . . . that a major part of British authority would rest henceforth less on power than on the appearance of power – theatrics, social elegance, pomp and cere-mony'.[2] And he had used this power, with the national project in the 'doldrums' of economic depression and political division,[3] to keep the national aspirations of 1867 alive and vibrant until 'nation-making' could renew again. Dufferin didn't create the nation (although he was not above thinking that he had) but at an early stage when the emotional commitment to the new state was tentative, he gave it expression. Under him the Crown provided a cultural focus as the political momentum was stalling in the wake of the Canadian Pacific Railway scandal. The two decades after he left would see a remark-able growth in Canadian loyalty to the British Empire. By 1900 'for

146

most English Canadians their British and Canadian identities were so completely interwoven that one could not be disentangled from the other'.[4] In his contribution to this lay Dufferin's triumph.

It also reflected the personal popularity of the Governor General, for when his term of office was up, Dufferin left on a tide of adulation. The farewell speeches in Parliament were predictably generous. In July they were back in Montreal for a 'week of ovation', culminating in their carriage being dragged through the streets by the students of McGill University. On the return journey to Ottawa their train was stopped at every station by crowds wishing to make their farewell and in the capital there were another three 'great goodbyes'. His voice was recorded for posterity on a new 'phonograph', an early prototype of the record player involving a needle and tin foil; Dufferin speaking so loudly down the cylinder that the needle tore the foil. And two authors, William Leggo and George Stewart, were locked in fierce competition to publish major assessments of Dufferin's 'reign', a mark of respect awarded to none of his predecessors or successors. 'The most popular of all the modern Canadian governors',[5] Dufferin was held to be so successful that he had to be replaced by royalty.[6]

All of which his critics in Canada found incomprehensible. His high flown speeches on the inherent genius of the Canadian people they dismissed as condescension and somewhat in jest. The crowds he attracted smacked of 'populism'.[7] Even allies such as Macdonald found him 'too gushing for my taste'.[8] 'I see you have been joining in the praise of Lord Dufferin's "administration"', Goldwin Smith wrote caustically to Gladstone:

> Lord Dufferin has not been called upon for any display of administrative ability. His energies have been devoted to cultivating popularity by speeches and entertainments. I believe that while he has advanced his own future, he has done this country harm . . . Lord Dufferin is lauded by the Jingoes and the Tories . . . but flunkeyise this country as they will, they will not prevent the ultimate union of the North American continent.[9]

And there lay the rub. With the United States celebrating the centenary of the Declaration of Independence, Dufferin's campaign against

'Yankification' had struck a popular chord. Dufferin took great care to talk the language of 'partnership in the future fortunes of the Empire', of the 'unity of interest', and of his respect for Canada's 'reasoning loyalty' to the Crown. This was a language that resonated.[10] 'If Scott created Scotland and Landseer the [visual proof?], you have certainly done so for the Dominion', wrote Granville. Later generations would redefine the nation in their own terms, but in its infancy the images that Dufferin wove helped to bind the myriad of loyalties into a common frame.[11]

However, Dufferin's appeal was on a scale that transcended his office. Recapturing the excitement of celebrity from centuries ago is an elusive task. Celebrity, as with all fashion, both draws off its context and is killed off by it: momentary, transitory, seemingly inexplicable, it briefly flares before leaving no lasting trace.[12] It was the popular response he aroused that stuck in the memory: unexpected, bewildering for a few, thrilling for many; but in retrospect for some in the establishment, also disturbing, even faintly embarrassing, something later to be denied. And for academics such as Professor Grant of Queen's and Goldwin Smith there was perhaps too a shard of the envy that comes when merit (theirs) is not rewarded with such popularity.[13] In focusing on his self-importance and on his failings as an administrator, they missed the key factor of his novelty.

For a start there was the fact of his presence: socially at the heart of the political capitals in the east – not least Quebec where he built his summer residence; physically too, in the isolated communities to the west of the Great Lakes, where his visits would live long in the folk memory. Few native politicians had shown such a commitment and it is impossible to play down the symbolic impact of his presence in the fringes of the empire. Just as novel was his manner. Part of his fascination was that he was quite unlike any Canadian. Fastidious in dress with his monocle catching the light, the elaborate courtesies and expressions delivered with a slight lisp, his winning combination of 'blarney, charm and gracefulness' all hinted at the gentlemanly ideal that flourished in popular English novels.[14] Also attractive was the Irish take he brought to metropolitan glamour, crucially retaining a degree of intimacy amid the elegance and sophistication. For all that he was grand, he never let himself become too grand; and Canadians were surprised by his accessibility and by how he sought to put everyone at their ease, without letting informality descend into liberty. In such a hierarchical age, this openness from the representative of monarchy was both novel and a measure of modernity. What marked him out was an intuitive ability to connect with the human in most people.[15] This went beyond mere flattery – though he never stinted on lashings of that. Rather it was the conviction that he shared the Canadian dream – which in part explains why his speeches became 'events'.

As a speaker, Dufferin's strength lay as much in his manner as in his message. An offspring of a family where words mattered, he spoke in a vocabulary seemingly beyond the experience of many of his audiences; yet thanks to the imagery, clarity of construction and his refusal to talk down, people listened. Also unexpected was the playful irony he would use to lighten the seriousness of an occasion, the risqué allusion to sharpen the attention and even some knockabout at the expense of reliable foes such as the United States. And all this delivered in a conversational approach: apparently spontaneous, strikingly self-deprecatory and always easy on the ear. The style was no different at smaller gatherings: where over dinner and amid the winning intimacy of shared gossip, 'anecdote would follow anecdote, now of . . . statesmen in Gladstone's cabinet, then of actors and actresses'. Either way Dufferin made the British connection fashionable, even inspiring, and certainly fun. In an age where outside of the large cities, entertainment was rarely to be found, there wasn't a show to match Dufferin's imperial circus.[16]

Still, for all that he was a natural raconteur, these were in fact the performances of a self-conscious actor and founded on hard preparation. Behind the lightness of touch, his recognition of the need to reduce the message to its essence and repeat it endlessly is quite a modern insight into the techniques of mass communication in an emerging democratic age. Dufferin appreciated that in a society created by the inventions of rail, steamship and telegraph, perception would travel more easily than reality; symbols and opinions could matter more than achievements. This was why he was attentive to ritual, and so assiduous in managing the press, alert to correct any error and ready in return to offer 'exclusives'. His attention to detail was such that the official draft for the press in advance of the speech would include 'applause' and 'hear, hear' at appropriate intervals. Or so his critics alleged.[17]

There is no doubt that as the celebrity cult grew, so did the promotion of the messenger.[18] The naming of streets, railways, even forts came with the post.[19] The proliferation of signed photographs was something else altogether. So valued did these become that in the case of the sea captain who took the Dufferins around British Columbia, one became part of his daughter's dowry.[20] Revealingly the last eight pictures Dufferin sent assured the recipient that they were the last person he was thinking of as he sailed away from Canada.

His preoccupation with his own reputation is illustrated by his secret contribution to the two biographies that accompanied his departure. Aware that both Leggo and Stewart praised Dufferin's 'rule' as 'the model of Colonial constitutional government', Dufferin produced not only three volumes of press cuttings but also appears to have written a detailed memorandum on key events such as the Canadian Pacific Railway controversy. Since Leggo allowed him to vet the final proofs, presumably Dufferin was happy to let the hostile tone towards Mackenzie stand. He was so involved that his fussing over the binding and engravings almost caused Leggo to miss his deadline. For a Governor General to collaborate while still in office (albeit at one remove) in the denigration of his prime minister was extraordinary. Although the publishers were instructed 'not to permit any allusion to your [i.e. Dufferin's] aid', the Liberals were quick to suspect collusion. Without confidential communication, many held that 'certain passages could not have been written', wrote Mackenzie to Dufferin in early 1879. Rather nobly Mackenzie denied the possibility. Instead in a delicious touch he sympathised with Dufferin over being so ill-served by these biographers and reassured him that 'already the books have dropped out of sight'.[21] But by then Dufferin had long gone and the copies sent to the Queen, Disraeli, Carnarvon and Lorne had already done their work. In a sense these books were merely shaping the record in much the same way as he had tried to do with his frequent memoranda and correspondence home. And, like them, they were in Hariot's phrase, 'seed sown'.

★

Caroline Norton and Helen Blackwood. 'Georgia's the beauty and Carrie's the wit, and I ought to be the good one, but then I am not'

The only surviving picture of Dufferin's father, Price Blackwood, 'swaggering away to the Downs . . . like the Flying Dutchman'

Georgiana, Duchess of Somerset, of whom Disraeli wrote, 'Anything so splendid I never gazed on [before] . . . clusters of the darkest hair, the most brilliant complexion [and] a contour of a face perfectly ideal'

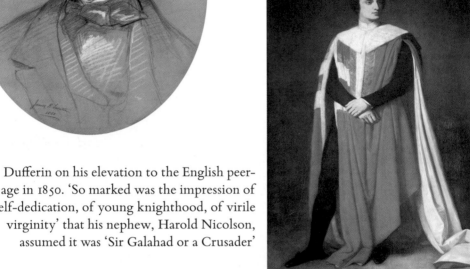

Dufferin at the age of twenty-four, by
James Swinton. 'Much too good looking
and captivating' was Queen Victoria's
verdict on her new courtier

Dufferin on his elevation to the English peerage in 1850. 'So marked was the impression of
self-dedication, of young knighthood, of virile
virginity' that his nephew, Harold Nicolson,
assumed it was 'Sir Galahad or a Crusader'

Dufferin's rooms at Oxford. 'Everybody is astonished at the luxury and taste which
prevails in my room and really I am myself beginning to tremble at it . . .
Granny would be quite aghast'

Marochetti's figure of the Duchess of Argyll from the prow of the *Foam*. 'If only she could have seen how the passionate waves of the Atlantic flung themselves up towards her lips'

The crew of the *Foam* en route to the Arctic

Dufferin's painting of the *Foam* anchored in English Bay, Spitzbergen. 'Its most striking feature was the stillness of this new world . . . a deadness [in a landscape of] Primeval rocks and eternal ice'

Hariot Hamilton with Lord Dufferin, *c.*1863. 'You said
that I may look upon you as at an elder brother'

'The return after the wedding' by Coke Smythe

Helen, Lady Dufferin, of whom the American diplomat J. L. Motley wrote: 'She has known everybody and tells peppery anecdotes, strikes out little portraits and talks of gay or grave subjects with [equal] brilliancy'

George, Earl of Gifford. 'Giff, the object of my guilty passion,' admitted Helen

The Earl of Dufferin

The Duke of Argyll

The Duke of Somerset

The Duke of Sutherland

Hariot, Countess of Dufferin, by
Anna Massey Merritt, 1874. 'Society
is, at present, my business in life'

Hariot with her children
in the snow. 'There are
over-stockings, over
boots, over etcs of all
descriptions to be put on,
but once out, it is delightful and most exhilarating'

Dufferin's watercolour 'Our Hut on the St John River near Gaspé'.
'With no one between us and the North Pole', the Dufferins could relax

'Curling in Canada', by William Notman, presented to
Dufferin (standing with Hariot in foreground)
on his departure from Canada in 1878

When Dufferin had first gone to take up his post in North America political opinion in Britain could not have been more hostile. More than once Tennyson had ridden to Dufferin's rescue in support of keeping Canada in the empire.[22] By late 1874, however, the mood had begun to change. Dufferin's speech to the Toronto Club on 2 September on Canadian loyalty and the potential of the Dominion was one he had reiterated many times. As ever it read well in the press the next day. What was new was the enthusiastic response in Britain. In the uncertainty over Britain's place in the world after 1870, a demonstration of colonial support for the Mother Country now resonated back home.[23] 'All fulsome in praise of Dufferin', noted Granville; and Argyll admitted to 'a lump in my throat and fine Argyllshire rain in my eyes'. The *Spectator* spoke of Dufferin's 'brilliant Toronto speech' with its 'mixture of Irish genius and English sagacity' providing a reaffirmation of 'confidence in the life of British institutions and the steadfastness of the British race'.[24] In this and subsequent speeches Dufferin assumed the role of a wordsmith for the emerging imperial ideal. Vital to this was his ability to make Canada seem everything Britain wanted the empire to be: strong, progressive, exciting and popular. Very quickly Canada had become 'a success' and with it the Governor General.[25]

'You must be surfeited with popularity', wrote a friend. In fact Dufferin was keen to press his advantage still further. Colonel Fletcher, his resourceful former ADC, had the contacts: be it, at Dufferin's direction, placing paragraphs in the *Pall Mall Gazette*, sounding out the editors of the *Daily Telegraph* and the *Saturday Review*, or leaking to *The Times* who always 'liked hearing from you'. It was Fletcher who saw that Leggo's biography was widely and favourably reviewed. When in 1878 a more direct approach was required, as after Goldwin Smith's fresh assault on Dufferin in the *Fortnightly Review*, another ally, George Brodrick, the Warden of Merton and sometime Liberal MP, was mobilised to write a major riposte in the subsequent edition. As a result, even at the height of the Balkan crisis, Dufferin's Canadian speeches were being quoted in extenso.[26] For as Brodrick reassured his friend, 'in this country [you] are certainly – if I may say so – a favourite with the Press'.[27]

'I never remember a speech being as well received as yours was in this country', wrote Granville in 1877.[28] Respected Liberals such as Childers wrote of Dufferin's administration of Canada as being 'the most successful government certainly this century'.[29] 'Her Canadian Dominion', declared the Queen, 'cannot be in better hands than his.' Despite Dufferin's Liberal loyalties, the Tory government considered him for India in 1875 and gave him a GCMG in 1876. Even old Tories such as Lord Cairns spoke openly of Dufferin's 'vice-royalty' in Canada as he wrote in 1878 to congratulate him on the 'magnificent harvest of golden opinions which you have reaped'.[30]

Where politics led, high society followed. If Dufferin had helped to make the empire stylish and glamorous, it was because he was so himself. He was the subject of adulation in such slavish publications as the *World*; in whose series of 'Celebrities at Home', hero worship knew few bounds: 'never in vice-regal or regal dwelling [Rideau Hall!] was there more of the grace that is the outward visible sign of mind to which art is a second nature and taste an hereditary instinct'. The fascination with celebrities could nevertheless ensnare some unlikely victims. 'Dufferins: a great break to see them . . . for Dufferin's reign has been a great success', gushed a starry-eyed John Bright after a stay at Chatsworth in November 1878. It is a moot point whether Dufferin shaped the perception of Canada more than Canada forged the perception of him. Together they established him as the glamorous, beau idéal of a largely mythical aristocratic empire.[31]

17

'The man for high latitudes'

DUFFERIN RETURNED HOME to find his family unusually quiescent: 'We had both your aunts at an afternoon lately and they did not come to a collision', wrote Elizabeth Argyll breezily.[1] Caroline's eventual marriage to Lord Stirling in 1877 and her death after a prolonged illness three months later provided a surprising, almost respectable, resolution to a life of stirring and sadness.[2] The loss of Elizabeth Argyll the next year was a heavier blow. For many years she had been Dufferin's closest confidante: part older sister, part stern mentor, she had been his fiercest defender and a faithful shelter from the maternal storm.[3] Other old friends were struggling too. Laid up in Cannes, Constance Grosvenor found Lady Jocelyn 'looking so young [as she stood] over the grave of her last child'. Within two months, noted Dufferin, 'my dear friend Fanny [Lady Jocelyn]' had died too.[4] Such deaths hit him hard.

Dufferin returned to diplomatic duty – this time as Ambassador to Russia, appointed by Disraeli's Tory government. Hounded by the Liberals in the aftermath of the Eastern Crisis over his aggressive, seemingly provocative policy towards Russia, Disraeli's poaching of the Liberals' star diplomat was an astute political move, which the Liberals could hardly resist.[5] Tactics aside, Dufferin was the right man for the job, 'capable of performing disagreeable duties in a pleasing manner', explained the Tory Foreign Secretary, Lord Salisbury, and one 'who can cope with the finesse which the Russians display in diplomacy'.[6]

What is less obvious is why Dufferin accepted the post. After all, the Tory government had barely a year to run and was increasingly unpopular. Yet, once approached by Disraeli through his Uncle Somerset, Dufferin accepted without consulting any of his Liberal friends, including Argyll.[7] The timing of the announcement of his appointment – as the Liberal hierarchy gathered in the Reform Club to laud his achievements in Canada – could not have been more awkward. Belatedly Dufferin wobbled and pleaded for time to consult his party. 'Too late', came Disraeli's brisk response. Anxiously Dufferin sought out from Granville Gladstone's reaction: 'peculiar', as it turned out, which Dufferin rightly surmised disguised considerable irritation.[8] Consequently in his speech he emphasised that his agreement with Disraeli 'left [me] quite free as to my politics' and reasserted his Liberal principles; taking cover in what Harold Nicolson dubbed 'the virginity of the public servant'.[9] But there was no gainsaying that 'there was something comical in my position'.[10]

Nevertheless there was much sense too. Revealingly, to begin with Somerset urged his nephew to accept because of the prospect of 'employment'.[11] With the last of the land sales that would finally clear his debts just a year away, he was now heavily dependent on a salary. At the same time Dufferin saw the Russian posting, in the interim before the Liberals returned, as a 'good opportunity of educating myself a little in European politics'.[12] Such experience would be vital to any further advancement, especially as he was something of an outsider in the diplomatic world, an intruder whose progress depended on his connections (of whom the latest, Salisbury, had been his fag at Eton).[13] What made such privilege tolerable was the reputation won in Canada. 'He is certainly charming and I suppose the most popular man in Europe', noted Regy Brett as he travelled up to London with Dufferin. 'But what a bore it must be, having to keep up such a reputation.'[14] And therein lay Dufferin's predicament. Bereft of wealth and exceptional political gifts, but blessed with the intuition and imagination that made him a distinctive as well as a talented diplomat, it was his reputation – what in modern parlance would be his image – that would make his future. But reputations won in distant parts need momentum to sustain their power at home. If he added European achievement to his record, his standing would be enhanced significantly. More than that, it would enable him to establish a unique position: a troubleshooter for the empire drawn on by all parties and a national figure. And so, for all that 'another spell of an Arctic climate is not a pleasant prospect',[15] two days after renewing his vows to Liberal ideals, at the behest of his Tory masters he set sail on 24 February 1879 for Russia.

In the aftermath of the war between Russia and the Ottoman Empire over the Balkans (1875–7), Russian ambitions to build a Slavic empire of satellite states had come to little following the intervention of the other Great Powers, not least Britain, at the Congress of Berlin. Fearful of falling foul of his pan-Slavic lobby, the Tsar had stalled on the implementation of the subsequent treaty and, almost a year on, Russian troops were still in the Balkans and the British Embassy was widely ostracised. It was in order to break this dangerous stalemate that Disraeli had called on Dufferin: 'a first rate man',[16] who had a 'rare tact and power of attraction . . . for work of political healing'.[17]

'The work here under Lord Dufferin is simply *nil*', reported one of his staff.[18] The new ambassador spent little time on official despatches, preferring to write private letters to Salisbury. Dufferin, viewing the embassy as a social arm of diplomacy, embarked on a major renovation of the building ('a hideous rhubarb-coloured house, unfinished within'). And when the Office of Works refused to pay any more, Dufferin simply exceeded (by more than a half) his official salary.[19] In the meantime he was rigorous in paying his calls and attending every reception and ball. 'The hours they keep are dreadful', lamented Dufferin to the Queen, after a dinner starting at 6 p.m. ended at 4 a.m.; as a general rule to leave before 3 a.m. was deemed 'unreasonable'.[20] Nevertheless the Dufferins proved 'indefatigable'.

To add to the stylishness of the British embassy, Dufferin chose 'to surround himself with young men of good fortune' and fashion, among them the Duke of Abercorn's son, Lord Frederick Hamilton, and Lord William Compton, the future Marquess of Northampton. But he worked them too, insisting that they were last to leave the dance floor.[21] To be fair, he led from the front: endlessly courteous, finding time for the least important as well as the grand, and impressing with the breadth of his interests and genuine admiration of Russian art and literature; and all laced with the magnetism that came with celebrity. It was an unabashed and relentless PR offensive and it proved irresistible.

By September 1879 diplomatic gossip had already picked up that 'where backs were turned to [his predecessor] Augustus Loftus, Dufferin [is] extremely popular and that Russian Society flock to him'.[22] The test would be Dufferin's first official reception of the season. He wore the blue swallow-tailed coat and epaulettes of a Lord Lieutenant of Co. Down, the riband and star of St Patrick as well as the star of the GCMG – seeking to further England's cause by emphasising his Irishness. Hariot produced her best diamonds, while all the servants wore 'State liveries, cocked hats and knee breeches'. The real coup was to appoint Prince Lieven as Grand Master of Ceremonies, thus ensuring strict adherence to Russian protocol (which was fiendishly complex) and impressing the aristocratic old guard. Equally impressive was a display of the golden spurs and roses, laid out in the dining room, their story of a 'most feudal arrangement' greatly appealing to Dufferin's guests. Stylish, aristocratic, different, this was an occasion not to be missed and nearly 550 attended.[23] Soon afterwards Odo Russell in Berlin was hearing from Princess Radziwill of how the Dufferins were 'the most charming and popular diplomatists that there had ever been in St Petersburg!'. Even allowing for the ribbing from his friend, there was no doubt that the British were in from the cold.

'Lord Dufferin is so very popular at St Petersburg,' noted the Queen, 'she trusts not too much so?'[24] But as Disraeli explained, 'What is desirable is that Lord Dufferin in his audience today may lay the foundation for a satisfactory settlement of every "burning" question'. In the event on their first audience the Tsar chose to deliver 'a great scolding'. Yet he continued to recognise his commitments arising from the Congress of Berlin; and two cordial meetings with Gorchakov suggested to Dufferin a willingness to consider a fresh start. After all, as he was quick to grasp, 'it is known that I am an anti-jingo and that gives me great pull'.[25] In close consultation with Salisbury, Dufferin began cajoling the Russians with promises and the occasional threat towards the final retreat from Turkish Europe. 'Partly from inherent slipperiness, partly from the disjointed character of the administration, you always have to deal with the Cabinet of St Petersburg', advised the Foreign Secretary, 'as you might have dealt with the firm of Quirk, Gammon, and Snap'. Dufferin was up to the challenge and a 'masterly' negotiation resulted in the final evacuation of Russian troops by 4 August 1879. To seal this advance in relations Dufferin asked Salisbury to insert in Disraeli's Mansion House Speech 'a panegyric of Alexander' – which remarkably the prime minister delivered.[26] Such astute gestures were typical of Dufferin and in this case were quickly rewarded. At a military review the following week he found the Tsar 'wonderfully pleased' and generals with 'nothing but praise for Lord Beaconsfield and England! Quite a new thing', Disraeli noted.[27] Of course both sides were looking for an escape from the Balkan impasse but it took Dufferin to steer them to a resolution; and in only five months.

> It is a fallacy to assume that within our lifetime any stable arrangement can be arrived at in the East. The upmost we can do is to provide halting places where the process of change may rest awhile. But what we have to do is rather to assume the probability of change and so shape our precautions that it should affect no vital interest of ours.

The pessimism in Salisbury's letter to Dufferin of 4 February 1880 reflected more than his natural perspective.[28] For a revival of the Great Game was in the offing.[29] Blocked now in the Balkans, Russia's attention turned to Central Asia and the easier pickings in the territories of the largely nomadic Turkoman tribes. Such activity inevitably brought Russian armies closer to India and stirred up a recurring nightmare of Britain's chattering classes of the 'jewel in the imperial crown' in peril. To combat this, Afghanistan was regarded as an essential buffer, to be kept within British influence. But it was also thought that protecting Afghanistan meant that the British should take a stand further north and in particular over Merv, an ancient Turkoman city in central Asia, which offered a potential base for an invasion of Afghanistan. Salisbury's attitude was altogether less anxious.[30] For a start he doubted whether the Russians genuinely sought to annex India. And even if they did, the logistics of supply lines stretched over hundreds of miles of near desert would have severely tested their military organisation.[31] Consequently he argued against the expense involved in defending Merv. In any case, he held that Afghanistan would be a more cooperative buffer if Britain insisted on Afghan independence rather than asserting British influence by force.

Unfortunately for Salisbury, the Conservative-appointed viceroy in India, Lord Lytton, thought differently. On his own initiative he ordered a full military occupation. This complicated enormously the series of talks Dufferin undertook with the Russian foreign minister,

Nikolai de Giers, over Russian intentions. Not surprisingly the Russians viewed British operations as potentially aggressive and asserted in turn their interests; not least over Merv, something Dufferin knew many in the cabinet would never concede. Only after eight meetings in July and August 1879 could Dufferin at last reassure London that the Emperor's ambitions did not stretch to Merv. 'Probably not now,' muttered Disraeli.[32]

But the stakes were raised much higher in late September 1879 by a 'startling' proposal from Bismarck: an alliance with Germany. Bismarck saw the prospect of a Russo-British conflict as an opportunity to woo Britain to an alliance, which with Austria would secure Germany's position in Europe. In the event the offer evaporated as quickly as it came.[33] But the affair was unsettling, especially with the Russians pressing ever closer to India. Interestingly, Salisbury sent Dufferin back in December via Berlin to test the mood there. On arrival Dufferin found the German Emperor openly hostile to Russia and delighting in 'our successes in Afghanistan'. Then Dufferin received an invitation to stay with Bismarck at his retreat at Varzin. They had met before but this was a signal honour; if one that involved travelling for eight hours in winter to see 15,000 acres of pine and a 'rambling, unpretending house of no style'. As it was, he arrived to find his host in his dressing gown and suffering from a 'pretty sharp bilious attack'. Whether out of indigestion or not, what followed was a 'monologue' breathtaking in its continental sweep and unabashed cynicism. By turns appalled and fascinated by the German Chancellor's 'very humorous and epigrammatic view' of recent events, Dufferin caught the measure of the German fear of Russia. In the belief that pan-Slavism was rampant and the Ottoman Empire being 'one of those things which has to go', the diplomatic fault line was now all too clear. With France itching for revenge on his western border as well, Bismarck was seeking to establish with Britain and Austria 'the party of les satisfaits' who would offer a 'sure guarantee of peace in Europe'.[34]

None of this eased Russian suspicions of British motives. 'Your visit to Varzin has created a deep sensation in the diplomatic world', wrote Odo Russell.[35] And especially in St Petersburg. If nothing else this established Dufferin as a major diplomatic player in the courts of Europe; or as Bismarck put it with his instinct for the human weaknesses of his opponents, their meeting has 'confirmed my first impression that you are the man for high latitudes'.[36]

August 1880 found Dufferin once again witnessing army man-oeuvres, this time in the company of the Emperor in preparation for the renewed attack on the Turkomans.[37] Back in Britain this provoked what his friend Argyll dubbed a fit of 'Mervousness'. Yet Dufferin remained convinced that India was not in danger and, for all their bluster, he also doubted the Russians would take Merv.[38] This was just what Gladstone's new government, which had campaigned against Beaconsfieldism and reckless adventures abroad, wanted to hear. 'He ought to be a good judge', recorded Hamilton in his diary and so he proved to be.[39] In January 1881 a large Russian army under General Skobeleff blew up the Turkoman stronghold at Geok Tepe. In the aftermath 4,000 tribesmen were massacred; news that was greeted back in Russia with the singing of Te Deums and 100-gun salutes in recognition of the restoration of Russian military honour. But Merv was left for another day.

In the meantime the return of the Liberals reopened the prospect of being made Viceroy of India. With Argyll confiding that Dufferin's appointment was 'highly probable whoever is in power', his hopes were high.[40] In both St Petersburg and Calcutta it was seen as a foregone conclusion by those not quite in the know.[41] A misinformed leak in four London papers claiming that Dufferin had ruled himself out of the post had him scurrying to correct the record and regretting that he was not in London to secure his case.[42] Ripon's appointment, therefore, came as a bitter blow. To his closest friends he did not hide his disappointment, naturally assuming it was in revenge for taking office under the Tories.[43] Argyll insisted otherwise: 'No! No!' he sought to reassure him. 'I have seen no indication of the smallest feeling against you.' In fact, it appeared that he had not even been considered.[44]

A sense of marking time now enveloped his Russian mission. With the Liberals in power the Russian fixation faded and with it Dufferin's sense of being at the heart of things. Gone too was the intimacy he shared with Salisbury but which never developed with Granville, the new foreign secretary. 'Weary of St Petersburg',[45] he rented a summer-house in 1880 in Finland, began to paint again, took up dancing lessons and, more adventurously, went on week-long bear hunts. On one of these he shot a 'pretty large bear' which had taken refuge in a tree, only to discover at the foot of the tree its three cubs. Even though after six months they 'roared, scratched and bit like fiends', Dufferin had them transported back to Ireland. One he gave to Maude, Lady Clanmorris in Galway. There it broke out of its stables and killed some sheep, thus instigating the first ever bear hunt in Galway. Another was gifted to Dublin Zoological Gardens where some years later it was to be seen looking a little forlorn and 'labelled dangerous'. The third was kept at Clandeboye in a specially constructed bear garden, where it lived for four years until one day it nearly killed its keeper (who was only saved by 'prompt and plucky action' from Archie). Promptly shot and stuffed, it was displayed less dangerously in the entrance hall at Clandeboye.[46]

Unlike in Canada, Dufferin could escape back to Britain. He calculated that within the first ten months he had crossed the English and Irish 'channels' twenty-six times. This enabled him to renew his connections with political society. It had been the Queen who had first raised the possibility of Dufferin going to India and he never failed to arrange an audience with her, indefatigable in his attentions as she bemoaned her loneliness; with an eye to the future he would also call on the Prince of Wales. The Queen had come to view him as one of the few Whigs she could trust and it says something of Dufferin's skills as a courtier that she could presume he agreed with her on foreign policy. After talking 'so confidentially' to Dufferin at Balmoral when she had blurted out her anger at the Liberals' lack of patriotic support for Disraeli's foreign policies, she assumed that the 1880 election results 'will astonish Lord Dufferin as much as everyone else'.[47] Ironically at this time he was looking to get closer to the leading Liberals. By August 1880 he had overcome his disappointment sufficiently to confide to Granville that 'I really believe that if the late government had remained in office another year, we should have been in dispute, if not at war, with all the world.'[48] Such reaffirmations of faith would see him invited to Hawarden in November. However, by now Dufferin was not simply out to protect his own future; he was also increasingly concerned about the growing radicalism of Liberal policy and especially in response to the land war that had broken out in Ireland.

18

Revolutionary Times

IN IRELAND A series of disastrous harvests saw the formation in October 1877 of the Irish Land League which escalated matters with rent strikes and boycotts on estates that refused to lower rents. In what was a 'New Departure' Irish Nationalist MPs led by Charles Stewart Parnell allied this land campaign to the political call for home rule, so that by 1881 the mood in Ireland had not been as revolutionary since O'Connell's day. From his estates at Coole Park in Co. Galway, Dufferin's friend, Sir William Gregory, looked on in despair at the 'malignant hatred with which [English] rule is regarded'.[1]

For all that his land sales put him 'beyond the reach of even a communist revolution',[2] Dufferin was desperate to return to England and engage with the debate first hand.[3] At Hawarden in early November 1880 a long chat on Ireland with Edward Hamilton, Gladstone's private secretary, revealed just how detached Dufferin had become from the political tide.[4] Next he found himself vigorously attacked when, in giving evidence to the Bessborough Commission, he attempted to denounce tenant right. His experience before the Richmond Commission (looking into agricultural distress) was an even more bruising affair with one of the commissioners later boasting of how he had 'smashed by cross examination Dufferin's evidence'. To be fair this was sport Dufferin was ill suited for but such indignities were all faithfully passed on by Granville to his master.[5]

Undeterred, Dufferin pressed on and, with Argyll's assistance, wrote a major article advocating land purchase and a peasant proprietorship – 'a wild scheme' in Gladstone's eyes but which was published with his acquiescence on 4 January 1881.[6] Remarkably Gladstone was keen not to hurt Dufferin's feelings: 'I do not think it tactful to object'[7] was the best explanation he could offer Granville. But nor did either seek

THE IRISH DEVIL-FISH.

"The creature is formidable, but there is a way of resisting it. * * * The Devil-fish, in fact, is only vulnerable through the head."
VICTOR HUGO's *Toilers of the Sea*, Book IV., Ch. iii.

Illustration from *Punch*, June 1881

to include Dufferin. What mattered for Gladstone was not Dufferin's political views but his diplomatic skills. And lest these be lost by a public stand-off over Ireland in December he offered Dufferin the major ambassadorial role in Constantinople.[8]

At which point Dufferin found himself the target of a smear campaign in Ireland. In February 1881 his former tenants in the Ards peninsula drew up a memorial denouncing their former master of deceit. In particular that, while heavily involved in the drafting of the 1870 Land Act, he had introduced new leases for his tenants (who were unaware of what was to come), which would free him from the constraints of the impending act – in effect denying them rights through a form of insider knowledge. While none of this was strictly illegal, it was deemed immoral and threatened his reputation as a good landlord and respected authority in Liberal circles on the land question. The irony of all this was not so much that the central accusation was untrue – the leases were drawn up three to four years before the act – but that they thought he was worth attacking. Suddenly not only were Irish Nationalists denouncing the 'English absentee', so too were socialists such as Jenny Marx (thus following in a family tradition) and articles appeared in the *Pall Mall Gazette* (known to be the prime minister's paper of choice).[9]

Such a personal assault rattled Dufferin, perhaps more than it should. Argyll rallied to his defence, assuring Gladstone that his friend was not 'the greatest rack renter in Ireland'.[10] Knowing that the charge could not be dismissed so lightly, Dufferin wrote an agonised defence to Gladstone ('I cannot tell you my dear Mr Gladstone what a pain and humiliation it has been to me to write this letter'), his embarrassment heightened by his assertion to Gladstone only in December that 'my rents have been cheerfully paid' despite no tenant right. Later, as the attacks persisted, Dufferin was too distracted by his own travails to focus on the land bill.[11]

'Dufferin . . . astonished and disgusted at Irish Land Bill', the Duke of Somerset relayed to Brinsley Sheridan, after 'Gladstone told him some months ago that he sympathised with Dufferin's paper'.[12] As recently as January 1881 Dufferin had been reassuring Lansdowne that 'my great hope is still in Gladstone'. Similarly exposed, Argyll resigned from the cabinet. This did put Dufferin in a quandary; after all, resigning was the last thing he could afford to do. 'Do nothing hasty', urged Argyll. 'I mean about resigning. A member of Cabinet is in a very different position from an ambassador who is never responsible for the policy of ministers under whom he serves.' It was a distinction Dufferin appreciated, reassuring his friend 'don't bother too much about me for I will know how to possess my soul in patience'.[13] In private was another matter. 'It is so like the English,' he raged to Gregory. 'They pride themselves upon their "generous" policy towards Ireland, their generosity consisting of trying to bribe the Irish population into loyalty with our money, and while they pretend to sit in sackcloth and ashes for their past tyrannies, they are simply repeating them.'[14] Prime among 'them' was the prime minister who paraded his moral conscience through the parliamentary debates as one divinely inspired and irresistible.[15] A year later and safely ensconced in Constantinople as the land war raged in Ireland, it still rankled: 'I wonder', Dufferin mused, 'whether the slightest gleam of light ever impinges on Mr Gladstone's conscience in regard to these exhibitions of his sense of justice.'[16]

Revolutions, however, were not confined to Ireland. On 13 March 1881 Emperor Alexander II was returning from a military parade accompanied by his usual escort of mounted Cossacks when they passed two or three men shovelling snow by the side of the road. Suddenly a bomb exploded under his carriage. Although a good deal shaken, both carriage and Emperor survived intact. Believing the attack over, the Emperor got out to see to the injured Cossacks. At which point a second bomb was thrown, landing just by his feet. The explosion tore off a leg and much else beside. Dufferin, who had earlier been conversing with the Emperor at the parade, heard the explosion and rushed to the Winter Palace. As he climbed the stairs, he was met by the Grand Duke Vladimir who told him there was no hope. Kennedy, his secretary, with a keener relish for the macabre recorded that at the lying in state 'all that remained of the late autocratic ruler of Russia was the head and the trunk'.[17]

The assassins were dubbed nihilists. Alexander II's (largely symbolic) liberation of the serfs in 1861 had fuelled unrealistic expectations, which by the 1880s gave way to frustration at the failure to reform the autocratic system and ultimately to revolution and assassination.

Actually this was their fourth attempt on the Emperor's life in the time Dufferin had been in post in St Petersburg.[18] Queen Victoria (who was attacked seven times in her reign – in each case by deranged individuals) was especially affected, not least because she had married her offspring into most of the royal families of Europe. With St Petersburg now 'full of stories of bombs and mines and explosions and conspiracies to blow up everybody', the Queen took fright, refusing to send the Prince of Wales to the funeral. It fell to Dufferin to win her round, pointing out that with the royal families of Europe 'flocking to St Petersburg' in a show of monarchical solidarity, it would look 'very ill if a brother-in-law and sister had been deterred . . . from fear of . . . personal risk'. She acquiesced but not before declaring him to be 'personally liable' should anything happen to them. 'Not a very pleasant message', he later recorded, since the 'Nihilists might [on this occasion] have cleared the European chessboard with a vengeance'.[19]

In the event the funeral was a shambles, and a missed opportunity to those like Dufferin who placed great value on the power of ceremony.[20] Not that the British royal family proved masters of ceremonial procedure either. Some days after the funeral the Prince of Wales and his party went to the Anitchkoff Palace to instal the new Tsar, Alexander III, into the Order of the Garter. Unfortunately the Tsar arrived in military uniform and trousers, which made the application of the garter more awkward than usual. As it was the Prince of Wales tied the garter to the right leg. 'Other leg, Sir' whispered an aide 'amid some gentle tittering on the part of the royal ladies . . . After the ceremony the Emperor withdrew with his left trouser leg tied above the knee in a most ungainly fashion.' Even so, Dufferin reported back to the Queen's secretary that it had been 'really a striking ceremony [which] went off admirably'.[21]

While the cabinet digested his first assessment of the new Tsar ('not a man of any ability, obstinate, rough and shy, and without experience . . . owing to his reclusive habits'),[22] Dufferin went to the trials of nihilists to assess the anarchist menace. Among the expected 'very low types of humanity' he was surprised to find a doctor ('very distinguished looking', even 'gentleman-like'). Much more perturbing were the two women who with their 'hair cut short, flat-breasted and sexless' appeared the very denial of femininity.[23] Sixteen years later he returned to the subject, exploring in a thoughtful article the origins of nihilism. Drawing parallels with Indian nationalists, he attributed such revolutionary protest less to the 'cleavage' between the aristocratic elites and the 'dumb millions' and more to the education of numerous professionals with high ambitions and few opportunities. 'Scantily endowed with this world's goods but saturated with all the most advanced radical, social, communistic, speculative or agnostic ideas which progressive Western civilisation has lately evolved', they were bound to 'chafe' at the 'paternal despotism'.[24]

It was his own country that he felt had started the rot. The tendency of the English radicals 'to buy the support of the masses by distributing among them the property of their own political opponents' was effecting a 'social revolution' and 'establishing . . . a precedent established in Ireland that is almost sure to be applied elsewhere'.[25] Very easily the Land League and nihilism became almost synonymous in his eyes. 'If every reform were to be made for which the country was fit, it would not disarm these blood thirsty scoundrels', he fulminated to the Queen in March 1881; actually about nihilists in Russia, but he was saying the same about the Land League. A year later the 'Irish Nihilists' struck, not with bombs but surgical knives, assassinating Gladstone's new chief secretary and nephew, Lord Frederick Cavendish, as he walked in Phoenix Park with his deputy.

The events of the early 1880s clarified much for Dufferin. The idealistic liberal who looked on bemused at the revolts of 1848 or the Paris Commune in 1871 now saw the global challenge to aristocratic rule for what it was. All of which would serve to relocate Dufferin's politics – if not yet formally. With Irish landlordism and indeed English Whiggery being sold out by radicals in what Gladstone called the conflict between the classes and the masses, the defence of authority became the focal point of his worldview.

In April 1881, Dufferin made a final visit to the Hermitage amid a flurry of farewells, and returned to England in time to attend Disraeli's funeral at Hughenden. His success in Russia had established his diplomatic credentials, while in the courts of Europe his social elan won many admirers. Cosmopolitan and well connected (his long stint at

Windsor ensured that he was welcomed by the Queen's many relations abroad), he was seen as the perfect English gentleman, and all
the more so for not being English. By now his reputation exercised a
fascination in its own right. It was partly the appeal of the heroic
explorer (it is surprising how many claimed to have read *High
Latitudes*). Even Bismarck, of all people, caught the celebrity bug, if
briefly. Passing through Berlin en route for the first time to Russia,
the Dufferins received a visit from the most powerful leader in Europe
(in full uniform and 'shining helmet'); so long did he stay that they
became 'a little anxious over the time'. Yet what amazed the attachés
at the embassy was that he went at all: 'Why Prince Bismarck does
not go out of his house four times a year', explained one. Even so, the
next day came an offer to dine, in the process of which two Pomeranian
aunts were put off because 'they would not amuse Lord Dufferin'.[26]

Back home, his appointment to Constantinople sealed his independence of the political parties and established a reputation as a
troubleshooter of the empire. A *Punch* cartoon (21 May 1881) sought
to capture the appeal of Dufferin, portraying him as a Turkish pasha
smoking a 'Chibouk', beneath which ran the legend, 'The Earl of
Dufferin, P.C., K.P., K.C.B., G.C.M.G., a man of many letters from
High Latitudes. Again he urges on his wild career . . . to Turkey'.
Unconventional, stylish, distinctly grand; compared to whom even
the radical republican Sir Charles Dilke, Gladstone's Under-Secretary
to the Foreign Office, knew his place: that of 'occupying the relative
position towards you that an ant does to an eagle'.[27]

19

Finding One's Assiette

The drawing room of the Summer Embassy glistened with Sheraton and fresh chintz. The chandeliers in the gallery tinkled as the children galloped along the upper corridors . . . [Their parents] dined under the magnolias, the candle-flames on the tables swaying lightly in the large glass globes. After dinner the young men of the Chancery would come across from their house along the quayside and there would be games . . . amateur theatricals, tableaux and picnics . . . and moonlight expeditions on the Bosphorous . . . Dufferin presiding, two fingers of his right hand tapping tranquilly upon the palm of the left, a slow remembered smile lighting his southern face. No man has ever absorbed or distributed so much enjoyment.[1]

THUS FIFTY YEARS after the Dufferins' arrival in Constantinople, Harold Nicolson tried to recapture the setting in which his parents would meet and marry. Arthur Nicolson, who was to catch the eye of Hariot's sister Katie,[2] was part of Dufferin's talented team, three of whom later became ambassadors and one, Charles Hardinge, Viceroy of India. All would trace their most formative years to this magical time spent under their chief.[3] Dufferin was always very open in discussion with his staff, often to the verge of indiscretion, and ready to share the tricks of his trade.[4] What they all appreciated was the way 'he took a broad statesmanlike view of political questions and left details to be worked out by his subordinates'. In one official's telling phrase, Dufferin 'had the capacity of utilising other men'. Control freaks such as Curzon, who would later deride such an approach for being too casual, missed the point that Dufferin could crack the whip, and all the more effectively for being so unexpected.

Nevertheless the ambassador's regime did not appear too arduous, allowing the Dufferins to lead an outdoor life: an hour's tennis every morning (with 'the Miss Bartholeyns') followed by long rides in the afternoon or better still hours spent in his 'yawl' exploring the coast-line or sailing around the Princes' Islands in the Sea of Marmara.[5] Occasionally Hariot would organise regattas with races between the ambassadorial caiques – long graceful water launches decked out in luxuriant colours and rowed by twelve men in the finest livery.[6] Dufferin's hospitality knew few bounds;[7] while at balls 'His Excellency always gave an admirable example by dancing with all the prettiest and youngest ladies until the small hours.'[8]

Yet such leisure belied the difficulties facing the British mission. To the outsider the Ottoman regime appeared mercurial, largely impene-trable, and intuitively deceitful. No one was held to embody this more than the Sultan, Abdul Hamid. 'A small man with a dark beard, soft eyes, and a gentle manner,' was Dufferin's first impression – and one humble enough to light the cigarettes of his guests.[9] But he was a more complex figure: 'a collection of antitheses' in the verdict of a recent historian; 'subtle and silly, brave and frightened, cruel and tolerant, modern and traditionalist, listening one moment to the Koran, the next to the adventures of Sherlock Holmes (read to him at night from behind a screen in specially commissioned transla-tions)'.[10] Preferring 'the use of the silken chord to the sword', he had tried to eliminate his rivals only to live in constant fear of his own assassination. Such was his paranoia that not only did he make his own medicines but he also pulled his own teeth. Rarely venturing from his refuge at Yildiz where he was protected by his six-feet-tall Albanian bodyguards, he governed his empire, surrounded by his pashas who would bow to the waist in his presence and hold their tongues. It was a private fantasy world of his own creation; and yet in it he suspected everyone.[11]

Abdul Hamid was not without talent. However, the problems facing the Turkish Empire meant that its disintegration was widely regarded as inevitable.[12] In Europe it was being undermined by Balkan nationalism; its financial system was so corrupt that the state declared itself bankrupt in 1876; while the recent war against Russia had ended in defeat and, at the Congress of Berlin, humiliating loss of territory.

Subsequent demands from the Great Powers for the Turks to guarantee the freedom of non-Turkish communities and in particular the Christians in Armenia (especially dear to Gladstone's heart) were deeply resented. Instead Abdul Hamid countered this by encouraging a revival of Islam; and at home by asserting an authoritarian rule, sustained by a vast network of spies.[13]

This posed two problems for Dufferin. Firstly, with the Sultan insisting that all matters be referred to Yildiz, Turkish administration had ground to 'a standstill'.[14] The second problem was that the British were an 'object of abhorrence'[15] to be frustrated by officialdom drawing on an inexhaustible pool of compliments as they played for time.[16] 'The Sultan makes me the most positive promises on the subject [Armenia] but time slips by and nothing is done,' lamented Dufferin to Layard in late January 1882.[17] And nothing ever would. But by then 'the subject' was already being overtaken by events.

On 9 September 1881, a colonel in the Egyptian Army, Ahmed 'Urabi, sealed off the 'Abdin Palace in Cairo and compelled the terrified Khedive, who ruled Egypt in the Sultan's name, to concede political reforms and the restoration of the army to its full complement. This was more of a strike than a coup, and a well-ordered, gentlemanly affair at that. But its consequences were to reverberate around Europe and to distort the politics of the African continent for over a century. At the time most saw it for what it was – primarily a local, even military matter. However, alongside calls for the replacement of hostile ministers and the restoration of army pay and posts, the demands for a popular assembly reflected a broader discontent: that of rural labourers (fellahin) who made up 90 per cent of the population and were ground down by taxation; government officials resentful at senior posts being taken by foreigners (who made up 2 per cent of the civil service but absorbed 16 per cent of the payroll); and Islamists shaken by France's recent seizure of Tunis. And all of these were deeply opposed to the oligarchy of Turkish and Circassian elites that had exploited Egyptians for centuries.[18]

To these traditional oppressors were now added European bondholders who had financed at ruinous rates a wildly ambitious drive for modernisation in the 1870s. By 1876 the country was bankrupt.[19] So lucrative were these loans that they were widely distributed among most investment portfolios from Vienna to Paris and London; to the extent that a default on the interest payments could have triggered a significant financial crash across Europe. To prevent this, Egypt was forced to cede control of her finances to the Dual Control of Britain and France. By 1880, 50–60 per cent of government revenues went to the bondholders. Britain's economic presence was even more pronounced for it absorbed 80 per cent of Egypt's exports and supplied 44 per cent of its imports in addition to a large stake in the Suez Canal. Defending such interests were up to 90,000 foreigners, who benefited from terms leaving them free from all tax and most legal constraints.[20] This was no less that an informal occupation; and out of such foreign exploitation 'Urabi was in time to draw on the resentments of the downtrodden to create a populist movement for 'national regeneration'. His rise from out of the ranks of the fellahin symbolised the aspirations of many Egyptians. And by December 1881 his appeal to the masses (who now hailed him as 'El Wahid' – the Only One) put him in a position to dictate the course of Egyptian politics.

To Arabists such as Wilfrid Scawen Blunt, who had pitched his tent outside Cairo to witness the excitement, 'Urabi was a freedom fighter, whose nobility of purpose, simplicity of manner and winning smile encapsulated the romantic ideal.[21] The British press initially took a similar line. As did Dufferin, who had happy memories of five months in the Nile Valley with his mother and a fascination for its culture ('to this day I have a book of hieroglyphics on hand'). As 'all his instincts [lay] with the national party in Egypt', to him the solution was in getting 'anything like self-government started'.[22] So, as 'Urabi made no direct threat to the bondholders' interests or the Suez Canal, the Liberal government in London, embroiled in Irish difficulties of their own, preferred to await events; while Dufferin, to soothe French nerves, dissuaded the Sultan from sending in troops.[23]

However, the situation was radicalised by two ill-conceived Anglo-French initiatives – a declaration of their right to intervene in Egyptian affairs and then in May 1882 the despatch of a squadron of ironclads to threaten Alexandria.[24] Since they were under strict instruction not to fire a shot, this naval force represented a bluff waiting to be called. What had previously been a myriad of reformist groups, now focused around an expanded army and a policy of rapid Egyptianisation.[25] Stirred up by Muslim 'shaikhs', the mood had turned distinctly ugly towards all foreigners and especially in Alexandria.[26] If the Europeans felt vulnerable, so too did Gladstone. Where once he confided his sympathy for the sentiment of 'Egypt for the Egyptians',[27] now he faced a horrible choice: come to terms with 'Urabi to the detriment of Britain's economic interests and prestige or intervene militarily and expose the hypocrisy of all he had stood for since 1877.[28] No wonder he accepted the French suggestion of an ambassadorial conference of the Great Powers to be held in Constantinople.[29]

Then came word that rioting had broken out in Alexandria. Ever since the arrival of the ironclads – in many ways the real provocation – the city had been ready to explode. Over two chaotic days (10–11 June) fifty Europeans were killed and hundreds more injured, including the British Consul, Charles Cookson, with a severe head wound.[30] Thousands evacuated the city leaving properties and businesses to be ransacked by Muslim mobs.

'International atrocity. Wholesale massacre to overrule the people of that country', noted Gladstone privately.[31] Yet there was never any evidence, as many of the cabinet would much later acknowledge,[32] that 'Urabi had anything to do with the massacres, let alone initiated them. Nevertheless at the time the Liberal leadership did not hesitate to make the link. In the prime minister's dramatic declaration to Parliament, 'Urabi had thrown off the mask'. Rather than 'Urabi leading a popular nationalist movement, 'everything was governed by sheer military violence'. Memories of similar massacres during the Indian Mutiny fuelled hysteria in the press, with even measured organs such as *The Economist* asserting that 'the contingency of anarchy' offered the government 'perfect freedom of action'.[33] Within four days of the riots the British cabinet effectively authorised in principle British intervention; the following week on 21 June, two days before the conference was due to open, Gladstone outlined a 'sequence' for military action.[34] Immediately Lord Hartington, the secretary of state for India, initiated a full alert in preparation for the deployment of Sepoys from India; the Admiralty sent two warships to the Suez Canal; and Dufferin was instructed to ask the Powers to 'sanction' an expedition by troops 'other than Turkish'.[35]

Yet it is not clear whether this represented a commitment to act. Certainly after the riots Gladstone had to be seen to be decisive. But his attitude to the forthcoming conference suggested otherwise. Privately he hoped it would act as 'a bulwark against precipitate follies'[36] – by other powers or cabinet colleagues.[37] Hence Granville insisted to Hartington, until its outcome was clear, 'the question [of intervention] is hardly ripe for discussion'.[38] But most important of all, recognising that some action was almost inevitable, Gladstone saw in the conference the legitimisation of what in Tory hands might have been denounced by him as military adventurism.

It also took the matter out of the hands of his political rivals and into those of his ambassador in Constantinople in whose abilities he had by now developed considerable trust: 'he is like a man who has at last found his assiette'.[39] Dufferin would need to have, for his mission was not easy. Gladstone's preferred outcome was the use of Turkish troops under the mandate of the Great Powers (to which both the French and the Turks were opposed).[40] Failing this, he proposed a 'joint action' (but with who?) to restore the Khedive's power and the status quo. He insisted that reparations for the damage done to British interests in the riots would be a 'separate question' and not for the conference; so too, more controversially, would be the Suez Canal.[41] This was a tall order.

Quickly the conference found itself in difficulty. Initially the Turks refused to participate.[42] Then Dufferin's efforts to authorise 'prompt and energetic' intervention on behalf of the 'suffering Egyptians' against a 'military usurper' who had brought 'absolute anarchy' to Egypt – very much the Gladstonian case – was rejected by all the other powers. After all, the Egyptian government was still intact and with 'Urabi as Minister for War extremely popular; taxes were collected, debts paid and justice administered. They also argued that it was not realistic to expect the Sultan to reassert Turkish control in Cairo with 'Urabi regarded 'even in Constantinople, as a champion of Islam'.[43] So much so that after the opening session of the conference, the Sultan invited Britain to send her troops to Egypt. Dufferin rejected it out of hand, fearing European reaction, and said that even if presented as a 'gift . . . with all Europe consenting', Britain wouldn't want the 'burden and the responsibility'. Granville and Gladstone were equally swift in their rejection. Interestingly, they did so 'without a Cabinet'; the first Hartington knew of this was when the Queen showed him Dufferin's telegrams – both furious at a missed opportunity. Thus rebuffed, the Sultan had no option but to procrastinate.[44] 'The Conference makes no way', Edward Hamilton recorded in his diary: 'Urabi shows no sign of giving in; the Porte still plays a totally dark game; and France cannot properly be relied on.'[45] To his credit on 6 July Dufferin managed to get the conference to make a formal offer to the Turks to send in their troops. Only for the Sultan to reject the offer, unmoved by Dufferin's frantic assertion that 'what is wanted in Egypt is immediate action'.[46]

Immediate action was certainly what Britain needed. On cue Admiral Sir Beauchamp Seymour in command of the British fleet in Alexandria harbour, seeing 'Urabi adding guns to the city's fortifications, sought permission on 7 July to bombard the new batteries.[47] Gladstone quickly saw the spuriousness of the threat and Northbrook too accepted that the guns offered no 'real danger' to his ironclads. Yet he did add a rider that suggested intent and has inspired conspiracy theorists to this day: 'but if we want to bring a fight on, we can instruct B. Seymour to require the guns to be dismantled'. Two days later Granville sent out two separate instructions: one to General Garnet Wolseley appointing him to command a land force to restore order in Egypt, and a second to Seymour instructing him to prepare for a bombardment.[48]

Worn out by long venomous sessions in Parliament and cabinet over his Irish Crimes Bill ('My brain is very weary'), Gladstone gave way in the face of a cabinet for once united and determined on action.[49] With events already developing a military momentum, the French fleet withdrew.[50] On 11 July 1882 with the expiry of the ultimatum, Seymour opened fire. After a ten-hour bombardment 'Urabi had no option but to evacuate his troops. In the vacuum, two days of looting and further destruction ensued; to the extent that on 13 July Seymour had to land a detachment of marines to restore order through summary justice. For all Gladstone's insistence that they be called a 'police force', the die had been cast.

Gladstone had hoped that this nineteenth-century version of 'shock and awe' would prove decisive. It certainly proved destructive.

Not only were most (but not all) of the forts put out of action but many of the historic buildings on the seafront were destroyed; as was much of the commercial and some residential districts in the city. Hundreds, possibly thousands of citizens were killed.[51] More than being a disproportionate display of force, it was also a remarkably inaccurate one. Of the 3,000 shells fired, it is estimated that only 10 hit the forts; the vast majority hit the city. Such inaccuracy has again stirred modern conspiracy theorists brought up in an age of 'precision bombing'. Cock-up and complacency are perhaps more realistic explanations; though not to prevent Seymour being rewarded with a peerage and a parliamentary grant of £25,000 before the year was out. Wolseley's damning of it as a 'silly and criminal bombardment . . . concocted [by] the Admiralty' could reflect service rivalry (and the frustration of losing 7,000 troops to the defence of Alexandria as a consequence). What is unquestionable is that in the days after the bombardment Gladstone quickly attributed the burning of the city to a deliberate policy by 'Urabi to torch Alexandria – proof of the prevailing 'anarchy' and thus the veracity of the British case. All in all, the crisis in Alexandria could not have come at a better time for those like Dufferin who wanted 'action'.[52]

Seen as a signal of British intentions the bombardment had the effect of flushing out the Great Powers. With his hand strengthened, Dufferin quashed an Italian proposal to neutralise the Suez Canal. Instead he persuaded his colleagues to reissue the invitation to the Sultan to send troops under the mandate of the conference. Should that fail, Dufferin was urged by Granville to 'devise other means'. The concern now was over letting the Sultan's troops into Egypt lest they formed an alliance with 'Urabi. So Dufferin, together with the French, insisted (with conference backing) on a tight agreement for any Turkish intervention – 'the military convention' – as well as a proclamation of 'Urabi as a rebel.[53] Not surprisingly, 'The Porte still dallies' recorded Edward Hamilton in his diary, '. . . and the hope now is that he will decline to send troops or else continue to dally so as to make it possible for the Powers to act independently and appoint other mandatories to settle the Egyptian question.'[54]

Privately Gladstone urged Dufferin to 'avoid the danger of seeming to ask the Conference for a monopoly or privilege'.[55] So (with the conference's understanding),[56] throughout July Britain and France sought allies for a joint operation if only to defend the Suez Canal. Italy declined the offer. And then French intervention evaporated with the fall of the government on 31 July. With her proposal the only one left on the table Britain (still officially acting on behalf of the conference) had the free hand she desired.

A formal mandate from the Great Powers had never been likely and could have necessitated significant concessions elsewhere.[57] Tellingly, for Gladstone, the authority of the conference was essentially 'moral, not legal'.[58] What Dufferin achieved through the negotiations over joint operations and through agreements on Turkish intervention was to neutralise Great Power opposition, at least in the short term. Also important was what the conference was steered away from: recognising 'Urabi; or an internationalisation of the Suez Canal. Crucially the conference was not allowed to break down, merely suspending itself in August, and thus enabling Dufferin to continue on its behalf talks with the Porte; and allowing Gladstone to hold on to the belief that 'we are discharging single-handedly a European duty'.[59] A fiction, no doubt, but one that would strike important chords at home during the long wait for the invasion force to arrive.

20

'A master of his profession'

BACK IN ENGLAND, Gladstone kept up the unrelenting demonisation of 'Urabi to sustain the popular momentum in Britain for the coming conflict.[1] And to keep at bay awkward 'truths' – not least the charge that this was a bondholders' war. 'It is an unpleasant reflection', remarked Salisbury when previously in office, 'that – as regards Egypt – France, Austria and Germany have all shaped their diplomatic action . . . purely to satisfy the interests of certain bankers who were able to put pressure on their foreign offices.' This may explain why these powers acquiesced in Britain's intervention. But was Britain above such calculation as Salisbury implied?

'What a mess in Egypt!' wrote Argyll to Dufferin in June; 'I am interested like many others as a stockholder'.[2] It is very likely that Dufferin was too, given the capital he had raised from his land sales. Remarkably sixty-five MPs held Egyptian bonds.[3] But few were so heavily invested in Egyptian bonds as the prime minister, with these bonds accounting for 37 per cent of his investment portfolio. In six months the outcome of the coming war would increase the value of Gladstone's Egyptian investments by almost 50 per cent. Yet there is no evidence of this swaying his actions and plenty of evidence later of him enacting policies over Egyptian loans that ran counter to his personal advantage. Nor was there any tradition in Britain of government support for bondholders caught out by foreign repudiations. That said, Gladstone was undoubtedly happier taking up the cudgels on behalf of 'order' in Europe and 'the general maintenance of all established rights in Egypt, whether they be those of the Sultan, those of the Khedive, those of the people of Egypt, or those of the *foreign* bondholders'.[4]

Sustaining this 'internationalism' over the coming months would be Dufferin's task.[5] While the convention provided a fig leaf of European authority for the invasion, the outward pursuit of Ottoman participation, however undesirable to British generals, remained a vital ingredient. For in the six weeks it would take Wolseley to confront 'Urabi, Britain's position remained vulnerable: from those powers which might seek to advance their ambitions in the Turkish Balkans or in Asia; and from the risk of a pre-emptive strike by the Sultan while the main British force was at sea.[6] In this phoney war the front line was Constantinople and the weaponry diplomatic.

With British troops en route, the initiative lay entirely with Dufferin.[7] Reflecting this, the Turks accepted in principle the terms offered by the conference for their involvement. And with this, on 14 August the other ambassadors agreed the suspension of the session, leaving Dufferin on behalf of the Great Powers to complete the deal. Yet it took him a further eleven days before he persuaded the Turkish delegates to sign up to the military convention; only for the Sultan 'to make difficulties' again. This set the pattern for the coming weeks with Dufferin patiently coaxing and occasionally threatening the Porte towards agreement.[8] By now Wolseley had entered the Suez Canal (past a 'gesticulating' de Lesseps on the quay), and Granville was secretly briefing cabinet ministers on the fast approaching 'critical moment when diplomacy must yield to arms'.[9] At the eleventh hour ('according to Turkish custom'), on 29 August, the Porte had declared its readiness to sign the military convention. 'Dufferin seems to do very well', noted Granville.[10]

Almost too well, for as Hamilton remarked candidly, 'We don't want now the Porte's assistance.' Once again it was Gladstone who insisted on the diplomatic benefits of Turkish involvement. Interestingly, when confronted by the Queen in full sail against any involvement for the Turks, he chose as his prime defence 'the desire to support and assist an ambassador who, in circumstances of the greatest difficulty, had shewn himself "a master of his profession" as a diplomatist'.[11] With Wolseley's attack expected daily, Dufferin now had to sit it out.[12]

On 13 September, after an impressively disciplined, silent night march (led by Bedouin guides), Wolseley's forces came across 'Urabi's base at Tel-el-Kebir. Attacked at daybreak, the Egyptians were taken completely by surprise and in little over forty minutes 'Urabi's army was destroyed. What followed was little short of a massacre with Egyptian losses being estimated at anything up to 10,000 (compared to British casualties of 57 dead and 22 missing). 'Urabi fled for Cairo pursued by British cavalry. But his cause was now hopeless and he and the city surrendered without a shot being fired.

That same day (and unaware of events in Cairo), the Sultan summoned Dufferin at 3 p.m. for what bizarrely turned out to be a last attempt to agree arrangements for Turkish military involvement. For eleven hours, with the Sultan in one room and Dufferin and a dozen pashas in another, they exchanged memoranda and amendments to the terms of the military convention, 'each one more impractical than the other'. By 9 p.m., after a second meeting with Dufferin, it appeared that the Sultan ('crouching over a table of ebony playing nervously with his beads') was 'weakening' and by midnight his ministers were very hopeful of a signature. Then at 1.15 a.m. 'the sinister figure of the Sultan's astrologer was seen creeping towards his master's study'. This was Sheikh Abu al-Hudaal-Sayyadi, from Aleppo, who denounced all deals with 'infidels'. Within minutes fresh concessions were being demanded. This was too much even for Dufferin, who summoned his launch after storming: 'One would think I was the representative of a Power whose armies had just been annihilated on the field of battle, rather than one whose generals had concluded a successful campaign by a brilliant victory.' As he got up to leave the pashas 'clustered around me, pulling me down by the coat tails, stroked my hand and almost patted my cheek, beseeching me not to ruin Turkey'. Finally by 2 a.m. he escaped and sailed back to the embassy at Therapia. There awaiting him was Granville's telegram with the news of 'Urabi's capture.[13]

'I congratulate you on your brilliant campaign, in which you have covered yourself with glory'. So wrote Kimberley who previously had never been much inclined to rate Dufferin's abilities.[14] In his verdict on Dufferin's contribution, he echoed opinion in Britain and in the foreign ministries of Europe. It was remarkable that barely four years after Russian intervention in response to Turkish misrule had brought Europe to the brink of a continental war, Britain was able to send an army into the Ottoman Empire with the apparent acquiescence of the Great Powers and the Sultan. In managing this Dufferin entered 'the very first rank of living diplomatists'. Through 'sound judgement, resolute action, and consummate tact', he had secured at the conference 'complete liberty of action' for Britain. Admittedly once Britain had decided to act there were no powers with either the means at the ready or the national interest to stop her. Nevertheless the opportunity for mischief was undeniable. As part of the Dual Control (and with her Tunisian colony) France would have expected a major role. Bismarck had little interest in Egypt but plenty in stirring up divisions that would keep Britain and France preoccupied. Instability in Egypt could find Russia and Austria manoeuvring to exploit a potential break-up of the Ottoman Empire. That events didn't unravel in the summer of 1882 owed much to Dufferin's negotiating the military convention and then sustaining the prospect of Turkish involvement as it decreed; and thus tying in the Great Powers until Tel-el-Kebir.[15]

Vital to this achievement was Dufferin's handling of the Porte and especially Abdul Hamid, whom Gladstone had long regarded as 'the greatest of all liars on Earth . . . a bottomless pit of fraud and falsehood'.[16] Hence the value London placed on reining him in. 'All that has taken place at Constantinople', wrote Hamilton on the eve of the conflict, 'clearly shows how impossible it is to deal with such a knave – and clever knave too – as the Sultan. If anyone could manage him, it would be Lord Dufferin who has exhibited throughout these difficult times extraordinary diplomatic acumen and great firmness.'[17]

Dufferin put it down to never 'resorting to a single dubious act or expression'.[18] So it was profoundly irritating that it was not for these virtues that he won the acclamation of the British press. Indeed quite the reverse. Instead it was for the adroit arts of delay and confusion by which he sucked the Turks and the Great Powers into complex negotiations, distracting them until too late from the covert advance of Wolseley's army. Undoubtedly there were those in the War Office and cabinet who did not want any Turkish involvement. Nor did trusted friends such as Argyll, who, convinced of Turkish duplicity, was from early on urging Dufferin to tell the Porte 'too late, too late, ye can't enter now'. And indeed by September nor did Dufferin.[19] Hence his extraordinary decision to go for a week's sailing on the Bosphorous in the final days of the crisis, which in hindsight looks like a determined effort to avoid any agreement.[20] As for the negotiations, Dufferin accepted that 'artificial delays' were a 'perfectly legitimate' tool of the diplomat's trade. By now the ambassador was 'so distrustful of the Sultan,' reported Ponsonby, 'that he dawdles . . . till Wolseley has struck a blow'.[21] In any case these were not negotiations in the proper sense but more of an ultimatum as Dufferin, out of necessity, couldn't deviate from the original terms imposed by the conference. Terms which were always known to be too humiliating for the Porte to accept and as such were for some commentators not intended to be accepted.[22]

Still the fact remains that in matters of delay the Porte and espe-cially Abdul Hamid needed no help.[23] Back in Britain, where there was little empathy for the precariousness of the Sultan's position in the Islamic world, his delay in allying with the irresistible force that Britain had sent out seemed incredible folly in a leader. And so only explicable in terms of a masterful sleight of hand: what Dufferin bitterly referred to as 'the diabolical astuteness of the British Ambassador'.[24] This in turn was reinforced by Wolseley's spectacular military strike: the extraordinary ambition of the night manoeuvres, the surprise attack, above all the astonishing speed of the campaign. With so complete a victory it didn't take much to presume the far-sighted diplomatic preparation that preceded it.

What took the Powers by surprise was not that the British excluded the Turkish forces; but the thoroughness of British control both of Egypt and the Suez Canal. What had been sold as an international police operation began to look like a British occupation. And with it, a redrawing of the strategic map of Europe towards the African contin-ent in what would become the Scramble for Africa.[25] In late 1882, as they waited anxiously for evidence of a military withdrawal, the Austrians were not the only ones to experience what Dufferin called 'a momentary doubt'.[26] And no wonder, for they would have to wait nearly seventy years for Britain's withdrawal. Dufferin may have been a beneficiary of unintended outcomes, but there were many across Europe ready to believe with the Porte that they had been duped.

'Your hesitation of yesterday', remarked Dufferin to the Sultan as Wolseley arrived in Cairo, 'has made my reputation as a diplomatist

A FRIENDLY GAME.

Sublime Porte (*Aside to* Khedive). "YOU'LL HAVE TO DO ALL YOU KNOW! HE'S BEST-ED *ME!!!!*"

Illustration from *Punch*, November 1882

but ruined it as an honest man.' A touch melodramatic perhaps (and dismissed by one biographer as 'retrospective family whitewash'), but there was no doubting that reputation mattered to Dufferin.[27] As in Canada, he always found time to nurture the press (and Mackenzie Wallace of *The Times* he found so congenial that he was even a regular in Hariot's theatricals). Similarly in his extensive reports back to London, there is more than a hint of his managing the narrative and his role in it. To a degree Dufferin was a prisoner of his own creation. Regarded in the press as the beau idéal of the English gentleman, in truth he looked anything but.[28] Nor indeed was he English (and therein lay a host of insecurities). But in the public eye he had come to espouse values held to be intuitively English: integrity, common sense, calmness under the greatest pressure, unrelenting in the pursuit of justice. Thus, for Dufferin, to be praised for 'having tricked the Turks in an un-English fashion' cut him to the quick.[29] Within days of the story breaking, he was corresponding to all his friends and writing an eighty-page report for the government to counter the 'suspicions . . . being put about in some of the papers'; although he admitted in a maudlin tone to Granville that 'no mortal soul will ever read it'.[30]

In the aftermath of battle such anxieties barely resonated in London as the euphoria swept up even the Liberals. Edward Hamilton confided in his diary to being 'quite Jingo-ish'. As for his boss, the good news had him ordering the bishops to ring the bells and the War Office to fire a celebratory salute in Hyde Park. 'I hope the guns will crash all the windows,' he exulted (to the dismay of those in his party still inspired by his Midlothian creed).[31] In similar vein the Queen pressed the case for a major honour for Dufferin. Gladstone talked of the Garter, Granville demurred preferring the GCB as more fitting of a diplomat. All to no avail. Dufferin, who had something of a collector's eye for such things, asked to be spared.[32]

21

Statecraft and the Art of Casting a Veil

> Above all things, I hope you will never imagine that I attach any
> importance as far as my own credit or personal interests are
> concerned to the publication of what I write. Such an idea as
> that is never present in my mind.
>
> Dufferin to Granville, January 1883

SOME MONTHS LATER the British position in Egypt was an
unholy mess.[1] Gladstone would not be the last British prime
minister to go to war with no plan for the aftermath. His insistence
that 'Urabi had led a military coup and not a popular movement was
becoming less convincing by the week. Liberating Egyptians had
been a crucial justification of the war: but what if liberal institutions
had already existed there (and certainly in a more advanced state than
Britain would ever concede)? In Britain, for all that the war remained
popular, criticism in Parliament and the press grew steadily, exposing
not only the frailty of the government's moral case for war (a war of
'bondholders against Egyptian peasants'), but also the consequences
of the British government's abdication from any new responsibilities
with the restoration of the Khedive. However constitutionally correct,
this proved a recipe for chaos. Gladstone remained deeply reluctant to
govern Egypt – not simply because of the added cost but because it
would only confirm what most European chancelleries already
believed, that the British were determined on 'a silent annexation à la
Bosnia'. As before, Gladstone sought relief in the demonisation of
'Urabi and, displaying surprising viciousness ('I shall be very glad if he
can be hung without real inclemency'), he eagerly awaited the execution that would vindicate his actions.[2]

As it was, the cabinet were split on future policy: with Chamberlain leading the radical charge for the imposition of Western liberalism on an archaic East, and the Whigs frustrated at the delay to impose imperial authority. The decision to appoint Dufferin as special commissioner was a revival of Gladstone's conference strategy of placing divisive issues off limits until Dufferin reported back.[3] Dufferin's popularity would also provide some respite from the press who lauded him ('a brilliant diplomat [who has] always emerged . . . covered in laurels') and drew comfort from 'his understanding of the occult processes of the Oriental mind'. Indeed, 'Lord Dufferin, more than any other', proclaimed the *Daily Telegraph*, 'holds at this moment the secret threads of the entire Eastern Question'. But for all that, *Punch* was closer to why Dufferin's appointment gave such reassurance. In its cartoon of 11 November 1882 entitled 'A Friendly Game', Dufferin is seen coldly shuffling the deck of cards as he measures up his next victim (see p.182). Meanwhile the Sultan whispers to the Khedive as he leaves the table, 'You'll have to do all you know! He's best-ed *me!!!*' One paper described Dufferin as 'a great magician', who might seek to restore order 'by spells of his own devising': a British oriental to master the East.[4]

He would need to draw on such powers if he were to master his brief, which was not discussed by the cabinet until the day after he set sail for Cairo. Not surprisingly the result was a collection of contradictions. It was insisted that the occupation 'should last for as short a time as possible' in order to secure 'peace, order and prosperity in Egypt'. Seconded for only three months, he was expected to re-establish 'the stability of the Khedive's authority' and encourage 'judicious development of self-government'. Add in the fulfilment of 'obligations to Foreign Powers', and it was clear that this catch-all of an agenda was designed primarily for public opinion. To be all things to all men – or at least appear to be – now fell to Dufferin in his capacity as 'primo tenore assoluto upon the charm of whose voice we could depend to command the applause of the stalls, boxes and amphitheatre'.[5]

In the royal 'boxes' keeping a keen eye was the Queen, who for all her intimacy in urging him to write 'as an old friend', set the bar of friendship quite high: Egypt must 'remain, short of annexation, *under our control*. As for 'Urabi's trial, 'Lord Dufferin must be very firm'.[6] And there lay his first problem. For to him, there was 'not a tittle of evidence' implicating 'Urabi in the Alexandria massacres. Soon Gladstone was pointing out to the Queen 'a rather strange reflux of sympathy in this country for 'Urabi'. After fifty-two days and with the prosecution floundering, Granville was urging 'to get a solution' (and one with 'as little reference home as possible').[7]

Within ten days of his arrival Dufferin had struck a deal. Sensing that the defence team were running out of funds and exploiting 'the weak point' in 'Urabi's case – that while he had not instigated the riots, he had done nothing to stop them (something for which in 1861 Dufferin had executed a Syrian governor) – he won agreement for 'Urabi to plead guilty and his death sentence to be commuted to exile in Ceylon. And as 'Urabi set sail on Boxing Day 1882, Dufferin seized the opportunity to declare an amnesty; and so 'the debris of rebellion [would be] cleared away'.[8] The Khedive had been powerless to resist. On hearing the deal 'Urabi's lawyer wired Blunt: 'Urabi delighted at result . . . Dufferin brick . . . Anglo-Egyptian colony furious'. So too were the Turkish and Circassian elites. And even more so the Queen. Tearing into Granville, she demanded: 'Is innocent Christianity to remain unavenged?' But with *The Times* through Mackenzie Wallace approving (and most Egyptians too), the issue died, much to the relief of the government.[9]

From his arrival in Cairo, Dufferin hit the ground running.[10] Within a month he had appointed Sir Evelyn Wood to re-establish an Egyptian army, supplemented by a new police force organised by Colonel Valentine Baker[11] (who had come with Dufferin from Constantinople). Perhaps the most important appointment was that of Sir Colin Scott Moncrieff, a distinguished Anglo-Indian irrigation engineer, whom Dufferin persuaded, when his ship docked at Port Said, to become Director General of Irrigation. Another key appointment was that of Dr Fleming Sandwith who established a sanitation department. The need for both of them was demonstrated by a serious outbreak of cholera where a major catastrophe was averted by emergency measures taken by British troops. On the legal side Dufferin, finding the courts 'so bad, so imbecile, so corrupt' set in train reform of the codes for civil and criminal proceedings and issued a decree banning the use of the kurbash (which Cromer called a 'staggering blow' against its use but, given its cultural hold, an initiative that proved largely symbolic). More significant was his drive to increase the number of native judges. Other proposals included schemes for the abolition of the slave trade (in Egyptian Sudan) and a reform of the tax system. Auckland Colvin remained in place as financial adviser but significantly Dufferin, to the fury of the French, abolished the system of Dual Control. It was one of the ironies of victory that, for all the talk of a 'European duty', Britain was quick to dispense with European involvement – not least with any consideration of neutralisation of the Suez Canal. 'Our permanent ascendancy in Egypt will be as solidly established as if we had annexed the country immediately after Tel-el Kebir,' Dufferin comforted the Queen.[12]

That was precisely what Gladstone had assured Parliament on 10 August would never happen.[13] And yet to most onlookers, 'Le Veritable Khédive d'Egypte, c'est Lord Dufferin'. Curzon, visiting in February 1883, found Dufferin 'the temporary King of Cairo, residing in a palace and surrounded by a court . . . As evidently a first rate diplomatist as he is an attractive man.'[14] Nevertheless Dufferin did not lose sight of his brief. His difficulty was that a war designed to secure political liberty in Egypt, destroyed not only the constitutional movement and its institutions in their infancy but also the authority of the Khedive. In the vacuum Britain had to accept immediate responsibility, an outcome that looked more permanent with each passing month. All this ran utterly counter to Liberal opinion in Britain. 'Pray make Chamberlain understand', Dufferin pleaded with Sir Charles Dilke, that he was as keen as anyone to 'emancipate the fellaheen, i.e. the real people of Egypt', but for the present, it would be a 'mistake' to 'force prematurely arrangements which we dare not apply to India'. Seeking to protect what little room for manoeuvre he had, Dufferin came right to the point: 'I quite understand the necessity of satisfying liberal opinion in England by the institution of something that will ensure the development of popular government in this country . . . but do not let them press me into recommending the appearance of the thing without the reality, merely because it will sound well in the constituencies.' By now Gladstone too had joined in ('the phrase "reasonable suffrage" is one which I read with a desire for more information').[15]

As it was, Dufferin had a clear sense of where he wanted to go. It is striking how far his 'tentative opinions' suggested within two weeks of arrival were reflected in his final report. And also how similar in approach they were to his proposals in Syria twenty years earlier. In both cases he was trying to restore law and order after a massacre of Christians. Both required a constitutional settlement as a prerequisite to the evacuation of a foreign army. And in both that settlement would be built on existing cultural traditions and structures to ensure greater popular participation and security against tyranny. Hence the confidence with which he attacked the practical task at hand. The main difference was the perception of the task at home: what Gladstone would later call the need to resolve 'how to plant solidly western and beneficent institutions in the soil of a Mohammedan community'.[16]

> It is true that from the commencement of the historical era the Valley of the Nile has been ruled by foreigners . . . its administration oppressive and the indigenous population emotional, obsequious and submissive. But there is no need to imagine that what has been must always continue even in the unchanging East, [or that its people should remain] eternally impervious to the teachings of civic morality, the instincts of patriotism or . . . the common axioms of government [held by] civilised mankind.[17]

An opening of such grandeur (as would have graced few state papers) not only asserted the presence of its author but also established from the beginning the central tenet that liberty was a universal, realisable for all through the instruments of progress, be they the rule of law, education, the dynamic of individual opportunity and responsibility, and especially time. As instructed, Dufferin ruled out annexation: 'The Valley of the Nile could not be administered from London.' Rather Britain sought to 'enable them to govern themselves, under the uncompromising aegis of our friendship'. As a statement of Liberal intent Gladstone could not have wanted for more.

And yet Dufferin was convinced that representative government in Egypt had to be founded on traditional local structures. Thus he proposed an elaborate interlocking set of provincial and legislative councils drawn from the leaders of village communities. These would review all legislation and budgets but only in an advisory capacity, save for a veto on all new taxes and loans. Otherwise the Khedive and his ministers retained full powers. To Dufferin, given the stage of development of society in Egypt ('a long enslaved nation instinctively craves for the strong hand of the master rather than for a lax constitutional regime [which] is more likely to provoke contempt'), it would have been impractical to do anything else. What he was seeking to achieve, he later told Baring, was 'to erect some sort of barrier, however feeble, against the intolerable tyranny of the Turks'.[18] For all his powers the Khedive would find it hard to ignore the institutions of public opinion. At the same time the hope was that a system of regular elections and public meetings would act as 'a course of constitutional training'.[19] However, this could not be relied on to fend for itself but required 'our sustaining hand'. At one level, that meant retaining the full complement of government 'advisers . . . to keep them in the paths of rectitude'. On another, it meant ensuring 'that no subversive [i.e. foreign] influence will intervene between England and the Egypt she has recreated'. With the government committed internationally to military withdrawal, Gladstone would baulk at this.[20] Nevertheless the inference, however implicit, was that Britain was in for the long haul.

Appreciating that such a verdict was unpalatable, Dufferin tried to get around this by turning his report into a literary event, immersing it in a tidal wave of liberal sentiment. In so doing he set out the characteristics that would, in his eyes, define British imperialism as a liberal force and reaffirm its civilising mission. For him it was about stripping away centuries of misrule and ignorance through administrative reform, the rule of law, and application of modern technology; educating and improving societies until they ultimately evolved into independent, self-reliant states. Thus imperialism in liberal hands was not about conquest and acquisition; nor was it exploitive, autocratic, egotistical or racist. Rather it was moral, liberal, respectful, responsible and uplifting. Or in other words it was not Beaconsfieldism. This was romantic tosh of a high order but it went down a storm, even when Dufferin's exuberant imagination took him almost beyond parody as in an eye-catching passage purporting to describe progress already active in Egypt:

The metamorphic spirit of the age, as evoked by the inventions of science, intercourse with European countries and other invigorating influences, has already done something to inspire the fellah with the rudiment of self-respect, and a dim conception of hitherto unimagined possibilities. Nor like his own Memnon, has he remained irresponsive to the beams of the new dawn. His lips have trembled, if they have not yet articulated, and in many indirect and half-unconscious ways he has shown himself . . . unexpectedly appreciative of his legitimate political interests and moral rights.

Such flamboyance reflects something of the late nights ('I am nearly dead') that drove Dufferin to produce his report within two months, while largely running the country by day.[21] But in the adrenaline rush, he was determined that this would be the best of him, producing a report that was not simply 'extraordinary'[22] in its mastery of the subject and dextrous in the subtle gestures to conflicting audiences, but, more impressively, one that (despite a brief that was fundamentally flawed) succeeded in promoting a strategy that was visionary, constructive and inspirational. For all the literary splash, this was, at least in spirit, a work of genuine statecraft.[23]

It was also a work of self-preservation. Aware of the reception that awaited his despatch,[24] Dufferin was determined not to be the fall guy for a government reluctant to take difficult decisions. Right from his arrival in Cairo he actively sought to steer public opinion. Central to this was Mackenzie Wallace, the leading foreign correspondent of *The Times* who had become a firm friend in Constantinople after Dufferin prevented his expulsion following some articles critical of the Porte. This was to prove the most important friendship of Dufferin's career. Once established in Cairo, Wallace effectively operated as Dufferin's press officer.

Also there was Moberley Bell, then resident correspondent for *The Times* in Cairo who, in the first two months of 1883, as Dufferin was writing his despatch, became a regular visitor. Granville must have been the only one who was 'surprised' when on 8 February *The Times* effectively published Dufferin's draft report 'before it arrived in England'.[25] Indeed it would be another six days before the

Foreign Secretary received the official version – too late to effect any changes without highlighting that they were his. Likewise Dufferin's efforts in January to reduce British army presence by 2,000 (from 9,000) in advance of his implicit argument in favour of continued military occupation, reflected the need to stage-manage the reception of an undesirable outcome in Liberal circles. At the same time, by frequent reference in the report to the constraints placed on him by the government, he was in effect protecting himself from some of the more unpopular suggestions. Lyall, his biographer, claims that Dufferin's remit denied him an opportunity to engage with the debate on government policy, restricting him to how best to implement it. No doubt, this was the impression that Dufferin wanted to give. But actually he involved himself quite actively in the debate, developing a number of implicit positions and detaching himself from the official line.

This was most blatant – the 'forced condemnation' in Baring's phrase – in his discussion on why, when looking at Egyptian administration, he rejected the arguments for replicating the Indian model. Not only did he concede that 'the masterful hand of the Resident would have quickly bent everything to his will'. But such was his enthusiasm for the Indian approach that the advantages appeared to far outweigh the flaws. Thus the official line was maintained but at the cost of opening (beneficial) speculation on Dufferin's preference. On the issue of withdrawal, the arguments were similarly loaded. And with the bulk of the report given over to the chronic state of Egyptian society and advocating a major programme of reforms, the case for a protectorate was clear, if necessarily implicit.[26]

On the publication of the report in March 1883 *The Times* was not alone in picking up 'a double current of thought running through the document'. The *Saturday Review* went further, claiming that Dufferin had 'recourse to the ornaments of style for a purpose' and highlighted a 'duet' between 'the astute man of the world . . . and the devotee of Radical commonplaces'.[27] Still most Liberals agreed with the *Spectator's* verdict that 'there is the beginning of a fine policy of reform' and the *Pall Mall Gazette* went as far as to see in Dufferin's attempt 'to regenerate a nationality' an aspiration to 'Home Rule for Egypt'.[28] Nevertheless for most commentators the constitutional scheme was at best 'impractical'. To the largely imperialist press, however, this was seen as being wholly intended: 'it was part of Lord Dufferin's task to construct a sham', insisted the *Globe*, and reflected the fact that 'he went to Egypt bound and fettered' by governmental instructions designed to appease radical opinion. His brief was in *The Times*'s verdict, 'to make ropes of sand'.[29] As a result, many questioned whether Dufferin actually believed what he had written, and that one needed 'to read between the lines' to appreciate his 'real convictions'. This was most obvious in his comments on the 'Resident's magisterial hand', which the *St James Gazette* recognised as 'a singularly impressive passage, meant to be remembered'. The *Daily News* went further: 'It is a most able and brilliant piece of writing; but the last thing which any paragraph of it suggests is an early retirement from Egypt.'[30] Indeed.

A decade later Alfred Milner was to give the final judgement: having praised Dufferin's 'extraordinary' mastery of the subject, he went on to elaborate that 'behind . . . the misleading catchwords, the impractical ideals, which he [Dufferin] felt bound to treat with respect, there is a manly grasp of the facts . . . To anyone who looks closely and critically at his words the whole truth is there.' As Dufferin affected surprise, even hurt, at being so misunderstood, his own actions during his short time in Egypt had all the hallmarks of a Resident. And with the ink barely dry on his report, he was soon advocating the continuation of his role in the form of a colonial governor, for 'The Khedive makes no way with the people'; a campaign that soon was echoed by *The Times* and the *Observer* and would eventually culminate in the appointment of Sir Evelyn Baring. Dufferin's Egypt, predicted *The Economist*, 'will be an Oriental despotism with a thin constitutional varnish' and so it proved.[31]

Yet, however thin, Dufferin's constitutional creation was not a pretence. Writing a year later to his former legal adviser in Cairo, Sheldon Amos (who had lost his library in the bombardment of Alexandria), Dufferin reiterated that his intention was never to introduce a liberal constitutional state. Given the 'characteristics' of Egyptian society, 'I reduced the dose to homeopathic proportions' and left the Khedive's government 'as untrammelled and as absolute as I found it'. But amidst the preponderance of practicality, he wished to plant 'the frail germ of liberty'. And so establish what for him was a fundamental principle:

> Though the East differs from the West in many respects, the great characteristics of human nature are the same all the world over, and it is folly to pretend that those circumstances which are recognised as necessary to the human happiness in one part of the world can be dispensed with in the other. I believe the right of nations to be consulted in reference to their own affairs to be as indefeasible in the East as in the West . . . Nor is it true that Eastern people are so absolutely incapable of conducting business through . . . elected assemblies.[32]

As the plaintive tone suggests, this was a vision that was fast being overwhelmed by events. Soon after Dufferin left in May 1883 the Egyptian government was struggling to control a major epidemic of cholera.[33] Worse was to follow in November when the Egyptian army under a British officer, Major Hicks, was wiped out when it marched into the Sudan to meet the threat of the Mahdi – an Islamic prophet who had mobilised a great following to eradicate the infidel in Egypt.[34] For now, British troops would be staying.[35]

Thereafter the logic of the situation asserted itself. Baring, the new Consul General,[36] adopted most of Dufferin's improvement schemes and with British civil servants running the administration of finance, public works, customs, posts, irrigation, police and army, he saw no need to alter Dufferin's constitutional regime and his all-powerful, ostensibly 'advisory' role. However, he never saw beyond the natives being 'a subject race' and by 1895 all pretence of 'Egypt for the Egyptians', of nurturing a nascent governing class, had been quietly dropped. Thus Dufferin's 'fragile germ of liberty' had been 'plucked up'. It had always been a long shot. Yet one that, as 'a declaration of a revolutionary principle', would in time prove significant.[37] Instead, in the short term, he found himself the architect of a 'veiled protectorate', and, moreover, 'a protectorate' that would remain out of French hands. All things considered, Dufferin had every reason to be pleased with this outcome. Asked to square circles, he had done so, and largely on his own terms.[38]

Certainly it appeared so back in Britain; and not entirely because his acolytes, Amos and Wallace, published detailed works on the Egyptian crisis.[39] Caricatured in *Vanity Fair* in 1883 as 'one of those extremely rare men who seem to escape detraction', for all his glittering career 'Lord Dufferin is in reality what he appears – not merely brilliant and kind hearted but is also simple, conscientious and true'.[40] Two years later the *World* was devoting three pages to Dufferin who has gained the name of 'our only diplomatist'. In a new age of celebrity, he continued to catch the eye. 'As a man he is eclectic, original, eccentric; very English in appearance, with a deceptive, Mephistophiles air.'[41] Popularity was one thing. But for those in power it was the unexpected evidence of the 'manly' virtues of spine, grip, relentless vigilance and resolve together with his ingenuity that made Dufferin the troubleshooter of choice. Displaying the courage to hold firm in negotiation, he had emerged from the Egyptian crisis as a major international figure. Luck of course had played its part and the strength of his hand too. Nonetheless for *The Times* what made him distinctive was more intuitive:

> Lord Dufferin possesses the imagination which distinguishes the statesman from the official . . . He has the invaluable power of placing himself at the centre of a novel set of facts and [then] following their natural causation and seeing them in their natural connexion. He has the sympathy which is the moral correlative of insight and looks upon the down-trodden fellaheen and the congenitally corrupt officials with the eye of a fellow man.[42]

It was a theme Dufferin took up in a speech to the Empire Club in London in July 1883. After a brief genuflection to 'this sceptred isle', whose manifest destiny was 'to possess and fructify the waste places on the earth's surfaces', he directed his audience's attention to 'the yearning' – 'scarcely realised' in Britain – among the colonies 'for due recognition of their kinship' . . . 'Only [if] they are properly dealt with [will they wish] to continue [as] co-heirs of England's illustrious past, associates in her empire, and sharers in her future fortunes.'[43] For all the rapturous reception Dufferin's remarks received, there was evidence that Englishmen were becoming impervious to such liberal sentiments.[44] The recent Egyptian crisis had reflected uglier realities that would reverberate long into the future. Intervening in the affairs of a small Arab state and in defence of major economic interests, a global superpower drew on the assumed moral superiority of the West – safeguarding human rights and promoting 'democracy' – to justify retrospectively a quick corrective war. In the event the justification proved imaginary. And without any clear plan for the aftermath, the consequences were the mobilisation of Islam and a series of strategic and military commitments in the surrounding regions, which would drain British resources and corrupt the politics of a continent for more than a century. Plus ça change.

As for Dufferin, happy now to accept the GCB bestowed on him, he returned to Constantinople to await the next call. Embassy life returned to idle pursuits, entertaining visitors[45] and the occasional interesting invitation from a Dr Heinrich Schliemann writing from 'Troy near the Dardenelles'. He was blessed with an escape of a different sort when his horses bolted down a steep street. Luckily for him the carriage collided with the open door of a mosque, thus enabling Dufferin to jump out before the carriage speeded up again, careering down the hill and ploughing into the bazaar causing many injuries. Saved by Allah, he was later rescued on 18 August 1884 by Gladstone who wrote to offer Dufferin the prize that he had sought for so long, the viceroyalty of India.

PART III

Kipling's Viceroy: Dufferin in India, 1884–8

The significance of the office was almost beyond ambition. The Viceroy of India had few peers in Asia. The Tsar of Russia, the Emperor of China were scarcely his superiors, the Shah of Persia and the King of Siam trod carefully in his presence, the Amir of Afghanistan and the King of Nepal were frankly at his mercy, the Dalai Lama would be well advised to respect his wishes and the King of Burma was actually his prisoner. He occupied the throne of Akhbar and Aurangzebe, he stood in the conquering line of Alexander and he was officially said to reign like a king in his own right. Yet it was a kind of exile for an Englishman . . . For all the pomp . . . it was all a kind of charade. The Viceroy was only a temporary Civil Servant on a five year term.

Jan Morris, Pax Britannica, pp. 279–80

22

An Indian Inheritance

You saw – what did you see from Bombay east?
Enough to frighten any one but me?
Neat that! It frightened Me in Eighty-Four!
You shouldn't take a man from Canada
And bid him smoke in powder-magazines;
Nor with a Reputation such as – Bah!
That ghost has haunted me for twenty years,
My Reputation now full-blown.

> Rudyard Kipling, 'One Viceroy Resigns'

INDIA HAD BEEN an appointment long in the coming.[1] Yet even now the cabinet considered others before 'finally our choice fell on Dufferin'. For as Kimberley would later reminisce, 'Granville was reluctant and Gladstone very reluctant' – only finally giving way when Kimberley raised the prospect of an imminent election resulting in a Tory viceroy.[2] By then Gladstone could have been forgiven, after Egypt, for thinking that that was exactly what he was being asked to appoint. In contrast to the cabinet, Dufferin's appointment was greeted, 'as was to be expected, with a chorus of approval by the Press' of 'England's one diplomatist'.[3] 'When unlucky shuffle the pack', was the advice of the *Evening News*, 'and when in doubt, play Lord Dufferin.'[4]

A celebrity appointed to the most glamorous of posts was always going to excite the pulses. 'Charming in manner, no shyness or awkwardness, a touch of blarney, a quick temper, a slight or more than slight lisp, and a very decided will', recalled Sir Mortimer Durand, head of the Foreign and Political Department in Calcutta.[5] Quick thinking and versatile, able to grasp the key point and act on it, these were skills that Dufferin shared with the best of diplomats. Unlike his two predecessors, he had held viceregal responsibility before – ostensibly in Canada and de facto in Egypt. So he knew the processes of imperial policymaking and was not naive in acting as if colonial policy had no impact on metropolitan politics, appreciating the need to manage public opinion both in London and in India. From his earliest days in Syria he had always insisted on direct access to the prime minister, and yet took time to nurture relationships with the foreign secretaries and influential advisers such as Sir Edward Hamilton. Above all, he never fell out, not even with Gladstone. Being accepted as above party did not make him apolitical. However impromptu the manner, every word he uttered was considered for its resonance; however obsessive he was over secrecy, every indiscretion or outright leak was carefully weighed.[6] And all this was carried out behind a facade of irrepressible geniality.[7] One Indian official (Lyall) would later recall: 'what struck him most was that Lord Dufferin seemed always to carry his point, yet he never seemed in antagonism with anyone'. Or as Lord Frederick Hamilton noted: for all the air of a dilettante, 'no man understood better the use of the iron hand under the velvet glove'.[8]

Setting sail on 12–13 November from London on a troopship, the SS *Clive*, the Dufferins accompanied by their eldest daughter, Nelly, and her cousin Rachel Thynne, arrived in Bombay on 8 December 1884. After disembarking at 4.30 p.m. onto a quay, 'bright with guards of honour, cavalry escorts, and . . . dignitaries in uniform'[9], the processional drive to Government House shaded by a golden umbrella – the ancient symbol of the Mughal rulers – provided their first thrilling glimpse of the subcontinent:

> Fancy a drive of five miles through a town . . . Fill the whole – the streets, the windows, the rows and rows of balconies, the trees, the tops of carriages – with a teeming crowd, natives of every shape and colour, dresses of the most brilliant hues, little children clothed in the whole rainbow; children clothed in nothing at all and parents with the nearest approach to nothing at all that I ever saw before . . . And when you can't imagine any more add the five miles of cheering and the ever-recurring

bands sending forth 'God save the Queen', the handkerchiefs waving, and say if it was not an exciting scene.[10]

Their entrance concluded in 'a curious Brahmin ceremonial' (Dufferin described it as 'like seeing a chapter of Leviticus in action'), which saw them being garlanded with wreaths of jasmine and roses and sprinkled with rosewater; including Nelly 'who wished to sink into the ground on the spot'.[11]

Then followed a two and a half day train journey, during which Dufferin caught a chill and, with a temperature of 102 degrees and seemingly 'very unfit', they arrived in Calcutta on 13 December. A guard of honour resplendent in their uniforms and a drive through cheering crowds did much to revive his spirits. After which Hariot expected something more from the swearing in: 'it is not an imposing ceremony. Several gentlemen stood round a table while the Warrant was read, and then they sat down while Dufferin signed it, et voilà tout.' That night, isolated within by the empty halls of Government House and without by the vastness of their new responsibilities, 'we feel rather lonely now'.[12]

In this they were not alone. One of the striking features of British India is how few Britons were to be found there. As late as 1901, the British in India numbered only 154,691; or barely a fifth of the population of Glasgow. Over half were made up of the Army and their dependants. Of the rest, many were concentrated around the major cities of Bombay and Calcutta and to a much lesser extent Madras, with the remaining 40,000 scattered over an area the size of Europe. In a sea of people, the British in India would feel distinctly isolated; an isolation given edge by memories of the Mutiny of 1857.

In the wake of the Mutiny, the utilitarian mission to anglicise India was abandoned for a policy of 'religious indifferentism'. But cultural toleration was essentially a tactical retreat rather than a reflection of new understanding. Anglo-India withdrew into itself – a hermetically sealed moral and social order, reinforced by a strict belief in racial hierarchy. The most racially vociferous may have been those of least standing in the British community: the tea planters, railway employees, journalists, businessmen, lawyers and professionals. Sensitive to snobbery from official Britain, they were only too keen to enforce their superiority over Indians. But even the senior members of the Indian Civil Service (ICS), 'with all their magnificent qualities', Northbrook warned Dufferin, 'have strongly ingrained in their minds . . . that no one but an Englishman can do anything [in India]'. By the 1880s, it was generally recognised that relations between the British and Indians were deteriorating into separate spheres, symbolised by the club. Hindu society was becoming just as exclusive, reinforced by a value system at points quite alien to British culture. This was most stark in the treatment of women but also in the religious constraints on certain foods and alcohol and symbolised by the washing of hands after a handshake as if the British were untouchables. Only at the very highest social levels was there much engagement.[13]

In fact most Indians never saw a Briton – except perhaps an assistant magistrate.[14] In addition large parts of the country were not directly governed by the British. These were some 680 princely states, some such as Hyderabad and Kashmir larger than England and Scotland combined, others no bigger than Hyde Park. Loyal in the Mutiny, the British chose to leave these 'natural' rulers alone under the guidance of a Resident. But, having been allowed to retain a semblance of their former independence, they required sensitive handling. Phenomenally wealthy (largely through exploitation of their own people) but stripped of their traditional martial role and resentful of the constraints on their independence, many princes led lavish and dissolute lives.[15]

If both princes and peasants were seen as reassuring forces of conservative tradition, the same could not be said for the educated elites, emerging ironically from the British strategy after 1858 of modernisation, especially in the expansion of educational opportunities.[16] In 1857 three universities were established (in Calcutta, Bombay and Madras) and by 1887 India had 60,000 graduates, with Calcutta soon to be the largest university in world. Inevitably this initiative fostered native elites (especially from Bengal and Bombay) well versed in Western thought and national identity. Realistically the separatist threat was non-existent; with only 0.5 per cent in national education and barely 2 per cent literate (hence a total newspaper circulation of only 150,000), and concentrated in just three or four main cities.

Most ambitious Indians saw British rule as an opportunity – a system to be part of rather than against. For the financially precarious middle class, government positions were crucial lifelines to advancing social status. However, by the 1880s there were too many graduates chasing too few jobs. Out of this would come a call for greater native entry into the higher ranks of the civil service who represented the officer class of the ICS.[17]

To English Tories, such as Salisbury, however, government by 'Competition Baboos' would be 'terrible'. 'Baboo' was a condescending term for all educated Bengalis – who were deemed presumptuous, pushy, ever-critical and provided, in Salisbury's phrase, 'the opposition in quiet times [and] rebels in times of trouble'. Such prejudices ran deep in the Anglo-Indian community. But in deciding to confront this challenge the Tories abandoned the strategy of quiescence that had stabilised the subcontinent in the two decades after the Mutiny. The architect of this was Lord Lytton, romantic poet and imperialist, who sought to re-establish the princes as a feudal bulwark to the meritocratic advance of the native elites; making his point most spectacularly at the Delhi Durbar, held in 1877 in celebration of the Queen's elevation to Empress of India. More prosaic was his attempt to make the ICS an exclusively British body and suppressing the native press. All of which, not surprisingly, only served to radicalise the elites he had been determined to sideline.

The Liberal counter-attack that followed the change of government would be every bit as aggressive. The new viceroy, Lord Ripon (1880–4), 'rejoiced to say that the effect of despotic power' made him 'more Radical every day', as he looked to advance the cause of the native elites. By 1883 Anglo-Indian discontent with Ripon was widespread: driven by class and racial snobbery, this descended into a turf war over the levers of power. Matters were brought to a head by the Ilbert proposal to allow Indian judges to preside over cases involving Europeans in rural areas. This should not have been controversial as it was already the practice in urban areas and would barely affect twenty magistrates. However, in the context of Ripon's rhetoric and all that had gone before, it became the trigger for a fundamental debate among the British on their role in India. In the uproar that followed, the viceroy was ostracised within the British community, now organised by the Anglo-Indian Defence Association in what was dubbed the 'White Mutiny'. No viceroy could rule without Anglo-India and ultimately Ripon was forced to back down, to the dismay of the native elites.[18]

Within seven years much that had been achieved in the previous twenty had been undone as political consensus gave way to 'two diametrically opposite views'.[19] Both positions were major divergences from the post-Mutiny consensus and both ended disastrously. The credibility of British rule now lay in jeopardy. It would be up to Dufferin to forge a new consensus. Moreover he would be attempting this as other Great Powers were beginning to challenge Britain's global supremacy and in so doing ensuring that India – economically, militarily, and strategically – would become increasingly important in the British World System.

23

Governing India

You've seen your Council? Yes, they'll try to rule,
And prize their Reputations . . .
They look for nothing from the West but Death
Or Bath or Bournemouth. Here's their ground. They fight
Until the Middle Classes take them back,
One of ten millions plus a C.S.I.,
Or drop in harness. Legion of the Lost?
Not altogether. Earnest, narrow men,
But chiefly earnest, and they'll do your work,
And end by writing letters to the *Times*.

Rudyard Kipling, 'One Viceroy Resigns'

IT WOULD BE hard to underestimate the grandeur attached to the viceroy. In Britain he cut a heroic, glamorous, all-powerful figure: being a romantic throwback to a pre-modern age and also the icon of Britain's global superiority – economically, militarily and culturally – in the late nineteenth century. It was an exotic mix. Appointed by the political elite and with the status of a senior cabinet minister, he was primarily 'a temporary autocrat of tsar-like magnificence, the liege-lord of 600 feudatory states and an Asian ruler with his own army and diplomatic service. [As such] he was hard to coerce and practically irremovable.'[1] But how far did reality match the image?

Firstly the viceroy was the representative of the Queen Empress and exercised monarchical authority in her name. But unlike the British Crown, the viceroy combined regal with governmental powers as head of state, assuming full responsibility for running the country. Indeed he exercised powers not held by the Crown in Britain since the seventeenth century. He governed through the Viceroy's Council, comprising mainly of the senior department heads in the ICS – all of whom depended on the viceroy for promotion and whose compliance earned Kipling's derision. But men of the calibre of Sir Mortimer Durand, Sir Charles Aitchison and Sir Auckland Colvin, were more substantial than Kipling would allow.[2] To administrative power the viceroy could add legislative authority through his chairing of 'my Legislative Council'.[3]

Yet for all this, the viceroy's authority was not without considerable constraints, not least his responsibility to Parliament through the Secretary of State for India. Who dominated that relationship depended on personality.[4] But it was also affected by exposure to public opinion in England. With the improvement in communications – Suez Canal (1869), electric telegraph (1870s) – and the growing public interest in empire and especially India, the government of India could no longer hope to operate in splendid isolation. From 1882–3 Irish Nationalists and English radicals, often in communication with Indian politicians, began asking more frequent questions in the House of Commons on imperial 'injustices'. Conversely in the Ilbert case *The Times* and the *Daily Telegraph* stirred up support for Anglo-India in London. 'Civilians' frequently complained of MPs and other grandees who came on fact-finding tours, drank them out of house and home and then denounced them when back in the comfort of London.[5] Also in London, and potentially more troublesome, was the India Council made up of retired old ICS hands who acted in the Indian administration like a board of trustees. In practice they could be overruled by prime minister and cabinet. But short of that, they could prove to be highly conservative and obstructive and it was they who largely did for Ripon. So with Indian affairs no longer, in Salisbury's phrase, 'a bagged fox' – only brought out when there was no better business in Parliament – inexorably the secretary of state became more assertive. Dufferin's predecessors may all have acted independently of the imperial government and British political opinion, but none survived for long once they had lost favour in London.

Even within India a Viceroy's authority was not all that it seemed.

Most viceroys, at some time or other, found managing the provincial governors difficult and Dufferin fell out spectacularly with Sir Lepel Griffin, the Agent to the Governor General in Central India. Unquestionably bright, particularly knowledgeable on foreign affairs and even quite witty (the government of India was 'a despotism of office boxes, tempered by the occasional loss of a key'), Griffin was 'an ass in externals' (Lyall). Having made an unseemly fuss over his knighthood,[6] his arrogance towards his princely charges only helped to generate frequent crises. Dufferin railed too at his 'pleasure in passing himself off as a destroyer of female virtue' and his 'habit of ostentatiously maintaining intimate relations with some vulgar second rate woman'. Lyall found him in Simla as 'an unblushing rake' courting the married Isabella Burton (the model for 'honestly mischievous' Mrs Hauksbee in *Plain Tales from the Hills*). Griffin, he judged, was 'a fine neighing stallion that wants castrating'. Since castration was not an option, Dufferin resorted to refusing him promotion and sabotaging his reputation in London. By 1889 Griffin had left India and was to spend the next ten years failing to get into Parliament.[7]

A more traditional form of obstruction could be provided by the central bureaucracy. Remarkably there were only ninety members of the Indian Civil Service operating in the main centres of power – Calcutta, Simla and the provincial capitals – illustrating the administrative capacity of the ICS. Less welcome was its resistance to viceregal initiative or even the acceleration of business: what Curzon dubbed the culture of 'tranquil procrastination'. The conservatism in the system contrasted with the increasing demands made on the administration since the 1870s. Like his predecessors, Dufferin struggled to avoid being overrun by the onslaught of reports, memoranda, telegrams, minutes, and statistics which contributed to 100,000 documents pouring out of the Indian secretariat every year – each providing opportunities for obstruction or 'paper-logging' the viceroy. And all this was in addition to his official correspondence with the Queen (who had strong views on Indian defence and the treatment of the princes and from 1887 was much advised by the Muslim Abdul Karim, the Munshi),[8] the Secretary of State, and councillors in London, and the provincial governors and residents in India. Any emergency and there simply wasn't time to keep up with day-to-day business. 'It seems to me that India is a kettle out of which the bottom is perpetually tumbling', confided Dufferin a little desperately to Sir William Gregory. Consequently, it was a rare viceroy who could escape dependency on the ICS.[9]

To this can be added the resentment most viceroys felt at the daily ceremonial tasks; or the five to seven months a year away from Calcutta on progress or at Simla. Behind the glamour lay many tedious acts of duty and courtly rituals – each seemingly more preposterous than the next. Whatever one's status, all were bound by the Warrant of Precedence, which firmly insisted on a bewildering seventy-seven separate ranks. However, for Dufferin, the ceremonial role not only stirred the imagination, but offered a symbolic focus of authority in a diverse continent of 2,000 castes and 200 languages and, in emphasising the monarchical nature of British India, reaffirmed the prevailing hierarchies on which British rule depended. While much has been made of the great Durbars of 1877, 1903, and 1911 as spectacular demonstrations of British imperial might, it was the daily exercise of courtly rituals, receptions and openings together with the annual progresses of the princely states that sustained the image and gave an imaginative presence to British rule. It was a routine that required great stamina for a punishing schedule made all the more draining by a climate that seemed to affect the vicereines especially. In the garden at Barrackpore, the viceregal retreat outside Calcutta, lay the tomb of Lady Canning; and the wives of three of Dufferin's immediate successors (Elgin, Curzon, and Hardinge) either died in India or prematurely afterwards.

It is in this light that Dufferin's style of government has to be judged, for historians have largely followed the verdict of one of his own council who declared the viceroy 'a dead lazy fellow'. Certainly he was overwhelmed, as most viceroys were on arrival, by the amount of work. Much to Hariot's disapproval, Dufferin frequently had to mix business with pleasure: 'He only comes in at the end of our dinner, has his breakfasts and luncheons cut short and is altogether busy.' Often Hariot would complain that 'it is quite impossible to get speech of him' or bemoan that 'Dufferin did not come with us, as he always rather dreads a holiday on account of the accumulation of papers that follows upon it.'[10] None of this suggests that

Dufferin was particularly idle. Yet while he could work very hard on a project or in the midst of a crisis, it is clear that he had little appetite for the 'grind' of day-to-day administration. For all his insight into the workings of government, his experience was not really in running governmental departments. It was as a diplomat that he had made his reputation and instinctively he looked to manage people rather than the paperwork.[11]

Nevertheless, even before he left for India, Dufferin was quick to spot the contradictions in the position, whoever was viceroy. 'Cast in the heroic mould of imperialism', the role required 'a man of unique versatility, who possessed, among other qualifications, an aristocratic background, a thorough understanding of English politics and the intricacies of Western as well as Eastern diplomacy, executive ability and the dedication of a loyal public servant. By the 1880s, the ideal of the Viceroy far transcended the capabilities of the Viceroy.'[12] So Dufferin made two decisions that would redesign the role in a way that would have shocked Ripon and later Curzon.

To deal with the tide of administration, he went with his instincts and chose to delegate systematically. All matters concerning social arrangements, progresses and protocol were left to Lord William Beresford. Despite holding the rank of military secretary, Beresford made himself indispensable to the Dufferins: 'From the highest military affairs in the land to a mosquito in my Excellency's curtain or a bolt on my door, all is the business of this invaluable person and he does all equally well.'[13] All government matters went through Dufferin's private secretary, Donald Mackenzie Wallace, whose duties included providing summary briefs of governmental papers, seeing many of the delegations and other visitors, and writing much of Dufferin's semi-official correspondence. He was even authorised to forge Dufferin's signature, which he did 'with lifelike fidelity'.[14] 'A good watch dog is the faithful Donald,' grumbled Kipling, but as the prime conduit to the viceroy Wallace was able to stamp a degree of coherence on policy.[15] For Dufferin, Wallace was 'the key to the whole business' and his success in running Dufferin's office earned him a knighthood in 1887. This approach left the viceroy free to coordinate policy and develop strategy; and to focus on the next crisis. It also allowed him to establish a daily routine, so enabling him (as the oldest viceroy ever) to retain his stamina. Nine hours at his desk every day, an hour to shoot clays or play tennis, dinner in the evening before retiring at 10 p.m. – this regularity was only disturbed by major celebrations or durbars and the autumnal progress. To Ripon and Curzon such a routine amounted to a dereliction of duty. Nor could they have tolerated letting private secretaries acquire positions of such influence.

Much more shocking, however, was his abandonment of the presumption of viceregal independence from London. This had always been de facto rather than *de jure* as distance had left the initiative with the proconsul in the field, in India and elsewhere. With the revolution in communications from the 1870s, Dufferin was quick to appreciate that the role now required managing English perceptions as much as Indian realities, and that vital to the viceroy was a good relationship with the Secretary of State in London. Hence his assertion that it was 'no longer within the province of a Viceroy even to suggest important fundamental changes in the system he has been appointed to administer, for matters of such gravity naturally fall within the competence of the government at home'. Hence too his assurance to Kimberley, his Eton contemporary and now his Secretary of State, that he was 'an excellent master to serve under'. Such flattery came easily enough; and of course there was an element of self-preservation in insisting that London accept responsibility as well as power. In accepting the reduction of the viceroy's role to that of a super-diplomat, his regime would be intentionally different from that of his predecessors.[16]

Even before his departure he endeavoured to reduce public expectations. Viceroys, he insisted, were 'no longer required by their superiors or compelled by circumstances to startle their countrymen by the annexation of provinces and all those dramatic performances which invariably characterise the founding of new-born empires'.[17] By contrast, and partly to offset the diminution of his political independence, he would promote the social prestige of the role for Indian and British consumption.

First, however, Dufferin had to deal with the fallout from the Ilbert affair. Huge crowds had been mobilised to bid farewell to Lord Ripon in a triumphant progress from Simla to Calcutta, ending in a massive gathering in Bombay. In Calcutta there was no mistaking that Ripon's departure had 'completely overshadowed Dufferin's arrival'. 'No Viceroy has ever left India amidst such general and genuine expression of goodwill on the part of the Indian population', Dufferin reported a little anxiously to Kimberley.[18] With Ripon gone, Dufferin set about defusing the row over the Ilbert affair; in the first instance by finessing the exceptional aspect of Ripon's regime. Key to this was the concept of 'continuity'. So Dufferin reassured Anglo-India by affirming in a speech to the Calcutta Trades' Association in January, that 'my policy will be guided by those ancient principles upon which the British Empire in India was originally founded'. But continuity was also applied to Ripon: 'The Marquis of Ripon has prepared the soil, delved and planted. It will be my humble duty to watch, water, and train.' Lest this appeared lukewarm, Dufferin specifically mentioned the 'principle of local self-government'.[19]

But as he reclaimed Ripon's ideas, he distanced himself from the man. 'The only mistake he [Ripon] has made', he explained with specious generosity to the Queen, 'has been in treating India too much as if it had been a Parliamentary Borough and canvassing the Natives. But India is not Midlothian.' The result was a diminution of viceregal dignity, something both the Queen and Dufferin felt keenly, and the division of 'the country into two camps, with the Natives and the Anglo-Indians yelping at each other from either side of a ditch'.[20] It is hard not to feel that Dufferin's interpretation of the Indian 'problem' was fully formed before he had arrived and was directed towards British opinion – in the media and among the metropolitan elites. Eventually (despite even the Queen being asked to 'destroy this letter'), Ripon got to hear of Dufferin's condemnation of him for 'Midlothianising' India.[21] Dufferin's reply ('in rendering yourself so popular with the natives, you have made the position a little difficult for your successor') was a touch rich from one who had done just that in Canada! But his positioning did help to quell the Anglo-Indian campaign in the press and gave him the breathing space he needed.

Determined to 'Avoid speechifying', Dufferin got away without a speech of any political substance for almost two years. Instead he was more concerned with bringing onside Ripon's acolytes such as Ilbert. Their interview barely two days after the new viceroy had arrived saw him at his most seductive. Acknowledging that Ripon was 'on the side of the angels', he nevertheless laid bare the hostility he aroused in Britain, only then to 'surprise' Ilbert with a violent tirade against jingoism. Thus he set the ground for the key message: the need to conciliate Anglo-India – 'both because you have to exist with and among them . . . and because . . . of the great power which Anglo-Indians have of influencing English opinion both in and out of Parliament'. Already exhausted by the vilification, Ilbert offered little resistance. As with many people before him, it was the manner as much as the substance that won him over. In a public life dominated by protocol and reticence Dufferin's startling frankness reinforced by the impression of going too far and swearing to secrecy was an intoxicating mix when acted to perfection.[22]

In tandem with this, the Dufferins, playing to strength, launched a major social offensive. With a new viceroy, Anglo-India was only too keen to escape their self-denying ordinance and return to Government House; and not least because 'their wives and daughters will want to dance and show off their new frocks,' Dufferin assured the Queen. As ever he directed his ADCs towards the 'elderly ladies', reassuring them that they 'need not trouble about the young and pretty ones. I will look after them myself.' With 1,800 at their first levee, Hariot recorded that people had passed by at the rate of 25 a minute – the fastest she had endured for ten years – and still they overran by twenty minutes. Predictably Calcutta society succumbed to the Dufferins' winning combination of glamour and warmth. Yet their receptions were not just aimed at Anglo-India, recognising that 'many inconveniences must arise from the division of whites and blacks into two hostile and vociferating camps'. So at the first levee the best was left to last with Dufferin especially appreciating the Indian officers saluting and presenting the hilts of their swords to him in respect. 'If Lord Dufferin had not come,' confided Rudyard Kipling's father, Lockwood, to Edith Plowden, 'I think poor Anglo-India would have gone crazy with vexation and apprehension but we have no end of confidence in the new man.'[23]

Calming the political temper would take longer and so Dufferin made it clear there would be no political initiatives.[24] Instead, he would despatch outstanding commitments, especially the Bengal Tenancy Bill, which was intended to protect the peasant cultivators from oppressive landowners or zamindars. The similarities with Ireland were not surprising for the bill was 'virtually in the hands of a parcel of wild Irishmen'. Inevitably Dufferin interpreted it as an Irish conflict translated to a foreign shore and got stuck in, removing 'nine or ten of the most obnoxious regulations' in defence of landlord rights. For this he received no thanks from the zamindars who resented *any* encroachment on their property rights. Nor from the ryots (small farmers), although he did increase their protection and indulged in lines of arguments, such as a provision of 'fixity of tenure at judicial rents' that he had resisted strongly when applied to Irish landlords! However, getting the bill on the statute book and within three months did win widespread respect in the Indian press. It had been an impressive start and in London Kimberley 'greatly rejoiced' in Dufferin's 'firmness and decision'. With his strategy of restraining aspirations, little legislation and working through consensus, Dufferin hoped for an 'uneventful' time in office, seeing his role as maintaining 'a low and steady pressure' on government. Such hopes were to prove unfounded, for by 1884 British rule in India was facing three fundamental challenges to its survival.[25]

The most obvious was the future role of Indians in the government of their own country. To the native elites, most of whom were anglophile, the successful counter-attack of Anglo-India exposed the hollowness of official rhetoric, while the naked racist language of the 'White Mutiny' was profoundly shocking.[26] In dealing with the controversy so efficiently, Dufferin had bought time but not very much time.

The other challenges were of longer standing. By the 1880s it was getting harder to balance the books. Fundamental to this was the extent to which the Indian economy was managed to meet British imperial interests. India provided a vital market for British exports (especially textiles and iron and steel) at a time of growing protectionism in Europe. Much of this involved major infrastructure projects – particularly railways and irrigation programmes – requiring large loans from the City. In turn, India exported to Britain key domestic commodities (wheat, raw cotton, jute and tea), thus providing the foreign exchange to pay the interest on British loans, which in turn covered British trade deficits elsewhere. In addition, the Indian government had to pay for much of the British presence: from the salaries and pensions of British troops and the ICS to the cost of running the India Office in London! Making matters worse, the depreciation of silver (the base of the Indian currency) against gold left the rupee victim to violent inflation, losing over a third of its value to sterling from 1873 to 1892 and declining particularly in the 1880s. Such falls had a significant impact on government loans and the many goods imported from the UK, all of which were paid in sterling.

By contrast, sources of revenue were relatively inelastic. Any re-imposition of an import duty on British goods had been ruled out in the 1870s in the interest of Manchester and the cotton industry.[27] Increases in salt tax especially affected the ryots and the very poor and risked disorder. Dependence on landowner support made governments reluctant to increase taxes on land. In turn income taxes were unpopular with Indian officials and the educated elites. It was they who dominated the Indian press and the lower ranks of the British administration. Keen to cultivate them, Ripon had actually cut income taxes. Even so, the government of India would find itself with little option but to impose greater taxation.

The only alternative, and one always appealing to MPs at Westminster, was to cut expenditure, especially in public works programmes, the instruments of modernisation in India. Dufferin's reign would see in 1887 the opening of a railway bridge in his name that ran for half a mile across the Ganges at Benares. Not a thing of beauty, but it represented the remorselessness of iron and steel which were the real engines of Britain's imperialism. Railways and irrigation programmes were also seen as vital to the alleviation of famine. As recently as 1876–8 famine in India had left 58 million starving and in Madras alone 4 million died. Taking up an idea from the previous administration, Dufferin's government proposed a scheme of Famine Protection Railways, comprising of 4,580 miles of track of which all but 770 had been constructed by the time he left. Such schemes by their nature were uncommercial, and came under heavy parliamentary pressure to be paid for by increased loans.[28]

Sacrosanct and claiming a third of all Indian government expenditure was defence. In this context unexpected demands, such as the Afghan expedition in 1879–80, which added an unbudgeted £5.9 million, could have a devastating impact on Indian finances. Even more worrying was the increasing use of the Indian army for Imperial

No. XII.   CELEBRITIES OF THE DAY—THE EARL OF DUFFERIN, VICEROY OF INDIA, AND THE COUNTESS OF DUFFERIN
DRAWN FROM LIFE

Illustration from the *Graphic*, March 1885

campaigns outside India but at Indian expense. Wolseley had drawn on Indian troops for the Egyptian occupation and in 1885 Dufferin would have to send troops to Suakin to fight the Mahdi at a cost of £1.3 million; of which the Treasury in London only paid back £800,000. In fact, since 1860, the annual cost of 66 per cent of Britain's standing army was paid for by Indian taxpayers (without which Britain's Great Power status would have been domestically difficult to sustain). It was vital for the government of India to retain control of defence policy and convince London that it could achieve military effectiveness without wrecking the Indian budget and the spectre of taxing Indians for 'British' adventures.

In April 1885 with Dufferin congratulating his staff on the successful session, these three challenges would come to a head, for his administration was about to be blown off course by events.

24

Playing the Great Game

Your business! Twice a hundred million souls.
Your business! I could tell you what I did
Some nights of Eighty-Five, at Simla, worth
A Kingdom's ransom. When a big ship drives
God knows to what new reef, the man at the wheel
Prays with the passengers. They lose their lives,
Or rescued go their way; but he's no man
To take his trick at the wheel again. That's worse
Than drowning.

Rudyard Kipling, 'One Viceroy Resigns'

ONCE MORE THE Great Game was coming to a head. The 'rules' of this game were founded on certain assumptions. The first of these was that India was too important for Britain to lose: economically (by 1900 it absorbed 20 per cent of her exports); internationally her credibility as a Great Power would not have survived its loss; and domestically, because, ever since the Mutiny, popular and press opinion decreed that India be defended at all costs. The 'Jewel in the Crown', India had become by the 1880s part of the national identity. Perhaps most important of all was the geopolitical dimension. In an age fast becoming dominated by great empires, India acted as a crucial hub for all British possessions in the East and was the springboard for future expansion. The concern therefore was not simply the defence of India, it was also fear that a Russian push beyond the Caspian Sea would endanger other British interests in the Gulf, while her expansion in the East might affect developing markets in China.[1] At the same time it was believed that Britain's hold on India was actually very vulnerable: latent native hostility in combination with a Russian attack might see Britain's authority implode across the subcontinent.[2]

But just how realistic was the Russian threat? With Russian armies now in range of Afghanistan – which guarded the mountain passes into India – a confrontation seemed a matter of time. Yet the logistics of attacking India with supply lines over such a distant and hostile terrain – let alone the expense – appeared insurmountable. Given the difficulties Roberts had in Afghanistan in 1878–9 and Britain's subsequent evacuation, why suppose that the Russian army, which Dufferin had observed in St Petersburg, would do any better? Hence some argued for withdrawing British defences to the Indus. Ironically, Roberts, now C-in-C in Madras, drew an entirely opposite conclusion. Rather than wait until the Russians were at the frontier, the British should act with purpose – expanding troop numbers and building defences – to keep Russia out and India loyal; both involving levels of expenditure that could cripple the Indian budget. 'It is one of those cases', acknowledged Dufferin later, 'where if we lose, we lose; and if we win, we lose.'[3]

This was not just an academic debate. In 1884 the Russians completed the conquest of Turkmenistan, capturing Merv (about which there had been much 'Mervousness' in 1879–80) only 600 miles from the Indian border. 'The Russians [are now] the masters of the situation', warned Roberts who, together with Durand and other 'bellicose' colleagues, tried to stampede the new viceroy onto the offensive. So too did the Queen: 'We are terribly troubled about this Afghan Frontier question, but I have written and telegraphed and warned and protested until [the government] have taken fright! But we are in a dreadful mess everywhere and on bad terms with everybody and every country. The Queen is well nigh worn out with it.'[4] With intelligence reports now warning that up to 23,000 Russian troops could be at Herat (now held to be 'the key to India') by 21 May, along with a mass of plainly inaccurate rumours, Dufferin decided to take no chances.[5] By March 1885 preparations were laid for 25,000 British and Indian troops to be stationed at Quetta, ready to advance on Herat.[6]

In London, the cabinet were already 'very bellicose about the

Afghan frontier', only for the stakes to be raised higher by the latest Russian offer of a settlement of the border – a proposal which even Gladstone considered to be so inadequate as to be 'little short of insolence'. For Gladstone, then up to his eyes in the Gordon debacle and sending troops to Sudan, the timing could not be worse. But Dufferin was by now becoming increasingly wary of a pre-emptive defence of Herat lest it become another Khartoum. 'It would be better, if that were possible, to make the dog drop his bone by throttling him, than by pulling it out of his mouth.' With his commander-in-chief (Sir Donald Stewart) offering support against the more gung ho, he sought to woo the Amir of Afghanistan at the coming durbar to be held at Rawalpindi. For the 'principal object' was the 'freeing of the hand' of Britain over 'the delimitation of the Afghan frontier'.[7]

The durbar at Rawalpindi, a military station by the Indus river in north Punjab, was intended to be a diplomatic version of shock and awe to keep the Amir from deserting to the Russians. Constructed on the same lines as Lytton's famous Delhi durbar in 1877, a tented town of interlocking camps was erected with the viceroy's predominant at the centre. But a week of torrential rain and hail had unexpectedly turned the venue into a quagmire. By the time the Amir finally arrived on 30 March, much had had to be cancelled, including processions of elephants and a day of military manoeuvres. Still the Amir did not disappoint. Given that Abdur-Rahman had never been beyond his country, Dufferin prepared to be greeting a savage tribal chief whose brutal reputation had gone before him. Instead he found himself face to face with a 'burly man, big rather than tall [and a] broad . . . pleasant face with no trace whatever of the hook-nosed, keen-eyed, Jewish Afghan type'. Lame from neuralgia in the leg, he wore a black half-uniform coat decorated with two diamond stars, long boots and a tall astrakhan cap. Here was a 'prince of frank and even bluff, yet courteous manners [who] was quite at his ease amid a crowd of foreigners'. But who also retained 'a look of implacable severity', leaving British officials in no doubt that they would be negotiating as equals. Such challenges brought the best out of Dufferin, and appreciating the importance of 'amour propre' to his guest, he arranged for the Queen's son (the Duke of Connaught) to welcome the Amir to his quarters. It was an astute move for which 'his gratification was undisguised'. That said, nothing did more to improve the Amir's temper than Dufferin finding 'Miller the dentist' to pull his guest's tooth.[8]

By the time the negotiations began on 2 April the Russians were known to be collecting around Penjdeh (a fortified town on the Kushka river ostensibly within Afghan territory). Any border incident with Britain formally committed to defend Afghanistan risked a major confrontation with Russia. It was Dufferin's task to release Britain with her honour intact or, much more dangerously, make a stand at Herat and call Russia's bluff. After a couple of tentative sessions Dufferin gambled. Pointing out the inadequate state of the fortifications at Herat, he again offered to organise its defence and again was refused. Seizing his chance, Dufferin then attempted to extricate his government from its 1880 commitment: 'If Your Highness rejects the assistance that we offer you under the terms of our Treaty, then Your Highness will have to make with the Russians the best arrangement you can. You will be unable, for instance, to maintain your claim to the Penjdeh district.' 'Better', he went on, 'to cut off a bit of your little finger . . . [than] suffer a fatal blow to the heart.' To everyone's surprise the Amir agreed, even denying he had ever made a claim to Penjdeh. With that a map was produced and a new line proposed around Zulficar. Dufferin could therefore report back to London, that by the redrawing of the border Britain had been left 'at perfect liberty . . . [and] with a free hand in the matter'. To his officials the viceroy had executed a masterstroke.[9]

Yet if so it was one that the Amir was ready to exploit. Having only just got the British out of his country, the last thing the Amir wanted was their return. What he did need, on the other hand, was arms and cash, both of which Dufferin now promised in abundance. The Amir's prime motive was to intimidate his opponents within Afghanistan; hence over the coming years it would be rival Afghan tribes and not the Russians who would fall victim to the guns given by the British. He was not going to let this opportunity go in order to retain Penjdeh, which was indefensible and with little strategic importance for him. Even his late concession to allow the British, in the event of Herat falling, to occupy Kandahar in the south still left him in control of most of his country while serving to give any invading Russian force pause for thought. If Dufferin had got what he wanted, so too had the Amir.

By now with the weather finally relenting the Amir could enjoy the spectacle of a military review – as well as making public his allegiance to Britain in his speech.[10] After the march past, Dufferin, indulging his chivalric instincts, presented the Amir with a diamond-hilted sword 'as a gift from myself'. Holding it aloft, the Amir declared 'that with the sword he hoped to smite any enemy of the British Government'.[11] As fate would have it, his fealty was about to be put to the test.

That night, word came through that nine days earlier, on 31 March 1885, Russian troops had attacked and captured Penjdeh leaving 300 Afghans killed and the Russians 100 miles from Herat. This raised the stakes very considerably. The Indian government knew that once news of this attack reached Britain, there was a real chance of war. For the Afghans, Penjdeh, so easily conceded only days before, now threatened to become a point of honour. It was extremely fortuitous that at this moment the Amir was Dufferin's guest. And it was a measure too of the trust the viceroy had built up in little over a week that the Amir was willing to listen to British entreaties that the loss of Penjdeh changed nothing. Sensing that the British were desperate to avoid conflict, he instead extorted more guns and money out of Dufferin. For the viceroy this was a cheap price to pay.[12]

Throughout all the negotiations Dufferin was largely out of communication with London. In the interim pragmatism had at last won over martial ardour within the cabinet. 'It really cannot matter to us very much,' noted Hamilton, 'whether the line [in the desert] is drawn a little further north or a little further south, provided we can secure the agreement of the Amir to it.' Hence the relief when four days later word came through of the Amir's concession of Penjdeh and virtually all territory the Russians demanded: 'a most unexpected deliverance from our difficulties'. Only later that day did they hear of the Russian attack. But with a solution to hand, Britain chose to limit its reaction to a seizing of the moral high ground.[13]

Nevertheless, if London viewed Dufferin's negotiations as 'very satisfactory', there was still consternation over his commitment to any future military intervention. In limiting any advance should the Amir not hold Herat to Kandahar, Dufferin had secured a practical forward base for India's defence. But this was admittedly a reconfiguration of policy for the benefit of the Indian government and one that would necessitate 200 miles of railway.[14]

To the cost of this would be added the funding of the Amir. This Dufferin put at £200,000 in subsidies on top of the 30,000 breech-loading rifles and 24 heavy guns ostensibly for the defence of Herat. Of course, as Dufferin was 'well aware', the Amir might be 'trifling with us . . . Unfortunately we are dealing with savages.' And yet, as only Dufferin could argue with equanimity, 'after all it is only money that we stand to lose'. More importantly he had secured a time out, a break in the slide to war and without any immediate British occupation. Because of what Hamilton called this 'breathing time', 'war is not likely now'. Even the Queen 'appears to be astoundingly inclined for peace'.[15] Back in Rawalpindi, the mood was celebratory. By now the Amir had 'absolutely thawed' and could not have been more effusive in his last speech. London's instruction to make him a Knight of the Star of India was 'the crowning drop that made his cup flow over' (even if the only medal to hand was the viceroy's) and he departed 'as pleased as a young bride with a diamond necklace'.[16] It was the beginning of the end of the Great Game.[17]

There is no question that Dufferin's performance at Rawalpindi had been masterful, extricating Britain from a potentially disastrous position and providing the opportunity for a lasting settlement. However, his achievement would be far greater if it were imagined that Britain and Russia were actually on the brink of war and the catastrophic events of 1914 might have occurred thirty years earlier. 'An attack on Herat would mean war with Russia everywhere', had been Kimberley's bleak verdict in early 1885. Soon he was reporting back that England was 'hovering on the very brink of war'. Many in the late nineteenth century assumed that the next continental conflict was more likely to be caused on India's North-West Frontier than the Balkans; among them Bismarck who looked for it to sap the strength of two major rivals.[18] Behind the rhetoric, there was plenty of evidence of war preparations. In addition to the 25,000 troops sent to Quetta, the navy made plans for the bombardment of Vladivostok; while in

England the reserves were called up and official announcements of war were printed in readiness. In Parliament Gladstone secured the largest vote of credit since the Crimean War and the stock markets in London and New York tumbled. Hence the assessment of some modern historians that there was in 1885 'a good chance of war' and significantly, Salisbury, ever the fatalist, was at the time primarily concerned that the responsibility be seen to lie with Russia. One historian has chosen to compare it with another stand-off where the Russians eventually blinked, describing the Penjdeh crisis as 'an extended Cuban Missile Crisis'.[19]

But, as with the Cuban Crisis, that war did not break out owed much to the fact that neither side ultimately wanted to fight. Russia simply hadn't the funds to attack India in 1885 and recalled a general in February 1884 who had suggested they should. Similarly Britain was too deeply embroiled in Egypt and especially the Sudan to consider a major war. Also it was actually very hard for both sides to inflict significant damage on each other. Logistics really ruled out a Russian invasion of India but equally an attack by Britain on Russian Asian territories would have no telling impact on Russia itself. And the last thing Britain wanted was permanent low-level conflict on India's frontier. Nor could they rely on Ottoman acquiescence should they choose to re-enact the Crimean War. Other than some gunboat diplomacy in the Baltic, there was little option but peace. Hence Bismarck's derision for the Rawalpindi Durbar: 'C'est Offenbach tout pur'.*

And yet 1914 would prove the folly of believing that a rational assessment of mutual interests would prevent a major pan-European war. Conditions still had to be created that would leave the Powers able to negotiate a solution, free from the pressures of opportunism, prestige and populism. This is what Dufferin achieved at Rawalpindi. It was an occasion when personalities mattered as much as armies, a brief moment when relationships and the ability to win immediate trust were the decisive instruments. As a result, calm heads prevailed and the normal sparring between foreign offices could resume.

---

* 'It is all pure Offenbach.'

25

Tiger Shooting with Churchill

Yours, with your stories of the strife at Home,
Who's up, who's down, who leads and who is led –
One reads so much, one hears so little here.
                    Rudyard Kipling, 'One Viceroy Resigns'

DUFFERIN ENTERED SIMLA on a wave of triumph but by the time he descended into the plains in the autumn his ascendancy threatened to be undermined by a new government and a different Secretary of State. For Kimberley's successor was a genuine political force, one who believed in radical action, of governments making things happen; but most importantly, someone who was determined that India would be made to serve the interest of the Tory party. Like the meteor, to which he was often compared, blazing across the night sky, Lord Randolph Churchill did not fight shy of the havoc he could cause. Dufferin, powerless to get out of the way, at least knew what was coming. For Churchill and Dufferin had 'previous'.

Despite Dufferin later recalling to Churchill's widow that her husband had 'quite won my heart' when visiting India, the viceroy had been livid at 'the mischievous wretch's meddling'. Churchill could not resist leaking for party advantage embarrassing information over Gladstone's policy towards Suakin, which he had learnt at Dufferin's table. Similar motives led him to support opposition in India to the Bengal Tenancy Bill and praise the crowds that bade farewell to Ripon. Yet perversely the men whose opinions he claimed to value the most were reactionaries and generals who had little faith in the natives and mostly wanted to fight Russia – men such as Roberts and Sir Lepel Griffin.[1] If there was consistency here it appeared to be an instinctive preference for action unconstrained by moderation or consequences for others.

Perhaps surprisingly, Salisbury and Churchill, with the Queen in support, made Dufferin's retention a condition on taking office in June 1885. 'Our one desire', Churchill insisted to the viceroy, 'is to be mainly, and even entirely, guided by your advice.'[2] Such was the extent of mutual flattery indulged in by both (largely in inverse proportion to the level of agreement between them), that it might be seen as a change of style rather than a shift in power. This was not a mistake that Dufferin was to make. In the months since his departure from India Churchill had become a powerful, dangerous figure in British politics, one who had made his reputation by breaking his leader in the Commons and then advancing through political intuition, bravura opportunism and brilliantly executed, violent, and often shamelessly unfair denunciations of his rivals. Harnessing such an elemental, ambitious force to the realities of government was always going to be a challenge. As early as August 1885 Dufferin was flagging up the danger, hopeful that with governmental responsibilities Churchill might 'get to see that there is something better worth living for than party management and electoral victories'. This was wishful thinking; with the Tories a minority caretaker government until the election due in November, the intervening months were always going to be an extended electoral campaign.[3]

'You can imagine the feeling of the old stagers here', Kimberley had written from the India Office on Churchill's appointment. Yet Churchill was soon exercising a very tight hold on his staff.[4] 'My great fear is that he should be got hold of by the wrong people', Dufferin had confided to Godley – 'almost the only friend . . . that I have in the India Office'.[5] The appointment that caught the eye was that of Roberts over Wolseley to be commander-in-chief of the Indian Army, rejecting the advice of Dufferin – who thought Roberts lacked 'political judgement' – and the India Council and the Queen. Dufferin only just managed to veto Griffin's selection for the India Council. Strikingly all Churchill's appointments were unreconstructed Lyttonists – hostile to any concessions to native India, and passionate forwardists.[6] Just as symbolic of the new order were those who

Churchill did not want. When Dufferin proposed with royal support the Duke of Connaught for the vacant Bombay command, Churchill refused. Dufferin's embarrassment was compounded by Churchill, quite intentionally, misrepresenting the viceroy as being equivocal on the appointment. The Queen would not be the last to complain of Churchill operating in 'a very shifty way'.[7]

Then, in order to spice up a speaking engagement, Churchill announced the Russian agreement on 3 September, four days before the agreed protocol was due to be published. There was next to nothing that Dufferin could do about this, other than do as he did, making plain that the 'ultimate settlement of all important questions must out of necessity be arrived at in London'.[8] Salisbury and Churchill were soon exasperated by his unwillingness to take responsibility; despairing of the very long, convoluted and ornate letters in which Dufferin would outline options rather than decisions ('he was just the same when he was a boy at Eton', Salisbury explained a little uncharitably). But such was London's capacity to intervene that to do otherwise would only expose him to becoming the fall guy for a high-risk policy of a renowned political gambler. One who, within months, would propel the Indian government into an invasion of Burma.

In doing so he was treading a well-trodden path. The British had been invading Burma for most of the century, acquiring the country in instalments and completing the process with this, the third, invasion. The pretext was the apparent decline of the remnant kingdom of Ava into anarchy. Epitomising Burmese misrule were the young King Thibaw and Queen Supayalat. The Victorian press caricatured Thibaw as a weak king addicted to gin, with Supayalat, his queen, portrayed as a reincarnation of Lady Macbeth: acquisitive, vindictive and ruthless. Admittedly in 1878 Thibaw had seized power in a coup that saw eighty members of the royal family murdered; clubbed almost to death by hired criminals and then thrown in a pit to be trampled by elephants. Such homicidal assertions of authority were almost an ancient ritual – a tradition broken, though, by Thibaw's predecessor. Hence the uproar in Rangoon, and such was the revulsion in British India that Lytton considered annexation in 1878 and 1879; indeed in 1879 the British Resident was withdrawn. Further hostility was provoked by the Burmese insistence on the superiority of their traditions, symbolised by their insistence on foreigners taking off their shoes in the presence of the King. Or by making European ladies stay on their knees as they played the piano for the Queen; whose acts of capricious cruelty towards women her husband may have cast an eye on were the stuff of legend.[9]

Most historians now question the accuracy of this moral assault. Since the rules of succession allowed any member of the royal family to apply, transfers were always bloody. As for Thibaw, he was found to be sober, religious, and a cricket lover. Admittedly Thibaw's 'generally haphazard rule' saw government ministers in league with dacoits – bandits who posed as defenders of the people yet actually terrorised the villages. Other parts of the country were in the hands of local warlords, while in 1883 the Shan states were in rebellion. The next year the Kachins invaded and Burma had to call on the aid of Chinese 'freebooters'. In the midst of all the chaos there was a second massacre of friends of the princes who had fled the first massacre; a prison breakout being the opportunity to eliminate hundreds of political rivals. To the outside eye this was a regime in apparent meltdown.[10]

This confusion would serve as a pretext for British intervention. Two events escalated the tension. Firstly in January 1885 Thibaw signed a commercial convention with France who had since 1882 established protectorates over neighbouring Vietnam, Cambodia and Laos. By June a French vice consul had arrived in Mandalay, which was soon awash with rumours of arms and railway contracts (to build a line from Hanoi to Mandalay) as well as loans through a French subsidised Royal Bank of Burma. In the midst of this, the Bombay Burmah Trading Company, the largest British company operating in Burma, was taken to court for illegal exporting timber and, accused of 'bribery', was fined so heavily (£250,000) that suspicions inevitably arose that Thibaw wished to reallocate the lucrative teak monopoly to French interests. News of these events provoked calls from the Rangoon Chamber of Commerce for the annexation of Upper Burma. Accompanying this were grandiose descriptions of trading opportunities, not only of increasing trade within Burma but also of a direct overland trade route to China, opportunities that would be lost to the French. Dufferin rejected these pleas, primarily on grounds of cost to the Indian taxpayer. In any case the economic

argument for invasion was unproven and the administrative respon-
sibility would be enormous. Nor was it clear just how significant the
French penetration was – especially as the letter from Ferry, the
French prime minister, to Thibaw which the Bombay Burmah
Trading Company produced in court as evidence of complicity was
widely recognised in official circles as a forgery.

'It is the French intrigue that has forced us to go to Burmah; but
for that element we might have treated Thibaw with severe neglect.'
So claimed Churchill. However, the French, preoccupied with
conflicts in Indo-China, had already recalled their envoy and were
plainly backtracking. It was commerce that fanned the flames, as from
July 1885 Churchill was lobbied by the British Chambers of Commerce
and the Bombay Burmah Trading Company. Yet what really caught
the eye of the Secretary of State was the electoral opportunity. For a
minority government facing elections, a war on behalf of British
trade in Burma would ensure that 'the large commercial interests in
their country will be warmly on our side'. He openly admitted to
Dufferin when the die was cast (18 November 1885) that 'a government never fails to derive a certain amount of credit for successful
war'. Similarly he was in cahoots with *The Times* to ensure a noisy
barrage of stories for annexation. Meanwhile his officials prepared the
ground in Whitehall: 'Thibaw's sins are many and great', one wrote
to his opposite number in the Foreign Office, 'and I feel quite sure
your able pen, aided by a few snarls from myself, could formulate a
Bill of indictment against him that would make every old woman in
London weep!' Predictably Salisbury's suggestion of a joint enterprise
with France was kept from Dufferin.[11]

Formally the decision lay with the viceroy. Dufferin remained
doubtful to the end as all the advice from India made clear the risks
annexing Burma would bring.[12] But with the cabinet, according to
Churchill, for 'annexation, pure and simple',[13] Dufferin felt he could
do little. Just how far the cabinet were fully consulted is a moot point.
But with Thibaw refusing to back down over Bombay Burmah on 13
October, Churchill had his pretext and ordered the ultimatum. Before
it arrived in Mandalay on the 30th, he had in effect announced the
war at a rally in Birmingham. The only irony was that the war, which
began on 8 November, was not completed until 1 December – too

late for the November elections. Nor did Churchill hide his desire from the outset for annexation. Dufferin tried to resist this too and as late as 22 December was promoting the idea of a protectorate under a compliant prince. 'The unwilling Viceroy' had to be dragged to the decision, with Churchill railing to Salisbury that Dufferin was 'impotent to take the smallest responsibility on himself; we have to decide everything and he gets all the credit'. He would not be the first to complain of this but it was a bit rich from someone who was never going to have to face the consequences of his actions. Conversely, Dufferin was letting Reay, the governor of Bombay, know how much he resented 'being driven into the Burmah business'. 'Once the ball is set rolling, one has very little control over the issues, as far as some of the principal interests of humanity are concerned.' For in truth he had little option (other than to resign). And with the Queen all for annexation, he gave in gracefully and in turn was rewarded amply.[14]

And yet, once again, was Dufferin protesting his innocence too much? For all that the regime seemed on the verge of anarchy, as Mackenzie Wallace makes clear the prime preoccupation was geopolitical and specifically the risk that France would seize the chance to intervene. Consequently he and Dufferin were open to any rumours of French conspiracies.[15] Reporting back to Kimberley after barely a month in post, Dufferin declared himself 'very anxious about the condition of Burmah'. While the 'idea of a military adventure up the Irrawaddy is extremely distasteful to me', now was the 'opportune moment' as both France and China 'have their hands full'. Moreover, he argued for 'complete annexation' to avoid a repetition of the 'troublesome frontier' with Afghanistan. Consideration of pre-emptive strikes suggests Dufferin was more hawkish than he later portrayed himself. However, by March the Russian threat had ruled out adventures in Burma.[16]

By the time Churchill resuscitated the prospect of intervention in the late summer, Dufferin had genuine reasons to be cautious: how easy would it be to incorporate Burma into the Indian administration? How could they afford Burma as well as the new fortifications in the north-west? That said, in October he echoed Churchill in favouring 'annexation pure and simple' and sought to avoid 'reduplicating' the buffer policy in the East.[17] While he noted the hostile opinions to annexation ('and in this view, I see, Lord Ripon coincides'), 'my own instincts point the other way'; and to him Burma lacked the 'elasticity' and 'power of resistance' to act as a buffer, being of 'soft and molluscous [sic] consistence'.[18] So for all that Dufferin might insist three days later on being 'naturally an enemy of annexation, war, and everything that can result in the loss of human life . . . I have taken the bull by the horns'.[19] In fact his ultimatum left Thibaw with little room for manoeuvre and would have made Upper Burma into a vassal state. Revealingly, in her journal, Hariot, describing Dufferin's nonchalant signing of the ultimatum in Simla after breakfast, refers to it as a 'declaration of war'.[20] Just as telling was Dufferin's ordering up the troops in advance of the Burmese reply. Not that Salisbury or Churchill waited even to read Thibaw's response before announcing the state of war.[21]

Yet, even as the troops were invading, Dufferin was still assuring Ponsonby, the Queen's private secretary, that annexation remained an 'open question' and denied acting from 'any Jingo impulse': 'The Burmese people are a nice people, easily managed, and I cannot bear the thought of making war upon them.'[22] So why after the invasion was there so much hesitation over annexation? The answer lies in the November elections in Britain. These had left the Tories dependent on Irish nationalist votes. But with the Hawarden Kite signalling Gladstone's conversion to Home Rule so tempting the Irish with what the Tories could not offer, it was almost certain that the Liberals would be back in power when Parliament reconvened in January. In the circumstances Dufferin could not afford to risk being portrayed as a Lyttonist, a prancing proconsul and a target for Liberal and radical ire. So when General Prendergast, commanding the invasion force, first pressed Dufferin for clarity over annexation, Dufferin replied that it would 'not be a very opportune course to take in the midst of a general election . . . nor . . . must my hand be forced'.

By November his letters to Churchill had reduced annexation to 'the lesser of two evils' and a decision requiring further 'deliberation'. Above all he claimed the decision as his alone ('as I am the responsible person in the matter') and that he would not be 'forced' to make up his mind. 'I have authorised you', he wrote to Prendergast (fully aware that Churchill was champing at the bit with the electorate slipping away from his party), to declare that British 'ascendancy [in Burma] will be permanent and supreme'; adding a little dismissively that this 'ought to be sufficient to answer most of the ends that you have in view'.[23] Later his insistence in December of getting the Law Officers to provide legal opinion on whether annexation would require special powers reflected the viceroy's desire to protect himself in such a fluid political situation. Nevertheless Dufferin didn't stall because he disagreed with annexation but because he knew that Churchill and Salisbury would do it for him. They were so desperate to get the annexation through before Parliament returned that they resorted to a royal proclamation in an effort to tie in the Liberals. That Dufferin submitted a draft proclamation which allowed for a return to Burmese independence was simply re-establishing his Liberal credentials and proposed in expectation that Salisbury and Churchill would strike it out (as they did). As he admitted to Kimberley on the Liberals' return to office: 'as far as possible in the circumstances . . . I have tried to avoid putting my hand further forward than I could take it back again, in the event of the new Ministry determining upon a change of front. The late Government . . . forced the running a little faster than I wished on the question of annexation.'[24] Actually, far from being steamrollered into a policy he disapproved of, Dufferin had elegantly finessed his political realignment without losing the policy – which he still felt 'the right one' after his visit to Mandalay. But from now on, the policy was regarded as a legacy from the Tories and Dufferin's tone was that of the reluctant imperialist: annexation would prove 'a great nuisance . . . it will breed nothing but trouble and annoyance'.[25]

The conquest was a straightforward affair. The 10,000-strong Burma Field Force advanced rapidly up the Irrawaddy in steamers. At one point the invasion force saw the Burmese troops: 'dressed brilliantly in red, white and magenta coats, the officers with gold umbrellas held above them' to keep off the sun, they retreated as quickly as they had formed up and in 'good order'.[26] The only serious opposition came at Minhla and overall the British suffered 4 killed and another 4 drowned; cholera would later be a greater killer. Such was the speed of the British assault that the Burmese had not had time to prepare the defences of Mandalay, the capital, and by 28 November

Thibaw had surrendered. Prendergast had delivered Dufferin the 'bloodless' victory he had called for. It was all, as the Queen wrote to him, 'admirably done'.[27]

Churchill's enthusiasm for all things military was not confined to Mandalay. As he was propelling the viceroy to war in Burma, he was urging expensive defences on the North-West Frontier. In the aftermath of Penjdeh, Dufferin's challenge lay in restraining a military confident of the Secretary of State's support. To Russophobes Penjdeh had confirmed their worst fears; fears that would be heightened by the arrival of the Caspian railway to Merv in 1886. The problem for Dufferin was that outwardly 1885 had come closest to the invasion of India since the time of Napoleon. On the other hand, the Penjdeh crisis made him realise the impracticality of defending a frontier a thousand miles away, and among a people who were corrupt, unreliable and hostile. Also making him question his early enthusiasm was the expense. He had been surprised by how much it cost to keep troops battle-ready so far from their supply bases; costs that would have to be borne by Indian taxpayers.[28]

And for no purpose. 'I am one of those', he confessed, 'who do not believe that Russia will actually invade India during the present century.'[29] Thus the Rawalpindi agreement was intended to scupper the forward schemes of annexing Afghanistan. The £200,000 paid to the Amir was a 'gambling transaction' but one far cheaper than the mobilisation at Quetta 'putting a fearful hole in our pocket'. Determined to avoid 'a deluge of expense every time that a wretched Cossack chooses to shake his spear on the top of a sand hill against Penjdeh . . . [which] is pretty much what has happened now',[30] Dufferin chose to draw the line on India's North-West Frontier. Thereafter Churchill's insistence to maintain military preparedness continually ran in conflict with Dufferin's desire to prevent expenditure falling on the Indian taxpayer. But he had to concede Churchill a circus in the form of military manoeuvres.[31] As it proved, it was an event more fit for the navy. For when it took place in January 1886 with 35,000 troops, Dufferin was fated again with the weather. Amid lashing rain, the salute of cannon at the viceroy's entrance was drowned out by the crack of thunder. But that same month saw the fall of the Tory government and the end of Churchill's brief spell at the India Office. For all the respite this offered a harassed viceroy, there was no escaping the legacy of these tumultuous months, whose consequences were to set the agenda for Dufferin's remaining three years of office.

Still, Churchill's departure allowed the restoration of viceregal authority in military matters and the freedom to develop a reasonably coherent defence policy for the North-West frontier.[32] In the aftermath of Penjdeh, the Anglo-Russian Border Commission sprang into life and with 'much jollity and vodka' settled the border in two years. Then, forgoing expensive forts, Dufferin persuaded Roberts to build a series of staging posts and to invest heavily in railways and bridges. In the event of a Russian attack, troops could be directed from the interior towards the point of attack. The native army was increased by 30,000, along with an additional 1,000 British regulars.[33] By 1888 Dufferin could confidently assert that Russian power in Central Asia 'is like a hollow drum'. But he continued to retain the option of being able to advance to Kandahar and Kabul in the event of a Russian assault, facilitating this by building a tunnel through the Amran range.[34] Even so, the potential cost of occupying Kandahar was by now dissuading Roberts; in 1887 he couldn't bring himself to calculate it.[35]

What Dufferin managed to achieve from all the competing pressures (as late as 1888 Dufferin was having to reassure the prime minister that Indian defence 'has been the chief object of my solicitude')[36] was a system of flexible response at reasonable cost. Not only did it meet India's needs, but it was also politically resilient. For what one historian has dubbed 'defensive forwardism' could be variously presented: 'It could appear more defensive than forward for Kimberley, more forward than defensive for the politically aggressive Churchill, and a balance of the two for the cautious Cross.'[37] It was a strategy that would serve viceroys well into the next century. Securing the northeast frontier, however, would prove far more troublesome.

26

The Military Consequences
of Lord Randolph Churchill

Perhaps you're right. I'll see you in the *Times* –
A quarter-column of eye-searing print,
A leader once a quarter – then a war;
The Strand a-bellow through the fog: – 'Defeat!'
''Orrible slaughter!' While you lie awake
And wonder. Oh, you'll wonder ere you're free!
Rudyard Kipling, 'One Viceroy Resigns'

FEBRUARY 1886 SAW Dufferin on SS *Clive* with his staff and family, winding their way up the Irrawaddy past banks 'covered with pagodas' within which 'Buddha is everywhere . . . always sitting there with the same calm smile'.[1] Perhaps not quite as evocative as Kipling's reaction four years later: 'lilac, pink, vermilion, lapis lazuli, and blistering blood-red under the fierce sunlight that mellows and modifies all . . . the hillside below me and above me was ablaze with pagodas . . . Far above my head there was a faint tinkle, as of golden bells, and a talking of the breezes in the tops of the toddy palms.' It was to prove the inspiration of his most famous 'Ballad', 'Mandalay'; though in truth Kipling never got closer than Rangoon and Moulmein.[2] Dufferin too was to find that all was not as it seemed in Burma.

'The Viceroy's State entry went off to perfection', wrote Brigadier General Sir George White to his wife, not least because 'it was left entirely to me.' Dufferin, who placed much store on the importance of the ceremonial, was duly impressed: 'Good! They were more than good, they were ideal – they were dramatic.' Later that night in conversation with the viceroy, White noted that Dufferin was 'evidently bent on making this a great success, and does not want to be restricted by expense . . . [and] takes more of a Palmerstonian view of England's position than Lord Ripon'. By contrast (and in character) Dufferin was at the same time wearily declaring to his new Liberal masters that he was 'perfectly unprejudiced by any Jingo sentimentality' and regarding the annexation as 'a great nuisance' which will cause 'for some time . . . nothing but trouble and annoyance'. Indeed Dufferin was already picking up on symptoms of the difficulties ahead.[3]

While marvelling at the Royal Palace 'with its acres of gilt roofing, and shining pinnacles, and forests of teak pillars all gold!', Hariot nevertheless couldn't hide her disappointment at the disappearance of the fabled treasure. A 'very poor prize it is! Thibaw's ladies were much too sharp for our soldiers and managed to walk off with everything.' Perhaps more disturbing, three months after the invasion, was the sporadic gunfire at night over Mandalay that Dufferin could hear from his steamer. He insisted that the Burmese should not prostrate themselves but show no more respect to the viceroy than Europeans or Indians, only for the Hlutdaw (or state assembly) to be 'openly defiant', refusing to present an address. Hariot too felt herself snubbed at a small reception she laid on for the ladies of the court as a gesture of reconciliation.

The next day rumours were circulating of plans for a general uprising. A 'photo-call', involving the artists of the *Graphic* and the *Illustrated London News*, then proved a shambles. The intended image of Dufferin in front of the throne surrounded by respectful Burmese was undermined by an inability to find the Burmese contingent, who had been secreted in a distant corner of the palace. As a result the whole charade had to be re-enacted. That night, at a formal dinner as he sang the praises of the senior Army staff and the success of the mission, Dufferin was already doubting the official line. Seeking out White afterwards, he was startled by the general's request for significant reinforcements just to protect the Europeans. And was even more so when he asked how far British power extended in Burma. 'Up to that man and no further,' replied White, pointing at a sentry on the ramparts above. For the first time Dufferin grasped the precariousness of the British position.[4]

This convinced him of the need to incorporate Burma into the Indian administration. Officially it was still an open question. Faced now with incipient lawlessness and what he saw as a disintegrating state, only direct rule and British troops could, he felt, secure civilisation in Burma. Watching Dufferin, at a reception in the royal Palace, formally proclaiming the new order, Hariot could not but 'feel very sorry for our new subjects . . . What they would have liked is a king of their own kept in order by us.' However, Dufferin dismissed talk of puppet rulers as an 'expensive, troublesome and contumacious fiction' (which might explain why Hariot chose to edit the comment from her published diary).[5]

If annexation was something of a foregone conclusion, it was still an odd one, given that the external threat had vanished (if it had ever existed)[6] and there was little now to constrain British trade. What made the occupation both inevitable and inevitably a failure was the omission to cultivate the one cohesive force in Burma, the Buddhist faith. The pre-eminence of Buddhism had not escaped Dufferin. Yet British Burma was to be forcibly remoulded by the imposition of Western values at the point of a bayonet. In so doing the British missed an opportunity to win the peace. Ever seeking the positive, Hariot concluded 'for better, for worse, Burmah is annexed. It seems a rich country and Mandalay is a lovely place, and we at any rate have had a delightful visit'; but the soldiers have 'a full and rather dreary prospect before them'. Symbolically on their departure the viceroy's boat hit a sandbank and they were stranded for a day. The British would find themselves stranded in Burma for far longer.

The policy of formally dismantling the state – the King exiled to India, the monarchy and the Hlutdaw abolished, the police and army disbanded – meant that the British were left to impose governance on an alien culture in a vacuum. Within months there were insurgencies in central and Upper Burma. The British gave the insurgents a general name of 'dacoits' (bandits) but in practice there were many different resistance movements and with no common focus other than to get the British out. That said, most of the disorder was in areas already lawless for decades and over half the arrests were of established brigands.[7] In time some cohesion and legitimacy would be provided by

Buddhist monks whose 'millenarian resistance' drew on the revival of ancient cultural traditions.

But for all the chaos of the resistance, there was no mistaking the viciousness of the terrorist war that followed in a terrain of endless rainforests and rivers. As it was the real killer remained disease. Around 1,700 troops were invalided back in the first eight months. The monthly death rate between May and October 1886 was 100 to 150. Three successive political agents in Manipur died in post from 1886 to 1891. Not for nothing did the Irrawaddy become, in Kipling's haunting phrase, the River of the Lost Footsteps. Moreover the troops got no support from the local population despite the dacoit terror. Very quickly the army resorted to bloody and random atrocity.

Back in Calcutta, Dufferin would take a break from increasingly gloomy meetings on the state of Upper Burma to direct the installation of the great gilt mirrors taken from Thibaw's palace; and 'amused myself' examining the large box of Thibaw's jewellery and crowns en route from Mandalay to Windsor.[8] But it would require more than treasure to manage opinion back in Britain. Indeed the mismanagement of it would present Dufferin with as grave a threat as any he faced in Burma.

'PS – I deported *The Times* correspondent for transgressing the Press regulations'. So added General Prendergast in a letter filled with the good news of military victory. To the media-sensitive viceroy back in Calcutta, however, the postscript could only spell trouble. The object of the general's irritation was E. K. Moylan, a lawyer by profession who was also the Rangoon correspondent of *The Times*. Initially his relations with Colonel Sladen (the army officer responsible for civil administration) had been good enough for Moylan to secure a private interview with King Thibaw; a scoop which *The Times* published on 5 December 1885. Included in Moylan's report, however, was a graphic account of a night of rioting in which various European consulates were attacked amid looting and violence on the streets. Moylan exaggerated for greater impact but did not fundamentally invent. On the other hand nor did he submit his report to the military censors as regulations required *before* despatching it to London. For this Moylan was deported on 3 December 1885. By 9 December *The Times* had retaliated, making this a cause célèbre. With the editor,

G. E. Buckle, an important confidant of Churchill's, there was only ever one outcome. Dismissing the treatment of Moylan as 'mischievous or silly', the Secretary of State ordered his reinstatement.

There the incident would have sat, but for two factors: the personality of Moylan who returned hell-bent on revenge.[9] And secondly an incident that would shape the popular perception of the war, which Moylan would learn over dinner with Melton Prior, an illustrator with the *Illustrated London News*. With the army struggling to contain the violence in the wake of marauding dacoits, soldiers had resorted to desperate measures, including summary execution of prisoners. By 1 February 1886 there had been twenty-two such executions in addition to mock executions to terrorise dacoits into becoming informers. One execution in particular, which had been witnessed by Prior, became infamous. With the dacoit facing the firing squad, on the command 'fire', a camera flashed. The photographer was Colonel Hooper, provost marshal in Mandalay. Later much was made of Hooper's military record and humanity but under Moylan's pen Hooper was described as an 'ardent amateur photographer . . . desirous of securing views of the persons executed at the precise moment when they are struck by the bullets'. To achieve this, Moylan claimed, the final command was often delayed for minutes until Hooper was ready to 'expose the plate'. This last point was almost certainly a fabrication but the exposé of these 'experiments' on 21 January caused outrage in London.

Dufferin, 'much annoyed' after his insistence to Prendergast to operate 'with exceptional humanity', quickly forbade all further military executions. But he knew that the damage had been done.[10] He was then further amazed to discover that Hooper had only been reprimanded – it was deemed that he was not on duty when he took the photographs. 'Be that as it may,' he acknowledged to Kimberley (now back at the India Office), 'the result is disastrous, [making] the war unpopular and . . . render[ing] public opinion in England very suspicious of all our doings.' Moylan may be 'an ill-conditioned cad' but his campaign had destroyed Prendergast's reputation (for all that he had 'just conquered a province bigger than the United Kingdom with the loss of a little over twenty men'). 'Everything he [Prendergast] does will stink and few reputations can withstand the erosion produced

by the constant droppings of a special correspondent's acid telegrams.'
So, Prendergast's command was transferred to White; and Charles
Bernard took over the civilian administration from the army. Although
this could be justified operationally, Dufferin had been forced to act
'shabbily', and Moylan had his first scalps. No wonder Dufferin began
to fear just where Moylan's campaign might end.[11]

In the short term events favoured the viceroy. By now the Home
Rule controversy had broken, blocking out all other considerations
in London. 'If there is any act of absolutism or illegality that your
government wish to commit', wrote Lady Gregory, 'now is your
time, for India is forgotten for the moment.' Such barbed comments
from Irish friends showed how bad the perception had become. If
anything the military situation was even worse and by the end of
August the army was barely in control around Mandalay. Cholera was
also taking its toll. So too were Moylan's latest attacks. First to go was
Captain Adamson, the deputy commissioner of Burma, quite 'broken'
by articles denouncing his management of military trials.[12] With The
Times's correspondent beginning to target Bernard, stopping Moylan
had become a priority for Dufferin. A private request in late July to
John Walter, the proprietor of The Times, asking him to replace his
journalist backfired in the face of the latest examples of official incompetence. In the spring, dacoit activity had seen a third of the capital
destroyed by fire. Now on 16 August the Bund that protected
Mandalay from the annual flooding of the Irrawaddy broke and
50,000 lost their homes.[13]

In response to 'the popular cry'[14] Sir Hubert Macpherson was
appointed as White's superior. As a well-known general, he would
have a 'soothing and reassuring effect at home'. His replacement by
Roberts barely two months later (after Macpherson had died of fever)
resonated even more. For presentational reasons Bernard's replacement by Sir Charles Crosthwaite was delayed until January 1887 but
there was no escaping that, in Dufferin's eyes, Bernard too had been
'discredited . . . by [Moylan's] deliberate system of perverse cunning
and malicious representation'.[15] The British in Burma, it seemed,
were buckling under a media witch-hunt in London.

However, the military campaign began at last to turn. Seizing his
opportunity Dufferin moved onto the offensive, tackling The Times

head on by writing a major defence of his Burmese policy. Initially composed as an aide-memoire for Sir Richard Cross, the new Secretary of State, Dufferin expanded it and had it privately printed as a pamphlet, which he then circulated to eighty people – a mix of the powerful (politicians, Indian experts and editors) and also to many of his friends. This was a classic tactic of Dufferin's. None of the controversies were ignored but with a wealth of detail he steadily exposed the exaggeration and misrepresentations. He sought to moderate public expectations by outlining the true nature of the conflict, and at the same time he repudiated that he had been guilty of trying to fight the war 'on the cheap'.[16] Instead he stressed the similarities to the disorder in the Irish land war about which his audience was only too aware, comparing the guerrilla tactics of the Moonlighters in Ireland with Burmese dacoits and the difficulties field armies had in defeating such foes.[17] Above all, the pamphlet was intended as a devastating critique of Moylan's journalism, and all the more deadly for being privately circulated. Finally, he reinforced his position as a servant of the empire carrying out a policy about which 'I never ceased . . . to have considerable misgivings'. A follow-up article written anonymously in the *Edinburgh Review* gave further weight to his cause. And with even White in November ordering his officers 'to avoid anything repugnant to public opinion', Dufferin had regained the initiative in the war of perception.[18]

So too on the battlefield. 'Affairs in Burmah are going on swimmingly', he could assure his daughter by the summer of 1887.[19] Crosthwaite achieved the resolution the British wanted with a ruthless and systematic 'pacification' of the country; crushing resistance by brutal tactics later to be adopted in the Boer War – burning out villages and abducting the families of dacoits until they surrendered – tactics whose impact White declared to be 'magical'. It was all part of a 'surge' with over 40,000 troops designed 'to make the [villagers] fear us more than the bandits'.[20] Within a year British authority was securely established through most of Burma, although the last pockets of rebellion were not quelled until 1892.

Was it worth it? When Dufferin left India in December 1888 there were still 35,000 troops in Burma and 8,000 police and the cost of £5 million was over ten times Dufferin's original estimate. Commercially, other than the Burmah Oil Company (formed in 1886), the annexation provided little trade of lasting benefit. Nor did the British ever recoup the enormous outlay on railway development in Upper Burma. As for the strategic imperative of conquest, this was not tested. The French were never interested in challenging Britain's hold on India or realistically her interests in Burma. Internally, the incorporation of Burma into British India never became anything more than an administrative arrangement. As one historian explained: 'The insouciant Burmese were quite unlike any of the Indian peoples . . . [and] the deposition of Thibaw dislocated the delicate interdependence of the monarchy and Therevada Buddhism and, from the highest motives, the British, by declining to interfere in religious matters, undermined and destroyed the Buddhist hierarchy.'[21] With the loss of so many traditional social and legal structures following the conquest, crime became an ever-present problem. Here was the reality of what Kipling would soon dub the 'White Man's Burden' in the service of 'Your new-caught, sullen peoples, / Half devil and half child'. The blessing of stable government barely survived occasional rebellion, evaporating eventually in the face of the Japanese invasion in 1942. Post-war independence brought little respite. For all that Thibaw's rule had verged on the 'lunatic', it is hard to deny in retrospect that the decision to annex in 1886 was a catastrophe for the native Burmese.[22]

The war would have important consequences for India too. 'I suppose the Burmah business will a little upset your calculations', Churchill had acknowledged in passing.[23] If the defence costs after the Afghan crisis were crippling enough, the Burmese war denied Dufferin the capacity for a domestic programme to settle India after Ripon. By January 1886, income tax had to be reintroduced. Not surprisingly Indians resented paying for Britain's war and Dufferin's viceroyalty came to be seen on the subcontinent as taxes and Lyttonism – precisely what he had wanted to avoid. With hindsight there would be those who argued that because of the Afghan and Burmese crises, Dufferin did not get to concentrate on domestic developments such as the Indian National Congress until too late.[24]

But in reality it had become more personal than that. On one level it was having to commiserate with his neighbour Viscount Bangor, whose eldest son had died fighting Dufferin's war.[25] On another, having invested so much of his reputation in the Burmese project, he came to be 'obsessed by Burma'. And not least by Moylan. Few, he noted, survived 'with such a liar and hell-hound as Moylan upon his tracks'. Having always enjoyed a glowing press, Dufferin had his confidence jolted by the assault. In the face of this criticism, he knew that Burma would come to define his viceroyalty back in Britain. It was a battle he literally could not afford to lose. Hence his intolerance of those less committed than he;[26] hence also his unabashed pride over the final victory in Burma. It was as if the sheer competitiveness of political survival had sucked dry his Liberal instincts. Nor did he see the irony of refusing honours in the wake of Egyptian annexation only to accept them over conquest in Burma. Denied 'Quebec' by the Queen, and preferring a Burmese rather than an Indian title, he was only concerned lest the addition of 'Ava' to his name sounded as if 'out of one of Offenbach's operas or the Mikado'.[27]

As it was, the final act of the Burmese tragedy would have graced any opera. Sixty years after the viceroy sent British troops into Burma, Fort Dufferin (as Thibaw's palace had been renamed) was destroyed by British bombers trying to flush out the last of Japanese resistance on 20 March 1945. Even more poignantly, five days later in the jungles surrounding Ava the 4th Marquess of Dufferin and Ava was caught in a Japanese ambush and killed.

27

A Very Public Private Life

I wonder now. The four years slide away
So fast, so fast, and leave me here alone.
Reay, Colvin, Lyall, Roberts, Buck, the rest,
Princes and Powers of Darkness, troops and trains,
(I *cannot* sleep in trains), land piled on land,
Whitewash and weariness, red rockets, dust,
White snows that mocked me, palaces – with draughts . . .
A hundred thousand speeches, much red cloth,
And Smiths thrice happy if I called them Jones,
(I can't remember half their names) or reined
My pony on the Mall to greet their wives.
More trains, more troops, more dust, and then all's done . . .
Four years, and I forget. If I forget,
How will *they* bear me in their minds?
Rudyard Kipling, 'One Viceroy Resigns'

IT WAS ONE of the oddities of imperial government that the
Viceroy of India spent so little time in his capital. Like a medieval
monarch, he seemed continually on the move. Barely three months,
from mid-December to March, would he reside in Calcutta. Another
three months were given to the progresses around the subcontinent.
The greatest portion of the year was spent at Simla: a hill town 7,000
feet above sea level, separated from the plains by mountains and
a hundred miles from a railway. And yet every April there was a
1,200-mile migration from Calcutta of files and officials as the government pitched its tent amid the clouds.

If the sweltering heat of the Indian summer drove government and society to the hill stations, there was also the beguiling prospect of a haven of apparent Englishness.[1] And in Simla the Dufferins would establish their 'home'. Surrounded by 'a hundred mountainous ridges that rise around us . . . like the waves of a confused and troubled sea', it comprised of numerous miniature Swiss cottages, perched perilously wherever they could get a foothold on the ridge of a Himalayan spur. 'That the capital of the Indian empire should be thus hanging on by its eyelids to the side of a hill is too absurd', Dufferin would admit but after Calcutta's stifling humidity 'the air is delicious, most healthy and bracing'; and with its 'charming walks along shady paths cut into the side of the mountain, rhododendrons thirty feet high [and] covered with blossoms', and in the trees above 'whole tribes of monkeys spring from branch to branch', it offered an idyllic escape.[2]

With nineteen-year-old Nelly and her cousin Rachel they attacked the Simla season of balls, dinners, gymkhanas and picnics with gusto, hosting 50 events in their own cramped quarters and attending another 200, making their mark by introducing the mazurka.[3] Simla under the Dufferins, as one long-serving government official later reminisced, became 'the brightest, wittiest, most refined community I ever knew'. There is a need to keep some perspective on this: at Lady Dufferin's Fancy Dress Ball the 'great feature of the evening' was the quadrilles arranged by Hariot 'in which the dancers sang Nursery Rhymes as they went through the figures'. Moreover, so elaborate were the costumes that more merriment was to be had when the vicereine genuinely failed to recognise her husband: 'I think I know your face but I cannot remember who you are.'[4]

In their enjoyment of such frivolities the Dufferins were unusual. Most viceroys despaired of the unrelenting tedium of the social frenzy. But after eleven months on the plains and often at lonely stations, two weeks at Simla offered a great release for the young and the unmarried; and for what moralists called 'breaking the Seventh Commandment'. And they were duly outraged over Kipling's recently published *Departmental Ditties* and *Under the Deodars*, which portrayed Simla as frivolous and loose. Actually, amid the social banality, the Kiplings became something of a lifeline for Dufferin. They met in Lahore en route to Simla in 1885. Dufferin enjoyed talking art with

Lockwood, Rudyard's father. But it was his wife, Alice, who was the prime attraction. Having declared that 'dullness and Mrs Kipling cannot exist in the same room', the viceroy never failed to take any 'opportunities of conversing with her'; even enrolling his daughter Nelly into Lockwood Kipling's drawing classes in part so that he could call on Mrs Kipling frequently.[5]

A different kind of distraction came from building. To Hariot, Peterhof, the viceregal residence, was 'a cottage', in which one could only entertain twenty-three people comfortably.[6] Their preferred site on Observatory Hill would be much more spacious and had a 'splendid view'.[7] And it would provide Dufferin with the chance to indulge his architectural imagination in schemes that lack of money had prevented him inflicting on Clandeboye.[8] To the dismay of the Public Works department, over the next two years this house became an obsession. He would visit the building site twice daily, and drag nervous house guests over the scaffolding, making them climb 'up the most terrible places, and st[and] on single planks over yawning chasms', recorded Hariot.[9] The outcome was an expansive three-storey mansion built mainly in an Elizabethan style ('English Renaissance') with towers and a cupola and a profusion of balconies. Dufferin's stamp was unmistakable; most notably (as at Clandeboye) with a scattering of faux medieval coats of arms and the carvings of heraldic beasts supporting the chimney in the great hall, which rose to the full height of the house. 'There is nothing makes such a pretty decoration as heraldry, as each shield becomes a spot of brightness and light, besides being very interesting', Dufferin reassured his eldest daughter. If this showed his age, the new house was paradoxically 'the first truly modern Government House' (in India) with its electric light, indoor tennis court, and 'European Kitchens' – white-tiled and in the basement.

Mary Curzon would famously dismiss it later as a home 'a Minneapolis millionaire would revel in'. In doing so, she was more right than she knew. For when Dufferin was Governor General in Canada, he and his wife had frequently visited the United States and never failed to comment on the luxurious homes of the rich or to marvel at the latest technology. His more snobbish successors would dismiss this as provincial, and it is hard to imagine their wives getting quite such a thrill as Hariot did from switching the electric lights on and off.[10] Or that they would summon two representatives from Maples of London to advise on the furnishings. In addition to the decoration of the great hall in teak, walnut and deodar, there were gold and brown silks for the drawing room, a lighter shade of yellow for the ballroom and Spanish leather in 'rich dark colours' in the dining room – colour schemes that would later make Maud Lansdowne 'shudder'. Why, she would protest, import the latest plutocratic fashions from the metropolis and ignore the vibrant colours and fabrics around them in India? Still, even their fiercest critics enjoyed the gardens and especially the view. Needless to say, Dufferin was oblivious to such charges. Writing to Nelly, he reported that:

> The house is almost finished . . . It will certainly be a very nice monument I shall have left of myself in this outlandish country, for it will be a very pretty house as well as very comfortable habitation, and many future Viceroys, and especially their servants, for all the domestic arrangements are exceptionally good, will bless me for the pains I have taken about it.

One person who didn't was Cross who had to foot the bill of £100,000. Characteristically, this was a house built with no serious regard to budget. For all that Dufferin might claim that the outcome was 'beautiful, comfortable, convenient [and] not too big', it was at least a 'palace' able to entertain a thousand at a time, as he did within a month of moving in.[11]

Surprisingly, India proved the 'most difficult of all the societies I have ever had to do with', lamented Hariot in her diary, with dinner guests showing them not 'a gleam of recognition' the next day. Unlike Canada, the viceroy was socially 'deified' and all contact rigorously regulated, symbolised by the levees where hundreds would pass by, acknowledging 'the presence' without conversing. Not that there were many safe topics of conversation anyway and there was always the risk of being ambushed by endemic racism and crude snobbery which they both found repellent. Instead days were an endless cycle of incessant work punctuated by balls, lunches, garden parties, and dinners in Calcutta; of paying calls in the heat; of ambitious mothers promoting unattractive daughters; above all of being constantly under the microscope: 'We never move anywhere that we don't see a photographer pointing at us from the top of a carriage.'[12]

The constraints of protocol were even greater when meeting the Indian princes. For all that Dufferin had mistakenly learnt Persian believing it to be the lingua franca of the princes, language was less of a barrier – most could speak English if they wished to – than princely dignity and status. But at least on tour there was often the excitement of hunting expeditions. In such a world, prowess with the gun was proof of manliness and aristocratic credentials – of one's fitness to rule and hence the obligatory photograph with the kill. Dufferin had come a long way from his timid blooding forty years before. When tiger-shooting in the Nepal Terai he shot six, including 'knocking over the biggest beast of the lot'. This shoot involved 170 elephants (mostly sent by the Nepalese government) which were used to drive the tiger from cover and ultimately trap it. Dufferin missed the first tiger because at the critical moment his elephant 'suddenly whipped round and I found myself entangled in a tree'. Eventually they cornered 'a magnificent male tiger [and] I had the satisfaction of rolling him over with a bullet from a 500 Express rifle which broke his back, while a second in the head killed him outright.' Afterwards he was 'duly photographed in a triumphant attitude with my tiger'. On the same expedition he saw his first peacock: 'you cannot imagine how beautiful they look sailing through the trees with their lovely tails glistening in the sun'. That said, he still shot it.[13]

Tennis provided another pastime and one shared with some of the princes. Dufferin would play with his staff most days, often on little more than courts of baked hard mud. At the viceroy's request the servants who picked up the balls were 'exchanged for small boys lightly clad'. As Hariot explained to her mother, 'Dufferin's artistic eye is in perpetual delight over the muscles exhibited by those who wear few garments . . . but a higher authority has commanded that they should be draped.' A similar authority in 1887 saw off a young lady whose conversation had so entertained the viceroy over dinner – her reputation not quite passing muster, explained Dufferin ruefully to Nelly. Such intrusions of petty respectability irritated him (if never to the point of resistance), for without stimulating company he was quickly bored. Society mattered to Dufferin: 'There is nothing like going out and meeting with one's fellow creatures for brushing away the cobwebs and harassing recollections of one's cares and worries.' Hence he looked forward to January and the stream of visitors to Calcutta and their news of home. A group that largely invited themselves, they were an eclectic mix. In 1886 Joseph Chamberlain's two brothers, and Sir William and Lady Gregory (for all their barbs over Egypt and Burma) visited.[14] The next year saw among others the Duke and Duchess of Manchester, Herbert Gladstone and a prolonged visit from the Roseberys. Dufferin relished political tête-à-têtes with the coming man of the Liberal party.[15] George Curzon also came that year, revelling precociously in the similarities of Government House with his family seat at Kedleston, as if establishing a future right of possession.

For most of the year the Dufferins were dependent on family and immediate staff. In addition to their seven children, Hariot's brother Fred was an ADC (with his wife Blanche). Another ADC became virtual family: Lord William Beresford was worshipped by Hariot with a devotion once reserved for Macdonald, and she would be constantly in fear of him breaking his neck in the Simla races. As with all new arrivals, family life was 'entirely ruled by the sun'. During the hot season they lived mostly indoors with the curtains drawn to keep out the sun; conversely the monsoon would see them shivering amid the high ceilings and draughts of Government House. While the temperature in Bombay had been 'exquisite' with 'balmy' sea breezes, Calcutta they found 'damp and muggy and more or less depressing'. Consequently 'we are all a little swinkey'. Yet surprisingly they often complained of the cold: when Dufferin caught a high fever staying with Lyall, the latter put it down to his sitting outside under an awning in the noonday sun 'like a Hindu ascetic'. They make no mention of the snakes, mosquitoes and cockroaches. Food was more of a culture shock. With little bread, fresh fruit, and meat in the hot season they resorted to a diet of spices, curries, and naan and chapattis. 'Becti hot, becti cold, becti of course', wrote Hariot of 'the only fish to be had in Calcutta'. That and little sense of culinary hygiene meant that usually one of the family was ill or 'seedy' at any one time. And death could strike very suddenly: from cholera, typhoid, snake bite; even the smallest cut risked going septic or being infected with tetanus. When Archie caught typhoid in 1886 Hariot fled Simla for Lucknow to nurse him (but not until after the Connaughts had departed).

More traumatic was the death of their friend Tennyson's second son, Lionel. Having just started at the India Office, Lionel was invited by Dufferin out to the subcontinent where he caught the fever that eventually would kill him on the sea journey back in April 1886. 'We regard attacks of [this] kind pretty much in the same light as we do colds in England, so you need not be uneasy', Dufferin had written in early February, and thereafter he felt keenly his part in a tragedy that had left his old friend 'broken'. Heroically, two years later Tennyson would dedicate a poem 'To the Marquis of Dufferin and Ava' in which any recriminations gave way to the generosity of a 'shared love found in sorrow':[16]

> But ere he left your fatal shore,
>   And lay on that funereal boat,
>   Dying, 'Unspeakable' he wrote
> 'Their kindness,' and he wrote no more;

Such sadness aside, India proved the making of Hariot. Still young in her early forties (and no longer constrained by childbearing), she really came into her own as vicereine. While remaining deferential to her husband (even in front of the children she called him Dufferin or 'My Lord'), she was (as were her children) highly experienced in leading the public life. Taking refuge from her natural shyness in the formality of her position, she thrived in the great state occasions and receptions that would intimidate others. Nor did she fail to find something fascinating in the round of official visits to schools, hospitals and local businesses. As with all their postings, they quickly gained the reputation of throwing the best parties. With her debutante daughter and a dashing officer son, together with an endless stream of visitors from Europe, she ensured that viceregal circles did not lack glamour. What was new was the authority she displayed in her own right in the public sphere. Dufferin would fondly recount the King of Greece's pronouncement that 'there was no lady in Europe who could enter a room like Lady Dufferin'. Her graceful curtsy with a court bow of the neck, straight back, and sweeping descent to the floor was apparently 'long remembered in India' – even if to modern minds it is hard to conceive the importance of such things.[17]

By now Hariot was quite expert at setting up a British lifestyle in foreign lands with a steady stream of at-homes, receptions, dinner parties, amateur theatricals, tennis parties, horse rides and picnics. India would prove no different. Other imperial habits asserted themselves with a brisk certainty. Nowell, their longstanding servant, was put in charge of the household because 'we find it is the greatest comfort to have one European head. The natives are excellent servants but they want a master hand over them.'[18] She was very much in charge domestically and had no qualms about rearranging their living quarters in the vast palace of Government House ('The kitchen is somewhere in Calcutta, but not in this house'). The 'great peculiarity' of Indian houses 'is the public character of all the rooms', Hariot would later remark. So she moved all the family into one of the wings of Government House where the rooms were comfortable. All the bedrooms were now adjacent and also close to Dufferin's office. A series of interlocking drawing rooms offered further privacy and with its tables and screens and plants and photographs and furniture draped in pink silk, 'I have made the room look "homey"', she declared with evident pride.[19]

Privacy it has to be said did not mean being alone: even their children had personal jemadars (a 'body servant' who followed wherever they went). In addition there were 'legions' of housemaids in red tunics, turbans and gold braid (and soon to be embossed with the letter 'D'), with responsibilities regimented by caste. 'One . . . arranges the flowers, another cleans the plate, a third puts the candles into candlesticks, but a fourth lights them; one fills a jug of water, while it requires either a higher or a lower man to pour it out. The man who cleans your boots would not condescend to hand you a cup of tea.' This attentiveness drove many a vicereine mad but Hariot revelled in the battalions at her command. And if she wished to get away, there was always Barrackpore – the viceregal 'place' twelve miles outside Calcutta which offered a haven with its English park (reminding them of Cliveden) and a pretty garden with large blue convolvulus 'creeping over everything'. Dominating it was a gigantic banyan tree, which provided shade for dining al fresco; and all the more 'beautiful' for setting off the 'scarlet liveries . . . moving in and out of this natural arbour'.[20] As such, it provided the perfect image of those fortunate enough to be living the imperial dream. Indeed all that it lacked were those she held most dear – her children.

28

Parents and Lovers

An Indian Childhood

FOR INDIA WAS continually separating families. What made Christmas at Barrackpore in 1887 so precious for Hariot was that it was the only time the family were together in India.[1] School, university and the regiment would see their sons leave home from the age of seven. As it was, when the Dufferins left for the subcontinent they only brought Nelly with them, leaving the younger children[2] with their grandmother. Consequently family life was an emotional roller coaster of departures and arrivals. Once Hariot had to leave a recuperating Archie at Lucknow and go to Bombay to see off Nelly and Rachel; compensated though by the knowledge that her other children were setting off from England that same day. On such occasions she was known to abandon all decorum and run the length of the pier to catch a sight of her returning children. Separation affected the wider family too and Hariot particularly missed the company of her sister Katie. Letters provided some compensation but in 1887 when Hariot was touring Karachi she caught a glimpse of the future. Allowed to make a direct wire to her sister, whose husband was now chargé d'affaires in Tehran, Hariot was 'really astonished' at the 'rapidity' of the replies, allowing them to 'converse'. In effect they were emailing each other. The wonders of this only made her frustrated 'that the machine was not able to accomplish just a little more and let me hear or see her'.[3]

By 1887 both Hariot and Dufferin were so busy that, especially in Calcutta, they lived separate lives for most of the day. Once it was only the refrain of 'God Save the Queen' from the courtyard below her window that reminded Hariot that her husband was leaving for a month. Consequently their children were largely dependent on each other. It was for her brother, Terence, leaving for London and the Foreign Office exams, that Victoria wept 'bitterly . . . her arm thrown so lovingly around his neck'.[4] Terence at least was steady ('I can trust him implicitly', acknowledged his father). Archie, the eldest son and unashamedly Hariot's favourite, was not. Dashing and handsome he may have been but he was also feckless whose gambling debts were the cause of parental despair. Always at hand to still 'anxiety over Archie' was their eldest child, Nelly. Hariot became increasingly reliant on Nelly to look after her siblings. In turn her siblings looked to her to sort out their parents, as she assumed the role of what Basil would later call the family's 'sheet anchor'.

And for no one was this truer than for her father. Her departure in November 1886 for the London season left him bereft. He would postpone writing important despatches to government and Queen in order to pen a letter for his daughter to catch the last post. 'I do not think I clearly knew until you left us how much I loved you', he wrote, 'and what an important element you were in my heart and in my life.'[5] And yet she had always held a special position, as the young girl who bore his mother's name came to assume much of her personality. Once Archie had been sent to Eton, Nelly was the senior child and saw her parents at work in Canada between the ages of seven and fourteen. This education would create the ideal imperial girl and by 1877, aged barely twelve, she was accompanying her parents on official tours of the west. From early on there were signs of the strength of character that would make her such a force in the family. Willing to manage rather than confront, her capacity to think independently and act decisively would make her indispensable. As a consequence her relationship with her parents was almost one of equals. 'You are not only a most sweet daughter but a friend, a playfellow and a companion', Dufferin would write.[6]

Nelly and her father shared interests, in art especially, and both liked to gossip. She knew how much he would enjoy the tale of his old friend Lord de Ros, on escort duty at the Queen's Jubilee, who bowed so deeply to the King of the Belgians that the carriage went off without him, forcing him to chase after it amid much 'hooting' from the crowd. She mothered him too, reminding him to take his quinine and nurturing his fragile confidence by reassuring him after an article in *The Times* that she saw no evidence 'that your popularity is "on the wane"'.[7]

At the same time she could be merciless on her father's vanity. Quick to notice that Archie was 'getting thin in the cheeks as I did', Dufferin had determined to have his son's portrait painted while he was in his prime. Conceding that his son was 'handsomer than his father ever was', he took refuge in judging the Swinton picture of Dufferin at a similar age the finer portrait.[8] All this Nelly sought to keep in check. She recounted seeing a picture of Dufferin that was only recognisable by his hands, knowing full well that he was particularly sensitive over them as a tightening of the tendons had left his fingers 'bent like a claw'. As a result her father resorted to surgery, enduring three painful operations ('I am being very much bullied'); all ostensibly to enable him to hold a sailing rope again.[9] Madame Tussaud's offered a fresh opportunity to mob him up. There she found Dufferin portrayed in the Star of India robes and surrounded by native chiefs and Afghans and a little way off a group of former viceroys 'discussing' his policies, a composition which Nelly thought 'ingenious'. However, not only is the hand not the hand that 'Mamma and I would recognise everywhere' but his hair was quite white. As intended, Dufferin was 'perfectly frantic' on receiving the news. For if 'to enter those halls, especially as the central figure, is the surest sign an Englishman can have that he has become famous', to be then portrayed as an old man 'is truly humiliating'.[10]

If much of this was tongue in cheek, a little more unusual and intrusive was his instruction to his daughter, telling her to write freely on 'your little cares and anxieties . . . any social . . . mortifications such as going to a dance and not getting a partner', promising to keep 'whatever you say quite private'. From whom one wonders? Hariot? In a trivial incident the viceroy was caught red-handed sending Nelly 'a surreptitious £10' against Hariot's expressed instruction. On another occasion he moaned to her that 'Mamma [replaced] all my prettiest watercolours' in her outer room with 'horrid portraits of the Queen and Prince of Wales'. And there were the private jokes at his wife's expense. At a dinner in Calcutta Dufferin sat beside a young lady who remembered him in Canada; to which Dufferin had replied:

'You were a child at the time which must be my excuse for not having made love to you.' To 'my great surprise, mamma did not approve'.[11] But then Hariot's Ulster proprieties had never approved of such banter.It was only with his daughter that he could indulge himself with these risqué confidences, assuring her when on tour without Hariot that he felt 'quite free to take advantage of whatever hospitality the Pondicherry virgins may offer'. More striking was his confession (perhaps only half in jest), after relaying a tale of a boy mistakenly brought up as a girl, that: 'At all events, I am convinced that Providence does sometimes make the blunder of putting women's natures into men's bodies. I have myself often thought that I was originally cut out for a young lady.' To which, unlike her mother, Nelly could respond in kind, gently teasing him with an episode over dinner, when an old 'Servian' gentleman on hearing Dufferin's name asked loudly: '"Dites donc, Lord Dufferin a-t-il marié sa fille?",* which made me blush, and every one titter, besides being such a barbarous way of putting it. I explained that you had *not* married me, and felt grateful that you at least were not there, for I know that you would have made some wicked joke about my still being at his "disposition" or something of this sort. Now wouldn't you?'[12]

In this of course she spoke just like the mother – not hers, but his. Dufferin's affection for his daughter was not a reflection of disenchantment with his marriage. He remained deeply in love with his wife and she records that as Donald Mackenzie Wallace, at a dinner in Simla, toasted them on their 25th wedding anniversary, they 'both felt rather chokey'.[13] Rather the special attraction of Nelly (and indeed for which she had been named) was that she seemed more and more like his beloved mother. 'You possess the greatest gift of all, which is that of tender and spontaneous humour. This is what my mother had . . . and it is so nice to see it bursting out again afresh in you.'[14] There were other similarities too – in the gentleness of manner not lessening the acuteness of her observation; in the loyalty to siblings and in the occasional change of tone to rein them in sharply; and in the desire to be loved by all rather than possessed by one. By the autumn he was writing: 'Among the many joys you afford me, one of

---

* 'I say, has Lord Dufferin married his daughter'?

the greatest is the fact that not only are you very like my mother in your looks and your expression, but that every day you are becoming more like her in mind. You possess both her delicate and spontaneous humour and, what is a greater gift still, her sobriety of thought and good sense, as well as her sweet amiability which made everyone love her who came near her.' Here was the fantasy of the boy, whose shared love with his mother had so shaped him, and who now longed to revive the intimacy with the daughter who appeared to be the reincarnation of his mother. It was an illusion that Nelly was happy to indulge but not succumb to, letting him know, for instance, that she wrote longer letters to her mother (which ironically was just the sort of comment her grandmother would say to keep the young Dufferin in check).[15]

Yet for all this, it is actually Dufferin who ends up sounding most like his mother. Fearing that his English relations may be pushing Nelly towards marriage, he suddenly displayed a moral ferocity in stark contrast to the levity with which he discussed matters of the heart. After warning Nelly that 'Most men are selfish, thoughtless and inconsiderate' and alerting her to 'the pirates of the ballroom', he urged her to return to India 'safe and heart whole'. And he assured her that there was no need to marry until she is '25 or 26', even offering to fund her should she never marry. By July 1887, so fearful was he for his daughter – innocent of the 'evil ways of the world' and adrift in a London society that had become 'so corrupt' – that he resorted to the creed imbued in him by his mother and his guardian when he urged her to 'remember that religion and prayer are the only real safeguards . . . Morality, pride [and] sense of duty . . . are barriers which sooner or later fail and give way under the pressure of temptation [and] excitement, whereas the fear of God and a simple faith in our Saviour will suffice to protect you from all the assaults of the world and the devil.'[16] His mother had written similar letters of dread and judgement to him in the 1830s and 1840s and to devastating effect. Nelly, however, was more than a match for this: 'if you are not in a hurry to get rid of me, I am not at all anxious to leave you, and besides, you are my only admirer, so you see I am very safe', she quipped.[17]

Was this just paternal jealousy? There is certainly a possessive air in the correspondence: 'My own Darling Little Nell, you know how tenderly I love you'; 'No one will ever love you better that your old father.'[18] But if so, what was the point of sending her away for the season if not to attract proposals of marriage? Moreover this was her second season and with each passing year her opportunities would dwindle. It is as much about the loss of innocence: of her 'being carried away in the stream'. Is it too fanciful to suggest that, having once lost his mother in marriage, he could not face losing her again twenty-five years later? It is a measure of her hold on him that twenty years on from her death, he should be looking to recreate her among his offspring.[19]

Back in Simla, marriage was attacking on another front. In 1886 Archie had met Kipling's sister Trix and a brief flirtation ensued. A year later they were reunited at Simla. Archie, having left his regiment to be an ADC to his father, renewed his suit only to be rejected. And not surprisingly, given how crassly he wooed her. 'He suggested that though I didn't think him up to much, it might amuse me to be a countess', Trix recalled later. 'Too expensive' was all that she could think of replying; only for him to take her seriously and explain 'at length in his stodgy school boy way that though of course I would have to be "presented at Court at my marriage", my wedding dress with a train of family lace would be A1 and a small tiara that belonged to his beautiful Granny would suit me far more than the "fender full of shamrocks Mother sports"'. Although only twenty-four, there was little of the Sheridan ancestry in this proposal (nor any of the ardour that might have quelled the occasional suggestion that Archie's instincts lay elsewhere).[20] Stung by this rejection, he confessed to his parents, with humiliating consequences. As Trix recounted it, 'Though Lord Dufferin loved me for my good sense, Lady Dufferin never forgave me . . . Of course a penniless daughter-in-law was the last thing she wished for, but she said openly that she had always thought me a really sweet and charming girl; but, if her "splendid Arch" was not good enough for me, she gave me up!' No doubt pressed by his wife, Dufferin then called on Alice Kipling and asked her to remove Trix from Simla, only to get the answer he fully deserved, with the result that by the end of July it was Archie who had to leave.[21]

This falling-out also led to official disenchantment with her brother's writing. 'His Excellency [is] an Angel of the first order', had noted Kipling in his diary in 1885 after Dufferin had wooed the mother with compliments for her son. There was admiration too for his *Departmental Ditties* and praise for the young Kipling's 'infallible' ear for rhythm and cadence. But by 1887 his performance in a farce was dismissed by Lady Dufferin as 'too horrid and vulgar'. In return, Kipling, who once described a woman as 'sincerely insincere as Lord Dufferin', portrayed him as a world-weary, cynical careerist as he advised his successor in his poem 'One Viceroy Resigns'. Yet there was never a complete breakdown and Kipling's celebration in early 1888 of Hariot's hospital fund in 'The Song of the Women' received in return a volume of Dufferin's poems and a photograph of his wife, striking with 'tiara, pink sash and scowl'. Nor would that be the end of Dufferin's generosity, and in 1890, after much pleading from Kipling, he secured a pension for his father, Lockwood.[22]

By now Dufferin was feeling his age.[23] And feeling 'too the gradual dying out of those amongst whom his mother spent her youth'.[24] In response to this, Nelly, while still in Britain, was despatched on a pilgrimage of his old haunts such as Dunrobin in search of his mother's letters.[25] The Duchess of Sutherland had long descended into high eccentricity. But as Annie Stafford as they had sailed past the Western Isles, her fair hair streaming in the wind, she had been for the young Dufferin the epitome of a liege lady. And arriving at Tarbat House near Tain, the first thing Nelly's eye alighted on in the hall was 'you, a little Marochetti bronze figure, waving a flag and with one hand on your heart saying all sorts of pretty things [in] homage for your Scotch island'.[26]

29

Dufferin's India

You'll never plumb the Oriental mind,
And if you did, it isn't worth the toil.
                    Rudyard Kipling, 'One Viceroy Resigns'

E VERY OCTOBER THE viceroy would set out from Simla with
his retinue. Their ultimate destination was Calcutta but their
route was circuitous, taking in, over nearly three months, distant
parts of the Indian Empire and its semi-independent princely
states in what were in effect royal progresses. Many viceroys found
the process of governing India on horseback frustrating and
longed to get back to the capital. By contrast, Dufferin leapt at
any opportunity to escape his desk. More charitably, he had
always been an inveterate traveller – fascinated by new lands and
peoples and ready to suffer the discomforts that came along.
These great tours were a highlight of his year and not since Lord
Mayo would a viceroy travel so extensively or enthusiastically
across the subcontinent.

The first expedition in 1885 saw them return to Calcutta from
Simla via Rajputana and Agra. Whether in vast encampments or in
ancient palaces, they found a world of unbelievable riches and arbitrary power, and the fulfilment of a fantasy they chose to see as
authentically oriental. Of all the courts they visited, 'the most
Eastern and splendid of all was Jaipur' with its 'beautiful palace and
courtyard, upon whose marble floors lighted by torches several
hundred young Nautch girls danced before us'.[1] In a grand gesture
Dufferin returned the fort that dominated the town of Gwalior (and
had even been a centre of the Mutiny in 1858) to the local

257

maharajah, in much the same way that he had, forty years earlier, returned the gatehouse at Killyleagh.[2]

The next year they left Simla on an epic journey to Lahore, then west to Bombay and Poona, before re-crossing the country to Madras in the south and finally returning to Calcutta by sea. In Hyderabad they were guests of the Nizam, then potentially 'the richest man on earth' and ruling a territory almost as large as Great Britain. There amid illuminated palaces they were feted with feasts and entertainments, the ubiquitous fireworks and the extraordinary spectacle of an elephant race: 'the great animals waddled along very fast, but without any apparent wish to get the one before the other'. Then followed one of those chance encounters that briefly made the empire seem small as Hariot discovered that the Nizam's children had a governess from Belfast. At Mysore they found the young maharajah 'one of the most enlightened of our princes'; not least for setting in train a significant programme of female education.[3] Further south at Tanjore, Dufferin, remarkably, was allowed behind the screen into 'a real zenana'. Amid the excitement he was ushered to a chair covered in a red shawl and was just about to sit on it when the shawl stirred to reveal a wizened old lady ('Fancy if I had squashed flat the Chief Ranee of Tanjore').[4]

The following year would see him in very different territory, the North-West. En route they spent a couple of days with the Maharajah of Kapurthalla who was inordinately proud of his drawing room, where Hariot was amused to find 'some lovely coloured photographs of Mrs Langtry'.[5] However, Dufferin's purpose lay much further west. Through the barren desert, its vastness punctuated by extraordinary rifts and hills sculpted by a hostile climate, he went to Quetta with Roberts on the new railway to inspect the new defences. Cantering to the top of a ridge, he looked over into Afghanistan: 'At our feet there stretched a great scarlet sea of sand, with black islands of basalt rising up here and there in the midst of it. Beyond were the blue hills that encircle Kandahar. It made me feel a little like Moses on Pisgah.'[6] So taken was he by the sight that he commissioned a tunnel through the Amran mountains so troops could get to Kandahar in a fortnight. This was an intoxicating and very expensive game, and one that Dufferin in the end couldn't resist. Fittingly the tour ended with a durbar at Rawalpindi where three years before he had met the Amir of Afghanistan.

Their last trek was the shortest and least ambitious – a journey of farewells. But it was not without incident. On the eleven-hour ride from Simla to the train, Nelly's horse fell dead. And after they attended the wedding of the local chief at Patiala, she woke up at 1 a.m. to find her tent ablaze. Getting out just in time with her maid, she looked on helplessly as the fire destroyed all her possessions within five minutes.[7] At this point they had also lost the viceregal train as by one of those cruel quirks of protocol it had deserted them to pick up their successors arriving in Bombay. And yet for all that it was a triumphal progress, with celebrations in all the towns they passed through and huge crowds greeting them in Calcutta.[8]

From the first Dufferin had been enthralled by what he found on these journeys: a kaleidoscope of colours, fabrics, architecture and people, all on a large scale. Yet a speech on the eve of his departure, strikingly entitled 'What is India?', demonstrated how powerfully British[9] his perspective had remained:

> Again among these numerous communities may be found at one and the same moment all the various stages of civilisation through which mankind has passed from the pre-historic ages to the present day. At one end of the scale we have the naked savage Hillman with his stone weapons, his head-hunting, his polyandrous habits, and his childish superstitions; and at the other, the Europeanised native gentleman, with his refinement and polish, his literary culture, his Western philosophy, and his advanced political ideas; while between the two lie, layer upon layer, or in close juxtaposition, wandering communities, with their flocks of goats and moving tents; collections of undisciplined warriors with their blood feuds, the clan organisation and loose tribal government; feudal chiefs and barons, with their picturesque retainers, their seigneurial jurisdiction, and medieval modes of life; and modernised country gentlemen, and enterprising merchants and manufacturers, and with their well-managed estates and prosperous enterprise.[10]

This was an India straight out of the novels of Sir Walter Scott. As they set eyes on the palace at Benares overlooking the Ganges with the maharajah's retainers crowded on the walls above, Hariot freely admitted that they 'were carried back to Sir Walter Scott'. It was an India that was as much about Britain as it was about the subcontinent. With the aristocratic verities in Britain wilting under the challenge of industrialisation and democracy, Imperial India offered for many Anglo-Indians a 'timeless' and 'unchanging' world in which class and caste mutually reinforced one other.[11]

Hence the assiduous courting of the princes. Not only were they extremely rich and powerful, controlling for the Crown a third of the subcontinent, they were also the overt embodiment of hierarchy. Here lies the origins of the government's keenness to engage with the extravagant and ancient ritual of the durbar, which established at its apex the Empress of India. Many of the ceremonies may have been pure invention but Dufferin recognised the durbar's importance as the formal demonstration of British authority. Soon durbars were highly regulated: determining how large a gun salute would be and whether Dufferin would greet a maharajah from the dais or descend to meet him halfway. This mattered because, by reinforcing the hierarchy among princes, they reaffirmed British pre-eminence over all, and traditional authority over modern presumption.[12]

Queen Victoria's Jubilee provided another opportunity. After a 101-gun salute, Dufferin inspected a military parade by the garrison in Calcutta before attending service in the cathedral through streets bedecked in flags. Then, as befitting any ancient despot, there was the celebratory act of mercy with 22,000 prisoners being pardoned as well as the release of all debtors owing less than a hundred rupees.[13] Later that afternoon there was a great assembly with half a million people mustering on the Maidan 'where I received innumerable congratulatory addresses which poured in from one end of the country to the other'. The highlight of the event was a firework display 'far superior' to any seen before in India (with 5 tons of fireworks and costing 22,000 rupees), culminating in a dramatic outlining in fire of the Queen's profile followed by similar portrayals of the Prince and Princess of Wales and even of the Dufferins – 'I thought I never looked so well.' Calcutta remained en fête the next day with immense crowds gathering to see sports and the march-pasts of cavalry and carriages; the crowd 'cheered and clapped much more than usual', Hariot noted with evident relief. 'They do like a tamasha! Dufferin and I both got severe blows in the face from the very large and very wet bouquets thrown at us from the roofs of the houses.'[14]

Such displays undoubtedly fed Dufferin's vanity. He loved sitting on the throne of Tippu Sultan, in the robes of the Star of India, receiving maharajahs, and the great jewels they would bring. But he never lost sight of the role he had to play. At a durbar in Simla for the local hill chiefs, Hariot captures this exactly when she describes Dufferin as 'in red with all his collars on, smart enough to satisfy even the Oriental ideal'. It was in rigorous attendance to such minutiae that Dufferin made an impact.[15]

Another vital weapon in the imperial armoury was the deployment of honours. The two main ones were Commander of the Indian Empire (CIE) and the more prestigious Commander of the Star of India (CSI). Within these were gradations of knight commander, grand commander, even knight grand commander. Crucially these honours were also offered to Indians – binding them into one common hierarchy. These were very sought after, with the grandest princes, such as the maharajahs of Mysore, expecting elevation to GCSI in every generation.[16] As a keen collector of such prizes himself, Dufferin understood their appeal. Few things gave him more satisfaction that year than to hear that he was the only person outside the royal family to receive a gold Jubilee medal from the Queen.[17]

The risk of this philosophy was that it simply encouraged the forces of reaction. Many Anglo-Indians did succumb, as Ripon found out to his cost; so did some viceroys such as Lytton.[18] The image of an India of maharajahs and their loyal servants had the virtue of being very exportable – especially to Britain. Fast becoming a staple of popular literature and press, one of the key events in its promotion was the Indian and Colonial Exhibition in London in 1886. Among those enraptured was the 'Kaiser-i-Hind'. For the Queen among 'all these different races who own her sway . . . The Indians take the palm [for] the very devotional way in which they bend their heads to the ground and touch and kiss her feet'. 'Their immense reverence' would tempt her to visit the exhibition two or more times. Ever one to spot a promotional opportunity, the viceroy advised her on the virtues of Indian servants (to the consternation of the old guard at Windsor) and after the Queen was so taken with her Indian escort at the Jubilee procession, he arranged for a detachment to be garrisoned permanently with her.[19]

The glaring omission, of course, was those Indians who were not at the beck and call of landowners and princes, the educated elites in Bengal and around Bombay. Dufferin had no doubt of their ability or coming importance; and socially his relations with them were perfectly civil and respectful.[20] Yet his attitude to the native middle class was never what it seemed largely because he was rarely sure himself. Ilbert was appalled to find Simla delighted at Dufferin's appointment as 'he'll grind down the nigger'. But such thinking was genuinely abhorrent to the new viceroy. Especially loathsome was 'that intolerable and vulgar brutality which the strong English race always manifest towards more inferior and sensitive populations'.[21] Among the many reasons for Dufferin's despising of Griffin was his revelling in being seen as the 'Hammer of the babus'. On another level, however, Dufferin appeared to share the presumptions and language 'typical of many Victorian gentlemen'. Key to this is a belief in the superiority of British civilisation – politically, morally, and materially – over other societies at differing stages of development. Fashion determined that this was in part due to the British character; what in the language of the day was loosely referred to as the British race. Such generalisations were also found in his attitude to the Catholic Irish (as opposed to the Protestant Ulsterman), his discussion on various 'Scandinavian races' during his Arctic voyage and similar comments when cruising in the Mediterranean. But none of this is specifically racist: for Dufferin any inferiority was cultural and open to progress, not inherent in the blood and immutable.[22]

What is more, while Dufferin never lost his belief in progress and the civilising mission, he didn't subscribe to the idea of fast-tracking what had taken centuries in Britain. Hence the tentative offering of his Egyptian constitution. At the same time he would go out of his way to defend people who others were seeking to eliminate; be they the Druze facing Christian revenge or Native Americans from white settlers. He could also recognise superiority among supposedly inferior peoples: the noble savage such as the Druze, the aristocratic Indian chief, the American millionaire, Indian maharajahs. And when recalling the Amir of Afghanistan: 'The Amir is a rough diamond, but that must not be taken to refer to his manners, which are those of a most polished gentleman.'[23] Class was a much bigger determinant of Dufferin's response than race. And particularly so when the inferiors challenged the aristocratic order. Much of his racial tone was directed at the Bengal babus and by 3 February 1885 he was already admitting to Kimberley that 'the Bengalee Baboo is a most irritating and troublesome gentleman'. But primarily because they were challenging the hierarchy and no different except in scale from nihilists in Russia, communards in Paris or land leaguers in Ireland.

By contrast, 'the loathing felt by the middle-class Calcutta Englishman [for the native elite] is almost ludicrous' (i.e. for being racist).[24] Among the senior ICS, social contempt for such Anglo-Indian vulgarity was on a par to that felt towards the aspirational Bengali; indeed the real objection to the educated Bengali was less his race and more that he embodied the worst characteristics of the English middle class – pushy, legalistic, disrespectful and challenging. Few were as blunt as Primrose (who had been Ripon's private secretary and would join Gladstone's office in 1886): 'Speaking generally the attitude of Englishmen to natives is intolerably offensive and overbearing – but the manners of middle-class Englishmen are odious everywhere, and most of us out here are terribly middle-class. Nothing strikes me more in Indian society than the badness of the manners except perhaps the dullness of the people composing it. So much for the Anglo-Indians.'[25]

None of this altered what was taken as fact, that Indians were incapable of ruling themselves and that in being dedicated to the service of the teeming millions, the British were the 'true guardians of India'. As a result, Dufferin didn't engage in any serious way with the concerns of native elites other than to bolster the traditional and the loyal. So in 1885 he declared that he was 'anxious to give the Mahomedans a lift in the world [as they were] being crowded out by the nimble-minded Bengalees'.[26] Dufferin preferred to operate through the forces of British rather than Indian modernisation and manifested in the quiet hum of steady administration and technological advance, especially the railway.[27] In this regard, engineers were the foot soldiers of British India, the most striking symbol of the civilising mission being the bridges they built. In Dufferin's day the two most spectacular were the new cantilever railway bridge over the Hooghly connecting East Bengal with the rest of India and the Dufferin railway bridge (now the Malviya Bridge) across the Ganges at Benares. The latter he visited twice, not simply because it would bear his name, nor just for the thrill of an 'alarming walk on thin planks at an enormous height over the river', after which they drove in some rivets with a 'hydraulic driver' – 'the least touch does it'. But there among the engineers he toasted in the large tent by the river was F. T. G. Walton 'the son of my old School Master who is still alive'.[28]

Other than famine response, there is little sense of a mission to remedy the social ills and poverty that were omnipresent. Despite the promise in the 1858 Proclamation, there had been no improvement in overall standards of literacy, health or housing, as Florence Nightingale would remind Dufferin incessantly. 'Lord Dufferin', she reported to his predecessor in 1886, 'is not obstructive, he has allowed every one of my reforms to go on, but he has not forwarded them – he is a diplomat, not an administrator.' A later attempt following the Burma campaign to scrap the Sanitation Commission (on the reasonable grounds that it was expensive and ineffective) didn't stand a chance once Miss Nightingale had alerted the viceroy to her views. It was remarkable the extent to which viceroys and secretaries of state felt the need to bow the knee to her. To his credit Dufferin managed by July 1888 to draw up a wide-ranging reform through a system of Sanitary Boards which even the 'Governess of Governors' begrudgingly acknowledged as 'no doubt a great step forward', before querying the funding and the government's commitment to the scheme (as it turned out quite perceptively).[29]

'Before breakfast drove around the slums of Calcutta in order that I may see for myself the insanitary state of parts of the town' (aided by a 'little tablet of camphor to smell at as he passed through them') recorded Dufferin in his diary.[30] Few of his predecessors would have risked this. More likely than not, his presence reflected the compelling force of the woman sitting alongside him. For Hariot would take a very different approach to Indian society.

30

Hariot's Indians

If she have sent her servants in our pain,
　　If she have fought with Death and dulled his sword;
If she have given back our sick again,
　　And to the breast the weakling lips restored,
　　　　Is it a little thing that she has wrought?
　　　　Then Life and Death and Motherhood be nought.
　　　　　　Rudyard Kipling, 'The Song of the Women'

IN MANY OF her attitudes, the vicereine followed where the viceroy
led – not least an appreciation of Old India. Hariot's letters home
detailed exotic animals and plants, ruins lost in the undergrowth,
ancient castles and palaces peopled only by glamorous maharajahs and
their faithful retainers. 'I have often mentioned the Rajah of Bahawalpur,
but he is such a magnificent and ideal rajah that I must tell you again
about him', she recounted breathlessly to her mother:

> His dark-coloured face is handsome. He has straight features and fine
> eyes, a short black beard, and long black hair resting on his shoulders.
> In front of his gold embroidered cap he wore a most magnificent
> aigrette of European cut diamonds, round his waist a diamond belt,
> and round his neck about seven rows of splendid jewels, emeralds and
> pearls and rubies and pearls strung alternatively. His coat was velvet
> and gold, and the skirt of it stood out a little over large loose white
> trousers. I have also seen him in a beautiful sage green moiré coat
> embroidered in silver. He is really more barbarian than the others, but
> his taste for gorgeous display makes him as interesting as a rajah in the
> Arabian Nights!

Every year on their tour of the princely states she would be enthralled by the re-enactment of such childhood fantasies; myths which the princes with varying degrees of resentment would indulge their masters.[1] Yet for Hariot the essence of the true Orient lay in such spectacles.[2]

But if the India Hariot responded to was largely a myth sustained to mutual advantage by ritual and wealth, it mirrored to an extent the rituals that sustained British myths too. Viceregal life was constantly creating tableaux and imagery that not only reinforced British power but also a particular view of India and one in which the British had the role they wished to play. This meant accepting the constraints that came with being under constant surveillance. Both Dufferins were very conscious of how events would look and how to generate spectacle and convey message; of how, whether it was entering a room or a great durbar, they were actors on a stage.

Hariot was to take this further by her mastery of photography. She took lessons with Sir Benjamin Simpson and was no doubt also guided by Lala Deen Dayal, the official viceregal photographer; but she had taken pictures before in Canada and was by now experienced in the techniques of light and composition. This was a private indulgence – she would go out on her own very early in the Simla morning. For someone who was aware of being looked at for most of the day, it was a rare chance to be the anonymous observer. Her ambitions were entirely conventional – a sightseer trying to capture the experience of what she was incapable of putting into words, but undone all the same by the vastness of a primitive landscape and by the colour and diversity and energy all around her. That buildings predominate, such as the Royal Palace in Mandalay or the palace of Udaipur rising from the water, also reflects the limits of the medium; and her determination to use the instruments of modernity to try to capture an ancient order. In her portrait of the Maharajah of Jodhpur and his extended family in their historic robes, Hariot felt that she had 'passed over into a thoroughly Oriental world'. By photographing the traditional India of maharajahs, peasants, ancient ruins, viceregal life and imperial events, she was reinforcing an India of her imagination. Her photographs were less about capturing reality as making it. But for all that, there is a startling clarity in many of her pictures and a sense of overwhelming immobility and timelessness and the people adrift in it. Literally in a scene of the Ganges at Benares with 'the people still bathing in it' but also in a picture of a monolith of a sacred bull 'with his Brahmin priests' on top of a high hill at Mysore; and it's there too in the desolate landscape around the new fort at the Khyber Pass with a mosque at the foot of a hill nearby (and in the background her military escort, impatient to get moving).[3]

And yet surprisingly Hariot was to prove much more ready to engage with Indian society (admittedly, mainly at its highest levels) than the viceroy. True she had more freedom than her husband but more than that she had a genuine interest to understand the society around her. So while Dufferin struggled with Persian, Hariot learnt Hindustani and not simply to speak to her servants (some of whom spoke English anyway); rather, at the consecration of a 'native church', in Simla, she took pride in being able to follow some of the service. Her daughters proved even quicker learners. However, it was the plight of women that brought her face to face with Indian reality: a reality of child-brides, disowned widows, purdah and incarceration. At Udaipur she deplored that the women bricked up in the zenana in the palace were also denied the stunning view of the surrounding lake. Similarly at a firework display put on in their honour by the Maharajah of Holkar, Hariot was surrounded by the children 'chattering away and so happy. I wonder if they will remember this night when, after a few years of liberty, they come to be shut up in a zenana.'[4]

In Bombay, at a party given by the Governor's wife, she met a women who is 'rather a celebrity in India just now'; highly intelligent, she had gone to court to avoid marrying the husband she was betrothed to as a child. It would be a 'test case' involving 'a great principle', Hariot had written excitedly only in the end for nothing to change. A delegation led by respected figures such as Sir I. Madhara Rao on the question of reforming the Hindu practice of infant marriages alerted Dufferin to the difficulties of confronting cultural tradition. 'We might wait till Doomsday till the Bengalis educate their native women,' raged Kipling. 'Meanwhile they are rotting in the zenanas, for sheer want of medical attention.'[5]

All of which only made Hariot's achievements more remarkable.

Eschewing direct cultural assault, she raised funds to improve medical provision for women. Firstly by increasing the number of female doctors and nurses (in the interim from Europe) able to treat women in purdah; and by providing dispensaries and cottage hospitals with women only wards; and by developing modern medical education rather than leave women vulnerable to local customs. The origins of what became the Countess of Dufferin Fund lay in a request to Hariot from Queen Victoria, when the Dufferins were staying at Balmoral in October 1884 prior to departure. They were also bombarded by Florence Nightingale, who sent Dufferin her pamphlet, *An Indian Education*, to read on his journey out and would write to Hariot 'by almost every mail'. Yet Hariot was ambitious enough to want to do more, to make a real difference and, more remarkably, attempt to do it on a national scale. Not even the Queen had expected this. By now Hariot was a very capable organiser, able to think strategically and with the self-confidence to operate effectively in a male society. With Dufferin often away or deskbound, she was ready to dedicate her life to the cause.[6]

By August 1885 she had established the National Association for Supplying Female Medical Aid to the Women of India. It had a structure of provincial committees responsible to the central committee with its resources divided between a central fund and smaller local initiatives. Needless to say, she was the only woman on the central committee. Other members included two members of the Viceroy's Council and various other senior officials, but she chaired it, keen that meetings should be thoroughly 'business like', and insisting on Indian representation (one Hindu and one Muslim). She also bravely asserted that her organisation would be separate from the government (even if it was dominated by its senior figures). More controversially she declared that it would be secular, in case it alienated either of the two main religions in India. But this also meant excluding Christian missionaries already working in the field; and, in doing so, infuriating opinion back in Britain. This decision was entirely at the private behest of the Queen.[7]

What gave the project life was Hariot's impressive capacity as a fundraiser. She had actually raised the initial funds, including £100 from the Queen, before the inauguration of the National Association.

Quickly she mastered the 'various little devices for exhorting money without pain to the victim', describing one fete to the Queen at which 'people looked very happy while they were being fleeced'.[8] Even so, for the fund to succeed meant recruiting the aid of the princes, many of whose traditions had, after all, created the problem that the Association was trying to resolve. And the funds required would be far beyond the usual expectations of social charity work. Above all, she would need the courage to ask and press, and yet retain the dignity of the vicereine.

Undaunted she set about her targets with some gusto. Through a combination of 'a most baleful and malevolent glare due to [her] short sight', together with a forceful personality and a near shameless exploitation of her position, she dragged donations from maharajahs and the wealthy, eager to demonstrate their loyalty. She would willingly endure the rigours of three days travelling if she thought a donation would come from it. Equally she had a keen awareness of the value of a viceregal visit and the status it would bring her host, setting her 'price' in her later years at the building of a new hospital, which she would then gracefully agree to open in person. By 1886 she had raised £23,000 of which £12,000 was under control of the central committee. The Queen's Jubilee in 1887 provided a golden opportunity, and one which she exploited to the full. The Maharajah of Jaipur (who had previously donated R10,000) provided the break-through, choosing to celebrate with a further R100,000 – 'my first very big sum'. More importantly this engendered a degree of competitiveness. So on the morning of the Jubilee celebrations, the Maharajah of Alwar donated R50,000 and the Maharajah of Bikaneer another R10,000, dwarfing the more modest cheque for R500 the Marquess of Aberdeen slipped under her plate at breakfast. Other substantial gifts would follow as all who wanted the viceroy's favour recognised the need to support his wife's fund. And not just princes: even Thomas Cook & Son held a fete to raise money for the Lady Dufferin Fund.[9]

By Sept 1888, after only three years, she had raised R700,000 and £3,560 from the UK. Of this R550,000 was invested (in India) and the remainder spent on building grants and scholarships. This provided grants for hospitals in Agra and Lahore, places at 5 medical schools for 200 female Indian doctors and nurses, 27 small hospitals and dispensaries for women, and the distribution of Florence Nightingale's *The Way to Health* to schools in north and central India.[10] By establishing a London branch she intended to sustain pressure on future vicereines to keep it going. Yet inevitably without her, energies waned and the Association was more reliant on government funding and it came to be seen as part of the imperial armoury, with only token native representation. Still by 1914 the Association's facilities had treated 4 million women.

Nevertheless Hariot's scheme faced criticism from the beginning, especially from missionary societies in India and in Britain, furious that their medical services were refused aid and the decoupling of aid from promotion of the faith. Ironically, in the next century it came under similar criticism from the national independence movement as secularism was held to challenge the place of religion in Indian culture. Recently, the fiercest criticism has come from some historians, especially Maneesha Lal, who question the scale of the achievement in terms of the overall female population and the impact nationally in terms of promoting Western medicine and healing patients. Moreover in its complete rejection of traditional medicine, the Association only reinforced Western prejudices of race and gender, was socially exclusive, and little more than a tool for perpetuating the condescending myth of Queen Victoria's concern for India and its women.[11]

It is hard to disagree that, having claimed to be a national organisation, it had not delivered a comprehensive national solution. And no doubt more could have been done in terms of the quality of hospital care and training. And yet there is a need for some perspective, since even the emergence of a nation has not made any significant impact, with Indian maternal mortality rates among the highest in the world according to the WHO in 2000. It was still remarkable in nineteenth-century India to aspire to a national organisation for women at all. The use of Western nurses at the start was simply a reflection of a reality in which female Indians were only 5 per cent of school population and there were only six female graduates in 1881-2. These were not her prejudices, and yet in this highly sensitive context Hariot found a practical way to confront the treatment of women. Similarly her insistence on secularism (at major political cost to her movement in

Britain) reflected respect towards local religions, not the contrary. Nor was she indulging in a cultural assault on local tradition. She did not attack the zenana per se, much as she might have wished to.[12]

However, it didn't help that some of her greatest advocates did see her campaign in terms of purging ancient practices and the denial of 'obvious' (i.e. Western) public benefit. Revealingly, the poem that Dufferin considered 'the finest verses Kipling ever wrote' was 'For the Women' – a blistering critique of the male values in Indian society that tolerated high maternal mortality. And the greatest venom was reserved for those educated middle classes with an à la carte approach to Western liberal values. 'I am told', Dufferin wrote privately in a similar vein to Ponsonby, 'that the Bengalee Baboo is especially indifferent to the comfort or even the lives of the women who administer to his pleasures. One had only to look at his corpulent, greasy figure and sensual face to understand that in all probability he has not been calumniated.'[13]

On another level, the popularity of the scheme led some to attribute to it Machiavellian intent. It was not simply the preponderance of the viceregal elite on her committee. The issue divided Congress with the modernisers enthusiastically in support. At a time of retrenchment it enabled the government at little cost to be both detached and advanced on a key question of domestic reform. Thus the Association became a 'powerful weapon in Britain's defence of its position against nationalist criticisms'. Did Hariot see it in these terms? Of course it was impossible for anything a vicereine did to be seen as 'non-political'. None of this lessened the surprise and hurt she felt at the criticism for what only aspired to be, in true Ulster fashion, a practical solution to a humanitarian problem.[14] Perhaps she should have taken it as a measure of her success. It was a striking organisational achievement not only to set up the Countess of Dufferin Fund but also to fund so many hospitals in so short a time. That it could never provide a national solution simply reflects the scale of the subcontinent. And she had established a national agenda where before none existed.[15] To have set in train the treatment of 4 million women over twenty years is still a great achievement for a private woman, albeit a well-connected one.

And her commitment was genuine. She was opening hospitals up to the last days, including in November 1888 in Simla and again in Lahore on her final journey back to Calcutta. She continued to fundraise for this cause for the rest of her life. In recognition of this, on the final viceregal tour of 1888, it was Hariot who was showered with gifts and addresses in her honour, including one in Lahore signed by 25,000. In Calcutta Town Hall, it was her portrait that was hung – the only woman among serried ranks of past governors. In the last days at Government House a deputation of ladies from Bengal, Bihar and Orissa came to present her an address. Expecting only twenty or thirty, she was astonished to find 'the ladies came in crowds', almost 700 of them.[16]

Her work was also immortalised in poetry. To Edwin Arnold's Nautch girl, she was the 'White Angel'. More famously, she was the heroine of Kipling's 'The Song of the Women':

> How shall she know the worship we would do her?
>   The walls are high and she is very far.
> How shall the women's message reach unto her
>   Above the tumult of the packed bazaar?
>   Free wind of March, against the lattice blowing,
>   Bear thou our thanks lest she depart unknowing.

Few would have expected that this woman, so conventional in many ways, should become such an energetic force for modernisation, and initiate a reform where governments had feared to intervene. For one historian, the National Association was 'the centrepiece of colonial philanthropic work into the twentieth century'.[17] She was, Dufferin wrote to his son Terence, 'the real hero of our Indian life'. 'The memory of Lady Dufferin', he declared to a Belfast audience greeting his return, 'will still live and flourish after the very fact of my ever having set foot in the peninsula will have been forgotten.'[18] And so it proved. She herself celebrated the National Association's 50th anniversary in London in 1935 as the guest of honour at a reception held in the India Office when she was ninety-two. The organisation was only dissolved with the assets transferred to the Indian government in 1957; the Fund itself was not finally wound up until 2002.

The Fund, Kipling would later write, 'was the thing of the Century as far as women in India were concerned'.[19] It did not, however, herald the coming out of a feminist. Hariot would have been horrified at the suggestion. She believed firmly in the separate spheres and held that Parliament should be 'a wholly masculine institution'. But her work opened up a communality with 'our Indian sisters' that transcended (at least in spirit) race and class. And with it came a number of close Indian friends such as Sunity Devi, the Maharani of Cooch Behar. By 1888 when Dufferin held all-male dinners, Hariot would get herself invited to 'native dinners' – all women, of course; where on arrival she would be dressed by her hosts in a sari and would eat with her hands, sitting on the floor. That she enjoyed such occasions is plain from her journal and to a degree she felt liberated by the experience; sufficiently so, at least, to ignore the anonymous letter deploring her mixing with indigenous women.[20] This independence took other forms too as she went 'roughing it' for five days in the Himalayan foothills with only 'Hermie' (and her staff) for company. In many ways India had been the making of her.

But what had it made? One of the first viceregal women who 'pushed the boundaries, enlisted the collective powers of women's organisations, and established national projects' and in doing so changed the role, is one recent verdict.[21] She effectively promoted this definition of the role through her publication of *Our Viceregal Life in India* (1889) and reaffirmed it with subsequent volumes on her activities in Canada (1891) and Russia and Turkey (1916). In time she would establish a dynasty of such women. When Nelly's husband, Lord Novar, became Governor of Australia, his wife proved herself to be 'the quintessential imperial girl groomed to be a highly successful imperial woman'. Like her mother she established a major philanthropic organisation, the Australian Red Cross, which owed everything to her drive, financial acumen and connections. Unlike her mother she was also politically astute and wrote or corrected all her husband's speeches.[22] Her youngest sister, Victoria, also followed her mother's example by promoting female health after her husband became Governor in New Zealand.[23] Like their mother, they would prove to be far more than 'great ornamentals'.

31

Face to Face with the New India

I told the Turk he was a gentleman.
I told the Russian that his Tartar veins
Bled pure Parisian ichor; and he purred.
The Congress doesn't purr. I think it swears.
                Rudyard Kipling, 'One Viceroy Resigns'

BY THE SUMMER of 1886 disenchantment towards the viceroy among native educated elites was firmly entrenched. Where once his charm had kept hopes alive, now the Indian press saw an imperial militarism as 'conceived by the Satanic imagination of Lytton'.[1] In the tradition of British wars being paid for by Indian taxpayers, in 1887 the Burmese campaign and the new frontier defence costs compelled Dufferin to impose a new income tax and increase the salt tax by 25 per cent. But disillusion with Dufferin had begun earlier, with a matter that had barely registered in Britain but went right to the heart of her imperial creed.[2]

During the 1885 war scare, there had been a call for the mobilisation of the militias, which were set up in 1857 to meet the challenge of the Mutiny and then fell into disuse. Historically they had been drawn from Europeans and Eurasians. But there was nothing legally prohibiting Indians from volunteering, and in Madras a liberal officer recruited four, only to be immediately overruled by the military authorities. Consequently there was a widespread campaign urging the government to allow Indians to defend their own country. Initially appreciative of this display of loyalty, Dufferin was soon persuaded by his council and by Kimberley in London that this was 'a craze . . . artificially stimulated by the press and the wire-pullers out to create a Citizen Army to be used hereafter for political purposes'.[3]

With resolution of the frontier dispute the agitation soon died out. But to one historian, this controversy was 'Lord Dufferin's lost opportunity'. Volunteering in defence of their country could have been the supreme badge of citizenship within the Raj and its denial was held to demonstrate their exclusion from the future of British India; which would have major ramifications over the next sixty years.[4]

So too would be the demise of two early initiatives: the opening up of entry to the Indian Civil Service and a review of the constitutional relationship with London – both of which were speedily killed off in the India Office. Disillusioned by Dufferin's apparent inertia, the educated elites in December 1885 formed the Indian National Congress – an event of enormous significance, in time coming to symbolise the beginning of the end for British India. It would prove an organisation capable of winning independence in 1947 and then go on to dominate the government for the next fifty years. This was a pipe dream in 1885 when a national congress first met in Bombay. It could not claim to be national and its membership was primarily drawn from the educated elites, was resoundingly middle class (with lawyers making up 33 per cent) and almost entirely restricted to the major cities. More disturbing perhaps was a religious fault line, for Congress was predominately Hindu.

Unlike the Hindus, Muslims felt particularly excluded from the opportunities of the British Raj. The importance of a Western education and mastery of English as the administration became more bureaucratic was a significant obstacle. Economically, in Bengal, even where Muslims were in the majority, most of the land and commerce was in Hindu hands. Consequently Muslims withdrew support for Congress policies such as the opening up of the ICS as it would merely increase opportunities for Hindus to dominate Muslims. Likewise Muslim organisations would argue for reserved seats not democratic allocation in any legislative reform lest they became, as Sir Syed Ahmad Khan put it, 'like the Irish at Westminster'. Thus British rule was better than Hindu rule – especially under a viceroy looking to do 'something' for the Muslims.[5]

There were divisions too over the ultimate goal. The majority of the members of Congress were essentially anglophile, seeking merely a greater constitutional voice and more opportunity within the most modern, global superpower. Those seeking substantial home rule for Indians were few; those aspiring to national independence fewer still. If, as Kipling believed, the gulf between British and Indian culture was immeasurable, so too was it between the educated elites and the masses with the former abandoning reform in favouring of unity and custom only in the 1890s. By then both Hindus and Muslims felt a need for a 'cultural rearmament' against the flood of European ideas in the last quarter of the nineteenth century: a revival of ancient languages and literature and the stricter enforcement of traditional values and rituals.

Tactically Congress was restricted to a limited (but not wholly ineffective) strategy of lobbying in Calcutta and stirring in London for a greater say in Indian government; and by defending 'India's interests', to establish Congress's right to speak for India (not least in British eyes).[6] In this propaganda war, key elements were the support of former ICS men such as Sir Charles Wedderburn and Henry Cotton who later formed a branch of Congress in London. And Allan Octavian Hume: an able, fractious and arrogant Aberdonian and disciple of Mme Blavatsky, whose hectoring letters to the viceroy were laced a little by his resentment of promotion denied.[7] More important for Congress was the contribution of newspapers in advancing their ideas. Again the scale of the influence should not be exaggerated. Serving a population of over 200 million were 319 vernacular titles with a total circulation of 150,000 and 96 English language papers with circulation of 96,000. But if the numbers involved in national debates were tiny, their influence within the national elites was profound. They set the public debate and provoked the Anglo-Indian press in the process. Managing the press had always been a priority for Dufferin and he would have long conversations with Banerjee of the *Bengalee* or take time to reassure Grattan Geary, editor of the *Bombay Gazette*.[8] If Dufferin was less attentive to Congress it was perhaps because it was little more than an annual conference whose membership didn't match that of the Cow Protection Society. It was the Anglo-Indian press that could cause him the most difficulty. Nevertheless Dufferin was much more attuned to Indian opinion than some suggest.[9] 'Though [the educated] class is at present small and uninfluential', he warned Cross, 'it is both wise and right to count with it, and we must remember that it is above all things a growing power.'[10]

As to what it might grow into, Dufferin instinctively drew parallels with Irish Home Rulers: India in his eyes replicated the pre-revolutionary Ireland of the 1830s and what elsewhere had become the conflict of the masses against the classes.[11] To him the Bengali babu was like the Irish nationalist – in that both were notable for their 'perverseness, vivacity, and cunning'. The link was often made explicit with Irish MPs raising injustices in India in the House of Commons.[12]

On hearing of the first Congress gathering Dufferin's instinct was to keep his distance. Privately he may have thought a nationwide gathering would moderate Bengali influence. And it would be like him to want to institutionalise channels of popular protest.[13] But his perspective was transformed by news from London in December 1885 of the Hawarden Kite. From this distance in time it is hard to imagine the shock Gladstone's conversion to Home Rule caused among Liberals. Isolated in Calcutta, Dufferin could only look on. Nor, as his postbag filled with the expletives of his Whig friends, could he risk committing himself publicly. Even after the bill had been defeated and the Conservatives had joined with the Liberal Unionists to form a majority government in July, he remained guarded. But at a dance eight months later when Lady Annesley declared herself a Home Ruler, Dufferin was uncharacteristically sharp, telling her 'not to talk like a little fool'. And his daughter clearly knew his mind when she wrote: 'Weren't you glad to hear of Mr Blunt being popped into prison.'[14]

The result was that Dufferin's attitude hardened considerably. 'In India we are passing into a new phase', he wrote to Maine in May 1886, aware that what might be conceded in Ireland would raise the stakes in India. 'The Indian Home Rule movement' would not, he admitted, be a serious force 'for a long time to come . . . but for all that we must not be blind to what is passing around us, and what is in the air'.[15] He became increasingly anxious as 'day after day hundreds of sharp-witted Babus pour forth their indignation against their English oppressors in very pungent and effective diatribes' in the press. In March he had pondered with Kimberley as to 'how far an absolutely free Press . . . is compatible with our existing regime'.[16]

Determined not to let matters slide, in a series of letters to Kimberley between April and June 1886, Dufferin outlined a strategy that he largely adhered to (as far as he was allowed) for the remainder of his viceroyalty. Interestingly, his response was not repression of the press but rather administrative reform. After studying the programmes of Congress and the moderate British Indian Association, he suggested that the British 'give quickly and with good grace whatever may be possible' and make an agreement that should be 'a final settlement of the Indian system for the next 10 or 15 years'. If this appears naive, the substance of his programme was startling. To 'mitigate disappointment' over the aborted parliamentary inquiry, he proposed a Public Service Commission to review opportunities for Indians in both arms of the civil administration. More striking was his arguing that 'now we have educated these people, their desire to take a larger part in the management of their own domestic affairs seems to be a legitimate and reasonable aspiration, and I think there should be enough statesmanship amongst us to contrive the means of permitting them to do so without unduly compromising our Imperial supremacy'.[17] More precisely he called for 'a large admixture of elective natives into the Legislative Councils'. Given that the 'facts [in the press] are either invented or misrepresented', and the government has no organ of reply, he was minded to give the 'native party' a 'right of interpellation' within 'the reconstruction of the Supreme legislative and the Provincial Councils'. This would also provide the government with a chance to correct the 'hallucinations' and cease to be 'an isolated rock in the middle of a tempestuous sea'. The driving force behind this was as much practical as ideological:

> I cannot help asking myself how long an autocratic Government like that of India – and a Government which everyone will admit for many a long year to come must in its main features remain autocratic – will be able to stand the strain implied by the importation en bloc from England, or rather Ireland, of the perfected machinery of modern democratic agitation.[18]

His concern was not that an Indian Parnell was imminent but rather to prevent one emerging by guiding such sentiments into the politics of cooperation.[19]

Such a strategy was never going to make much headway amid the storm enveloping Westminster. Kimberley declared interpellation 'a serious innovation' which sealed its fate and with it the reform of the Legislative Councils. With Irish Home Rule causing convulsions in Parliament, no Liberal was going to open up the prospect of constitutional change in India and leave their party exposed to the charge of dismantling the empire. Similar fears affected the returning Tories, although Dufferin did press again for a broadening of the representation on the Legislative Councils. The best he could achieve was the concession of a Public Service Commission. Given the resistance to the reform of the ICS, its remit would be limited. Also conceded was an extension of the Legislative Council system to the North-West Provinces (alongside the councils already in Madras, Bengal and Bombay). For the moment devolving further powers to the Legislative Councils was condemned, from the perspective of Westminster, as sounding too much like the Indian for home rule.[20]

32

Counter-attack

> . . . If they rise
> Get guns, more guns, and lift the salt-tax . . . Oh!
> I told you what the Congress meant or thought?
> I'll answer nothing. Half a year will prove
> The full extent of time and thought you'll spare
> To Congress.
>
> Rudyard Kipling, 'One Viceroy Resigns'

HE MAY, FOR his Tory masters, have branded it a 'Home Rule Movement', but as late as December 1888 Dufferin viewed Congress as little more than 'a small Bengalee clique in Calcutta, whose organ was the *Indian Mirror* under S. N. Sen', and who were capable of little more than 'bastard disloyalty' – outwardly with a hatred of England but 'in their own secret hearts' no aspiration to independence or revolution.[1] But the viciousness of the denunciation hinted at private anxieties. And not without cause, for two developments had upped the ante.

Firstly the third Congress in Madras in December 1887 proved much more significant: not simply because of the numbers (604 delegates including 83 Muslims) but for the social range of the delegates and the involvement of many major towns. Dufferin was so concerned at the attendance of Sir Madhara Rao that he offered him a seat on the Supreme Legislative Council – only to be politely refused. Just as worrying was evidence of financial support from some princes, particularly the Maharajah of Mysore (which earned a private vice-regal rebuke).[2] Anxieties were not alleviated when the (euphemistically titled) Thugee and Dacoity Department, a branch of the intelligence service, set up to monitor Congress activity, began reporting a myriad of other political meetings the length and breadth of India.[3] In hindsight the challenge was greatly exaggerated; yet in 1888, even cool heads such as Colvin (recently appointed lieutenant governor of the North-West Provinces) were becoming rattled.

Then on 9 February 1888 came the announcement of Dufferin's retirement.[4] Fearful of becoming a lame duck ('everyone talks as if we are going tomorrow whereas we really have nine months more to stay') and with 'the papers still . . . exhaust[ing] themselves in imagining why we go', Dufferin had to recall the editors of the *Pioneer* and *Indian Daily News* to quell misreporting.[5] All this filtered back to Cross in Westminster who asked: 'these congresses or conferences, or whatever they call themselves. Will they grow or lessen? . . . Is it wise to take action in any way?'[6] Congress had now become the prime political consideration of the government in India.

Dufferin was deeply irritated by the nationalist press yet he recognised the legitimacy of their grievance and the extent to which their emergence was due to British policy. 'Under our auspices', as he reminded Cross, 'an educated class' was 'created' and it was only natural after twenty-five years 'they are beginning to take an interest in public affairs'. In a paper in August he made the same point more forcefully. While British India 'must remain a benevolent bureaucratic despotism for some time to come', 'the only way' to prevent 'the abuses inherent in all despotisms . . . is by the Government giving legitimate facilities to the educated classes to proffer their complaints and make known their wishes. The existing Councils do not afford these facilities.' Hence, while the press were 'villainous', there was no other outlet for free speech and he would 'not dream of docking in the slightest degree the right of the publicist to criticise . . . the words, acts or policy of the Government'.[7] Brave words and not really what the Tory Secretary of State wanted to hear, agitated as he was by the news that Charles Bradlaugh and other radical MPs were planning a fact-finding visit to India in 1889. But in Cross's anxiety, Dufferin was scenting an opportunity. That said, the difficulty of securing any reform is illustrated by the fate of the report of the 1886 Public Service Commission. Set up on Dufferin's initiative, its main recommendation (to increase the age limit from nineteen to twenty-three for entry into the ICS, so enabling Indians to compete on more equal terms) was delayed by London for six years. All that was conceded was the transfer of 108 posts from the ICS to a Provincial Civil Service where they would be open to Indians.[8] Not surprisingly, educated India was underwhelmed by these proposals.[9]

Instead Dufferin chose to wait until Congress overplayed its hand. In the meantime he courted the Muslims and the moderates within Congress in an effort to isolate the 'Home Rule section of the Bengal press'. He (despite later claims) did not seek to foment religious division, indeed he feared the consequences.[10] 'The diversity of races in India and the presence of a powerful Mahomedan community are undoubtedly circumstances favourable to our rule', he acknowledged to the proprietor of the *Pioneer*, 'but these circumstances we found and did not create . . . It would be a diabolical policy to exacerbate race hatreds.'[11]

By the autumn this strategy seemed to be bearing fruit as a Congress recruitment drive, led by Hume, in the Muslim heartlands in April 1888 backfired, provoking Sir Syed Ahmad Khan to form the United Indian Patriotic Association to defend Muslim interests. Fearful lest Congress's intrusion into his territory stir up sectarian violence, Colvin took Hume to task publicly. In a heated correspondence he declared that the educated elites of Congress were as alien in the North-West 'as an elephant would be out of his element in Scotch mists or a banyan tree in Parliament Street'.[12] Dufferin was quick to notice how these arguments put Congress on the back foot.

It is in the light of this that his resurrection of the idea of opening up the Provincial Legislative Councils with a greater, but 'not predominating', number of 'Native members' should be judged. Not only had educated India 'set their hearts' on this but it would reinforce the localism of Indian politics, providing a channel for most political activity and preventing in years to come the establishment of 'a Home Rule [i.e. national] organisation . . . on Irish lines under the patronage of Irish and radical Members of Parliament'. He had raised these ideas with Kimberley two years before and knew they were even less likely to appeal to his Tory masters who would never countenance any policy of popular devolution. Hence Dufferin could not have been more tentative in his raising of it, initially as an Indian desire and later as something he would have proposed 'if I had remained a year longer'.[13] Nothing in this correspondence would have led Cross to suspect that Dufferin intended to pursue such a course in any meaningful way. Even when in late August Dufferin wrote for clearance for a small and secret committee to explore the issues – more in the tone of preparing a briefing document for his successor – Cross insisted on 'great discretion' lest anyone might assume that this was policy.

In fact Dufferin had been preparing for another tilt at reforming the 'Indian Councils' as early as 11 February 1888 – barely two days after his retirement date was announced – when he sounded out friendly journalists on the matter. As for the committee, it had been set up months before permission had been requested.[14] Furthermore its personnel,[15] all advocates of Legislative Council reform, had by late October a striking plan to create bicameral councils with a mix of elected representatives on a property and income franchise, together with nominated members to ensure communal representation and government support; and with powers of interpellation and budgetary review. If the report was predictable, the way it was used was not. For, as Dufferin confided ('this is strictly between ourselves') to his friend, Lord Arthur Russell, 'before I leave . . . I shall hope to have framed a plan which will settle satisfactorily all the questions and difficulties raised by the native Home Rulers, if only it is applied with a little judgement, tact and firmness.'[16]

His strategy for dealing with Congress now depended on coupling a final denouncing of the movement's political pretensions with a constitutional reform that would deflate the agitation and relocate 'the centre of gravity of native political activity' in its 'legitimate home amongst the really responsible classes',[17] and so demonstrate that the initiative still lay with the British. For the denunciation he had a date in mind – 30 November when he was due to give the St Andrew's Day address at a dinner 'given by the Scotchmen of Calcutta'. Yet he knew that Cross and even more so Salisbury would refuse to let any proposal for reform of the Legislative Councils go forward.[18] With time running out, he resorted to deception. On 20 October, Dufferin forwarded the committee report, claiming that it was 'provisional' and hadn't yet been discussed by the Viceroy's Council. In fact by the end of the month he was spending his last days drawing up the recommendations to go as an official submission to the Secretary of State. Cross was startled when a month later he received a formal proposal from the Government of India 'for the liberalizing of the Provincial Councils'; and the opportunity in the Supreme Legislative Council for a debate on the annual budget (and not just new taxes) and the right to raise questions on domestic and not just imperial matters.[19] To make matters worse, such a proposal now required an official response from the India Office. That need not ensure it would become public. Instead, according to Lady Gwendolyn Cecil, Dufferin's minute 'had been illicitly made public'.[20] Who by was never ascertained, though plainly Dufferin was suspected.

In any case he left a considerable trail in his St Andrew's Day speech. Although he protested to Cross that he had made no reference to the proposal as he 'had no right to breathe a syllable which could in any way . . . commit the government at home or my successor to any policy . . . which might . . . prove impossible of fulfilment', short of announcing it, he could hardly have been more specific. After referring to his speech on the Queen's Golden Jubilee in 1887 when he expressed his desire for reform of the Legislative Councils, he went on: 'the more we enlarge the surface of our contact with the educated and intelligent public opinion in India, the better . . . we could with advantage draw more largely than we have hitherto done on native intelligence and native assistance in the discharge of our duties (Loud applause) . . . I have now submitted officially to the home authorities some personal suggestions in harmony with the foregoing views (Cheers).'[21] Cross and especially Salisbury were appalled at the folly of English ideas being applied to Indian government – and they later tried to repress Dufferin's minute. But in the event there was little they could do but prevaricate, as the radicals in Westminster and nationalists in India kept the issue live until 1892 when the legislation was passed for fear of worse should the Liberals win (as they did) the general election.[22] As for Dufferin, he was for a brief moment untouchable. Recently elevated to a marquessate, he had barely a week to go in India and, with his next posting to Rome already announced, his timing had been masterly. If further protection were needed, the very tenor and focus of his speech ensured that immediate attention was directed elsewhere.

For what caught the eye was an astonishing and lacerating attack on Congress.[23] Urged on by Colvin and Chesney, he brutally dismissed the pretensions to a 'democracy . . . which England herself has only reached . . . through the discipline of many centuries of preparation'. Since he had not heard such views 'seriously advocated by any native statesman of the slightest weight and importance . . . who and what are the persons who seek to assume those great powers – to tempt the fate of Phaeton and to sit in the chariot of the Sun?' Then he dismissed their claim to represent the people of India as 'groundless'. Amid a subcontinent of 200 million almost all 'still steeped in ignorance', the educated activists represented 'a microscopic minority' (a phrase that would sting for decades). Worse, he denied the very concept of national cohesion. Instead the continent was populated by 'a large number of distinct nationalities, professing various religions, practising diverse rites [and] speaking different languages'.[24] Along with the obvious fault line between Hindu and Muslim ('the most patent peculiarity of our India "cosmos"'), there were other distinct cultural communities: 'the Sikhs, with their warlike habits and traditions, and their theocratic enthusiasm; the Rohillas, the Pathans, the Assamese, the Biluchees, and other wild and martial types on our frontiers; the hillmen dwelling in the folds of the Himalayas; our subjects in Burma, Mongol in race and Buddhist in religion; the Khonds, Mairs, and Bheels, and other non-Aryan peoples in the centre and south of India; and the enterprising Parsees'.

Dufferin's purpose in emphasising the diversity was to re-emphasise British rule as the only force capable of providing the 'external, dispassionate, and immutable authority to weld . . . each separate element of empire into a peaceful, co-ordinated and harmonious whole'. Saving the best for last, he then openly chided Hume ('the principal secretary, I believe') and ridiculed his 'silly threat' that 'he and his Congress friends hold in their hands the keys not only of popular insurrection but of military revolt, even [though] . . . they do not intend for the present to put these keys into the locks'. In threatening this Hume had overplayed his hand, as Dufferin always suspected he would. For this was a threat that most of Congress neither desired to make nor had the means to implement. More to the point, it enabled Dufferin to portray Congress as a revolutionary movement. Together with the proposed reforms of the provincial civil service and Legislative Councils and appeals to moderates in India to 'be more largely associated with us in the conduct of the affairs of their country', this represented the culmination of a year long campaign to detach moderate, educated India from the more radical in Congress.

To Congress the assault was both a surprise and surprising in its deliberate offensiveness. Nothing over the previous three years had hinted that Dufferin had such opinions. Hume felt particularly aggrieved. 'After professing sympathy with the Congress', he fulminated to Ripon, Dufferin 'at the last moment, spat in our faces and bolted, because with all his accomplishments, with all his talents, – his lordship is an ass, and a weak and touchy ass to boot.' To Hume and his friends, Dufferin's speech was a taking of revenge, a timid and deceitful act by a flawed character, craving of popularity and wounded by the campaigns of papers such as N. N. Sen's *Indian Mirror*, which Dufferin did regard as 'cleverly-conducted but vicious'. There is more than a hint in the speech of Dufferin indulging himself.[25]

And yet, if he craved popularity, it made no sense abusing Congress so publicly barely weeks before his departure.[26] His proposals were not last-minute gestures to give a liberal hue to a regime steeped in military conquest, for he had been pushing these ideas for over three years. From the outbreak of the Home Rule controversy in December 1885, the challenge of popular participation to imperial authority became the touchstone against which all colonial initiatives would be measured by Tory governments. That Dufferin should persevere with his schemes for increasing Indian participation, however slight, spoke of his intent. That he advanced them in the way he did told of his astuteness, in terms of timing and manner of approach. Put simply, if his imminent departure meant that he couldn't be sacked, his criticism of the nationalists had also made it harder for Tories and Anglo-India to condemn the liberal commitments given in the speech. And, of course, as with his constitutional proposals for Egypt, he had form with such tactics.

With faux-innocence, Dufferin hoped his speech would 'clear the atmosphere and render [his successor Lord] Lansdowne's position easier and pleasanter'. In fact he had by bringing such proposals into the open set the agenda for his successor. However much they prevaricated, Salisbury's government had to concede eventually. In truth these were relatively minor reforms in terms of the impact they had. Their significance lay in the principle that they set. Reminiscing forty years later, Banerjee pondered that:

> It is curious that Lord Dufferin, who encouraged the idea of an Indian National Congress and sympathised with its aspirations at the outset, should have, before he lay down the reins of office, described the educated community as a 'microscopic minority'. Indeed while he was condemning the Indian National Congress at the St Andrew's Dinner in Calcutta, he was writing a secret despatch supporting its recommendations for the reform of the Councils. Strange are the ways of statesmanship. Nevertheless we can forget and forgive much in the case of a Viceroy who first recommended a scheme for the reconstitution of the Legislative Councils upon a popular basis. His confidential despatch, which I was the first to publish in the *Bengalee* in March 1889, formed the basis of the Parliamentary Statute of 1892.[27]

As with any good editor, he knew how to look after his sources.

33

Conclusion

Kipling's Viceroy?

I'm old. I followed Power to the last,
Gave her my best, and Power followed Me.
It's worth it – on my soul I'm speaking plain,
Here by the claret glasses! – worth it all.
I gave – no matter what I gave – I win.
I *know* I win. Mine's work, good work that lives!
A country twice the size of France – the North
Safeguarded. That is my record: sink the rest
And better if you can . . .
I envy you the twenty years you've gained,
But not the five to follow. What's that? One!
Two! – Surely not so late. Good–night. *Don't* dream.

Rudyard Kipling, 'One Viceroy Resigns'

IT WAS AND remains a seductive conceit. In 'One Viceroy Resigns' Kipling portrays Dufferin in his cups: bored, lazy, cynical and keen to be off as at the last he shares his experiences with his successor. A vivid and clever portrayal, it provided an image so striking that it has prevailed ever since in the minds of contemporaries and later historians alike. Needless to say it bore little resemblance to Lansdowne's memories of their actual debrief ('Nothing could have been kinder or more thoughtful than he has been and I have really learned a great deal from him in a very short time'.)[1] More to the point, as Harold Nicolson would later protest, it is wholly unlike Dufferin in tone and manner; and its views were Kipling's not the viceroy's. In spite of his

St Andrew's Day speech, Dufferin was not hostile towards Congress in principle – unlike Kipling who deplored Dufferin's sympathies. Nor would Dufferin have limited his achievement to border defence and the conquest of Burma. Defusing the political crisis he inherited and setting an agenda for emerging India, which reflected his faith in liberal evolution and specifically Legislative Council reform – these mattered as much to him. The manoeuvrings during his last year were plainly incompatible with someone who 'followed Power to the last'. As for the oath by the 'claret glasses', this was just an Irish stereotype; for by now Dufferin drank very little if at all. If anything, 'One Viceroy Resigns' depicts the viceroy Kipling always dreamt of being.[2]

Yet Nicolson also picked up on a sense of disappointment; that somehow Dufferin's career had not lived up to cherished hopes. There were some obvious frustrations. All Dufferin's previous roles had been hands on, even in Canada. By contrast in India the scale of the responsibilities, together with greater interference from London, meant that the viceroy's role became far more constitutional and monarchical. Even Dufferin could have his fill of a stiflingly formal society. 'It is an odd thing to say,' he admitted to a friend, 'but dullness is certainly the characteristic of an Indian Viceroy's existence. All the people who surround him are younger than himself; he has no companions or playfellows; and even the pretty women, who might condescend to cheer him, it is better for him to keep at a distance.'[3] If the major crises or challenges brought out the best in him, the routine work began to irritate.[4] Equally wearing was the incessant pressure of governing such a vast continent of 300 million people, even if, as Wallace insisted, Dufferin could 'throw off his cares . . . as easily as he does his great coat. Nor is he ever worried or made fidgety by heavy responsibilities.' And yet, appearances aside, two and a half years into the post, he was confiding to Granville that he still felt 'like a man riding a very dangerous steeplechase'. While so far he had 'scraped through', he feared coming a 'cropper' at any time, so much so that 'one feels that there can be neither rest nor peace nor breathing time until one has got safe past the winning post at the end of my five years'.[5] Such insecurity often took contemporaries by surprise, especially when to Granville Dufferin appeared to be 'winning hands down'.

Yet these anxieties must not be exaggerated. There is certainly no evidence of morale being low in September 1887 when he gave warning of his intention to resign in a year's time. In the year that followed he proved anything but a lame duck, with the result that he felt able to look back on his efforts with pride. Writing to Cross on the eve of his departure, he judged: 'There is not a cloud on the horizon, and we have succeeded in all our undertaking.'[6]

On the other hand, Dufferin's own explanation for his early resignation – a desire to be near his children 'in order to start them on their respective careers'[7] – appears entirely plausible. They were a close family, with both parents feeling the absence of their children keenly. It cannot have been a coincidence that the months prior to the decision to resign were dominated by emotional turmoil over their eldest daughter.[8] In any case, at sixty-two Dufferin was older than any previous viceroy and, although both of them managed the climate, Hariot was suffering from the cold weather and draughty palaces to the extent that Dufferin tried to persuade her home in the winter of 1887–8. As early as May 1886 the relentlessness was beginning to take its toll on him too: 'The Viceroy never gets a holiday', he railed in his diary after the Jubilee celebrations.[9]

As ever with Dufferin there was a political dimension. As the seismic nature of the Home Rule crisis became clear, Dufferin knew he couldn't afford to stay too detached. 'I personally rejoice at the result', he wrote of Gladstone's defeat to an English friend; claiming that had he still been in Parliament he would have resigned the Liberal whip – brave words, though of course cheaply spoken. Always conscious of all Gladstone had done for him, he nevertheless acknowledged that 'I have hardly ever conversed with him [about Ireland] that I have not felt my face burn with irritation when I left his presence.' As viceroy he didn't have to choose sides but with the virulence of party feeling, could he rely on the Conservatives for future employment if he stayed on the fence? For Dufferin simply could not afford to retire.[10] Needing to get another post, it was best to act while his school friend, Salisbury, was still prime minister. Had he heard that Rome might be coming available? He certainly mentioned in his letter to Salisbury that Rome and Italy was an attractive post and also 'the land of my birth'. This might explain why he gave notice so far (fourteen months) in advance of his departure. As it was, few viceroys served the full term and four years was quite standard. But to announce it after barely three years was bound to spark rumours (as it did) and made no sense other than to seal the deal. Even so, he still felt the need to ask Salisbury to make clear that there had been 'no difference with the Government' or that he had 'lost your confidence'.[11]

Such angst only reinforces the impression of his obsession with reputation that is so pronounced in Kipling's portrayal. Where Kipling led, others followed. W. S. Blunt, never a generous critic, deemed Dufferin 'a farceur' but one who would prove 'a successful viceroy' – but only in the sense in which an actor milks the applause of his audience.[12] It was a theme that would never quite go away: 'I do not believe he has been in any single place of responsibility and authority in which he did not more or less purchase popularity by leaving to his successors unpleasant legacies', was one cabinet minister, Lord George Hamilton's startling verdict.[13] An odd assessment of someone who had not allowed three years of personal abuse in the native press to deflect him – no matter how much it had riled him. Admittedly his public standing in India mattered far less than his reputation in England. 'This much is certain', Churchill assured him, 'that you can do more with the British public than any Viceroy has been able to do since the days of Lord Lawrence.'[14] Dufferin never felt that secure in his popularity but it did explain why Salisbury, Churchill and the Queen made his retention a condition of taking office. Moreover for the Queen he remained one of her more important confidants, whether on European diplomacy, Irish Home Rule or the merits of Indians as servants.[15]

Even so, Dufferin couldn't ignore his image. Public opinion in High Victorian England held that in background, career, looks and manner, he represented the perfect ideal for an imperial proconsul. And with his appointment there was the added frisson of a glamorous role being filled by a glamorous figure. Just as he was trapped by the image he had evolved over thirty years, so was he dependent on it. Few viceroys would have survived so easily a military campaign that after three years was ten times over budget and, bedevilled by a guerrilla campaign, was still not under control; resulting in increased taxes for Indians, who were now in cahoots with radicals in London. So while Dufferin's vanity was beating strongly under the surface, the management of reputation mattered if the viceroy was to have any leverage in London and India.

None of this would protect Dufferin from the perception that lingered of his having 'a touch of Oriental flashiness'. For all his potential to be one of the greatest viceroys, his 'chief failing was his indolence' was the verdict of one authority. He was felt to have delegated often where he shouldn't have, rarely worked after dinner, and spent too much time revelling in the round of receptions, dinners, balls and durbars that most serious viceroys despised.[16] 'No wonder he knows so little when he never talks to a man', bitched Colvin to Lady Gregory as the viceroy led off the quadrille at a Calcutta ball; 'watch him and you will never see him do so'. When later accused of being too grand, Curzon would protest that he was only following the protocols established by Dufferin; except that he did not take 'pretty widows into corners as Lord Dufferin did or slip [his] arm around their waists and call them pretty dears'.[17] Thus the viceregal court appeared little more than a circus designed primarily to feed the voracious vanity of the viceroy – 'The Great Ornamental' – as he sat 'enthroned under a canopy of State surrounded by scarlet-clad attendants bearing the peacock fans and other symbols of royalty'. His crime lay in relishing too obviously the theatre and the trappings. This made it too easy for such indulgence to be seen as the mark of the career diplomat, ready to enjoy the opportunities of high office and not inclined to risk their loss by rocking boats.[18] Typically, in October 1888, as he was accepting his new post from Salisbury, he was writing to Gladstone congratulating him on his golden wedding anniversary and inviting him to Rome. No wonder that Mark Bence-Jones suspected that there was 'something a little calculating about him'.[19]

Perhaps there had to be. With four changes in government in London during Dufferin's four years in India, the arts of political survival would be critical. And yes, he needed the money. But then so did most of his successors; not least the Lansdownes who managed to save £20,000 in four years. And there lay the difference. For Dufferin never took money seriously enough to be guided by it, preferring instead a position of extravagant ignorance. He was certainly ambitious; but for the responsibility and not just the rewards. If his position necessitated occasional pragmatism, he was nonetheless no government lackey, as Churchill and Cross both discovered. Six years on and Churchill was still bemoaning that he had got 'no help from Lord Dufferin', who was never going to be the fall guy for Westminster politicians on the make.[20] At the same time he recognised that a viceroy had to work more closely with the government in Westminster. This wasn't weakness but wisdom. And in the midst of this enormously complicated, often hostile situation, it was he who set the British strategy on defence and, politically, on Congress and more generally on London–Calcutta relations for the next thirty years. In this regard Curzon was to be the exception that proved the rule.

Still that didn't stop Churchill, admittedly bristling at his own demise, condemning Dufferin's viceroyalty as 'a great failure, a time of inaction and indecision and stagnation when the opposite elements were essential'. The issue is less the hypocrisy of one whose narrow electoral preoccupations did so much to sabotage Dufferin's room for manoeuvre, but rather the charge of administrative incompetence. In Bence-Jones's damning judgement, 'The work of ruling India was beyond him.'[21] Certainly, Dufferin was not a natural administrator and, unlike Canada, in India he found himself at the head of a government. It didn't help that it was 'an inveterate habit of my mind never to allow any opinion upon any subject to crystallise until it becomes necessary to arrive at a practical decision'. Nor did he relish the day-to-day management of business. 'It is the greatest grind I have ever experienced', he complained once to the Secretary of State.[22] In general, where he could, he delegated and thus a reputation for idleness was born.

But those who worked under him saw his 'method' in a much more positive light. 'By far the best Viceroy I have ever seen . . . A Viceroy who is as bold and resolute as he is patient and courteous', was Durand's verdict. It is facile to dismiss such judgements as what you would expect from officials given a free hand and especially by one appointed Foreign Secretary at only thirty-five. Yet it was a near universal opinion among his staff. To Dufferin it was folly to immerse oneself in the detail to the extent that initiative was killed off. By trusting in his experts he would be free to tackle major issues and keep an eye on government strategy. Nor, on the drawing up of policy did his staff doubt his energy and commitment. Such an approach depended on the quality of his colleagues and Dufferin was 'a very shrewd judge of character with "an almost uncanny flair for [spotting] anything like insincerity or weakness"'. Mackenzie Wallace's experience he had long valued. But it was typical of Dufferin that he appointed to the Viceroy's Council, Anthony MacDonnell, a fellow Irishman whose views on tenant rights and Home Rule he abhorred but whose abilities were clear.[23] Determined not to let the charge – in the *St James's Gazette* – stick that he was not 'the absolute master of my own house', Dufferin mobilised Lyall to write a telling rebuttal in the *Edinburgh Review*, which with Mackenzie Wallace's official history of his viceroyalty and Hariot's extremely popular *Our Viceregal Life* restored the record.[24]

Nor should the endless social round be seen as leisure. Those viceroys who found it wearisome became progressively (and in the case of Ripon fatally) isolated. For all the Dufferins' enjoyment of these events, it is easy to ignore the professionalism that went into them. In making duty appear fun Dufferin was playing to his strengths as a diplomat: reassuring and steering opinion by saying the right thing, making the correct gesture, above all making it personal. No one did it better (as opposed to bigger) than the Dufferins.

Ultimately the measure of an executive lies in the achievement of its goals. In a letter to Salisbury of 1888, Dufferin reviewed his administration. In addition to the successful defence and expansion of empire in 1884–5, which he claimed 'has been the chief object of my solicitude since I came to this country', all the new frontier railways were in place, the army increased, the Reserve 'initiated', and the most vulnerable part of the North-West Frontier 'rendered inexpungible'.[25] The benefits of such investment would never be put to the test. But a possible European war had been avoided and India was more secure that it had ever been. Burma, he claimed, was now 'thoroughly subdued' and, while robberies will continue 'for many a long day', 'there is no longer a shadow of resistance'. On internal security he had established an Intelligence Department for the whole of India. He took pride in establishing two commissions on retrenchment and also on the Civil Service which have 'thoroughly eviscerated these

'The Great Ornamental':
Dufferin, the new viceroy

The viceroy and his councillors

'You've seen your Council? Yes they'll try to rule,
And prize their Reputations.'

Rudyard Kipling, 'One Viceroy Resigns'

Dufferin with the Amir of Afghanistan at Rawalpindi, 1885.
'Unfortunately we are dealing with savages'

Thibaw and Supayalat of Burma. According to Hariot, 'Like a queen [out] of ancient history, she was a very violent and passionate woman, governed entirely by impulse and caprice . . . if she liked you, she loved you; if she hated you, she killed you'

'In the afternoon we made a charming expedition to see the great bell at Mengdoon, which is only second in size to the Moscow bell . . . All the Special Reporters went with us'

Dufferin 'duly photographed in a triumphant attitude with my tiger'

The new Viceregal Lodge in Simla. 'The first truly modern Government House', and one that Dufferin claimed was 'beautiful, comfortable, convenient [and] not too big'. Mary Curzon later dismissed it as 'a home a Minneapolis millionaire would revel in'

Hariot's 'Splendid Arch': Lord Ava. He was much admired by his parents for his dashing good looks, but his debts and failure to marry would mean there was always much 'anxiety over Archie'

Nelly Blackwood. 'Not only are you very like my mother in your looks and expression,' wrote Dufferin of his eldest daughter, 'but every day you are becoming more like her in mind'

Dufferin picnicking at Simla

Taking up hunting again in Rome in his sixties, Dufferin felt 'five and twenty'

Sailing at Cowes: 'the exultation one experiences . . . is almost maddening'

'Honours accumulate on him'. This portrait by Troubetzkoy was commissioned on Dufferin's appointment as Warden of the Cinque Ports

Dufferin being painted in the studio of Henrietta Rae

Ulster hero: in addition to the Rae portrait hanging in Belfast City Hall, outside in the grounds stands a statue of Dufferin in all his imperial pomp

'Above the mantelpiece in the library at Clandeboye there hangs a portrait of Richard Brinsley Sheridan. It is a cautious picture.' Harold Nicolson on the painting by Richard Morton Paye

The Outer Hall at Clandeboye in 1900 with the statue of Amun visible at the top of the stairs

Tennyson's 'beautiful lines on Helen's Tower will render my mother's name and my own immortal long after the memory of anything that we have been or done has been swallowed in oblivion'

The christening of Sheridan, the 5th and last Marquess of Dufferin and Ava. Nelly (Lady Novar) stands at the left; her sister Hermione stands far right. Maureen and Basil sit with their children at the front. Missing is Brenda (wife of the 3rd Marquess) who had just attempted to dash out the baby's brains in order to exorcise the 'bad Sheridan blood'

important subjects'. He enacted three land acts for Bengal ('a gigantic Land Bill'), Oudh and Punjab with provisions to protect tenants over rent, tenure and compensation for improvements. In the North-West Provinces he introduced a university and a Legislative Council; and did 'a good deal' for Muslims, including protecting their 'pilgrim traffic'. Relations with 'all' the native states were 'very friendly' and the native press 'more reasonable and less abusive' – 'all the more creditable' in Dufferin's eyes as he twice had to add to the taxation system. As for the Indian finances, most of the problems came from policies initiated in London in the safe knowledge that they would be paid for in India. In the circumstances Dufferin did well by 1888 to reduce the annual deficit to just under R700,000 by increasing the revenue stream by R4.7 million. Hariot's hospitals would leave a remarkable and lasting legacy. Finally the 'animosity' between Anglo-Indians and 'advanced natives', the defusing of which had been his primary objective, has 'considerably calmed down'.[26]

The modesty of the last point aside, this résumé did not lack for gloss. Still, for all that, he deemed it 'not a very brilliant record', a 'sensational policy' was never his 'ambition'. Sent out to restore the equilibrium of British rule and thereafter drive India 'at a low and steady pressure', he could, as he expressed it to Salisbury, 'come home with a clear conscience'. More than that, he had set the strategic policy in two key areas for the rest of the century: in defence with the restraint of the Forward School;[27] and politically with the challenge of Congress met not by outright resistance but by the involvement of Indians in the Legislative Councils.[28] Yet for all this, his reputation, once the paeans of earlier hagiographers had died away, was of a viceroy who, in the words of the renowned Indian historian Sarvepalli Gopal, passed like 'a pale shadow' over India; who compared to Canning, Mayo and Ripon, 'did little more than track a minor orbit in the order of the vice-regal universe'.[29] Later observers were to accuse him of being guilty of throwing away two opportunities; turning points where British India failed to turn. Firstly, both over the volunteering question and later with Congress, Dufferin had a rare opportunity to integrate the forces of the New India into the British state and set in train its evolution into a self-governing nation within the British Empire. But he baulked at the task and by the time John

Morley finally extended the elective principle to the Legislative Councils in 1909, it was twenty years too late and the radical wing of Congress had reverted to terrorism.[30] Yet this ignores both his room for manoeuvre and the reality of Congress, for it was not until the 1920s that Congress was ever a mass movement on any significant scale.[31] In fact Congress was hampered by its very elitism and by the deep reluctance of most of its adherents to risk posing a genuine threat to British administration, in case it also endangered their primacy within Indian society. In effect its leaders were 'boxed in'. Dufferin's opening up of the prospect of reform and greater involvement in the Civilian Raj, made this fate palatable, even desirable to the leadership.[32]

In any case Dufferin's approach towards Congress had to be largely determined by the wider needs of the empire, rather than the desires of a minority in India.[33] His Councils proposal, while possibly opening the way for representative government, was primarily aimed at the improvement of the British system and involved drawing on native expertise without any significant concession of power. That independence came within sixty years of Dufferin's departure would have surprised him but so would the two world wars that revolutionised the situation. This, after all, was precisely the kind of catastrophe that he had successfully worked to avoid at Penjdeh.

As befitted the man, Curzon's charge was on a far grander scale. To him, the crime was a failure of imperial imagination; for the chance existed since the 1880s for Britain to secure not simply its position within the subcontinent but also, through India, to expand her influence throughout the East. Never one to understate matters, he held that in 'The Empire of Hindustan' lay geopolitical opportunities – by constraining Russia (from the Persian Gulf as much as India) and opening up opportunities in China and the Far East – for 'the mastery of the world' to be 'in the possession of the British people'. Opportunities that were 'systematically shirked by every Viceroy for 30 years'. Among these, Dufferin found himself damned by faint praise: his viceroyalty being a 'monument to the saving grace of tact'.[34] Not for Curzon 'low and steady pressure'. In an impressive display of executive zeal he carried through twenty-four major reforms in seven years, as well as encouraging major investment in infrastructure projects.[35] Compared to this Dufferin appeared very idle. Yet in contrast to this programme of modernisation, socially Curzon proposed a revolution of spectacular reaction, famously hailing the princes at the Dehli Durbar in 1903 as 'colleagues and partners'.

If Dufferin failed to imagine such possibilities, it is because he would have strongly disapproved of much of this programme. For all his love of Romance he was no reactionary. Almost immediately, strategic domination of the East seemed wholly fanciful in the wake of the Boer War. Within ten years very little of Curzon's perspective or his initiatives had survived. And ironically in 1917 it would be Curzon who would have to draft the declaration promising India self-government. 'A delightful literary humbug', was George Hamilton's snide judgement, 'he [Dufferin] has never long held any post in which he has not more or less been found out'.[36] Well, if so, it was not the case in India.

On arriving in Calcutta, the Lansdownes were surrounded by military escorts, bands playing and guards of honour. At Government House they discovered Dufferin at the top of the steps ready to greet his successor. Lansdowne found such solemn theatricality faintly comic but had the good manners not to let it show. Nor did his wife who comforted Dufferin as he led her inside with recollections of how, when she was a child at Baronscourt, he 'used to race [her] up and down the stairs, she sitting on my neck'.[37] Determined to play the role to the last, Dufferin delayed swearing in the new viceroy until his own point of departure. The ceremony complete, the Dufferins endured the 'inevitable historic group photograph'; and since Lansdowne was now viceroy, 'we took lower places at once'. After which, they made their way 'almost in tears' down the steps amid their cheering staff to the carriages waiting to set them on their way to England. For all his anxiety, Dufferin was rewarded with 'a most enthusiastic leave taking, the streets being lined with troops and all the windows and balconies crowded with people'. Then two days by train to Bombay where, he reported to his son, they 'had a splendid reception. It was like the old Canadian days . . . never been so much cheered in my life, which is saying a good deal.'[38] He was also chuffed by the decision by the Calcutta Corporation to erect a statue of him: 'an honour', as he told his son, 'conferred on a Viceroy who has given satisfaction'.[39]

Back in London even his critics accepted that he had fulfilled his brief: as Curzon later acknowledged, 'no other man could have so soon or so triumphantly smoothed the ruffled surface of Indian life. [For] as Lord Northbrook wrote to me, when Dufferin died: "I almost think the greatest of the many services he rendered to his country was the quiet way in which he managed to restore the confidence between the Indian Civil Service and the Government of India, which had been seriously shaken at the end of Ripon's administration – and Dufferin did this without crowing over Ripon."' Interestingly Kipling too would later reconsider his assessment. Visiting Dufferin (who was 'kindness itself') in Sorrento in October 1890, Kipling was entranced as Dufferin, 'sliding into a reverie', spoke on his work in India: 'I had seen administrative machinery from beneath, all stripped and overheated. This was the first time I had listened to one who handled it from above. And unlike the generality of Viceroys, Lord Dufferin *knew*.'[40] 'Dufferin . . . has not backbone enough for such a post', Kimberley had recorded in his journal when Dufferin was first considered for the role of viceroy in 1872. Such fears had also been raised as the cabinet deliberated his appointment in 1884. In the margin of the journal, however, lies a later annotation (dated 22 February 1892) which simply reads: 'we were quite wrong in thinking this. K.'[41]

PART IV

Making it Up, 1889–1902

34

Roman Holiday

DUFFERIN ARRIVED IN Rome in need of a quiet sojourn in a diplomatic backwater.[1] Only to find the city in late December bone-chillingly cold.[2] Within a week Hariot had left for London and Dufferin was confined to his bed with a chill. Yet when the weather lifted he appreciated the delightful garden and the embassy's position by the Porta Pia which, opening directly onto the Campagna, enabled him to gallop his hunters almost to his front door. Soon he was at the theatre to hear Sarah Bernhardt and where, during the interval, he would go 'from box to box like a gay young fop'[3].

As he had hoped, in Rome the diplomatic demands were slight.[4] While an insignificant power, Italy was not without significant pretensions, wanting to acquire the imperial trappings of a Great Power. Embodying this ambition was the prime minster, Crispi. A Garibaldian revolutionary turned establishment autocrat: 'His conspirator's temper . . . leads him to political gambling [and makes him] a danger to world peace', Salisbury had warned. The Italian threat to Britain (in hindsight little more than an irritant) lay to her Egyptian interests and particularly to Abyssinia and Sudan. Having to take Italian posturing seriously was always going to be wearing. Salisbury suffered particularly ('Crispi reproaches me like a neglected lover'). Eventually a protocol was signed in March 1891 which would last, thanks largely to the Italians' humiliation at Adowa (1896), until 1935.[5]

This was easy work, made easier by Dufferin's international standing. The change from viceroy to ambassador (and from subcontinent to peripheral peninsula) represented a sharp diminution in power and status. Yet Dufferin was 'delighted with my post beyond measure'. Along with regular evenings at the theatre and opera, afternoons were spent exploring the chapels and galleries within the Vatican. Unable to resist the temptation, Dufferin was soon buying pictures to adorn Clandeboye, spending £500 in one afternoon. And when all else failed, he could happily 'pass . . . an hour in arranging my collection of miniatures of Native Indian Princes'.[6]

Yet such sedentary activities could never fit the energies released after four years in the spotlight in India. Free from these strains Dufferin was a man rejuvenated. Taking up hunting again after thirty years made him feel 'five and twenty'. For one supposedly so cautious, he had little fear of physical danger; his determination to keep up with the hounds was almost frenetic. Nor was this restricted to horses: 'I have taken to bicycling violently'. None of these activities could match the exhilaration of sailing. Every summer he would decamp to Sorrento and spend months sailing among 'the lovely islands' on his latest boat, *The Lady Hermione*. Refitted before being sailed out to him in Naples, she was a decked boat with a well into which the ropes were led and attached to all sorts of levers, tackles and winches, to enable her to be sailed single-handedly. Thus equipped and being 'at this moment deep in Homer', he struck out into an imaginary Mediterranean of the Classical past where 'as you look across the harbour' (at Syracuse), 'it seems filled with shining triremes, the splash of oars and the cries of the Doric and Ionian combatants'.[7] Again it was the physical challenge, the testing of oneself against the elements, which would draw him out of port into a storm when most sailors stayed put.

Under these circumstances it is impossible to describe one's sensations, especially when you yourself have designed and constructed what seems to be the living creature to whose honour and guardianship you have entrusted your life. There you are, utterly detached from your ordinary existence, with hills and cliffs and shores already distant, enveloped in clouds and storm, and seeming to belong to a separate world from the tumbling raging tumult in the midst of which you are contending, while from time to time the struggle becomes so fierce that you know it is only your skill, experience, and presence of mind, in conjunction with the mechanical skill and deftness of the ship itself, that stand between you and eternity. The exultation one experiences on such occasions is almost maddening, for it is the victory of invent-ive ingenuity, vivified by moral force, that overcomes, and not just overcomes but makes subservient to one's purposes, the brute phrenzy [sic] of the adverse elements. Add to this the inexpressible beauty of billows with their steep blue walls and fringes of roaring foam, which encompass you for miles in every direction; and finally the subsequent pleasure of returning safe and sound to port, letting go the anchor in a quiet harbour, and then finding one's self a few minutes afterwards tranquilly reading a book over the fire, with all the recent turmoil of the sea floating vaguely before you like a distant dream.[8]

Few of his family shared his enthusiasm or his sea legs; not that that let them off having to learn Morse and semaphore codes so that he could communicate with them on shore. But on board they were quickly made to feel a liability.[9] More seriously, tragedy struck two months later when 'my Italian sailor boy, Michael Esposito' asphyxiated as he slept on the boat having, because of the cold, resisted putting out the charcoal fire. He had been warned of the danger, but it had never seemed to strike Dufferin to find him somewhere dry and warm to sleep in late October.[10] Whether this proved the final straw for his family or not, by the next summer Dufferin would be found sailing most of the time with the Amazonian Miss Ivy Neville Rolfe.[11]

Rome offered echoes of the past, including reminiscences with Prince (Joseph) Napoleon, now in exile, over their 'race' to Jan Mayen Island. The attractions of the city ensured a steady stream of visitors to the embassy. Among the guests he showed round St Peter's was the sculptor Sir Edgar Boehm, in Rome to execute a bust for a bronze statue of Dufferin for Bengal.[12] This bust was to play a decisive role in a scandal involving one of his regular royal guests, Princess Louise. Her marriage to Lorne had largely broken down, partly out of sexual incompatibility: she vigorous, if conventional and he homosexual, if not very often. Under the tuition of Boehm she had emerged as a talented sculptress and in the process an 'amitié amoureuse' had developed. Scandal broke after he died of a heart attack when alone with her in his studio, her lady-in-waiting having just been dismissed. Louise insisted to her mother that Boehm's death had been brought on by the exertion of carrying over at her request his new bust of Dufferin for her to see; distracting the Queen from any further enquiry with 'the ghastly details of his last shriek, fall and gurgle'. However, gossips and the press had a field day, pointing out inconsistencies in the official story in *The Times*. Given Boehm's reputation for affairs with his students, it was widely presumed that he had died making love to the frustrated princess. It was one of those stories that were too good to let probability get in the way. As to the fate of the bust, history doesn't relate.[13]

Dufferin found himself being feted on the social circuit by young, fashionable hostesses such as Charty Ribblesdale; and invited by the dining clubs of rising politicos such as the Blue Posts founded by Asquith and Haldane; or at the House of Commons, where he regaled the up and coming Alfred Milner with tales of Disraeli. Among the more enthusiastic of his new acolytes was Margot Tennant, a leading light of The Souls: an exclusive, self-important coterie renowned for being freethinking and quick-witted, and who took pride in apparently effortless displays of their intellectual superiority. 'Would you consider me bold if I asked you to lunch here [with] Oscar Wilde . . . you said you would come and see me?' she would cajole. 'Tiny' parties would follow (without Hariot, Margot would request, 'as she has had enough of us'), books exchanged and favours asked ('I know that you will forgive me anything [and] I have a sort of idea that you can get what you want – there is no doubt that some people can and do'). This was restorative company for an old man, especially as she listened: 'I shall never forget our talk and your advice to me this summer . . . send me the best photograph you have of yourself and sign it please'. Visiting him in Rome later that year she hinted at the nature of that advice: 'had a delightful talk with Lord Dufferin. He advised me to marry; said I was too nice to be alone and too clever not to be helping some man. He begged me not to be led away by personal attraction and said respect was the first thing and love the second.'[14]

By now he was regarded as something of a grandee. 'Honours accumulate on him', noted Gathorne-Hardy a little wistfully. After receiving the Freedom of the City of London on his return from India, he was soon appointed to be Warden of the Cinque Ports (with which came Walmer Castle, near Dover). As the 150th warden since Earl Godwin died in 1053, he would be part of an ancient line as the symbolic defender of the nation. In addition to numerous honorary degrees, he was elected Rector by the students of St Andrews University. As ever, leading his praises were the broadsheets. '*The Times* has always been wonderfully kind to me', wrote Dufferin to Mackenzie Wallace, now back in post – a relationship the ambassador was happy to nurture with secret information on Russia and Bulgaria which he had only just despatched to Salisbury.[15] When the new Kaiser came for a state visit in 1891, it was not always clear who was the star attraction. At a luncheon at the Londonderrys, the young Emperor came across to Dufferin, remembering being 'shown to me' by his mother when he was 'a little boy at Berlin and Potsdam'. Afterwards Dufferin went on to the reception at the Guildhall. 'Modestly entering the big chamber' he was embarrassed by being announced by the herald. 'Much worse' followed as 'I walked up the aisle and found myself being greeted by thunderous cheers. In fact as the papers say, I received quite an ovation. When I got to the dais I found Lord Salisbury, and I eventually took refuge amongst the foreign ambassadors.'[16] The following year Salisbury appointed him to Paris.

Dufferin left Rome on a tide of goodwill. Even the Pope requested a final audience (and would later send Dufferin a volume of his own poetry), while the King and Queen called on the embassy to say a last farewell. With most of Roman society on the platform to bid them goodbye, Dufferin could be forgiven for pondering on what he was giving up, as he left 'to re-enter upon the heavy work of a first rate embassy'.[17]

35

The Great Prize

Paris for any diplomat provided an irresistible climax to a glittering career. Even Churchill had asked to be considered.[1] It was, of course, better paid and much more glamorous than Rome, and with it on Rue du Faubourg Saint-Honoré came the loveliest of British embassies. Despite being only five, Harold Nicolson never forgot his first sight of a bewildering world of liveried footmen with powdered hair, of his uncle's private brougham with its electric light, and of the numerous gendarmerie protecting the entrance. There with his wonderfully named nanny, Miss Plimsoll, they came across dinner tables laid for fifty on which, beneath 'vast twisted candelabra', family icons – the golden roses and spurs and 'a regiment of caskets in silver and enamel, in ivory and gold, which had once contained addresses of welcome from Madras or Mandalay' – sat alongside relics of national triumph from the Empire plate to the 'épergnes and étagères of Pauline Borghese'.[2] For Hariot it was hard not to be intimidated by this. Fretting that 'even London pales before [Paris]', she feared being too provincial in this supremely confident and fashionable city.[3]

On the other hand, for her husband this was not the 'plung[ing] into a new and unknown world' as he protested at the time. Paris offered a return to old friends and haunts he had frequented with his mother. The embassy was also was a port of call for visitors of influence; from Andrew Carnegie to Baron Pierre de Coubertin with his plans for an international sports meeting.[4] The Queen and prime minister regularly recuperated in France. As 'almost the only one of her old friends left with whom she could talk', in March 1895 Dufferin was summoned to the south of France to hear a wild scheme the Queen had of sending for the Conservatives despite a Liberal majority in the House. Imperceptibly Dufferin guided this potential constitutional crisis into the long grass.[5]

As always he surrounded himself with clever young staff. Hardinge returned and as before the ambassador left matters 'entirely in my hands'. Not all his appointees were so tried and trusted. It was somehow typical of Dufferin to give a post to a young philosopher just graduated from Cambridge, even though he admitted that he had no intention of taking up a diplomatic career. Years later, Bertrand Russell would recall Dufferin as 'a delicious man – so perfect and well-rounded'.[6] Such men would leave Dufferin free to enjoy Paris's numerous galleries and modern inventions such as the Kinetoscope: 'the most wonderful thing that I have ever come across'. Every morning he would bicycle with his son Basil in the Bois de Boulogne, where on the smoothest of roads they could 'float off into a dreamland of exquisite motion'. In the evening he might head for the opera to hear the likes of 'Mme Melba' sing *Lohengrin*. Meeting her afterwards was the first time Dufferin had ever been backstage. It became a habit; meeting on one occasion the corps de ballet 'who despite being lightly clad, seemed eminently respectable and . . . remarkably ugly'. No doubt the same could not be said of Miss Mabel Stewart who at the Folies Bergères performed the 'skirt dance', which Dufferin returned to eagerly the following month. Or of Miss Mabel Sheible, another dancer, with whom he entered into a correspondence on the matter of her 'very transparent dress'. And no doubt he was duty-bound to attend a reception at the American Embassy to see Miss Loie Fuller act out her 'famous American Serpentine dance.'[7]

It was also in Paris that Dufferin claimed that an event took place that was not only extraordinary but in later years used to terrify his nephew with each telling. Staying in 1849 in a house in the west of Ireland, Dufferin had retired to bed when he heard a carriage draw up outside. Inquisitive as to who might be arriving so late, he drew back the curtain and looked out his window. There he saw a large hearse with two horses. The driver of the hearse then glanced up at him. Dufferin recoiled in 'cold panic; the face below him, the eyes that had met his, were the most sinister he had ever seen'. He quickly drew the curtains and a few moments later the hearse drove off into the night. The next morning his hostess insisted that there had been no such visit, breezily telling him that local tradition had it that when he next saw the apparition he would die. Forty years later he was in Paris visiting a friend in the Grand Hotel. Directed to the new modern innovation of a lift, he suddenly froze, 'chilled with fear', for the lift attendant was the same man who had driven the hearse four decades before. Muttering about taking the stairs, Dufferin hurriedly stepped back as the doors closed. As he ascended the stairs, there was a tremendous crash: the lift cable had snapped and all the occupants were killed. What was particularly odd was that none of the hotel staff were sure of the attendant's name as he had only joined them that morning.[8] This is the gothic horror beloved of Dufferin's relative, Sheridan Le Fanu. And it would appear that the ambassador was being equally imaginative. The only recorded fatality in a lift in the Grand occurred in 1878 when Dufferin was still in Canada. It would be typical of Dufferin to personalise and improve a local legend – cultivating his myth was second nature by now but as a metaphor of the impending dangers awaiting him in Paris, it would prove very prescient.[9]

'No British Ambassador can so perfectly have fulfilled the French ideal of a grand seigneur,' recorded one guest to the Embassy. 'He brought to the discharge of his duties tact, charm, knowledge of men and affairs and . . . a radiant kindliness, that in combination can never have been equalled. Though by no means tall, he was still straight and graceful, and his presence made most men look common.'[10] Dufferin may have looked the part but his assumption of what lay ahead would prove highly complacent. 'England and France', Dufferin wrote to his friend, the anglophile French diplomat Waddington, 'are very like a husband and wife', whose marriage was beset by 'occasional bickering'. Their reconciliation would be for him, he assured Mme d'Harcourt, 'a labour of love'.[11] The French though were in no mood for courting. Past memories enabled the press to paint Dufferin as a long-standing enemy of France. After all, in Syria in 1861 Dufferin had engineered a French withdrawal. Twenty years later he deceived Freycinet over British intentions in Egypt; then in 1885 he invaded Burma to block the spread of French influence. Even in semi-retirement he had spent the last three years courting Italy who was Germany's ally in the aggressive encirclement of France. Such hostility was only to be expected from someone who had been granted the rare honour of an invitation to Varzin by Bismarck. In diplomatic terms it was the most undiplomatic of appointments and Dufferin was not in for an easy ride.[12]

For these were volatile years for the French Republic. Twenty years on from the humiliation at Sedan, the desire for 'revanche' was as strong and yet as hopeless as ever. Internally the republic was beset by political instability with few governments lasting beyond a year (which Dufferin attributed to the French being one of 'the Celtic races' and so 'an inflammable people').[13] Tensions were further heightened by a scandal involving shares in the Panama Canal which indicated endemic corruption. 'The whole of France is one wild sea of denunciation, suspicion, mutual recrimination, and even the phrases of 1793 are coming back into use', Dufferin reported. With the assembly tearing itself apart, anarchism thrived. 'Paris very dull', he remarked laconically to Princess Louise, except for their windows being smashed (apparently in the belief that it was a Rothschild home).[14] Some months later in June 1894 the anarchist campaign came to a head with the assassination of President Carnot – stabbed through the heart by a young Italian who had sprung onto the step of his landau pretending to be presenting a petition. Further ratcheting up the discontent was a press, recently liberated from the controls of the Napoleonic era, and now violent, irresponsible and ruthless in its attacks on its enemies.

Prime among these was the British Empire. In such an atmosphere, Dufferin was a red rag to the Gallic bull. A vicious assault greeted him from the start, led by *Le Petit Journal*'s allusion to Dufferin's 'special business'. Just what that was saw the French press compete to establish the most lurid conspiracy. The prime components appeared to be a determination to divide France and Russia; a 3-million-franc slush fund to bribe the Assembly, of which, it was asserted, the Quai d'Orsay had documentary proof; and regular meetings between Dufferin and the Kaiser during Cowes week, whether lunching at Osborne or dining on the Imperial Yacht, on the eve of the ambassador's departure for France. Even *Le Figaro* described Dufferin as 'that acute and dangerous man'.[15]

The sheer hostility of the media threw Dufferin. 'Quite extraordinary how stories of this description seem to "catch on" to use the vulgar expression in this country.' Having tried to ignore it, by February 1893 he was determined to act. Since no one in Britain believed the accusations, this was, Dufferin acknowledged, a 'very risky thing'. But 'this abominable lie [was] credited even in good society' in France and thus, he felt, threatened his usefulness. Having cleared his speech with the Foreign Office, he carefully chose to deliver it as Gladstone would be 'expatiating on his Home Rule' bill, thus providing a good day for burying bad news if it went wrong. Typically he decided to make his point by making a joke out of it:

> The fact is that since I have arrived in Paris I have not spent a sixpence that has not gone into the pocket of my butcher or baker, or of that harmful but necessary lady, the avenger of the sin of Adam, whose bills every householder who values his domestic peace pays with alacrity and without examination – I mean the family couturière.

In the event this was well received in Paris. If dangerous he remained, at least *Le Figaro* was willing to recognise in Dufferin 'l'épithète gentlemanlike' and 'un délicieux humoriste'. Still the next night only 150 attended his reception, 'principally [the] English'.[16] However, as he feared, his response caught the eye in Britain. Consequently he found himself giving regular interviews to English journalists and challenged every inaccuracy, however minor, in the press.[17] In the end what brought the furore to a close was the public exposure of the bribery documents as forgeries and their being openly ridiculed in the French Assembly. Ironically, if Dufferin had waited a couple of months his vindication would have been complete. Instead his reputation never quite recovered from this public display of touchiness. Gleefully Blunt recorded the gossip doing the rounds: Dufferin 'has been an undoubted failure [in Paris] . . . He is too fond of paying little insincere compliments and his wife too uncongenial. There is a very bitter feeling in all classes against England, and just at this moment it is at fever pitch over Siam.'[18]

The Siam crisis was, as the anti-imperialist Blunt took pleasure in pointing out, 'a robbers' quarrel over their spoils' but serious for all that. Its origins lay in France's long-standing territorial dispute with Siam, which culminated in April 1893 with gunboats being despatched to Bangkok to persuade the Siamese regime to concede two-fifths of their country. The French demand made Rosebery's 'blood boil'. But with British interests (retaining 75 per cent of the European trade with Siam and some sort of buffer between French Indo-China and Burma) largely secure, the Liberal prime minister was reluctant to be the 'police of the world'.[19] That said, when the French upped the ante on 26 July by imposing a blockade of Bangkok, giving all ships, including the British navy, three days to leave, Rosebery called the French bluff by ordering HMS *Linnet* not to comply. Reluctant to provoke a war, the French backed down. 'It is half the battle', Dufferin declared to his friend on hearing the news, 'when you feel you can count on your chief' – which for once was not mere flattery. By 1 August with an agreed protocol signed, he met with Develle 'at which we virtually settled the Siamese question', Dufferin recorded in his diary.[20] This would prove a little premature.

It then fell to Dufferin to negotiate the details of the Siamese buffer, with an eventual agreement to make the Mekong River the demarcation of French and British interests. It was a torturous process with the French, fearful that Dufferin would once again deny them their colonial opportunities, being so duplicitous at times, as in 1895, to force the suspension of the talks. Despite Dufferin making 'a very good fight', he was disappointed when the returning Tories, seeking to clear the decks, simply conceded many French demands. Alongside this were other spats as French ambition clashed with British interests in Morocco, Madagascar and the Congo.[21]

By February 1894 public enmity to Britain was so bad that Dufferin had to ask the French president to guarantee the Queen's safety as she passed through France. He himself had felt it necessary to withdraw temporarily from Paris.[22] Yet throughout he remained outwardly at his most conciliatory. He offered to attend the ceremonies in Orléans which sought to revive the worship of Joan of Arc. A speech that won particular praise saw him dismissing as 'desultory troubles' when 'we occasionally run up against each other in the cane brakes of Africa or the fever jungles of Indo-China'.[23] In October 1896 his accompanying the Russian ambassador to military manoeuvres on the plains of Châlons for the Russian Tsar was noted favourably as demonstrating British acquiescence to the Franco-Russian alliance – and as such a typically inspired diplomatic gesture. It would prove the last of his career.

By now he felt keenly that the diplomatic world was changing. It was certainly shrinking. The Siam settlement may have rankled but what told more was that ultimately 'I had nothing to do with it. Lord Salisbury did it all himself with Courcel in London.'[24] It was also a more dangerous world. In 1896 in what he rather grandly called his 'last dying speech and confession' on the role of diplomacy he portrayed an international system on the edge: 'The whole of Europe is little better than a standing camp numbering millions of armed men, while a double row of frowning and opposing fortresses bristle along every frontier. Our harbours are stuffed and the seas swarm with ironclad navies . . . Thanks to the telegraph, the globe itself has become a mere bundle of nerves.' In a bleak conclusion he declared to an audience in Belfast that after thirty-five years' service abroad, his 'one conviction' was that 'force and not right is the dominant factor in human affairs'. So much for the Christian civilising mission and the liberal empire that he had dedicated his life to promoting.[25]

This was also a world in which Britain could no longer assume superiority – be it technical, economic or moral. While most saw the main challenge coming from Germany, Dufferin looked instead across the Atlantic. A dispute with the United States over Venezuela led him to predict an Anglo-American war, declaring 'the sooner we fight the better'.[26] Interestingly the threat was seen as being ideological rather than strategic, springing from America's position in the vanguard of democracy, encouraging populist politics at home and the 'insane irredentism' of the new powers abroad. For Dufferin, this was the class threat to established authority he had witnessed in Russia, India, France, Italy, and especially so in Ireland. Thus he insisted that an Ireland with Home Rule would bring to power 'the violent American party'. And to Northbrook he declared it was the experience of parliamentary government in republican France that 'has made me a stronger Unionist than ever'.[27]

Letting him down gently, the Foreign Office told him that Salisbury did 'not take a very serious view' of the danger, preferring 'to sit still'.[28] It had been the violence as much as the content of his views that startled some in the Foreign Office and helped to fuel a growing perception that Dufferin was beginning to lose it. As early as July 1893, Blunt, never admittedly a sympathetic source, was recording Philip Currie and Curzon making fun of Dufferin leaving Paris 'in a huff'. Earlier in the same year Algernon West called in on Rosebery at the FO 'who said all was very quiet; that Dufferin, who was the enfant gâté [i.e. spoilt child] of diplomacy, went on writing about two zinc tubs and some billiard balls lost at Rome, and that was all. Hope things were quieter elsewhere.'[29] Dufferin's famous despatch in which he denounced the French press as 'the worst in Europe' had in the 1890s more than a ring of truth to it but there was also a sense among Foreign Office insiders of just deserts for someone who had played the press to his advantage all through his career. Admittedly, as Dufferin took plum job after glittering post, he was never going to be popular with the career diplomats. And yet privately even Dufferin himself was becoming aware that the times were passing him by. The French press had rattled his confidence. On the back foot every day with the latest snide comments in the morning papers; never quite sure who would next take offence; or who was going to turn up at his receptions and who in this aloof, cynical, judgemental metropolis would not – it all wore down the outward self-assurance that had sustained him through his career.[30]

His moan to close friends that 'Our age is becoming more and more hysterical' suggested that culturally he felt out of touch. At one exhibition he was bemused by a 'horrid picture, of a young girl being cut in pieces by Jews, by a considerable Austrian artist'.[31] Checking out the artist commissioned to paint his portrait for Walmer, Prince Pierre Troubetzkoy, Dufferin found two 'abominable pictures . . . I am afraid the gentleman is an impressionist'.[32] In literature he could not finish Hardy's *Tess of the d'Urbervilles*: 'I so dread the heartbreaking way in which I feel sure it will end. I do not think an author has any right to make one so miserable.' Even more surprising, for the first time in his life he found himself rather prudish. A present from Hariot of a new edition of *The Decameron* was sent back because the illustrations, though 'perfectly executed', proved too shocking. At the opera, he was startled to find the young bride strip to her shift. 'Nowadays no play is considered complete unless the ladies unclothe themselves.' Yet as recently as 1890 his take on the Parnell 'drama' had been more tolerant than many. Rather than profess moral outrage as the salacious details of the affair with Kitty O'Shea were dragged out in the divorce court, Dufferin chose to point out that 'most of the instances of his escapade are common to all the transactions of this kind as a good many people must know from their own experience'. What put Parnell 'beyond the pale [was his] allowing Mrs O'Shea to accuse her sister of adultery with her [i.e. Mrs O'Shea's] husband. The man who could do this without apparently the slightest justification must indeed be a brute. I suppose they adopted it as a dodge to frighten O'Shea.' That Mrs O'Shea was quite capable of adopting this stratagem on her own simply never occurred to him.[33]

However, it was the evidence of physical decline that distressed him most. By the time he arrived in Italy he was 'mortally afraid I am getting deaf'. Twice he went to hear the great Sarah Bernhardt and both times he heard nothing. 'He is very wise, but like all deaf people, pretends to hear and [as a result] has lost much of his social éclat and reply in general conversation', Margot Tennant noticed two years later.[34] Then he had a 'very severe fall', skating in the Bois de Boulogne in 1894. At least on that occasion the cause was a pretty girl crashing into him. It was the 'tumble' when waltzing with Mrs Ward, 'a Canadian lady [who] skated beautifully', that really hurt.[35] Inevitably he felt keenly the intimations of mortality. His old friend Stafford's death – after his catastrophic second marriage – came as something of a relief.[36] In 1894 he visited in his parsonage his 'poor old Oxford friend, Hepburn', whom he hadn't seen for forty-five years but who had never failed to send Dufferin a letter on his birthday – now paralysed and bedridden for eighteen months. March 1895 would see him lay a white wreath on Lady Jocelyn's grave at Cannes 'on a beautiful morning, everything bathed in sunshine and the landscape lovely on every side': 'the earliest and dearest friend I ever had' who has 'always been a living presence to me'; but whose gilded existence was to be crushed by relentless tragedy. And yet, they had rarely communicated for decades.[37]

This gloom mustn't be overstated. He had many friends in Paris and shot regularly (and now quite competitively) with the leading aristocracy and politicians. The last garden party saw 3,000 invited and despite the rain, his guests 'enjoyed themselves very much, French people being always so gay and good humoured'![38] Nor was his work in France a failure. But the fundamental tensions between two competing empires had not been dispelled and the military stand-off at Fashoda was but two years away. Perhaps symbolically, his last year would see him seek solace in visits to the battlefields of Poitiers, Crécy and Agincourt. However much he was lauded on his return and friends composed triumphant verse in his honour,[39] this had not been the heroic finale of which his mother had dreamt. But then Sheridan would never have been a diplomat.

36

Making Sheridans

The Sheridans are much admired but are strange girls, swear and say all sorts of things to make men laugh. I am surprised so sensible a woman as Mrs. Sheridan should let them go on so. I suppose she cannot stop the old blood coming out.

Lady Cowper

There is no doubt that we are in a certain degree what our forefathers have made us.

Lord Dufferin[1]

BUT BEING A Sheridan was never quite what it seemed. To most outside the family Richard Brinsley Sheridan was the embodiment of a rackety century – a vibrant, decadent life filled with elopements and duels, dramatic orations and brilliant wit, suitably brought low by drink, louche dalliances, and financial ruin. To his family, however, this was a travesty. While Helen and her sisters took pride in the continued popularity of his plays, the task of rehabilitating their grandfather's political reputation remained the touchstone of family ambition.[2] It was the task to which Dufferin's mother had dedicated his life.

That Sheridan was a political 'genius' was an article of faith. Yet for all his achievements and talents, he had always been denied cabinet rank – something his grandchildren put down to the social exclusivity of the Whigs, ensuring that Sheridan would always be an outsider.[3] Similarly his granddaughters, in making their mark on society, only fuelled the prevailing belief that, as Melbourne cattily put it to the young Queen, 'All the Sheridans are a little vulgar.'[4]

By the time Dufferin returned to Europe in the late 1880s, the Sheridans' reputation for scandal was undiminished. The ructions over the Duke of Somerset's will rumbled on as late as 1893. With both his sons dead, Somerset's bequeathing of the family fortunes to his eldest son's illegitimate children and to his daughters instead of his legitimate heir, was so controversial that inevitably society gossip saw in it only the scheming of his wife.[5] In branding her the 'Sheridan Duchess', the name itself was held sufficient to convey the extent of her depravity.[6]

The same decade saw a return of the charge against Caroline Norton that she had sold to Delane of *The Times* the cabinet decision in 1845 to abandon the Corn Laws, which allegedly had been confided to her by her then lover, Sidney Herbert. This charge was rekindled by George Meredith in his barely disguised portrayal of Caroline, *Diana of the Crossways* (1885), and again in the 1890s by Sir William Gregory in his autobiography. As if that were not enough, Carnarvon was not the only one intrigued to hear rumours, widespread at that time in club land, that Disraeli was Dufferin's natural father.[7]

However much they craved respectability, ironically, to observers a respectable Sheridan was always going to be something of a let-down. Even Dufferin's daughter Nelly, in England for the 1887 season and staying with Brinny Sheridan (who had so famously eloped with an heiress in the 1820s), was disappointed to find 'the whole household is very good and rather narrow-minded', having later taken up with the Evangelical revival. In this they were not alone in the family. Nelly delighted in recounting to her father the travails of her 'Aunt' Gwen[8] who in 1887 wanted to improve the moral temper of her local village, by subscribing for the local library to an evangelical journal entitled *Mother's Companion*. Only then to discover its leading article on 'Inherited Wickedness' claimed that the 'best' illustration of this trait were . . . the Sheridans! As if to prove the point, while Nelly was staying with Aunt Rica, her cousin Henry shot himself. 'A softening of the brain . . . aggravated by a subsequent craving for drink' was how it was explained to her. Almost as shocking was the viciousness of the press, with *Vanity Fair* being particularly 'odious' in openly blaming Aunt Rica for her son's suicide. Later that summer, staying in Wicklow with her maternal relations, Nelly discovered that even the

Hamiltons viewed the Dufferins as part of the 'smart people' who are 'terribly worldly, and all marry for money and flirt with one another's husbands'. That year saw the publication of Percy Fitzgerald's *Lives of the Sheridans*. 'Making it sell' required him 'to rake up all the scandal he could', wrote a furious Dufferin. But then what other story was there to tell?[9]

It was to meet this question that Dufferin would dedicate the next decade, to an epic attempt at rebranding the Sheridans; and through a historical reconstruction to realise the longstanding aspirations of a maligned family. First, though, he sought to nail the 'lies' over Caroline with a fierce rebuttal in the *St James's Gazette*, pinning the blame on Lord Aberdeen and arranging Henry Reeve (Aberdeen's private secretary) to confirm this in the *Edinburgh Review*.[10] This only produced a flurry of further stories. As for Meredith's portrayal of Caroline, at Dufferin's insistence the author agreed to include a note in further editions that the Corn Laws slur was a 'calumny' and the book should be read as 'fiction'. None of this stopped the book running to many editions and establishing Meredith's name, leaving Dufferin to ruminate on how 'a lie of this sort, once started, seems to be irrepressible'.[11]

He had better luck with his own parentage. A 'long confidential talk' in the House of Lords in 1896 with Lord Rowton, Disraeli's secretary, produced evidence that Helen and Disraeli did not meet until six years after Dufferin's birth. It was a measure of Dufferin's anxiety that not only did he get Rowton to confirm this in society (Blunt heard within days) but he also felt it necessary to 'insert it' in a memoir of his mother. In a similar vein, fifty years on he investigated his father's death, calling in on General St John Foley 'who was the last person to see my father alive, having travelled with him to Liverpool' and collecting evidence to reinforce a verdict of accidental death.[12]

To a greater or lesser degree these were searches after truth. By contrast his treatment of his mother's memory drifted, consciously or unconsciously, into an embalming of the past. The return to Italy would see him make what he called a 'pilgrimage' to the 'little old medieval castle in the Apennines' which his parents had taken after his birth. There he 'conceived my mother . . . so proud and happy with her baby in her arms, she herself being almost still a child'.[13] Such places did not bring back memories in themselves but fired vivid imaginings that he contrived to mould into a memory; not just of a mother's intense love but more importantly of a time of innocence and joy when they were almost young together, as in later years they would pretend to be almost lovers. Lost were the moral strictures, the self-absorption, the sharp asides that would cut to the quick and rein him back in. Lost too the pressures of expectation she had placed on him that would undermine his confidence and initially held back his career. And there would be no hint of his anger towards a mother who, having virtually arranged her son's marriage, deserted him to marry without any warning his close friend (whose funeral Dufferin would later refuse to attend). Gone too was any recognition that his mother's devotion had been strictly on her terms; for her death had left him free to reconstruct their past.

As he sat down to write 'A Sketch of My Mother' in the introduction to a collection of her poems (which he published privately in 1894) Dufferin would create the myth of an unbroken bond and establish himself as the embodiment of her aspiration. Included with all her published works were the expressions of love she wrote to him on his birthday, thus establishing the exceptionality of their relationship, in which a son's first memory was apparently his mother's 'coming of age'. At the same time the stresses and admonitions would be erased, the hurts finessed. His youth was 'years of great happiness' at the heart of which was a woman whose beauty was 'divine – the perfection of grace and symmetry', whose 'charm and brilliant conversation . . . and involuntary appreciation of the ridiculous' lit up any company but whose 'natural impulse was to admire, and to see the good in everything, and to shut her eyes to what was base, vile, or cruel'.[14] Whether leaving London for Clandeboye or on perilous expeditions by sea to the Middle East, she is shown loyally by his side.

All of which made it crucial that his mother's marriage to Gifford was reconfigured into a sublime act of self-sacrifice. Portraying her affection as like that of 'a clever elder sister towards a younger brother', she had, Dufferin insisted, married Gifford only out of 'a passion of pity' and only after the doctors had confirmed there could be no recovery.[15] Furthermore the betrayal was now his, not hers. For with his marriage 'she had ceased to become the sole object and preoccupation of her son'; and thus her open acceptance of Hariot was a triumph of 'unselfishness'. Then, as if to seal the point, he rearranged the dates, declaring that 'I was unable to be [with her], my own marriage having taken place but a few days before Lord Gifford's case was declared hopeless.'[16]

If this left him free to deify her, it would now be on his terms. Helen became a symbol of virginal purity, a gentle liege lady, beguiling in her innocence and 'gaiety' whose 'very laughter was a caress' and whose capacity for love was 'inexhaustible'; yet also quietly religious, submitting her regency wit to a becoming modesty in her writings and instinctively displaying the tact and taste that Victorian respectability required. It was but a short step from here to beatification – 'her loving radiant face . . . my childhood's Heaven, as indeed it never ceased to be'. Even after death she would not desert him: and, quoting from her last journal, he relayed how she promised on her deathbed to 'continually be with my darling . . . in your walks or by your fireside – the fervour of my love . . . will surely encompass you!'.[17] And so it proved. A generation on and Harold Nicolson would remember 'even as a little boy, [being] conscious at Clandeboye of a vanished influence of great potency. From the windows, across the lakes, above the woods, Helen's Tower rose as a constant reminder of my uncle's mother . . . to be mentioned only with hushed reverence . . . The Tower was surrounded with associations which were intangible, awe-inspiring and remote. It checked our gaiety and our excesses with the raised finger of sobriety and even painfulness . . . It brooded with insistent mystery over all our escapades.'[18]

In the process of reinventing his mother he began to reread his own diaries ('it is like living one's own life again'), preparing them for printing, and in the process unable to resist the temptation to edit and improve. This was more than the excising of the embarrassments of youth. Gone too would be any criticism of his mother: the rows over his will, the 'engagement' to Nelly Graham, the naming of Helen's Tower, his jealousies over Giff: these were thoroughly obliterated or cut out.

This was but part of a much greater design to realign the past with the present. On a dull, rainy day in October 1890 he had set down in Sorrento to begin 'a short sketch of the Sheridan family, which I have long in my mind to do'. The drive to recovering the family history was a desire to establish an ancient lineage and quell the impression of adventurers who had come out of nowhere, a sensitive issue for he could never forget that he was the *first* Baron Dufferin and Clandeboye. In France he would 'trace the French Blackwoods to their lair in Poitou' and the chateau once owned by 'the only Sheridan who ever made any money since the time of Queen Elizabeth' in the West Indies. He would make 'pilgrimages' to hallowed sites of past Sheridans in Bath, London and Hampton Court; 'and even went as far as to inspect that little tumbledown house at Quilca where Doctor Sheridan and Swift had wrangled together and composed quips and madrigals and riddles'.[19] Out of this would come an attempt to build a redoubt of academic respectability around the family's reputation. Firstly by establishing Sheridan as supremely talented, noble and respectable;[20] and secondly by placing Dufferin in a literary family that by his calculation had produced over two hundred works from twenty-seven authors since 1665, and an ancestral line he traced back to 1550 and Donald Sheridan of Cloughoughter Castle. And of this lineage of 'very remarkable men' Dufferin was the latest manifestation. At the heart of all of this was an audacious conceit: consciously or unconsciously, instead of aspiring to emulate Sheridan, he sought to realise his mother's mission by remoulding Sheridan to be more like him.

This ambition inspired him to draw a parallel between Sheridan and Miss Linley and himself and his mother. Both men made their mark as men of letters and as orators; while Helen and 'her angelic ancestress, Miss Linley'[21] were both portrayed as 'child-women, innocent and seductive at the same time'. Despite rarely seeing his mother, Sheridan shared Dufferin's obsession with mother love, famously declaring that 'filial piety [was] the primal bond of society'. Other connections could include that both men were proud Irishmen making their way in an English aristocratic world; both felt keenly matters of personal honour and their status as 'gentlemen', even if it meant 'puffing' the press; and, through lavish generosity, both were frequently in debt. More importantly, both exuded a charisma, with remarkable powers of persuasion enabling them to enchant, flatter and disarm. Ultimately both were social actors, playing parts and inventing personas until it became instinctive.[22]

Yet their differences could not seem starker. Politically Sheridan was one of the great parliamentarians, able to hold the Commons in the palm of his hand for five hours; Dufferin could barely hold the Lords for five minutes and loathed the cut and thrust of parliamentary debate. While Dufferin nurtured his career carefully, Sheridan was genuinely independent, courageously holding to his views to the very brink of being arraigned for treason. Nor in terms of their literary talents can *High Latitudes* be compared with plays like *The Critic*, *School for Scandal* and *The Rivals*. And then there was the rakish lifestyle of duels fought, elopements, heavy drinking and frequent liaisons and scandals. Dufferin by contrast was the epitome of Victorian rectitude and now a teetotaller to boot. Symbolising all of this was the irony of a descendant of Sheridan, who had heroically impeached Hastings and the administration of the East India Company, becoming the Viceroy of India.[23]

Undisturbed by such caveats, in 1892 Dufferin commissioned the author Fraser Rae to write a new biography about my 'ill-used and maligned ancestor'. Previous biographers were dismissed as 'libellous' or tainted 'with jealousy'.[24] For 'in his best days [Sheridan] evidently possessed a power of fascination both for men and women which has probably never been rivalled and this can only have proceeded from real loveable qualities'. And then, just to make clear where this point was heading, he added, 'I have seen the same characteristics in his descendants.'[25]

To charisma Dufferin wished to add character. For to him the key to resuscitating Sheridan's political genius was to demonstrate there was substance as well as show. Hence his delight when Fraser Rae 'exploded the fiction about Sheridan's speeches smelling so of the lamp', worked and polished 'to the outmost' – much like Dufferin's. He praised the book for being a 'solid, virile and close-grained work' and not 'a flashy, flimsy and what the world calls a "brilliant" performance'. To Dufferin Rae's portrayal of Sheridan as a 'hard working, industrious public servant' and not 'an idle flighty creature' was completely convincing.[26] All of which proves that you get what you pay for.

Of course Dufferin denied any connection with the book, which was perhaps as well, as the critics panned it for making Sheridan, of all people, supremely dull.[27] To counter this, he mobilised the aged Gladstone to write a review and for once the old man obliged, placing Sheridan (along with Pitt, Fox and Burke) as one of 'the four superlative names of the years that follow the fall of Lord North'. Rather than perceiving Sheridan as 'a meteor that blazed with almost intolerable splendour in the great oration on the Begums of Oude and then sank into . . . obscurity', Gladstone asserted that 'the theatrical manager was the great working horse of the team'. No wonder Dufferin hailed this as 'a vindication of Sheridan's fame and character'.[28]

Two years on even Dufferin was forced to recognise that Fraser Rae's biography was only 'adequate'. So the culmination of the reinvention of Sheridan as a paragon of Victorian duty and public service would be an address given in 1898 by Dufferin himself, delivered in Bath, the setting for so much of the family drama and 'sacred ground'. In keeping with this, 'Miss Linley' is described as 'angelic', a 'sweet songstress who ravished the ears' whose love affair with Sheridan – from their elopement to final rapprochement at her deathbed – he portrayed as if part of an Arthurian romance.[29] To Sheridan's genius his plays were 'sufficient witness' while in politics he 'always fought on the side of liberty and humanity'. It would have been absurd to ignore the womanising and drinking but Dufferin's treatment could not have been more generous: 'With regard to his private character, I can truly say that it was a compact of noble, brilliant and most lovable qualities, marred – and when is it otherwise with poor humanity? – by occasional lapses and foibles, which the virulence of his political enemies and the contemporary tittle-tattle of the clubs have greatly exaggerated.'

Dufferin chose to emphasise certain characteristics. 'In an age far more savage and brutal than our own', when political conflict was 'conducted with an animosity and unscrupulous violence', Sheridan's 'good humour, unwillingness to give pain . . . and delicacy of offence stand pre-eminent'. Needless to say, if this had been the case, he would have been as ineffectual in politics as his descendant. Then there was his 'engaging manners and irresistible personal charm', which made him 'a welcome guest abroad'. The same of course could be said of Dufferin. Dufferin also stressed his 'extraordinary powers of application'. Of the image as the 'idle, casual dilettante', he insisted 'nothing could be further from the truth'. It was a charge that had been thrown at Dufferin. However, the trait 'of which I am prouder than of any other' was that, despite 'living in the Georgian era, a time when morality was at a low ebb . . . his writings were never tainted by the slightest breath of impropriety or indiscreet or immodest allusion'. An extraordinary claim that denies much of the wit and thrust of *A School for Scandal* and forgets the 'ribaldry' or 'low quibbles' he had to excise after the first performance of *The Rivals*. Finally, with his 'many-sided nature and talents . . . he lived in many different worlds and . . . shone with brilliancy in all. In whatever society he frequented he moved like a star.' As Dufferin did: a celebrity in the world of power as well as of fashion, artists and writers and, like Sheridan, a favourite at court.

This was an imaginative creation of a mythical lineage to which he was the heir. And to complete the vision Clandeboye was to be transformed from a Blackwood home to the ancient seat of the noble family of Sheridan. Dufferin commissioned copies of many of the famous Sheridan portraits. In particular the three great Gainsboroughs of Elizabeth Linley (including the one of her sitting beneath an oak tree which hangs in the hall today) together with Romney's portrayal of her as St Cecilia. Intermingled with them would be studies of his mother and her sisters, the 'three neat 'uns' in their prime, while in the dining room various Sheridan ancestors would vie for prominence. At the heart of these rooms would be enormous official portraits of Dufferin and Hariot – from Canada through to Walmer – formidably grand in pose and resplendent with decorations. It is striking how few Blackwoods survived this makeover. Naval heroes such as Uncle Henry of course, and Dorcas, whose fortune first propelled the family on, remained; so did Aunt Anna, but – overdressed and over large – she seems to bristle at finding herself in such company. His mother, who as a young bride endured long dinners with her Tory Blackwood in-laws, would have enjoyed this little triumph. While centre stage above the fireplace in the library hung the portrait of Richard Brinsley Sheridan – less a portrait than an icon of veneration in a family shrine.[30]

Guarding the entrance to this shrine was the great hall.

Purpose-built and inspired possibly by his excavations at Deir el-Bahir in 1859–60, it appears to replicate Egyptian tombs in design. Its large gallery is awash with treasures telling the story of Dufferin's life.[31] Here are 'curios' collected from his travels: a 4,000-year-old altar from the tomb of Mentuhotep II, ancient Egyptian inscriptions on the walls and a temple bell from Burma, curling stones and Indian paddles from Canada, an intricate model of Mandalay, another model, this time of the *Foam*, alongside its cannon and a bust of one of the liege ladies, two stuffed bears, the tigerskin from India stretched out on the floor, and a vast array of swords and shields, spears and lances (including the vicious 'katara' dagger from India), and a Buddha, imperturbable despite finding itself surrounded by carvings of fearsome beasts. Flying above it all was a flag of the North Down Militia – still in the great houses of Protestant Ulster the respectable symbol of loyalty. Beneath this, standing proudly, was a small terracotta maquette of the statue of Dufferin in his imperial pomp that still stands outside Belfast's City Hall; while above the baronial fireplace hung the portrait of the young knight.

Off the main gallery were a series of small waiting rooms and museums, each with further 'curios'. But the eye is led towards the 'processional route' and an ascending staircase with, at its head, his greatest treasure: a limestone statue of Amun, the god of Thebes, gazing down on all who dared to enter. Beyond, past the bed of King Thibaw and the sweeping staircase framed by towering narwhal tusks, lay the main reception rooms and the iconography of past Sheridans. Clandeboye was to be Dufferin's greatest tableau and one intended to establish himself in the Sheridan pantheon.[32] In the 1890s all the bedrooms were named after his postings, while on the estate 150 places – from copses and clumps to fields, lanes, rivers and hills – were renamed to reflect his life. Nor were his efforts in vain. 'The greatest of the O'Sheridans, the most illustrious of the Dufferins', Francis James Biggar would hail him in his obituary.[33] As fictions go, Dufferin couldn't have wanted for more. By the time Harold Nicolson wrote *Helen's Tower* in 1937 the family myth was well set. 'In my uncle's own veins', he declared, 'the Sheridan blood seethed and tingled like champagne' – a phrase the next generation would particularly treasure and take to heart.[34]

Yet at the very core of this conceit lay a revealing irony. 'Above the mantelpiece in the library at Clandeboye', recalled Nicolson:

> There hangs a portrait of Richard Brinsley Sheridan. It is a cautious picture. The artist was obviously intent on concealing from posterity the more convivial aspects of the Sheridan temperament. There is no suggestion, for instance, of the man, who, when found by the watch in a condition of complete collapse and asked his name, hiccoughed . . . 'W-W-Wilberforce'. There is no indication even of that wild liberal spirit, nor yet of 'that heart which has no hard part'. True it is that over the features of his subject the artist has cast a purple glow; yet this . . . implies the open-air aspect of a fox-hunting squire; there is no hint of the candle-laden atmosphere of Brooks's, nor of the mulled claret at Carlton House, nor yet of those unending brandies and soda with which, at late Parliamentary sittings, he would wash down Mr Bellamy's veal pies. His right hand, with a weak gesture of affirmation, indicates some oratorical point. It is not compelling. Nor would the observer deduce from this portrait that it represented one of the kindest and most amusing men that ever lived.[35]

Dufferin, by his choice of picture, had transformed Sheridan into a Blackwood.

37

Funding Sheridans

MAKING NEW MODEL Sheridans out of his children would prove considerably harder but at least at Clandeboye he could seek to inspire the next generation by creating a family seat fit for a great name. By now his woods and lakes were well established, as too was the family ritual of marching up to the Tower from which, on a good day, they could look up to Kintyre and across to the Isle of Man 'as plain and as near as the shores of Antrim'. Around the house there was further landscaping with terraced lawns, new vistas opened up through the trees; and by way of indulgence a new rose garden in the shape of a D.[1]

As for the house itself, he had long desired to knock it down and build a great seat to rival those of his aristocratic friends. Architects such as W. H. Lynn would be commissioned from time to time to draw up wildly ambitious schemes for Elizabethan mansions or French chateaux (or even combinations of both); none of these came to fruition, it proving cheaper just to bind the plans into an elegant volume for the library. But the urge never left him. In the late sixties, by relocating the main entrance to the west end, he was able to create a library. Here elegant shelves stood tall, filled with the gilded spines of learned tomes and speaking of serious scholarship were they not so neatly arrayed. With its high south-facing windows and welcoming fire in winter, this uplifting space became 'the convivial heart of the house' (as it remains to this day).[2] Outside some coach houses were turned into a banqueting hall; never very practical, it was mainly used by the local Women's Institute. Nor was the new real tennis court, decorated with Dufferin and Hamilton heraldic emblems, much used for real tennis. More successful was the chapel built to the west of the house. Its exterior ('almost Methodist . . . in its austerity') was softened by the arched entrance, giving the impression of a 'smaller and more Celtic version of the portal of San Michele at Pavia'. Nor was there anything Methodist about the interior. On the walls were hung 'huge oil paintings in the style of Luini' in heavy gold frames. The vestry curtain was 'Medicean in its grandeur', while the altar was 'draped in red velvet cloth patterned with unashamed pomegranates'. And as if to emphasise the 'pagan', to the left of the altar let into the wall was a tablet with the cartouche and title of Tirhakah, King of Ethiopia. Outside hung a large Burmese bell. If all this had 'too much about Rome' for local tastes, so much the better.[3]

Sustaining this would depend on considerable funds. The priority was to be the Earl of Ava (as Archie was now styled) and the perpetuation of the line. In particular Dufferin was anxious lest Archie be left with insufficient inheritance to sustain his new rank. On his elevation to the Marquisate in 1888 Dufferin let his other children know that they would have to make their own way. 'I could have wished him a good deal richer', he wrote to Nelly on first hearing that 'when his back was turned' she 'had engaged herself to be married'. Still he had never refused her anything and her fiancé, Sir Ronald Munro Ferguson, a former soldier turned Liberal MP for Leith and a close ally of Rosebery, was sufficiently connected that Dufferin even ignored his support for Home Rule.[4]

If she was happy enough with her bargain and the chance to manage his political career, for her father the wrench was far greater. At the end of the wedding with the departing couple lost finally from view, Dufferin 'pushed his way through the crowd of strangers in the hall, and [feeling] quite savage at their obtrusive good nature' he made for the woods and a solitary walk around the lake. This and more he shared with his daughter, his 'friend, companion, [and] playfellow':

> Somehow, my little Nell, I feel as if I were the only one ['except of course your mother' is deleted here] who really knew what a treasure has been carried off, and indeed in thinking of you, your poor father gets quite romantic and feels inclined rather to talk in the strain of a lover than a Papa. The only difference your marriage will make will be that you will have two lovers instead of one.

In this, he was as true as his word. Within a month he visited his daughter in Scotland; and he would treat the Munro Ferguson estate at Raith as a second home, where his relationship with his favourite child could continue almost unimpeded. In its possessiveness and violence of emotion, there are shades of his mother's self-centred turmoil over his wedding. In marrying Hariot he had recreated the difference in age but not the relationship. His eldest daughter, however, had the name and the mind (and something of the look), and around her he could remould the fantasy; and, having lost once before, it was as if he was determined now not to lose 'her' again.[5]

Victoria, for all her 'prettiness and originality', did not seek a glamorous (i.e. lucrative) match, falling in love with Willie Plunket, one of Dufferin's attachés in Rome and the son of the Archbishop of Dublin. 'Your Majesty would hardly consider him good looking', Dufferin reported back to Victoria's godmother. By way of compensation Victoria produced grandchildren (unlike virtually all her siblings), the first in April 1895 being predictably christened 'Helen'. Hermione on the other hand would never marry. Selfless and 'altruistic' almost to a fault, she became a nurse, Dufferin finding her in her London hospital 'so bright, gay and caressing'.[6]

Terence married Miss Flora Davis with 'no money to speak of'. Below stairs Nowell and Miss Plimsoll regarded such a liaison with an American as akin to the Fall, but at least it provided an excuse for a glamorous wedding in the Paris embassy.[7] As for his other sons, they were proving to be unreconstructed Sheridans. When dining after watching Beerbohm Tree as Svengali, Dufferin's joy at being placed beside the extremely pretty leading lady was tempered by the discovery that she was 'an intimate friend of Basil's'. To his father's relief, at Balliol Basil turned out 'extremely clever and literary. He has got some of the real Sheridan blood in him, but I am happy to say without its lawless effervescence.'[8] The Sheridan blood couldn't get him adopted for the local parliamentary seat, and he drifted into a sedentary life as a solicitor with time to illustrate brilliantly several of his friend Hilaire Belloc's books.[9] After which he joined Milner's 'kindergarten' in South Africa and eventually became colonial secretary in Barbados. Dark-skinned and with a slow drawling voice and 'irresistible' smile, he was the image of his father in more ways than one.[10]

His younger brother Freddie was not as bright, barely surviving Eton and failing entry to Sandhurst twice. With his son forever getting into scrapes, Dufferin feared a repeat of the 'ruin and misery' his Norton cousins had brought. But Freddie was more charming than that. Sent to India to escape one romantic entanglement, he had to be sent back to escape another. Hence there was relief when eventually Lansdowne (now at the War Office) telegrammed to say that despite failing the exam by one mark Freddie would get his commission into the cavalry.[11]

Thus the rescue of the family's fortunes came to depend on Archie. Strikingly good-looking, he was high spirited and good fun,[12] as well as a natural courtier when he put his mind to it ('Royalties delight in him', purred his father). But quickly bored, Archie's interests soon dwindled to polo and gambling. His response to his father urging him to 'give some thought to duty as well as pleasure', lest he become 'a mere aimless loafer', was to throw up his military career. 'I wish my son had been going to your ball,' Dufferin wrote in regret to Lady Londonderry, 'instead of rattling off to Canada as he has just done'; and not least because it meant that the flirtation with Lady Helen Stewart would come to nothing. Even worse was the news he learnt from Consuelo, Duchess of Manchester, that Mrs Vanderbilt had been so anxious for her daughter to marry Archie, that she asked him to dinner and placed him beside the girl; all to no avail as Archie paid her no attention. Instead it was the Marlboroughs who were to benefit from all those dollars. It is quite possible that Archie was gay, although Dufferin would never have regarded that as an obstacle to marriage. It was more his moral fecklessness towards his familial duty that depressed him. And, as it would turn out, the consequences of Archie's reluctance would prove devastating. 'Why aren't you my eldest son?' Dufferin lamented to his favourite daughter.[13]

A retirement pension of £1,700 p.a. was perfectly respectable but inadequate for Dufferin's needs.[14] Complicating matters further was the 1896 rent review by the Land Courts arising out of Gladstone's 1881 Land Act.[15] Aware that he would need additional resources when he retired, and with Archie failing to marry, he had no option but to bolster his income from directorships in the City.[16] For companies seeking to raise capital, the endorsement of a high profile celebrity, one whose respectability might reassure nervous investors, was worth paying for. And since they didn't come more respectable (or by 1896 desperate) than Dufferin, he was inundated with offers.

There followed an unholy struggle between the riches offered by the City and an honourable reputation that could be lost in a day. At which point he met with Lord Loch (the former high commissioner of South Africa) who was seeking a replacement for himself as chairman of the London and Globe Finance Corporation.[17] The deal was everything Dufferin wanted and more: £3,000 p.a. and at liberty to miss most board meetings, together with an undisclosed signing-on fee, possibly as high as £10,000.[18] The London and Globe was the brainchild of Whitaker Wright – a veritable Croesus in the City, whose name was 'a synonym for success and magnificence' (*Daily Telegraph*) and who, having been left penniless at twenty-one, was by thirty worth £250,000. His speciality lay in mineral exploration and his estate at Lea Park, near Godalming in Surrey, had a fortune spent on it. Hills were lowered and a lake built with a boathouse designed by Lutyens. Beneath the water, reached by tunnels from the house, were smoking rooms and a billiard saloon, all with glass ceilings to offer views of the fish or swimmers above. Also installed were an observatory, a theatre, a velodrome, a private hospital, and stabling for fifty horses. His London address was in Park Lane adjacent to Londonderry House. Here in a drawing room inspired by Louis XV's Cabinet des Rois at Versailles, he threw lavish parties for high society. At Cowes his yacht *Sybarita* would race and defeat the Kaiser's *Meteor*. 'Everything was swagger', it would later be recalled. 'The whole thing was a glorious vulgarity – a magnificent burlesque of business.'[19]

For one so fastidious in matters of taste, Dufferin was far from repelled by such company. He had always been thrilled by the fabulous displays of limitless wealth by Indian Princes or American magnates. And Whitaker Wright could be very persuasive. Sixteen stone and with his Northumberland burr, he was a veritable image of solidity and reassurance who would command shareholder meetings with the air of a man who knew what he was talking about. Meetings were held in the Savoy where maps were produced of gold finds in Australia. Afterwards there would be weekends at Lea Park to keep

Dufferin sweet and on one occasion *Sybarita* was sent over to Bangor for him to sail.[20]

As a result Dufferin not only accepted the offer but was sufficiently convinced to invest heavily himself. There is no record of his total holding but a partial schedule in 1899 had £72,380 of shares in five of Wright's companies and he was encouraging his son-in-law to do likewise. As for the London and Globe, Dufferin proved 'the ultimate guinea-pig director of the era' whose prestige was such that on his appointment the value of the shares immediately doubled. And with the company a seeming success following the sale of the Ivanhoe mines for £900,000, there followed the formation, somewhat at Dufferin's encouragement, of the British American Corporation, which was floated in December 1897 with Dufferin in the chair. He was paid such a high sum for partially underwriting the new company that he checked to make sure it was legal. Suddenly he had money. After decades of land sales he bought McBurney's farm in 1897, and months later Wright's farm, which adjoined Clandeboye. By 1899 he had acquired the ultimate status symbol, a luxury yacht, *Brunhilde*. Time would tell if this was propitious, but for now it was all onward and upward. 'Certainly', he wrote to Munro Ferguson, 'we must build adjoining palaces in Park Lane as soon as our fortunes are made.'[21]

38

Decline and Fall

H E HAD RETURNED home to an Ireland at its most stable since the Famine: Gladstone had been defeated, Parnell ruined, and the Home Rule movement utterly divided. Free now to come off the fence, he openly espoused the cause of Ulster Unionism, distinguishing 'We in the North' from the nationalist turmoil elsewhere in the island and highlighting the role of many Irishmen within the British Empire. 'I believe there is no power on earth', he wrote to Rosebery, 'which will be able to keep Belfast and all the industrial communities and the sturdy Presbyterians who are the life and soul of Ulster under the heel of the Celtic peasantry of Connaught . . . What I feel is felt by thousands and thousands of other Ulstermen'; their leaders all 'strenuous opponents of Orange fanaticism'. In his absence the Tories had taken up the strategy of land purchase, which he had advocated as long ago as 1881. 'I almost consider it a patriotic obligation to sell, for it is by getting the Protestant population rooted as owners in the soil that we shall erect the best bulwark against Home Rule', he would argue with all the radicalism of one who had little of his estate left to sell.[1]

By now he was something of a local hero. The dinner in his honour in Belfast to celebrate his return from India (19 September 1889) was the fifth so far. They were at it again on 20 October 1896 in Ulster Hall with Lord Pirrie, as Lord Mayor, in the chair. On this occasion no expense would be spared with Pirrie charting a special boat to sail to Belfast with the entire staff, cutlery and 'napery'; for, as he declared, Ulster took 'peculiar pride' in Dufferin's achievements and claimed him as one of their own. Plans were laid for a statue of Dufferin to decorate the new City Hall in Belfast. His popularity in the North in the 1890s was not due to social deference; nor was Ulster especially imperial before the Diamond Jubilee of 1897.[2] Instead, as a genuinely international figure who had walked with the great for thirty years, he was 'a celebrity . . . enriching the Society of the country by his presence in our midst'.[3] As in Canada, he brought a cosmopolitan allure to a fiercely provincial community, wooing them with his self-deprecating wit, range of allusion and theatrical lisping drawl, accompanied inevitably by flattery, so rococo as to be almost beyond parody. Winston Churchill, speaking in Belfast in 1900, was introduced by 'the venerable Lord Dufferin . . . No one could turn a compliment so well as he. I can hear him now saying with his old-fashioned pronunciation, "And this young man – at an age when many of his contemporaries have hardly left their studies – has seen more active service than half the general *orficers* in Europe." I had not thought of this before. It was good.'[4] He had the air of the exotic about him, but that was part of the appeal. He was one of their own if still from a different world.[5]

But he was an Irish figure too. He was at the tercentenary celebrations for Trinity College and later became both Chancellor of the Royal University of Ireland and a trustee of the Irish Literary Theatre (on account, Lady Gregory insisted, of his Sheridan ancestry). When the Queen came to Ireland in 1900, he was there to greet her as he had been nearly fifty years before when he had set eyes on Fanny Jocelyn.[6] Nor had he cut himself off from London society. Admittedly he was by now 'so deaf I am scarcely fit for human society, except, in a tête à tête talk'. A visit to a 'country house . . . has now become simple torture to me'.[7] Yet for all that, among close friends he could still be the 'life and soul of the party'.[8] He rarely attended the Lords now; except at the behest of his daughter for a debate on votes for women in local elections ('terribly beaten but I am in hopes that Nelly will be pleased').[9] In the public eye his reputation as a grandee was undiminished. By 1898, not only had he been honoured with the freedom of Bath and Edinburgh (alongside Lord Kitchener) but he could also claim doctorates from Oxford, Cambridge, Trinity Dublin, Edinburgh, Harvard, St Andrews, Laval, Lahore, Toronto. He was made President of the Royal Geographical Society, and held the same rank on the newly formed National Trust. On great state occasions he could still cut a dash. In A. C. Benson's waspish review of Gladstone's funeral ('There were a number of red-nosed people, like half-pay officers, who shambled in – earls, I think') there was one exception: 'Lord Dufferin, very splendid.'[10]

Back at Clandeboye Nicolson would occasionally find his uncle on the staircase, where hung the grants of arms, quietly contemplating his achievements:

To Frederick Temple Hamilton-Temple Blackwood, Baron Dufferin, Baron Dufferin and Clandeboye, Earl of Dufferin and Viscount Clandeboye, Marquis of Dufferin and Ava, Earl of Ava, P.C., K.P., G.C.B., G.C.S.I., G.C.M.G., G.C.I.E., D.C.L., LL.D., F.R.S., Governor-General of Canada, Ambassador to the Courts of Russia, Turkey and Italy, Ambassador to France, Viceroy of India, Lord Warden of the Cinque Ports, Vice-Admiral of Ulster, Lord Lieutenant and Custos Rotulorum for the County of Down, a Justice of the Peace. Greeting.

As Dufferin once privately admitted to Nelly, 'public applause was very pleasant to anyone in public service'.[11] When this began to ebb away in retirement, he could always take succour from the triumph of the Blackwood upstarts who had become the very equals of their Downshire and Londonderry neighbours.

Into this idyll came distant sounds of war. The war that broke out in the dispute with the Boer republics caught much of Britain by surprise.[12] Not wishing to miss out on what could be a short conflict, Archie secured a post as ADC to Colonel Ian Hamilton and almost immediately was in action with the Gordon Highlanders at the 'battle' of Elandslaagte (October 1899). Soon afterwards Dufferin would be proudly reading in the *Daily Mail* of his son's valour. However, barely a week later, as he was saying goodbye to Basil, Dufferin heard that Archie was 'surrounded', caught up in the siege of Ladysmith. By December it was clear that the British Army had a real fight on their hands and they suffered three defeats in what became known as Black Week. The Dufferins at that time were staying at Viceregal Lodge in Dublin where among the guests was Joseph Chamberlain – seen by many as the architect of the war. The next day Dufferin called on Lady Roberts who was 'dreadfully anxious' about her injured son; barely had Dufferin left her than news came of his death. Not surprisingly the mood was very sombre that evening at Viceregal Lodge. And into the midst of this gloom came a telegram from Archie, high-spirited and very much alive.[13]

A week later came another telegram. Archie had been hit in the head 'very dangerously' in a Boer attack on Waggon Hill on 5–6 January 1900. The family gathered in hope at Clandeboye only for a second telegram to arrive on 12 January 1900, confirming his death. Condolences poured in. 'There is something in the calm dignity of death – especially if it has been nobly won', commiserated Betty Balfour, as if chivalric cliché could offer much comfort. 'We are paying a terribly high price for Empire', Evelyn Baring wrote from Cairo the same day; a brutal truth to confront for one, like Dufferin, synonymous with that empire. A private memorial service in the chapel was all they could face, presided over by the Dean of Down (who would lose his son fighting at Pretoria). Two months later came three letters Archie had written from South Africa – heartbreaking in their exuberance. With them came a letter from Colonel Frank Rhodes. The older brother of Cecil, under fire he had bravely carried the wounded Archie to cover. He told of how his friend had never regained consciousness and after four days had died; and enclosed a lock of Archie's hair. 'I long for the advance of victories to begin again' was all Hariot could write to her mother that evening.[14]

Dufferin sought solace in his woods. There beside the ruined crypt of a seventeenth-century Blackwood, he had built a family burial ground, Campo Santo. Circular in design, he surrounded it with cypresses planted at intervals of twelve feet to 'add to its solemnity and seclusion'. And at its centre he erected a tall granite Celtic cross; on one side of which he engraved his son's name, looking south to the far-off land where he lay. At the same time he designed a window in Archie's memory.[15] Yet such stoicism as they could muster would not protect them from a second blow. Just after Christmas they received information that Freddie, then serving with the 9th Lancers, had been 'severely wounded in the chest at Gelegfontein'. Immediately they heard the news Dufferin cancelled all his directorships and he and Hariot booked a passage to South Africa. Two days later a second telegram arrived. It was from Leman, his solicitor – the London and Globe Company had been declared bankrupt.[16]

'Unknown to me and to all his colleagues, Mr WW has engaged in a gigantic gamble in Lake Views which has broken down and the company will have to be wound up', Dufferin explained to Munro Ferguson.[17] But if Dufferin was startled, few in the City were surprised. As early as June 1898 there had been an open attack on Whitaker Wright in the *Critic* as 'a past master in the art of arranging figures'. 'This apostle of mystification is fully aware that the public dearly love a share which is at a premium and yet "looks cheap."'.[18] Among the devices highlighted was the stimulation of the capital value of a company by substantial share purchases, creating a momentum and then, as demand exceeded supply, selling for personal profit thus depressing the price. But such was Wright's reputation as a moneymaker a credulous public remained keen to invest in each new company or issue flotation, and even increasingly to accept these new shares in lieu of dividends. Many of these companies were very high risk or pure fictions to raise capital. And many were under the umbrella of the London and Globe Company. As it turned out, Wright would raid one company's assets to shore up another without referring the matter back to either set of directors. Indeed he would take this further; on one occasion he transferred shares worth £1.25 million from one company to another prior to its balance sheet being issued before returning it two days later. Such devices often explained the large cash surpluses that so reassured Dufferin.[19] Wright portrayed the investments in terms of a gold rush, and in 1896 floated Lake View Consols with capital of £250,000. Through this company, he would buy up small mines cheaply and float them in London dearly: thus the Ivanhoe mine in Kalgoorlie was capitalised at £50,000 and refloated with capital of £1 million in London. The next year he formed the British America Corporation with capital of £1.5 million to exploit mining interests in British Columbia and the Yukon – an arrangement that *The Economist* all but denounced as a scam. All in all, in the six years before 1901, he created some forty finance or mining companies with a total share issue of £22.36 million.[20]

To all this and a later attack in the *Pall Mall Gazette* (in which Wright was accused of attempting to bribe their City editor – as he had done many others), Dufferin was oblivious. Trusting Wright, he accepted that this was the work of rivals (such as Horatio Bottomley) seeking to 'bear' the company and so 'most unfair'.[21] As Dufferin addressed the shareholders in his 'capacity as a City man' in January 1898 Wright could not have asked for more. 'Like the skilled diplomatist that he is', noted *The Economist*, 'he has displayed conspicuous ability in making rough places plain, and in glossing over apparently difficult points in such a way as to impress the average shareholder with the conviction that things are really much better than they look and that "everything is for the best in the best of all possible" enterprises.'[22]

That summer the practice of secret payments to aristocrats to secure their endorsement was exposed in the sensational Hooley bankruptcy hearings. In response *The Times* produced a stern editorial; its reminder of the expectations of noblesse oblige was apparently 'designed to make Lord Dufferin blush'.[23] If so, he didn't seem to notice. By December 1898 Dufferin was back in London for the Le Roi flotation. The advent of war a year later, however, depressed an already overheated market and by late 1899 the City was rife with rumours that Wright had seriously overextended himself. He had invested very heavily in the 'Baker Street and Waterloo Railway', which had been shunned by the public and cost London and Globe £600,000. This had been more than compensated by Lake View shares soaring in the early part of 1899 from £9 to £28 when a major find was rumoured. By December this had been exhausted with the consequence of a further loss of £750,000 to London and Globe. But disastrous though these losses were, it was Wright's response that would prove fatal.

The first hint of this was a frantic note from Lord Loch on 29 December 1899 after he had just learnt from Wright that to compete against the 'bears' he had 'raised upward of two million!!! He said he had pledged everything he had.'[24] Actually everything they had, for they would later discover that Wright continued raising funds through false accounting over the next year, with any dividends paid from pillaging other companies. Still as late as 17 December 1900 Dufferin recorded 'a very successful [shareholders] meeting' despite the lack of a dividend and the disturbances of a minority of 'bears'. He himself had been frequently cheered especially when declaring that he had no intention of 'deserting the ship'. And his defence of Wright could not have been more robust: 'Never have I seen any man so devote himself, at the risk of his health, and at the risk of everything that a man can give to business of the kind, as Mr Whitaker Wright.' Yet that night the bears were selling Lake View by the thousand and knocked a further £3 off the share price. To counter this Wright bought over 60,000 Lake View shares and spread word of a syndicate determined to do what it took to defend London and Globe against the assault. In fact they had only agreed to provide a limited loan of £500,000 and with the end of month settlement looming the company could not meet its commitments. Dufferin's sudden resignation in order to be with Freddie in South Africa may have removed the last fig leaf of credibility but nothing could now prevent the London and Globe from hitting the rocks.[25]

This was among the greatest scandals to hit the City in the nineteenth century and, although advised that there was no need, Dufferin cancelled the passage to South Africa to face the shareholders in January 1901. In spite of the anxieties about his son, there would be no escaping his public duty. Too ashamed in the interim to show his face in public, he shut himself up in his London hotel. In the event the shareholders received him with 'loud cheers'. 'Instead of tearing me to pieces as I expected,' he reported to a friend, 'the two thousand gentlemen assembled in Cannon Street received me as if I had been Lord Roberts. One is proud of such an incident for the sake of human nature.' For all that he feared disgrace, oddly it would bring the best out of him. He impressed many by his courage and dignity, for staying with the shareholders when he had every reason to leave for South Africa, and also for offering, despite his own heavy losses, to pay the smaller losses. 'How fine tempered was the metal [of his qualities]', Sir Edward Grey would recall.[26]

Yet old habits died hard. To Pattisson (his former secretary and financial adviser), he wrote of 'a terrible catastrophe [that] has over-taken us . . . Things were going quite well with us until lately, and then in a single day Mr W.W. embarked on a gigantic gamble on the Stock Exchange without saying a word to any of us and has . . . in fact ruined us.' Pattisson expressed sorrow at Dufferin being 'let in by your Managing Director' and reassured him that 'throughout all circles, both City and social, the blame has been put on the right horse'.[27] This was a defence that Dufferin would elaborate on to any who would listen. Having assumed that he had been involved with a genu-ine mining enterprise, he found himself 'entangled with a set of people' – from Wright to accountants, clerks, secretaries, solicitors and auditors – 'all of them engaged in . . . a fraudulent conspiracy', 'all in WW's pocket'. Then the solicitor he put on the board to 'see that things were kept straight' proved to be 'a weak and incompetent idiot'. Dufferin would even insist that 'the mining enterprise itself had proved very successful, and everything would have gone well if only our Managing Director had not taken to playing the Stock Exchange'. Acknowledging that people may blame him for touching the business at all, he would plead 'but persons who serve their country abroad cannot make money'.[28] He was, judged his official biographer, undone by his 'rule, where he had given his confidence, to give it absolutely; and on this occasion it was lamentably misplaced'.[29]

Such protestations of innocence wore thin quite quickly as more and more was uncovered of London and Globe's dealings. Even allowing for the fact that admitting to an ignorance of company finance was perhaps not as unusual as it would become, Dufferin was at fault for not creating structures to cover this. Putting his solicitor on the board to watch over his interests, he compromised the arrangement by insisting that Wright pay the man's fees.[30] Perhaps more remarkable was his continued support after Loch revealed the previous December Wright's unauthorised loan of £2 million. Admittedly he had been distracted then by Archie's death. But when the 'gigantic gamble' failed in late 1900, Dufferin had been sitting on the possibility of exposure for almost a year. Perhaps he had no option, having been landed with a fait accompli. Still, even as late as 16 January 1901 Dufferin was talking of the people who had 'betrayed WW'.

In 1893 Dufferin had reminded Hermione of her promise that 'you will never speculate: first because it is ruinous; and secondly because it is wrong'.[31] Odd advice for a nurse perhaps; but what is odder still is that, if he believed this, he should be investing in Whitaker Wright who was a high-risk speculator. As Wright would later protest, 'not one mine in a hundred pays. Anyone who knows anything and goes into a mining speculation ought to know that there is a more than even chance that he will lose. If on the other hand, he wins, he wins heavily. And yet, when the slump comes, [investors] look on their speculative counters as if they were special deposits in a savings bank.' It was an argument that had considerable sympathy in the City.[32] Dufferin may have been naive but he wasn't innocent of speculating. He bought and sold shares as the market rose and, what is more, encouraged his son-in-law to do likewise, even on occasion overcoming Nelly's strong scepticism. Thus in September 1899, on Dufferin's advice, Munro Ferguson took 'another plunge into Lake-Views'. When his London stockbroker warned in December 'that it is no time to be bullish', there was much bravado between father and son-in-law over 'croakers'. That said, Munro Ferguson bought and sold a block of Lake-View shares on 12–13 December and escaped with a profit. Not so his father-in-law.[33]

Ultimately all arguments for the defence paled as the scale of the disaster sank in. Originally Dufferin put the losses at 'nearly a million of money' (January 1900); by December 1900 it was put at £1.7 million. It was only when the matter went to court that the true horror became clear. It transpired that £5 million had been lost in the last two years of trading in addition to associated debts of another £3 million. Assets that had been valued by Wright at £7 million were in fact only worth £1.5 million. The collapse bankrupted twenty-nine members of the Stock Exchange, liquidated many of London and Globe's associated companies and ruined 'countless' private investors. There was no escaping the realisation that this scandal for Dufferin was 'an indescribable calamity which will cast a cloud over the remainder of my life'. Part of that was the threat of prosecution. For the rest of his life Dufferin would be dealing with inspectors asking questions he couldn't begin to answer. Not yet in the 'dock', he reassured his daughter in June 1901 but 'outlook is very unpleasant' and became even more so in July with the liquidator's official report – 'a most damnatory document'. Remarkably the shareholders 'still friendly to me as they have been all along'. But soon he was recording 'stormy' meetings and, with his resignation inevitable, his noble if wholly unrealistic attempt to clear up the mess had ended in complete failure.[34]

Not until 1904 was Wright brought to court under a private prosecution. Sensationally found guilty on all counts, he was sentenced to seven years' penal servitude. Generous to the last, as he waited to be transferred to prison, he handed his solicitor his gold watch and chain, saying 'I will not need these where I am going.' And then in a last defiant gesture he drew out a large cigar. He had barely time to light it when suddenly he collapsed to the floor, having taken, as it turned out, enough cyanide to kill three men. In his pocket was a loaded revolver – silver, of course – should the poison have failed. 'Even in death he was larger than life.'[35]

39

At the Last

ALL THIS DUFFERIN found deeply humiliating. A reputation nurtured over a lifetime could not prevent him looking a foolish old man in a matter of weeks. St John Ervine, writing nearly fifty years later, recalled the grim City jest of Wright having 'let a duffer in' before recounting how 'Ulstermen felt this exposure keenly, for they had taken great pride in Lord Dufferin, a man of high affairs; and the spectacle of one so distinguished revealing his incompetence . . . dashed and disturbed them'. If Dufferin's fate evoked genuine sadness beyond Ulster, it was at the tarnishing of a noble ideal – of honour, probity, wisdom – a romantic image which all had indulged in, now exposed as distinctly human, if not a little tawdry.[1]

The crash broke him financially too. The Italian pictures were sold for £2,000 (having been bought, it should be said, for £500). So too were shares of any value, leaving only a portfolio of worthless mining stock and four Suez bonds. Candelabra were sent to Garrard's and the yacht put on the market. This left him 'still very much to leeward of my normal financial status'. As it was, these economies barely covered Archie's gambling debts, with Coutts owed £15,000.[2] All his life he had fought to overcome the constraints of dreams unmatched by funds. Now he was facing the grim prospect of ending his days like Sheridan with the bailiffs hammering at the door. Inexorably, as they discussed 'economies over breakfast', the conversation turned to the leasing or selling of Clandeboye.[3] With the farm now closed, the labourers let go and the land leased out, the sense of energies draining away was omnipresent.

And not just at Clandeboye. On hearing of the Queen's death, he waited all week for the invitation to the funeral, dreading the reason as none arrived. When the call did finally come, it was so late that

Dufferin left for London within the hour without his wife. Arriving fatigued by the rush, he then had to fight through the crowds on the station to get to Windsor. There he waited in St George's Chapel by the West Door 'miserably cold and in a great draft for nearly three hours', so much so that he feared 'an attack upon my chest'.

At last, however, the doors were flung open; the Duke of Norfolk with his heralds fluttering round him entered and soon after came the coffin. As it passed before me, I could think of nothing but the poor dear Lady who was lying within it, who had been so kind a friend to me for fifty years and had never changed . . . Indeed so absorbed was I in these thoughts, that the throng of princes who followed passed quite unobserved, and I did not come to myself until all that was left me to look at was the tail of the procession.[4]

At the reception afterwards in St George's Hall, Rivett-Carnac, who had served under Dufferin in India, 'was horrified at the change that his recent troubles had wrought on this distinguished man. It was a raw day, and Lord Dufferin, who felt the cold severely, had got right inside one of the great fireplaces in the Hall and was trying to warm himself. His heavily embroidered uniform hung about him as on a skeleton, so thin had he grown. It was a Collar Day and he seemed weighed down with the Collars of five Orders of Knighthood which he wore . . . even then [it] seemed as if death had claimed him.'[5]

But not yet. Three months after they first heard of Freddie's injury, Dufferin waited with Nelly and 'Hermie' to welcome him back at Southampton dock. Watching him disembark, Dufferin could see Freddie was 'very happy; but [then] . . . we saw he was lame – couldn't stand upright or walk without a stick'.[6] Still nothing would stop him organising a triumphant welcome home to Clandeboye for his son in the traditional manner.[7] Such defiance would carry him through the rest of the year. With his 'one poor eye . . . dotted over with spots' (he had cataracts as well as being almost blind in one eye), he still stuck to the treadmill of public duty, receiving in October another degree from Glasgow and conferring others in Dublin; and then travelling overnight from Ireland to Oxford for the unveiling of a window in memory of Sir William Hunter. There Alfred Lyall saw Dufferin for the last time, on Magdalen Bridge 'looking down the stream towards the sunset, absorbed, as it seemed to me, in the remembrance of bygone days'.[8]

Days later he collapsed and was confined to bed in a London hotel for a fortnight. Determined to attend the ceremony of his installation as Lord Rector at Edinburgh (for which he had defeated Asquith by 257 votes back in 1899 when he still counted), he ignored his doctor's advice and travelled north. After a further two days in bed, he staggered up to deliver his lecture in front of a boisterous audience of students and professors. Too weak for the task, he soon sat down to read his speech, only with enormous effort standing again at the end. Still he wouldn't give in and went to attend the student songs in the concert hall. That night when the doctor called he was in great pain. Yet the next night he got up to speak at the Conservative Students' Banquet. Surprisingly he was 'quite revived for this', speaking wittily and well and was 'enthusiastically received' as he mobbed up his son-in-law's adherence to Home Rule. It would be his final public engagement but for one last time he revelled in the showman's thrill of having an audience in the palm of his hand.[9]

By now the stomach cancer that was to kill him was well advanced. On 30 December he could barely walk to the Lake and had to lean against a tree. Yet he was determined to shoot the first drive of pheasants towards the guns the next day. Despite looking 'frightfully ill', he was driven to the stand where a chair was ready for him. After shooting 'wonderfully well', he retired exhausted to bed – never to rise again. By 18 January he could no longer read and the doctors told him that he had no hope of recovery. Sir William Broadbent, the London specialist and friend, had come over to support him, deadening the pain with regular doses of morphine. And there was a flurry of comforting telegrams from Margot Asquith. On 4 February the Dean of Down administered the Last Sacrament with Broadbent repeating the prayers as he knelt beside Dufferin so that the old man could hear. For another week Dufferin held on, before drifting into unconsciousness and passing away at 6.30 a.m. on 12 February 1902.

His passing was not without one last flicker of the charm that had so defined him. The last letter he dictated was to Salisbury, ostensibly to resign all his posts: 'being as the doctors seem to say on my death bed . . . I suppose in the circumstances ill health will be a valid excuse'. But he also sought at the last to 'thank you for the great kindnesses and considerations you have never failed to show me since the time you started me on my diplomatic career, for having kept the Italian Embassy so long open for me, and more innumerable acts of kindness. I don't think you ever knew how much I liked you from the time you were a thin frail little lower boy in Cookesley's, even then writing as m'Tutor used to say, such clever essays.'[10]

40

Mythmaking and the Biographers

Lord Dufferin's death is in the papers. His end was tragic, but carelessness in money matters was the weak point in his character. When he came of age, I remember hearing, he had a quite unencumbered estate of £20,000 a year, but he muddled it away, Heaven knows on what, for he was not a gambler, nor a runner after women, only he kept no accounts and liked to do things on a grand scale . . . In all things else he was singularly high-minded, with a chivalrous devotion to his mother, the one passion in his life. He trifled with women rather than made love to them, and when his mother died his chief affections went to his children. A faithful friend, retentive of old memories and rightly beloved of all; [whose] marriage was arranged for him by his mother . . . and he accepted it as he would have accepted anything else from her hands.[1]
Wilfrid Blunt

UNCHARACTERISTICALLY GENEROUS, BLUNT'S assessment was all the more damning for what he left out: the traveller and man of letters, the politician and imperial diplomat whose achievements were the substance of obituaries all over the world. As self-appointed keeper of the flame, Hariot had no intention of letting her hero's reputation be lost amid an image of human frailty. With a major biography (by C. E. Black) already far advanced, she commissioned Alfred Lyall to write the authorised life. It was a good choice. Lyall had served under Dufferin, admiring him greatly, and now in retirement had emerged as an accomplished author and scholar.[2] Moreover he was willing to put up with Hariot's distinct vision and crucially her control of her husband's papers.[3] What emerged was elegant and scholarly. It stuck closely to the official public life, and was written with the understanding that comes with considerable experience of imperial governance. Conversely there is barely a mention of the London and Globe.[4] Restricting itself to all that was admirable, impressive and noble, this was the autobiography Dufferin never wrote but which the public expected to read. In securing Dufferin's reputation for a generation and more, Lyall's biography served her purpose well.[5]

'Miss Plimsoll, is Uncle Dufferin a great man?', the young Nicolson once asked his nanny. 'She turned and faced me . . . enraptured. "He is", she answered slowly "the greatest man in the world."'[6] It was not until after Hariot had died in 1936 that Harold Nicolson felt able to revisit this in his memoir, *Helen's Tower*. Strictly speaking, this was not intended to be a biography of Dufferin but an autobiographical sketch of Nicolson through his childhood memories of Clandeboye and his uncle along the lines of Proust's *À la recherche du temps perdu*. 'Yet everything Clandeboye [once] meant to me', he reported to his wife, 'has disappeared beyond capture, and it now seems a muggy, ugly place entirely hedged in by damp overgrown trees . . . This *à la recherche* business is not really much fun when the *temps* is as *perdu* as all that.'[7] Arriving at Helen's Bay railway station he now found it 'deserted and forlorn', the heraldic decorations eroded and the arrow slits hidden with ivy; entering the waiting room with its rusty lock, he found 'dead flies innumerable on the mantelpiece'. The house itself had the air of a mausoleum. Not even the Tower was sacred – having become 'a resort for Belfast tourists . . . [with their] charabancs and ginger beer'.[8] What followed was an attempt to reconcile the uncle that he had hero-worshipped as a child and believed into adulthood to be 'one of the leaders of the Victorian age' with this decay and oblivion. Instead of placing this demise in the widespread decline of country houses after the First World War, he chose instead to see it as a metaphor for fallen gods.

Nicolson portrays an attractive man of great versatility and talents but without quite the achievement to match.[9] Thus the aspiring poet had 'declined into a pleasing aptitude for vers de société'; while the able artist never progressed beyond 'a quite agreeable habit of painting little watercolours in the 1830 manner'. If his landscaping of

Clandeboye demonstrated 'unquestioned proof of (his) foresight and composition', as an architect he would 'display immense, if misdirected, energy'; and never more so than at Simla. As a man of letters, however, he wrote 'with fluent grace' (if over abundantly), was well versed in the Classics and knowledgeable on Egyptology. Yet his obsessive desire to master the Persian vocabulary – a pursuit begun in error but maintained doggedly for the next twenty years – suggests much that was narrow and pedantic. As yachtsman and sailor 'he had few equals even among the less distinguished members of the Royal Yacht Squadron'. By now Nicolson was getting carried away by his theme. Dufferin was a better and wittier painter than Nicolson allowed. Acquainted with Carlyle, Thackeray, Browning and Dickens and longstanding friend of Tennyson, Dufferin was a genuine littérateur in his own right.[10] Clandeboye may not be an architectural treasure, but most of his improvements there – the library, the chapel, and Helen's Tower – retain their attraction to this day. Moreover he made a genuine name for himself as an explorer and sailor in the 1850s and 1860s and never lacked physical courage.

But the question never went away. At Balliol Nicolson would be accosted by Sligger Urquhart: 'Was Lord Dufferin a *great* man? I have never been sure . . . He was certainly the most agreeable.' Writing in the ruin of the Clandeboye of his childhood, Nicolson concluded:

> He was certainly one of the kindest men that ever lived. He possessed immense gifts and tremendous charm of personality. In the final crisis of his life he showed integrity and moral courage. But did he possess vision as well as imagination; was he a great statesman or only a great diplomatist? He was certainly a very great diplomatist.[11]

Later historians wouldn't even grant him that. Andrew Harrison sees Dufferin, for all his attractions, as first and foremost a careerist, the consequence of failures elsewhere which meant that financially he could not afford to risk his position. Hence in India he was 'A professional pro-consul [who] would adopt whatever policy was dictated to him, for he wanted his political career to continue after India – for financial reasons if nothing else.' Harrison's Dufferin is ultimately reduced to being 'A dignified showman who gloried in pomp, circumstance and public approbation'; even going so far as to suggest that the last letter to Salisbury 'may have been written with an eye to the biographers'.[12] Subsequent historians have accepted the flaws even if they are more open to appreciating the style.[13]

But if Dufferin had been as weak and insubstantial as this, he would have been found out long before. How are we to explain 'the most glittering of all diplomatic careers'?[14] It is hard to gainsay a record whose highlights included: a lasting and peaceful settlement in Lebanon; being a major catalyst in keeping Canadian identities British and the Dominion under the British flag; the restoration of Anglo-Russian relations after the Congress of Berlin; and the preparation of the diplomatic ground for the invasion of Egypt. If his scheme there for representative government was too optimistic ('a dead letter' as indeed he knew it would be, with or without Baring), it had served its immediate purpose, providing a justification for Britain's continuing occupation – a considerable advance, in Dufferin's eyes, on the tyranny of the Turkish pashas. Then, after preventing an Anglo-Russian confrontation on the Afghan border escalating potentially into a world war, he secured the defence of India and incorporated Burma into the empire. In India, despite a very hostile political environment at home, he set in train the beginnings of representative government with the reform of the provincial councils. In an increasingly intolerant world these were the actions of a statesman.

For all the manner of a dilettante these were also the achievements of a very effective operator. In his dealings with foreign powers, he was assured, insightful, subtle and patient, able to negotiate directly with world leaders and emerging over three decades as one of the leading international diplomats of his day. For Britain he became the troubleshooter of choice for both parties (dubbed by his friend, George Brodrick, as Britain's 'pacificator General'); one who was resourceful and sufficiently connected to hold his own with governments of whatever hue. Lansdowne, who twice succeeded Dufferin, later declared that the most remarkable feature of Dufferin's career was 'the unbroken continuity of his success'. Furthermore it was the variety of the briefs that he mastered – some imperial, others diplomatic and almost all in most pressing areas of foreign policy – that made him stand out. However much they had rowed over Irish policy, to Gladstone Dufferin was 'the best man we have got' precisely because of this versatility: 'Indeed', he judged, 'I have never known so able and excellent an all round man.'[15] The influential journalist and historian T. H. S. Escott summed up the contemporary verdict in his *The Story of British Diplomacy* (1908), hailing Dufferin as 'the most recent of our greatest ever Diplomats'.

Part of that 'glitter' came from the public acclamation that followed him throughout his career. It is remarkable that as a diplomat he should become a national celebrity.[16] 'There is nothing dramatic in the success of a diplomatist,' Salisbury once pointed out:

> His victories are made up of a series of microscopic advantages; of a judicious suggestion here, of an opportune civility there; of a wise concern at one moment, and a far-sighted persistence at another; of a sleepless tact, immovable calmness, and patience that no folly, no provocation, no blunders can shake.[17]

In an age when the titans of popular appeal were the political figures or military heroes such as Wolseley and 'Bobs' Roberts, the arts of the diplomat were not obvious attributes to stir the populace. Hence from Goldwin Smith in Canada in the 1870s to Gladstone's Liberal cabinet a decade later, many politicians were quite nonplussed by Dufferin's popularity, especially in the eyes of the press.[18] It helped that he looked the part. Watching as Dufferin received his guests at the head of the staircase in the Paris embassy, Viscount Mersey was struck by how he 'looked the ideal ambassador, distinguished, cryptic and urbane'. It helped that he appreciated the evolving importance of the media in an age of rapid technological change; quick too to grasp its needs as well as its opportunities. Those who deplored the active nurturing of reputation forget that those working abroad left themselves very exposed to shifts of opinion at home. 'All my life long', he confessed to Nelly, 'whenever I have made a speech I have had to consider at least two and sometimes three audiences, like the circus riders who have to stand on the backs of several galloping horses at once.'[19] His mastery of cultivating public opinion, drawing on techniques of presentation he developed in Canada in the 1870s, would become the staple for democratic politicians for the next century.[20]

And yet if by the 1880s and 1890s Dufferin was a national figure, it was because he encapsulated the imperial zeitgeist. 'And now I have to hail to you as a sort of retired Alexander', wrote Argyll on his friend's return from India in triumph: 'the conqueror of millions and the absorber of new empires! . . . What a destiny it is, "The policy of annexations", as it used to be called.'[21] A tease maybe, but it was also an indication of how far Dufferin was a creation of his own times as the public mood shelved the civilising mission to became more jingo-istic and overtly imperial. Securing Canada for the empire, his role in the annexation of Egypt, and his conquest of Burma established him in the public mind. Moreover he contributed to a popular language of empire which allowed a liberal country to make the imperial chal-lenge seem a noble, invigorating, even moral destiny. This was a role that by the 1890s was giving way to more brutal creeds and would come to bitter fruition in the Boer War. But it was a tide that Dufferin had ridden with panache for thirty-five years.

Ultimately the 'glittering career' would be a triumph of personal-ity. To a degree Dufferin embodied the dichotomy between glad confidence and doubt which was so characteristic of the age. One of the things that surprised those he worked with was the sudden bursts of insecurity over his position that would overwhelm him even at the height of his reputation. To understand this most of his contem-poraries would look no further than his closeness to his mother, what one historian described as a lifelong worship of 'Oedipal intensity'.[22] This misunderstands the relationship, even if it captures the depth. The appeal was never sexual, nor did he hate his father. Still, for all the undoubted strength of her love, Helen could be exceptionally manipulative and it would be the burden of her expect-ation, gnawing away at him through all the years of grandeur and applause, which would lead him to the Faustian pact that would eventually bring him down.[23] In retrospect, as a consequence of her ambition, his adult life was a series of inventions which grew into a public persona which he could barely control and against which in the end he would be cruelly judged. Even on his retirement when at the height of his fame, *Punch* portrayed Dufferin on stage taking his final curtain under the title: 'The Well Graced Actor'. For all his efforts the Sheridans were players still.[24] The tragedy of Dufferin, if

'The Well Graced Actor'
Presented to Dufferin by the artist, Linley Sambourne, 6 June 1896

so it was, lay not in that he was far more able than some contemporaries and later historians give him credit for. Rather it was that he was not as great as he seemed outwardly to be. Dufferin was only too well aware of this. The fascination lies in the strategies he adopted to overcome this and in his fate as one who succeeded too well and as a result in the end not well enough.

However true this may be, it is a portrait that few who met him would have recognised. For above all Dufferin was good company. Alongside the rigours and achievements of his public life, he was 'gloriously versatile' and unashamedly eccentric at times. Few, if any, international figures declaimed in Greek to the students of 'McGill University, skated Sir Roger de Coverley on a Montreal ice rink, made a lifelong study of Egyptian hieroglyphics, scandalised St Petersburg society by hopping and grunting like a pig while playing Dumb-crambo, startled Paris by bicycling publicly, and conversing in Persian with the Shah'. 'I am', he once happily confessed to Lady Russell, 'a great believer in frivolity.' But this, which made him such fun, also blinded the serious in his profession to the seriousness with which he took his responsibilities;[25] and overlooked how his personality would inspire his staff, win over his fellow diplomats, and occasionally woo nations.

In 1892 Dufferin tried to comfort Tennyson's widow with his appreciation for 'the beautiful lines on Helen's Tower [which] will render my mother's name and my own immortal long after the memory of anything that we have been or done has been swallowed in oblivion'.[26] And so it has proved to be. What was most winning about Dufferin is unavoidably the most elusive.[27] It is difficult to recapture the peculiar attraction of a public speaker who once held a crowd enthralled or the raconteur who sparkled over a dinner table.[28] More to the point, no enduring reputation can be built on these. The universality of Dufferin's appeal to those who met him combined generosity as well as manner. 'He had read enormously, and his knowledge of books, pictures, and music was unbounded', but what Lady St Helier would admire most was that for all his erudition, 'no one was too insignificant . . . for him to be kind to'.[29] Fate may have required him to rely heavily on his capacity to understand people: a subtle perceptive art which underpinned a remarkable ability to make

and sustain friends. But it was his kindliness and a nobility of character, which was never lost as he acquired the steel to make his way, that
none who met him would choose to forget. Those who mocked his
chivalric attention to women failed to appreciate that it was shown to
all women, irrespective of status or looks. Miss Plimsoll, the Nicolson
governess, was treated 'as if she were an exiled member of the House
of Bourbon'.[30] It was an integrity that people trusted because of (or
despite) a manner that spoke nostalgically of past times. 'His courtesy', Lord Rossmore recalled, 'would be an exaggeration in anyone
else.' Critics assumed that such overt charm had to be deceitful but
those who knew him well spoke of 'his unconscious art of impressing
upon those who he met that he had been waiting all his life for that
moment'.[31] Such talents are immeasurable and indeed lost in the
moment. But they were his mother's. They were Sheridan's too.

Epilogue

In the Shadows of Ancestors

DUFFERIN WAS BURIED in Campo Santo on 15 February 1902. With his family and many local dignitaries in attendance, he was laid to rest 'in the fresh soil of his own beloved Clandeboye': interred amidst the woods he had planted, with their vistas of lakes and meadows that he had designed, and over which Helen's Tower still stood sentinel. As befits the life, this landscape was a triumph of naturalism made by man. 'Everything is so full of him', Hariot wrote that March, as she looked out over Clandeboye 'so pretty' bathed in the spring sunshine. Desolate at her loss, she nevertheless upbraided her mother: 'I do really hope that you will not indulge [in] grief.' Hariot would choose to endure, dedicating the rest of her life to 'keep[ing] this place' in the face of Terence's plans for housing developments and to preserving the memory of her husband.[1] This she would do without faltering for another thirty-five years.

As she stood firm, however, her family disintegrated around her. Having been 'grievously wounded' on the Western Front, Basil had reluctantly accepted a recuperative post as a private secretary to Lord Wimborne, the Lord Lieutenant of Ireland. As soon as he was fit again, he returned to the battlefields only to be killed in 1917. A year later in the influenza pandemic that followed the war Terence died too, a victim of pneumonia and the weak heart first diagnosed in the 1890s.[2] By the time Freddie inherited Clandeboye, it was starved of funds and in a high state of gothic decay.[3] In his granddaughter Caroline Blackwood's merciless portrayal of 'Dunmartin' in her novel *Great Granny Webster*, everything leaked, nothing worked, in what felt now a crumbling, gloomy prison of a home. Adding to the despondency was Freddie's wife. Brenda Woodhouse was 'lovely [but] fragile'; wildly eccentric, she soon descended into a near permanent depression in which she quite literally felt away with the fairies. A dreadful embarrassment to her children (who sought far distant corners of the house to avoid her) she may have been, but her war-broken husband never ceased to love her. However, by 1930, he too was dead – killed in a plane crash.

When Freddie died, his son Basil, known to his friends as Ava, was on his honeymoon, having married Maureen Guinness. One of the Golden Guinness Girls, there are shades here of the Sheridan sisters – though crucially, unlike them, Maureen brought serious money. Eventually she would buy out the debts of Clandeboye and put what remained of the estate on a sound financial footing for the first time in a hundred years. With her would come the hedonism of the inter-war years and a fatuous lifestyle given over to parties and friends, snobbery and selfishness, and in the case of Maureen a sense of humour that rarely ascended above pranks and practical jokes. There would be good deeds and honourable causes too but she would never lose that whiff of danger and the little arrogant cruelties that excessive wealth protects. She would have appalled the 1st Marquess (and no doubt been bored by him in return). Basil, however, with his satur-nine looks and 'liquid eyes', immense charm and impressive scholarship at Oxford, would have been much more what Dufferin had in mind when considering the future of the line. But by the end of the 1930s his political career was stalling as alcoholism and gambling told hold. His escape in the Second World War to serve courageously in Burma behind Japanese lines mirrored that of his namesake, Ava, forty years before. And it was perhaps fitting that he should die outside Ava, having liberated Fort Dufferin. It was remarkable that all those who had held the courtesy title of Ava had died prematurely – a circum-stance that would lead Caroline Blackwood to claim with some relish that the family had been cursed in retribution for her illustrious ancestor's brutal colonialism.[4]

Cursed or no, the same would hold true for the last marquess. Sheridan Dufferin, diffident and self-contained for much of his child-hood, was subtle, acute and elusive. An astute observer of others, his civility, wry expression and love of the absurd won many admirers. And yet, as with many intensely private people, he would remain a little detached unless in the company of close friends. With them he would party hard and (in contrast to his lack of ambition in the world outside) everything would be unexpectedly competitive, whether it was bridge, croquet or after-dinner games. Like the 1st Marquess he was a fine tennis player and a teetotaller. More importantly, he was highly cultured, an arbiter of taste, sharing with his forebear an intuitive appreciation of art. As part owner of the Kasmin Gallery he encouraged the development of new artists, as well as being a trustee of the National Gallery and the Wallace Collection. With his wife, Lindy Guinness, Sheridan was at the heart of a glittering sophisticated circle, largely aristocratic and wealthy but including artist friends such as David Hockney and Duncan Grant, along with other unexpected elements that made up the social scene in Sixties London. With the old guard giving way to the new, it was a time of exhilaration and savagery as society escaped the confines of one generation without yet appreciating the boundaries of the next. House parties at Clandeboye became the stuff of legend; remembered fondly for their warmth, eccentricity and exuberance – and for their droll, enigmatic host, mercurial as ever amid the fray.[5]

'We are all very Sheridanish', his sister would explain in later life and the idea of them being victims of 'bad Sheridan blood' was as much part of the family myth as in Dufferin's day. It was to exorcise this blood, Caroline insisted, that Brenda apparently tried to dash out the brains of her grandson against a wall at his christening.[6] Yet the success of Nelly and Victoria driving their men on to great imperial responsibilities dispels such convenient fatalism. Without their Protestantism and purpose (or indeed their mother), others would be overwhelmed by the shadow of the 1st Marquess and the expectations that family piety had raised to intolerable levels. Most coped through a combination of escape, ridicule or drink – or as Caroline called it, 'being Sheridanish'. To a degree, this was the latest stage of an ancient struggle of Blackwoods and Sheridans that had started with the marriage of Dufferin's parents and had continued ever since, with periodic infusions of Guinness money to sustain a house where glamour, creativity, scandal and a certain nobility too, sat increasingly out of kilter with its Ulster setting.

Oddly the first to relieve the oppression was Sheridan. For him Clandeboye came to be 'an enchanted place'. And part of that enchantment lay in a house infused with the spirit of his great-grandfather. He embarked on an ambitious restoration programme, returning the house to how it had been in the 1st Marquess's day. This was not a pedantic enterprise; kitchens were moved and heating added. More importantly 'pantechnicons' of fine furniture, paintings and carpets were 'blended imperceptibly' with all that Dufferin had brought back from a lifetime abroad. For both men were passionate collectors – 'magpies' – and in this revitalisation the intervening decades melted away. Nor was the empire to be a source of embarrassment. The display in the outer hall was improved, the Burmese and Indian treasures and the model of Mandalay restored and made prominent. In so doing the house regained its original confidence.[7] And it was to Clandeboye that Sheridan returned when his life was cut short by illness. In his last months he, with Lindy, designed a garden in the woods around a small stream that ran into the lake. To this he came for a last time, carried out by a loyal retainer, to see his work. Nearby was Campo Santo where the 5th and last Marquess of Dufferin and Ava was buried without issue in 1988 – exactly a hundred years after his predecessor had taken the title. Like his ancestor, Sheridan had returned to the grounds that had succoured them.

Twenty-five years on and Clandeboye has never looked finer. The house has been fully restored, Helen's Tower revived and revisited, and the surrounding estate carefully managed. A vignette of empire it may be but the place is alive with young enterprise – teams of Conservation Volunteers, in tandem with the Woodland Trust, revitalising the woods of Ulster; or local herdsmen breeding prize-winning pedigree Holstein Frisians and Jerseys. Young writers and artists are supported with regular exhibitions in the Ava gallery; while in the summer musicians come from all across Ireland for masterclasses and concerts with Camerata Ireland (unique for having the joint patronage of the Queen and the President of Ireland). A similar relationship has been developed with the Royal Botanic Gardens at Kew encouraging local horticulturists.[8] Together these activities reflect Clandeboye's re-engagement with its Irish surroundings, free at last from the constraints of planter and native, landlord and tenant.

Now the ambition is to look further afield and find ways to reconnect the estate with Dufferin's empire – the countries in which he served. For while the house remains a remarkable icon of the British Empire, it also reflects the reconfiguration of imperial values in the modern era. Not least in the exploration of new societies and different cultures for, unlike most imperialists of his day, Dufferin retained a fascination with what was 'other' and local: the modern challenge of cultural integration and the pursuit of unity in divided communities Dufferin had himself faced in Syria, Canada and India. Over three decades and across hemispheres and continents, he had witnessed the empire as a forerunner of global citizenship. Such diversity of terrain also instilled a deeply felt engagement with the natural environment, alongside an excitement in the transformative power of new technology and ideas. At the heart of this, providing the energy and creativity, is a chatelaine, who still finds time to exhibit her pictures in London and Paris. Like the 1st Marquess, she is an enthusiastic planter. As with the house, so with the estate, the desire has been to recover Dufferin's romantic vision, refreshing the original woods, clearing the lakes, establishing an arboretum to connect with one he planted in the 1850s. Again the approach is respectful, not pietistic or imitative – an engagement instead of like minds. And nowhere is this more so than in their respective designs for informal gardens around the Lake, both in terms of scale ('gardening with JCBs') and in their approaching them as they would their 'paintings'. In essence the last Marquess and his wife have reshaped the legacy of the 1st Marquess, as he before them had redefined Sheridan. A last hurrah it may prove to be but noble and heroic in its aspiration and execution and which leaves Clandeboye hopeful of its future. Dufferin would only have approved.

Acknowledgements

M Y FIRST DEBT is to Roy Foster, not only for being an inspiration and a mentor over many years, but also for proposing that I should write the biography of the first Marquess of Dufferin and Ava. That was in 1990. For this book, as my adult daughter gleefully keeps telling me, is in the gestation almost as old as she is. Not for much longer. A colleague of mine once dedicated a book to the boys in his house who distracted him for so long. I fear I cannot blame the boys in my house – I need no help when it comes to distraction – but they may be surprised to discover that this book was not, after all, a figment of myth. That this proved true is due in the first instance to many people in numerous archives who gave very generously of their time. In particular I would like to thank the generations of staff at the Public Record Office of Northern Ireland who were unfailingly helpful; not least Anthony Malcomson, Gerry Slater, Aileen McClintock and, more recently, Ian Montgomery and Lorraine Bourke. But first and foremost I am especially grateful to the late Dr Andrew Harrison. It was he who assiduously established the Dufferin and Blackwood archives as well as collecting Dufferin material from archives throughout the UK. Out of this came his PhD thesis which – with his authoritative grasp of the manuscript sources – remains the starting point for all scholarship on Dufferin. Sadly he did not live to write the biography he had intended. Whether or not he would have recognised the Dufferin on these pages, it certainly owes much to his scholarship and support.

I am indebted to the gracious permission of Her Majesty the Queen for allowing me to consult the Royal Archives at Windsor and to cite certain passages. For access to other manuscript collections and permission to quote from them I am grateful to the Marchioness of

Dufferin and Ava and the Deputy Keeper of Records at the Public Record Office of Northern Ireland, the National Archives, the Bodleian Libraries of the University of Oxford, the British Library, Devon Heritage Centre, National Library of Scotland, Stella Panayotova and the Syndics of the Fitzwilliam Museum, Patrick Zutshi and the Syndics of the Cambridge University Library. I would like to thank the Society of Authors for a grant towards the research of this book and to Tim Connor, Sir Eric Anderson and Tony Little for grants of study leave. Lois Sumner, Judith Nash, Janet Easterling and recently Carolyn Raeside have shown patience beyond the call of duty in typing and editing innumerable drafts. Thank you to Charlotte Villiers and Denis Wallis for their suggestions for maps and to Emily Gailey, Chris Gailey and Kay Deane for their comments on the text. Long ago I learnt much from discussions on imperial India with James Walmsley; and from many insightful conversations with Joe Spence, Paul Bew and John Young. At John Murray I am grateful for Caroline Knox's earlier support and that Roland Philipps didn't baulk when after many years I suddenly presented him with a script. I have appreciated the input of Juliet Brightmore as picture editor and Lyndsey Ng with publicity. Equally valuable has been the contributions of Martin Bryant my copy-editor, Douglas Matthews who has compiled the index and Nick de Somogyi who has proofread the whole text. But, most importantly, Caro Westmore has a remarkable talent in pulling everything together while somehow keeping her authors sane.

Clandeboye is a special place wherein live some special people. Thank you to John Witchell and Dick Blakiston-Houston for their local knowledge and friendship; and to Robbie John and all his staff for feeding and looking after me for many a year. Many thanks to Robert Malone, for the photographes from the Dufferin and Ava Archive. This book would have been impossible without Lola Armstrong's wholehearted commitment to Clandeboye, and to this project in particular. I really appreciated her invariably positive response to every research request and imprecise query. Nothing was ever too much for her. In this she mirrors her mistress. Lindy Dufferin is a force: irrepressible, mesmeric, panoramic in her imagination and boundlessly hopeful. She has stuck by this book and its author long after she had any reason to, and throughout she has never ceased to be enthusiastic and encouraging – indeed effervescently so. Together this book has been such fun to write.

Finally I owe my greatest debt to Shauna and Emily. What was initially supposed to be a one-year project has become, over the decades, the fourth member of the family. Where they might have despaired at the obsession that overtakes most writers, they have displayed only wry humour and unceasing support, and more love than I deserve.

Illustration Credits

Most of the pictures are reproduced courtesy of The Dufferin and Ava Archive at Clandeboye.

Additional Sources
Mary Evans Picture Library: page 6, page 9 above left, text page 162. Arthur Fish, *Henrietta Rae*, Cassell & Co., 1905: page 14 centre and below.

Notes

Abbreviations

D1071/W/27	Dufferin, Draft Memoir
DD	Dufferin, Diary
DNB	*Oxford Dictionary of National Biography*
HD	Hariot Dufferin
Letter Books	Letter books of Dufferin's mother
MDACQ	*The Marquis of Dufferin and Ava's Correspondence with the Queen 1871–1888*, in Helen's Tower Library
MIC	Dufferin Archive (microfilm collection)
OHBE	*The Oxford History of the British Empire*
QVD	Queen Victoria's Diaries
RA	Royal Archive, Windsor
TNA	The National Archives

PROLOGUE

1. 15.7.1894, D1071H/W1/27, p.114.
2. Sir Alfred Lyall, *The Life of Lord Dufferin* (1905 Nelson ed.), p.501.

CHAPTER 1: A CONFLICT OF TRADITIONS

1. Much of the family history that follows has been drawn from Dufferin's Draft Memoir, D1071/W1/27; Lizzie Ward's reminiscences which Dufferin commissioned in 1884 and reside in a printed volume in the Helen's Tower Library; and Dufferin's 'A Sketch of My Mother' in his edition of Helen, Lady Gifford, *Songs, Poems and Verses* (1894). In addition his mother's Letter Books in Clandeboye, which were typed up and bound in 1894, contain many notes and pen-portraits by Dufferin. See also Andrew Harrison, 'The First Marquess of Dufferin and Ava: Whig, Ulster Landlord and Imperialist', N.U.U. PhD thesis, 1983, pp. 9–26.

2. This may have reflected a delicate conscience, particularly as his father-in-law, Sir John Foster (Lord Oriel) was leading the defence of the Dublin Parliament.

3. Her experience of great men denied included a glimpse of Napoleon immensely stout under a huge straw hat, prowling in captivity on St Helena.

4. Mrs John Marshall, 'Memorandum on Tom Sheridan', D1071B/D4/1.

5. Helen to Caroline (her sister), October 1826, Helen, Lady Gifford's Letter Books, Helen's Tower Library, i, 4.

6. For the correspondence between Price and Hans and James Dufferin, see D1071D/12.

7. Helen to Caroline, 4.3.26, Letter Books, i, 3; Georgiana Sheridan to Brinsley Sheridan, 27.7.26, D1071B/D5/43.

8. Dufferin, 'Sketch', pp. 54–5.

9. Helen to Brinny, 17.8.27, Letter Books, i, 8.

10. Helen to Lizzie Blackwood, 1 and 14.6.30, Letter Books, i, 14. Diane Atkinson, *The Criminal Conversation of Mrs Norton* (2012), p.69.

11. Helen to Brinny, 30.7.28 and 10.11.29, Letter Books, i, 9 and 12. Rev. William Blackwood, Dufferin's uncle, was most famous for his retort to Melbourne when the latter was rejecting his claim for a bishopric. Delicately the prime minister (of all people) hinted at widespread rumours of a mistress. 'Not a word of truth in it, my Lord,' came the indignant reply, 'I wish to God there was!'

12. D1071H/W1/27, pp. 61–7. Dufferin's note after Helen to Brinny, 30.7.28, Letter Books, i, 9.

13. Helen to 'Muddle' (her mother), 20.11.30, 30.12.30, Letter Books, i, 22–5.

14. Helen to 'Muddle', 23.11.30; Price to Mrs Sheridan, 4.12.30, Letter Books, i, 23–4. Helen to Price, 'Friday 1831' and 27.10.31, Letter Books, i, 33 and 40.

CHAPTER 2: THE TRIUMPH OF THE SHERIDANS

1. Macaulay to Mrs William Penrose, 24.1.54, D1071B/D1/22.

2. Dufferin , 'Sketch', pp. 34–5. Helen to Brinny, 30.7.28, Letter Books, i, 9. Helen to Lizzie, 7.12.34, Letter Books, i, 90.

3. Helen to Brinny, 30.7.28, Letter Books, i, 9. Helen to Lizzie Blackwood, 8.5.31. Letter Books, i, 31. Disraeli to Sarah Disraeli, 21.2.1833, cited in Moneypenny, *Disraeli*, p.231. Philip Ziegler, *Melbourne* (1976), p.227.

4. 'Mrs Norton and Mrs Blackwood, beautiful Greeks', Disraeli to Sarah Disraeli, 20.7.35, Moneypenny, W. F. and Buckle, G. E., *The Life of Benjamin Disraeli, Earl of Beaconsfield* (1910–20), vi, pp. 302–3. Alison Adburgham, *Silver Fork Society: Fashionable Life and Literature, 1814–40* (1983), p.198. James Pope-Hennessy, *Richard Monckton Milnes: The Years of Promise* (1949), pp. 109–11.

5. Pope-Hennessy, *Milnes*, p.111.

6. Moneypenny, *Life of Benjamin Disraeli*, vi (1910), p.231. *Silver Fork Society*, p.193.

7. Lord Ronald Gower, *My Reminiscences*, p.552. Sarah Bradford, *Disraeli* (1983), pp. 152–3.

For the correspondence with Disraeli, see John Gunn (ed.), *Letters of Benjamin Disraeli*, (1982), i, 323–50. Moneypenny, *Disraeli*, pp. 232–3.

8. Creevey to Miss Ord, 26.5.36, John Gore (ed.), *Creevey's Life and Times* (1934), pp. 406–7. Lizzie Ward, 'Reminiscences', pp. 33–5. Helen to Frederick, 13.6.35, Letter Books, i, 95. Dufferin, 'Sketch', p.32.

9. However, there is a reference to Somerset having to take up the challenge from Grant (after helping the old general over a stile 'onto the field of battle'). Neither hit, Somerset purposely aiming wide. H. R. Grenfell to Dufferin, 7.9.97, D1071/H/B/G/404/1. Diane Atkinson, *The Criminal Conversation of Mrs Norton* (2012), pp. 124–9.

10. On the Norton marriage and much of what follows see Alan Chedzoy, *A Scandalous Woman: The Story of Caroline Norton* (1992). Ziegler, *Melbourne*, pp. 231–9. Diane Atkinson, *The Criminal Conversation of Mrs Norton* (2012).

11. Helen to Caroline, 'June '36', Letter Books, i, 109.

12. Diane Atkinson, *The Criminal Conversation of Mrs Norton* (2012), pp. 146–206, 423.

13. Helen to Lizzie, 16.1.40, Letter Books, i, 137.

14. 'The whole family of Sheridans had a disposition opposite to prudery', *The Satirist*, 12 June 1836. Atkinson, *Conversation*, pp. 175, 252.

15. Dufferin's note, Helen Dufferin Letter Books, i, 8 and 45.

16. Helen to Price, 5 and 13.11.31, 28.3.32, 6 and 21.6.32, 3.9.32, Letter Books, i, 46, 50, 61, 64, 66, 67.

17. 'I remember [over 60 years later] the day of my mother's coming of age, for I had poisoned myself with some laburnum seeds and my mother told me afterwards it had spoilt the anniversary'. Dufferin's note in Letter Books, i, 8.

18. Helen to Dufferin, 21.6.32, Letter Books, i, 65

19. Dufferin note, Helen's Letter Books, i, 8. Helen to Dufferin, 21.6.33, 30.5.36, Letter Books, i, 78, 108.

20. Harrison, p.29. Helen to Dufferin, 23.3.42, Letter Books, i, 184. DD), 19.1.42; 14 and 21.2.42.

21. Helen to Dufferin, 14.10.39, 7.2.40, 14.4.41, Letter Books, i, 127, 138. Helen to Lizzie, 19.6.40, Letter Books, i, 142. Price to Helen, 26.6.41, D1071D/6.

22. Lyall, p.39. Andrew Roberts, *Salisbury*, p.815.

23. DD, 8.2.42. Lyall, pp. 38–9.

24. Helen to Lizzie Ward, 10.3.38, 6.12.39, i, 119, 132.

25. Helen to Price, 25.7.35; Helen to Lizzie, 12.4.40; Letter Books, i, 101, 141. Helen to Brin, 30.9.31 and Dufferin's later marginal comment on his mother being subject all her life to 'attacks of low fever'. Letter Books, i, 37.

26. Pope-Hennessy, *Milnes*, p.111. Helen to Lizzie Ward, 15.10.39, Letter Books, i, 128. Brin to Helen, 'December 1840': 'Frederick quite perfect . . . there is a dash of modesty about him that does not in the least remind me of his father – Hem!' D1071F/B2/4.

27. Price to Dufferin, 24.11.37, D1071 D/6.

28. DD, 21.6.39.

29. Only then to join Brin and the Kilmoreys sailing off Southampton. For someone who never failed to deplore the horrors of the Irish sea passage, this was rich indeed.

30. Helen only seems to have visited him at Eton twice: once to deliver him to Cookesley (to whom she took an instant dislike) and at his confirmation where due to her short-sightedness 'some smart blue waistcoated Jacob got the blessing which I had intended for my blue waistcoated Esau'. Compare this to the support his father offered when his son was being bullied at school. Price to Dufferin, 7.11.39, D1071 D/6.

31. Dufferin to Helen, 11.8.40, D1071F/ B1/1.

32. D. Walder, *Nelson*, pp. 342–3, 498.

33. Price to Helen, 4.7.41. Dufferin to Price, 4.6.41. D1071D/6.

34. Gifford Journal, 21.7.41, D1071G/A/16. Dufferin 'A Sketch of My Mother', pp. 69–71.

35. Harrison, p.21.

CHAPTER 3: THE BIRTH OF 'AUTHENTIC' DUFFERIN

1. DD, 29.5.43(?). Harold Nicolson, *Helen's Tower* (1937), pp. 35–41.

2. Boyd Hilton, *The Age of Atonement*, p.249.

3. Helen to Dufferin, 9.12.43, Letter Books, ii, 5; Dufferin to Helen, 25.7.(84?), 'Hampton Court' (1844?). D1071F/B1/1-6.

4. Dufferin to Helen, 'Sunday Oxford', D1071F/B1/1-6.

5. Helen to Mrs Nugent, 9.3.43, Letter Books, ii, 2. Helen to Gifford, 4.9.41, 2.12.41.

6. Helen to Gifford, 1.9.42, 21.6.43,; Helen to Dufferin, 'Saturday [September] 1843', Letter Books, ii, 4.

7. Helen to Mrs Nugent, 22.7.44, Letter Books, ii, 8. 'In all reading it is of the first consequence to be in good health and spirits'. Somerset to Dufferin, 22.7.(44?), D1071H/B/S/204/4.

8. Dufferin, 'A Sketch of My Mother'. 'They were able to fuse the Victorian dogmas of parental discipline and filial piety with a twentieth-century sense of companionship'. Nicolson, *Helen's Tower*, pp. 61–3. Jane Ridley, *Bertie: A Life of Edward VII* (2012), p.163.

9. Helen to Mrs Nugent, 22.7.44, Letter Books, ii, 8.

10. Nicolson, *Helen's Tower*, p.67.

11. Dufferin to Helen, 24.1.45, 3.?.45, D1071F/B/1-6. Helen to Dufferin, 2.2.45, Letter Books, ii, 17.

12. Of Kimberley, who would play a major part in his later career, Dufferin's first impressions captured an intimidating aspect that would never quite disappear: 'I do not like him particularly but he is very clever and a great talker'. Dufferin to Helen, 24.?.1846, D1071F/B1/1-6. Six of his Christ Church contemporaries were to achieve cabinet rank. Lyall, p.54.

13. Dufferin to Helen, 1.2.45, 20–2.2.(45), n.d. (February 1845), 24.?.46, D1071F/B1/1-6. In the last letter he denounced at Christ Church 'the monstrous monopoly which [Eton] now enjoys'.

14. Sheridan Gilley, *Newman and his Age* (1990), pp. 224–8.
15. Dufferin to de Ros, n.d. (1845?), D2903/1.
16. Nicolson, *Helen's Tower*, p.69. Jelf to Dufferin, 28.7.46, MIC 22/1.
17. Gilley, *Newman*, pp. 156, 189, 211, 236–46.
18. DD, 12–13, 17, 24, 26.10.45; 11, 12, 16, 29.11.45.
19. DD, 4.12.45, 9.5.46. Thomas, Bishop of Ely to Dufferin, 9.5.46, MIC 22/1.
20. These included Guizot, Victor Hugo, Balzac and Louis Philippe – none of whom were near eighty!
21. DD, 12.1.46.
22. 'Gil Blas [the eighteenth-century picaresque novel] would be as good as any. Do not imagine that it is with any interested views that I suggest this. The birching, I assure you, has no attraction to me'. Dufferin to Helen (February 1846), D1071F/B1/1-6.
23. DD, 27.6.46, 24.7.46. Dufferin to Helen, n.d., 3.12.46, D1071F/B1/1-6.
24. Harrison, pp. 30–2.
25. Helen to Dufferin, 10.2.45, 21.4.45, Letter Books, ii, 19, 27.
26. Dufferin's note in Letter Book, ii, 16. Dufferin to Helen, 7.6.46, D1071F/B1/1-6. Helen to Dufferin, 'Saturday' (1846?), Letter Books, ii, 41.
27. Lyall, p.520.
28. A. N. Wilson, *The Victorians*, pp. 98–104. W. E. Houghton, *The Victorian Frame of Mind, 1830–1870*, (1957), pp. 64–9, 84–5, 348–9, 355–6.
29. Dufferin to Helen, '1845', 'Oxford, Saturday', D1071F/B1/1-6.
30. DD, 20.10.45, 17.3.46. Dufferin to Helen, 'Oxford, Saturday', D1071F/B1/1-6.
31. Lyall, pp. 46–7. Nicolson, *Helen's Tower*, p.68.
32. Dufferin to Helen, 'Sunday', 'Tuesday', 7.6.46, 24.11.46. DD, 12–15.6.46.
33. Lyall, p.52. Dufferin to Helen, 8.2.47, D1071F/B1/1-6. Francis Hepburn to Dufferin, 24.4.48, 29.11.48. 'I can quite enter into your feelings for her [Dufferin's mother] and believe that she has spoilt you for a wife', 20.6.48. MIC 22/1.
34. Intriguingly, cruelty to animals was the least of his arguments, he preferring to stress the risk to humans, the time wasted and 'the vacuum which generally prevails in a fox hunter's mind'. DD, 5.1.46.
35. Richard Faber, *Young England* (1987), p.167. Robert Blake, *Disraeli* (1966, 1978 ed.), p.218. Admittedly, while Disraeli was writing, Dufferin was more interested in 'contraband entertainments' of punch and champagne in the rooms above. DD, 23.2.42, 2.3.42: 'Party in the evening, nearly nailed. (1/6).' The same period also saw him develop an aesthetic interest in book-binding, ordering a bookcase to set off his first volumes.
36. DD, 4.11.45; 21.1.46; 24.2.46; 1, 6, 13.3.46. Dufferin to Helen, 15.4.45, Letter Books, ii, 26.
37. Lyall, p.48. DD, 7.5.46.
38. Lyall, pp. 55–7. Harrison, pp. 135–6.
39. Lyall, p.50. Nicolson, *Helen's Tower*, pp. 69–70.

CHAPTER 4: 'THE ONE GREAT PURPOSE AND INTEREST OF MY LIFE'

1. Dufferin to Helen, 'June 1847', D1071 F/B1/1-6.
2. Dufferin to Helen, 'Sunday', D1071F/B1/6.
3. Since she still denied him a key to their London home and continued to send letters exhorting him to wear flannel (making sure that it was 'thoroughly aired whenever changed'), her son may have had some cause.
4. Dufferin to Helen, 'Thursday', D1071F/B1/6 for a description of the Legges' ball which seemed to be largely conducted in the dark to the music of one drunken fiddler.
5. D1071/W/27, pp. 94–6; Peter Carr, *Portavo* (Belfast 2003), pp. 277–9.
6. Dufferin, *Narrative of a Journey from Oxford to Skibbereen* (Oxford, 1847), pp. 7–11, 22.
7. Lyall, pp. 59–62.
8. Harrison, p.138. Lyall, p.58.
9. John Cartmell to Dufferin, 19.12.48, MIC 22/1.
10. Harrison, pp. 139–42. After hearing Dufferin on his tenants, the Queen recorded that 'the Protestants are far more truthful than the Roman Catholics but not entirely so.' RA VIC/MAIN/QVJ: 1869, 23 February.
11. Pakington to Dufferin, 4.5.48, MIC 22/1.
12. Lyall, pp. 67–8. Nicolson, *Helen's Tower*, pp. 91–3. Harrison, p.146.
13. DD, 13–30.8.49. Dufferin to Helen, 'Dunlowe, Wednesday', D1071F/B1/6. Lyall. pp. 69–70. L. P. Curtis, *Apes and Angels*.
14. Dufferin was far from alone in viewing the Famine in such apocalyptic terms. Gladstone famously decreed the Famine to be 'a calamity most legibly Divine' and Dufferin's uncle and guardian, Sir James Graham, who as Peel's Home Secretary had received the first reports of the catastrophe, was equally biblical in his response. Hilton, *Atonement*, p.249.
15. Dufferin to Helen, 17.8.49, D1071F/B1/6.
16. On this, see Harrison, pp. 162–80.
17. Dufferin to Helen, 21.2.48, D1071F/B1/6. 'I have a kind of intense satisfaction in the certainty of my conviction'.
18. DD, 2.9.46. Even after the Young Ireland rising, he retained some sympathy for gentlemen rebels such as Mitchell (whose trial he attended) 'for doing what he considered right'. Harrison, p.146.
19. *Belfast Newsletter*, 4.1.48.
20. Such as he found in Galway on his 1849 expedition with Abercorn, which had left him resentful of 'our gruff Northerners'. Dufferin to Helen, n.d., D1071F/B1/6.
21. Actually Scott titled them 'Clandeboy': 'Ah Clandeboy! Thy friendly floor / Slieve Donard's oak shall light no more . . . And now the stranger's sons enjoy / The lovely woods of Clandeboy!'

22. Helen to Dufferin, 'Thursday', 1849, D1071F/B1/6.
23. DD, 19.9.50.
24. Dufferin's note (1899) accompanying a volume of plans describing the development of the house and grounds.
25. Dufferin to Janie Ellice, 10.11.55, D1071H/B/E/59/2. Dufferin to Helen, 25.12.?, D1071F/B1/6.
26. Dan Cruickshank, *The Country House Revealed* (2011), pp. 181–2, 201. Mark Bence-Jones, 'The Building Dreams of a Viceroy', 1, *Country Life* (1.10.1970), pp. 816–19.
27. DD, 29.3.50, 2 and 8.10.50, 20.11.50. Nicolson, *Helen's Tower*, pp. 86, 96–7, 138–41. Gavin Stamp, 'Helen's Tower', in Peter Rankin (ed.), *Clandeboye* (Ulster Architectural Heritage Society, 1985), pp. 29–33.
28. A. Rowan-Hamilton to Dufferin, 10.2.60. This was particularly generous as he was 'continually cursing his ancestors' for giving up Killyleagh for Ballyleidy. Dufferin to Helen, 'Sunday', D1071F/B1/6. The original proposal was for 'The lord of the castle to send every year a rose to the ladies of Clandeboye' in lieu of the gatehouse. DD, 4.10.55.
29. DD, 6–12.10.50, 22–26.12.50, 16.8.52. Patrick Bowe, 'James Fraser and Clandeboye', unpublished paper, 5.8.94.
30. As a consequence of cutting off the public highway, Dufferin was in conflict with an overzealous post office official in Belfast insisting as a consequence on moving the post box from the Clandeboye avenue. 'Even Euclid would have been impressed with your mathematics', reassured the Postmaster General, who happened to be his old friend, Canning. 'I hear that you have been standing on your head and singing songs in female attire. Euclid never did that', he jested as he overturned the local scheme. For this 'abuse' of privilege, Anthony Trollope (who was that official) later told Dufferin that he then 'held me in the greatest aversion'. Explanatory note in Helen to Giff, 'Jan 1855', D1071F/A2/4.

CHAPTER 5: IN SEARCH OF FAVOUR

1. Helen to 'My Duckling' (Dufferin), 'Friday 1847', Letter Books, ii, 69.
2. Ibid.
3. Nicolson, *Helen's Tower*, pp. 86, 115.
4. DD, 3, 6–7.6.49.
5. DD, 8, 31.7.49.
6. DD 5–10.8.49. Dufferin to Helen, n.d., 'Baronscourt' (August 1849), D1071F/B1/6.
7. For what follows, see Dufferin to Helen, 'Laggan Sunday' (September 1849), D1071F/B1/6. DD, 1–30.9.49. Harrison, pp. 52–3.
8. Helen to Dufferin, 18.9.49, 25.9.49, 'Sunday' (October 1849), Letter Books, ii, 108, 113, 115. Dufferin to Helen, 'Inverary Thursday' (September 1849), 'Glenquoich' (October 1849), D1071F/B1/6.

9. DD, 13–23.11.49. The lily was the creation of his gardener Joseph Paxton.

10. Helen to Dufferin, Bretby, 'December 1849', Letter Books, ii, 125. DD, 10–14, 24.6.49, 26.12.49. Sir James Graham to Dufferin, 26.12.49, MIC 22/2.

11. Even if Nicolson thought the picture which still hangs in the outer hall at Clandeboye 'execrable'. Nicolson, *Helen's Tower*, pp. 77–8.

12. Dufferin to Helen, n.d., D1071F/B1/6.

13. Dufferin to Helen, n.d. (September 1849), D1071F/B1/6. DD 28.1.50, 30.6.50, 6–8.8.50

14. DD, 20.7.49, 5–9.12.49, 13 and 22.4.50, 15.7.50, 5–6.2.51.

15. DD, 7.1.50. Dufferin attempted unsuccessfully to obliterate this reference. He was more successful with entries for 11,17,18.12.49, which were also about Lady Jocelyn. All of which might suggest that his mother's instincts were sound. Helen to Dufferin, 'Friday' (December 1849), Letter Books, ii, 124.

16. Hepburn to Dufferin, 20.6.48, MIC 22/1. Dufferin to Helen, 25.12.?, D1071F/ B1/6.

17. At a Howard family gathering in 1850 the only addition was 'the bright liveliness of Dufferin to enhance it'. *Journals of George Howard, Earl of Carlisle* (1871), 23.8.50.

18. It would certainly have failed to have wooed Jane Eyre. Having initially despised such 'active heroines' Dufferin had come to 'love' her by the end of the novel: 'yet I could never have married her. I should feel so inferior, such a sponge compared to her.' Dufferin to Helen, 6.2.48, D1071F/B1/6. DD, 2.1.50.

19. DD, 4.2.51.

20. Dufferin to Helen, n.d., D1071F/B1/6. Helen to Dufferin, 19.1.50, Letter Books, ii, 138. DD, 17, 22, 24, 26, 27.1.50. He took his seat on 31.1.50.

21. DD, 23–5.1.51; 3, 15, 26.4.51; 8–9.5.51; 3 and 8.6.51

22. DD, 28.12.50–6.1.51. Dufferin to Helen, n.d. (1852?), D1071F/B1/6. 'The Duchess [of Bedford] at dinner asked me whether she was to congratulate herself on my becoming her son-in-law and called me Freddie on the strength of the anticipation.' Dufferin to Helen, 'Thursday' (October 1849), D1071F/B1/6.

23. DD, 9–12, 21, 23, 26–7.6.51, 8.8.51. DD, 1–6.9.51; 11–24.10.51. Sir James Graham to Dufferin, '1851', MIC 22/2. Helen to Dufferin, 13.2.52, Letter Books, iii, 19. DD, 17–21.1.52.

24. DD, 26–8.9.50.

25. Helen to Dufferin, 26.9.51. Letter Books, iii, 6. Harriet, Duchess of Sutherland to Dufferin, 1.10.51, MIC 22/2. Constance Gower, to Dufferin, 27.4.52, MIC 22/3.

26. DD, 17.2.52. Georgy to Dufferin, '1852', MIC 22/3.

27. Despite this, he quickly forgave her, writing 'I can speak to you as if . . . in silence to my own heart'. Dufferin to Helen, 14.3.52, D1071F/B1/6.

28. Dufferin to Helen, 14 and 26.3.52, and n.d. (1852), D1071F/B1/6. DD, 17–30.6.52.

29. Dufferin to Helen, 'Thursday 1852', D1071F/B1/6. Later she was to marry (and run) Lord Carnarvon ('Twitters') and establish a reputation as a Tory hostess of considerable influence; sufficiently powerful indeed to forbid her mother from marrying Disraeli.

CHAPTER 6: THE POLITICS OF ROMANCE

1. Dufferin to Helen, 'Saturday' (1850), D1071F/B1/6.
2. Lyall, p.82.
3. Lady Russell to Dufferin, 17.6.50 and 12.11.50, MIC 22/2. 'They seemed to think that my nervousness was an advantage', DD, 1.7.50. Harrison, pp. 56–7.
4. Dufferin to Lady Russell, 27.10.51, D1071H/B/R/442/41. Lyall p.74. Nevertheless he did admit that the Austrians had preserved the 'old palaces' from predatory local developers.
5. Harrison, pp. 178–9.
6. Lady Russell to Dufferin, 27.11.51, MIC 22/3. Argyll to Dufferin, 19.8.53, MIC 22/4. Helen, of course, could be just as bad, describing to Giff a reception at Clandeboye for the Lord Lieutenant, Lord Carlisle, in November 1855, at which were 'a heap of Professors, Arian Ministers, Catholic Bishops, and "kittle-cattle" of all sorts not to mention 1000 fools – the indigenous population of the soil to whom we gave a concert afterwards.'
7. Dufferin to Helen, 21.2.48; 'Saturday' (1850); 'Genoa' (1851), D1071F/B1/6.
8. Lyall p.83.
9. Cited by Davenport-Hines in DNB.
10. Helen to Giff, 23.8.53, D1071F/A2/4. Caroline to Dufferin, '1853', MIC 22/4. Alan Chedzoy, *A Scandalous Woman*, pp. 220–1, 232–43. Ultimately time was to prove Caroline correct and 150 years on, divorced wives continue to be in her debt. Atkinson, *Criminal Conversation*, p.424.
11. Elizabeth Argyll to Dufferin, 10.12.53, MIC 22/4. Helen to Georgy, 'Tuesday 1853', 12.10.53, Letter Books, iii, 39, 42. Chedzoy, pp. 262–5.
12. Reviewing his papers in the 1890s he commented: 'Though my mother and Caroline got on very well together, Caroline was always a very uncertain quantity and a source of disturbance and worry to her relations'. Letter Books, ii, 16.
13. For this section see DD, 10.7.–18.8.54. Sir Arthur Otway (ed.), *The Autobiography and Journals of Admiral Lord Clarence Paget* (1896). Dufferin, 'A Last Letter from High Latitudes', *Cornhill Magazine*, November 1898.
14. Sir James Graham to Dufferin, 24.11.54; Lord John Russell to Dufferin, 8, 14, 16.2.55, MIC 22/4.
15. DD, 3–4.3.55; 19–28.3.55.
16. DD, 22, 30.4.55.
17. Dufferin to Helen, 22.3.55, D1071F/B1/3. Janey Ellice to Dufferin, 20.1.56, MIC 22/6. Lady Jocelyn to Dufferin, '1854', MIC 22/4. Caroline to Dufferin, 8.4.55, MIC 22/5.
18. Helen to Dufferin, 7.3.55, Letter Books, iii, 104. Although only Caroline would have put it quite so shamelessly on Dufferin's return from Vienna: 'My dear Lord! Fall in love with a Lichtenstein.'
19. Janey Ellice to Dufferin, 5.9.55, MIC 22/5. Dufferin to Helen, 'Friday', D1071F/B1/6.

CHAPTER 7: THE THRILL OF ESCAPE

1. Lady Russell to Dufferin, 4.7.56, MIC 22/6. DD, 1–2.6.56. Interestingly he did make a will leaving everything to his mother (but only to be produced if challenged by his family!). DD, 5.2.56.
2. Dufferin to Helen, 21.6.56, D1071F/B1/5.
3. Dufferin speech notes on 'Northmen', D1071H/W3/1.
4. Dufferin to Helen, 21.6.56, D1071F/B1/5
5. Dufferin to Helen, 'Tuesday June 1856', D1071F/B1/5. Dufferin, *Letters from High Latitudes* (1903 ed.; 1989 reprint), pp. 10, 15–16.
6. DD, 18.6.56. *High Latitudes*, p.16.
7. *High Latitudes*, pp. 35–42. Dufferin to Helen, 'Reykjavik', D1071F/B1/5.
8. Ibid.
9. *High Latitudes*, pp. 87–91.
10. HIH Prince Napoleon was a nephew and the image of his uncle Napoleon I (and a cousin of Napoleon III).
11. *High Latitudes*, pp. 114–29.
12. Dufferin to Helen, 2.8.56, D1071F/B1/5.
13. *High Latitudes*, pp. 149–50, 161–85. Dufferin to Helen, 22.8.56, D1071F/B1/5.
14. And inspired some to recreate his expedition, most notably James Nixon in 2006 and, more frivolously, Tim Moore, *Frost on my Moustache* (1999).
15. G. W. Dasent to Dufferin, 24.10.56, D1071H/B/D/42/1–7.
16. Too much so for one poor teacher in Barnes who in 1876 lost his post for reading 'indecent' excerpts to his class. John Green to Dufferin, 24.1.76, D1071H/B/G/372/1.
17. *High Latitudes*, p.169.
18. *High Latitudes*, p.155. Nicolson, talks of 'a neo-gothic strain to Dufferin's temperament'. *Helen's Tower*, pp. 106–12.
19. DD, 27.8.57. Lyall, p.98.

CHAPTER 8: 'ANY PEARL?'

1. Elizabeth Argyll to Dufferin, 18.8.58, MIC 22/7.
2. Helen to Dufferin, 6.2.57, Letter Books, iii, 141.
3. DD, 26.7.58. Archibald Rowan-Hamilton to Dufferin (April 1857?); David Ker to Dufferin, 15.4 and 15.7.57, MIC 22/7; Rowan-Hamilton to Dufferin, 15.2.59, MIC 22/9.
4. Lewin, Letters, ii, 164.
5. Tennyson to Dufferin, 19.9.58, MIC 22/9. Henrietta Todesco to Dufferin, 17.7.57, MIC 22/7. Lord Ronald Gower, *Old Diaries* (1902), p.59.
6. W. Richardson to Dufferin, (April) 1857, 2.8.57, MIC 22/8. John Hamilton to Dufferin, 'July 1857', MIC 22/7.

7. DD, 25.11 and 17–18.12.57. Elizabeth Argyll to Dufferin, 20.12.57, MIC 22/8. Dufferin to Helen, 'Wednesday' 1857, D1071F/B1/6.

8. Helen to Giff, 17.1.54, 'September 1855', 24.9.55, 15.10.55, 'November 1855', 12.11.56, 17.2.57. D1071F/A2/4.

9. Helen to Giff, 17.9.58, D1071F/A2/4. *Correspondence of J. L. Motley*, pp. 263–8.

10. DD, 9.1, 6–9.2, 8.3, 1–6.4, 20–9.7, 16.8.58.

11. DD, 5–10, 25.8.58, 3–4.9.58. Nelly Graham to Dufferin, 13.1.58, MIC 22/8; 3.7.58, 30.8.58, 8.9.58, MIC 22/9. Elizabeth Argyll to Dufferin, 8.10.58, MIC 22/9. The portrait remains in the gallery in Clandeboye.

12. DD, 25.8.58.

13. DD, 10–15, 22–8.8.58, 25.9.58. Cossy Graham to Dufferin, 28.12.57, MIC 22/7; 12.9.58, MIC 22/9.

14. Sir James Graham to Dufferin, 17.9.58, MIC 22/9.

15. DD, 2, 10 and 19.9.58.

16. Stafford to Dufferin, 2.11.58, MIC 22/9.

17. Elizabeth Argyll to Dufferin, 3.6.59, MIC 22/9.

18. Argyll to Dufferin, October 1858, D1071H/B/C/95/1. DD 19–20.10.58.

19. DD, 9–12.12.58.

20. Said Pasha (d.1862) was the son of the great reformer Mohammed Ali. DD, 24.12.58.

21. DD, 6–7.1.59.

22. DD, 6, 17, 19, 22–7.2.59; 20.3–18.4.59, 29.4–1.5.59. Dufferin to Aunt Anna, 7.5.59.

23. DD, 5–16.6.59.

24. Helen to Giff, 6.8.59, Letter Books, iii, 166, 169. Helen to Giff, 28.8.59, D1071F/A2/4. Helen to Georgy, 15.7.59, Letter Books, iii, 164. Helen to Aunt Anna, 2.1.59, Letter Books, iii, 162.

25. DD, 8–11.7.59.

26. DD, 7–29.9.59. Protestant instincts were easily suppressed on Mount Athos – 'such a genuine bit of medievalism had an irresistible charm for me'. Dufferin to Helen, 16.9.59, D1071F/B1/3. Dufferin to Aunt Anna, 9.8.59.

27. Where Wilson was overheard introducing himself: 'I am Wilson, Sir, The Wilson, Sir, His Lordship's Valet'. Dufferin to Helen, 9.10.59, D1071F/B1/3.

28. DD, 11–16.10.59.

29. DD, 16.10.59.

30. DD, 18.10.59. Dufferin, 'Description by Lord Dufferin of his visit to Damascus in 1859 and subsequently as British High Commissioner after the massacres' (1898), p.2.

31. 'Description', pp. 3–5, Lyall pp. 102–3. Dufferin to Aunt Anna, 2.12.59.

32. Chedzoy, pp. 267–70.

33. Helen to Georgy, 27.9.59, 24.11.59; Helen to Giff, 24.11.59, Letter Books, iii, 175–6, 179, 185–6. 'I don't know how I live, My Giff, without seeing your face or hearing your voice for so long'. Helen to Giff, 8.12.59, D1071F/A2/4. Giff to Dufferin,

16.12.59; Georgy to Dufferin, 13.12.59, MIC 22/9. DD, 25.11.59. Dufferin arrived on 25th but chose not to set sail for London until 31.12.59.

34. John Hamilton to Dufferin, 7.9.59. Stafford to Dufferin, 7.8.59, MIC 22/10.

35. Although she would remain his mistress for some years to come, Stafford did encourage Dufferin. 'She always talks of you with great affection. I wish you would have seen more of her – you are everything that is kind and good and I am just the contrary – you would have done her good and perhaps got her to take care of herself [she had a weak heart]. She says that she has heard from you several times.' Stafford to Dufferin, 7.8.59, MIC 22/10.

36. Jeanette Prosser to Dufferin, 20 and 30.3.60, MIC 22/11. The details of this affair are hard to come by thanks to later censorship. In the bound letter books at Clandeboye letters from Annie Gilbert, Stafford and Caroline Queensbury (who was to act as something of a go-between) between March and June 1860 are recorded in the written index but have been cut out of the volume. Similarly the diary entries for 2–30 June have been cut out or obliterated. The cover-up was extensive if rather crude and so from the remnants of some of these letters and the occasional oversight, it is still possible to piece together the probable turn of events.

37. Emma Buck to Dufferin, n.d.; 5 letters Caroline Queensbury to Dufferin, n.d. (one dated 4.6.[1860?]), MIC 22/11. Elizabeth Argyll to Dufferin, 14.6.(1860?), MIC 22/9. Caroline Queensbury to Dufferin, 26.6.60; Stafford to Dufferin, 12.8.60, MIC 22/12. DD, 22–30.6.60.

38. Camille Silvy Daybook Album 1 (1860), no. 833–4, National Portrait Gallery, AX51438-9. Presumably Dufferin destroyed these photographs when the crisis unfolded, hence these requests.

39. Spencer to Dufferin, 17.10.94, D1071H/B/S/476/51: ('I knew the poor lady slightly').

40. R. J. Gilbert to Dufferin, 11,19, 23.10.94, D1071H/B/G/143/1–8; Emma Buck to Dufferin, 5.6.96–21.10.1901, D1071H/B/B/866/1–5.

41. Nelly Graham to Dufferin, 3.8.60; Cossy Graham to Dufferin, 8.10.60; Brin to Helen, 22.2.61, MIC 22/11.

42. Dufferin to Helen, 15.1.60, D1071F/B1/6.

CHAPTER 9: DANGERS ABROAD

1. Philip Mansel, *Levant: Splendour and Catastrophe on the Mediterranean* (2010), pp. 97–101. Eugene Rogan, *The Arabs: A History* (2009), pp. 93–8. Hervey to Dufferin, 6.6.60, MIC 22/4.

2. Cyril Graham to Col. A. J. Fraser, 10.1.61, MIC 320/1.

3. Rogan, *The Arabs*, pp. 93–8. Mansel, *Levant*, pp. 97–101. Ann P. Saab, *Reluctant Icon: Gladstone, Bulgaria and the Working Classes* (1991), pp. 24–7.

4. Cyril Graham to Dufferin, 6.8.60, MIC 22/5. Saab, *Reluctant Icon*, pp. 30–41.

5. Janey Ellice to Dufferin, 7.8.60; Elizabeth Argyll to Dufferin, 10.8.60. MIC 22/12.

Characteristically his mother's response was not all it seemed: 'A flaming panegyric on you [in the] *Brechin Review*'. Helen to Dufferin, 8.8.60, Letter Books, iii, 211.

6. Together with much advice from his guardian, Sir James Graham, including the blunt 'protect yourself, copy everything'. Sir James Graham to Dufferin, 29.7.60, 15.8.60.

7. Dufferin to Nelly, Aug 1890 in Lyall, p.503. In her boredom as Dumas banged on egotistically over dinner, his young lover would decapitate flies and slip them into his drink when he wasn't looking. Then she would fill up his glass and turning to him 'in a winning manner', 'reminded him that he had not refreshed himself, upon which Dumas, still eagerly talking, used to drain off the decoction!'. Dufferin, 'Description', p.9. R. H. Meade, Journal, 14–15.8.(1860), D3044/J/7.

8. DD, 14.8.60.

9. Dufferin, 'Description', p.5. Graham to Dufferin, 6.8.60, MIC 22/12. Lyall, pp. 110–11. Harrison, pp. 88–9.

10. Dufferin, 'Description', pp. 5, 8–13. Col. Fraser to Dufferin, 24.9.60, MIC 22/12. Dufferin to Russell, 21.4.61, TNA, FO 78/1628.

11. Argyll's PS in Elizabeth Argyll to Dufferin, 27.9.60, MIC 22/12.

12. Meade Journal, D3044/J/7. Dufferin's delegation consisted only of 'Bobsy' Meade from the Foreign Office, Col. Fraser (military attaché), Cyril Graham, James Kennedy (Dufferin's private secretary), and Wilson 'salaming' theatrically.

13. Dufferin to Helen, n.d., 17 and 28.9.60, D1071F/B1/6.

14. Helen to Georgy, 6.11.60, Letter Books, iii, 219.

15. Russell to Dufferin, 22.9.60, MIC 22/12. Dufferin to Fraser, 15.1.61, MIC 320/1.

16. Harrison, pp. 88–99. Dufferin, 'Notes on Ancient Syria', 20.1.64. Lyall, p.115.

17. Palmerston to Dufferin, 2.8.60, MIC 22/12.

18. Prince Albert to Baron Stockmar, 4.3.61. Helen to Giff, 27.1.61, D1071F/A2/4.

19. Helen to Giff, 15.2.60, D1071F/A2/4. Helen to Georgy, 19.4.61, Letter Books, iv, 10. John Hamilton to Dufferin, 24.4.61, MIC 22/12.

20. Sir Arthur Hardinge, *The Life of Henry Howard Molyneux, 4th Earl of Carnarvon, 1831–1890*, p.169. Lyall, p.116.

21. Fruma Zachs, '"Novice" or "Heaven-born Diplomat"? Lord Dufferin's plan for a "Province of Syria": Beirut 1860–61', *Middle Eastern Studies*, vol. 36, no. 3 (July 2000), pp. 160–76.

22. Jasper Ridley, *Palmerston*, p.536. Russell to Dufferin, 26.3.61, MIC 22/5. Harrison, p.92.

23. Harrison, pp. 91–4.

24. Mansel, *Levant*, pp. 100–1. But see Zachs, ' "Novice" or "Heaven-born Diplomat"?', pp. 163, 171–2.

25. Shaftesbury to Dufferin, 26.6.61, MIC 22/5; Russell to Dufferin, 27.5.61, TNA, FO 78/1624. Sir James Graham to Dufferin, 3.8.60, MIC 22/12.

26. DD, 6.2.62. Lyall, pp. 131–2. Granville to Dufferin, 3.1.62, 8.2.62, MIC 22/6. Lord Crewe, *Rosebery* (1931), vol. 1, pp. 16–17. QVD, 7.2.62, 51, p.32.

CHAPTER 10: FAMILY POLITICS

1. Helen to Anna Dufferin, 11.3.62, Letter Books, iv, 39. Cyril Graham to Dufferin, 7.2.62, MIC 22/7.
2. Helen to Giff, 19.9.61, D1071F/A2/4. Helen to Dufferin,13.1.62, Letter Books, iv, 33. DD, 23.12.61, 16.1.62, 20.1.62. Dufferin's memorandum, 1888, Letter Books, iv, 45.
3. DD, 7.2.62.
4. Lyall, p.133.
5. Carnarvon to Dufferin, 15.2.62, MIC 22/7. To his great-aunt he declared that separation from his mother was not worth 'the treasure and power'. Dufferin to Lady Anna, 18.2.62, D1071H/B/B/449/17.
6. Janey Ellice to Dufferin, 27.8.61, MIC 22/13.
7. Hariot Hamilton to Dufferin, 1856, MIC 22/6; 14.10.61, MIC 22/13. 18.(12.61), 2.1.62, n.d. 'Monday 2nd'), MIC 22/14. DD, 14.10.61, 27.10.61,17.1.62.
8. Helen to Lady Anna Dufferin, 23.7.62, Letter Books, iv, 42. Argyll to Dufferin, 8.9.62, MIC 22/16. Hariot to Dufferin, 6.8.62, MIC 22/16.
9. Hariot to Dufferin, 20.2.62, MIC 22/16.
10. DD, 12–19.4.62.
11. Elizabeth Argyll to Dufferin, 8.9.62, 17.2.62. Argyll to Dufferin, 8.9.62, MIC 22/16.
12. Helen to Lady Anna Dufferin, 10.9.62, Helen to Lizzie Ward, 10.9.62, Letter Books, iv, 43–4. Lady St Helier, *Memories of Fifty Years*.
13. Helen to Hariot, 7.4.66, Letter Books, iv, 225.
14. Nicolson, *Helen's Tower*, p.143.
15. Dufferin to Lady Anna Dufferin, 3 and 10.9.62, D1071H/B/B/449/13–14.
16. *Downpatrick Recorder*, 25.10.62.
17. These scenes were all recorded in a sketchbook by an artist, Coke Smythe, who had been already commissioned to paint a mural at Clandeboye. Helen's Tower Library.
18. Helen to Annie Harvey, 25.10.62; Helen to Lizzie Ward, '1862'; Helen to Lady Ulrica Thynne, 'October 1862', Letter Books, iv, 46–8. *Leaves from the Diary of Henry Greville*, p.77.
19. Elizabeth Argyll to Dufferin, 16.4.55, MIC 22/5. Dufferin, Memorandum, 1888, Letter Books, iv, 45. Lady Dufferin, *Poems and Verses*, pp. 83–95.
20. Helen to 'My dear kind Friend', 9 September (1863), D1071F/A4/16. In the immediate aftermath of Giff's death, she would confirm this directly to her son. Helen to Dufferin, 26.12.62, Letter Books, iv, 54. In fact Lady Jocelyn had already passed this on: Lady Jocelyn to Dufferin, 31.10.62, MIC 22/13. Charles Nettlefold, *Lords of Yester* (2014), pp. 320–2.
21. Helen to Marquess of Tweedale, 13.10.62; Helen to Dufferin, 'December 1862',

Letter Books, iv, 45 and 55. Helen to 'My dear kind Friend', 9 September (1863), D1071F/A4/16.

22. Helen to Annie Harvey, 25.10.62, Letter Books, iv, 46.

23. Helen to Dufferin, '1862', D1071F/A4/18. Only half of this letter survives.

24. Dufferin (ed), *Songs, Poems and Verses by Helen, Lady Dufferin* (Countess of Gifford), (1894). See also the unpublished memorandum that Dufferin wrote in 1888 on his mother's marriage; Helen to Marquess of Tweeddale, 13.10.62, Letter Books, iv, 45.

25. And so too in death: 'Certainly no wife ever worshipped the memory of a loved one she had lost so constantly and fervently as my mother mourned Lord Gifford's tragic and untimely death.' Dufferin's memorandum, 1888.

26. Helen to Giff, 24.9.61, D1071F/A2/4.

27. Georgy to Dufferin (1862), Elizabeth Argyll to Dufferin, 17.1.63, MIC 22/18. Brin to Dufferin (1863), D1071F/B2/6/1-21. Helen to Rev. Charles Ditton, 30.3.63, D1071F/A4/19.

28. Helen to Dufferin, 22, 24 and 26.12.62, Letter Books, iv, 51,53. Georgy to Dufferin (1862), Lady Jocelyn to Dufferin, 11.1.63. MIC 22/13.

29. Elizabeth Argyll to Dufferin, 31.7.63, MIC 22/18.

30. And all the more miraculous for the fact that, a month before, she had been the only uninjured party in a serious carriage accident after the horses had bolted down Highgate Hill.

31. Nicolson, *Helen's Tower*, pp. 143–7. 'All last week the servants in a state of rebellion'; Hariot's Journal, 12.2.65; 10.7.67 D1071H/V/18.

32. Rupert Christiansen, *Tales of New Babylon* (1994), pp. 19–36. Nicolson, *Helen's Tower*, p.147.

33. Helen to 'Lal', 'Sunday October 1863', Helen to Dufferin, 22.11.63, Letter Books, iv, 91, 96.

34. Hariot's Diary, 22.2.68, D1071J/C2/4/1.

35. Helen to Dufferin, 1.4.64, Letter Books, iv, 107. Hariot's Diary, 5.2.68, D1071J/C2/4/1.

36. Hariot's Diary, 28–29.5.67, D1071J/C2/4/1. Elizabeth Argyll to Dufferin, 13.4.67, D1071H/B/C/88/18.

37. By now even Seymour was writing to him to take greater care of Hariot. Somerset to Dufferin, 14.8.68, D1071H/B/S/204/8. Elizabeth Argyll put it down to 'the confinements having come so quickly'. And then offered 'a little advice . . . I am sometimes afraid of your being on the wrong tack about her. You think she is so much younger than you are that you must give her change and gaiety etc. Now I believe she is much older in many ways than you are and had better lead you and not you her about this.' Elizabeth Argyll to Dufferin, 17.9.68, D1071H/B/C/88/36.

38. 1–6.10.68, Hariot's Diaries, D1071J/C2/4/1.

39. Dickens to Dufferin, 1868–1870, D1071H/B/D/139/1–2. C. Aspinall to Dufferin, 'April 1869', D1071H/B/A/291/1–4. W. Holman Hunt to Dufferin, 9.7.64, D1071H/B/H/692/1.

40. Hariot's Diary, 13.5.69, 27.7.69, 2.8.69, 11.8.69, 23.10.69.

41. Lady Frederick Cavendish, *Diaries* (1928), vol. 1, pp. 162, 292; vol. 2, p.97.

42. Helen to Dufferin, 6.5.64, 'August 1864' ('Dear, dear abroad'), 7.9.64; Helen to Lal, 'August 1864', Letter Books, iv, 110, 124, 125, 134.

43. Such was her pain by the end that on one occasion Dufferin had to leave the room. Atkinson, *Conversation*, p.407.

44. Dufferin to Helen, 'Easter Day, 1866', D1071F/B1/4. Helen to Dufferin, 'Saturday, April 1866', D1071F/A4/20.

45. Dufferin to C. S. Parker, 30.10.61, in C. S. Parker, *The Life and Letters of Sir James Graham* (1909), vol. 2, p.462.

46. Nicolson, *Helen's Tower*, pp. 138–43. Alfred, Lord Tennyson to Dufferin, 19.3.68, D1071H/B/T/101/3. On the fashion for 'woman-worship' in the 1860s, see Walter E. Houghton, *The Victorian Frame of Mind* (1957), pp. 350–1.

CHAPTER 11: MISSIONARY POLITICS

1. Helen to Dufferin, 'August 1864', Letter Books, iv, 128.

2. 'You are no longer a beginner.' Helen to Dufferin, n.d. (October 1864), D1071F/A1/5. Helen to Dufferin, 11.8.1866, Letter Books, iv, 233. A. I. Dasent, *John Delane, 1817–1879*, (1908), p.120. Harrison, p.133.

3. George W. Dasent to Dufferin, 1867, D1071H/B/D/428/7.

4. Harrison, pp. 198–201. But see David Fitzpatrick, *Irish Emigration 1801–1925* (Dublin, 1985), pp. 37–9.

5. Hariot Diary, 18–20.9.67, D1071J/C2/4/1. Elizabeth Argyll to Dufferin, 26.9.67, D1071H/B/C/88/23. Harrison, pp. 203–20.

6. These sought to prevent provocative marches and flags. On what follows, see Harrison, pp. 185–96. B. M. Walker, *Ulster Politics: The Formative Years 1868–86* (1989), pp. 61–2. Henry Patterson, *Class Conflict and Sectarianism* (1980), pp. 1–6.

7. Thomas MacKnight to Dufferin, 22.11.68, D1071H/B/F.

8. 'Long talk with Spencer over LL for Ireland'. Dufferin 'was thought too yielding and not "great man enough".' It was between Spencer and Dufferin. Angus Hawkins and John Powell (ed.), *The Journal of John Wodehouse, 1st Earl of Kimberley* (for 1862–1902), Camden, 5th Series, vol. 9 (1997), 11.12.68, p.229. D furious that Spencer got Lord Lieutenant. Spencer wrote 'I cannot thank you for writing so frankly . . . I had fully expected your disappointment', Spencer to Dufferin 11.12.68, D1071H/B/S/476/1.

9. Delane to Dufferin, 12.12.68, D1071H/B/F.

10. On Gladstone, see H. C. G. Matthew, *Gladstone, 1809–1898* (1999); Roy Jenkins, *Gladstone* (1995); and Richard Shannon, *Gladstone* (1982, 1999).

11. Jonathan Parry, *The Rise and Fall of Liberal Government in Victorian Britain* (1993), pp. 257–60.

12. Gladstone 'had to dominate [and had an] obsession with power: power to dictate events, power to smash opponents across the floor of the House of Commons, and power to sway vast audiences. Gladstone would not let power go.' Parry, p.255.

13. Parry, p.251.
14. Shannon, vol. 2, p.63.
15. Or as he preferred to put it: 'leave behind those who cannot keep up with me'. He 'regards the rest of us as children', wrote one cabinet colleague in 1880. Parry, p.254.
16. Argyll to Dufferin, 24.11.68, Parry, pp. 251–7.
17. Harrison, p.226.
18. Dufferin to Ellice, 8.9.68, MIC 326.
19. Dufferin to Argyll, 11.1.69, D1071H/B/F.
20. Harrison, pp. 232–6.
21. W. E. Vaughan, *Landlords and Tenants in Ireland, 1848–1904* (Dublin 1984), p.20.
22. Harrison, p.233.
23. Shannon, vol. 2, p.77.
24. Harrison, pp. 238–9.
25. Spencer always acknowledged Dufferin's 'authority' on matters of Irish land and by May 1870 was declaring 'How much I like your speeches upon all Irish Matters in which you stand out as our Champion.' Spencer to Dufferin, 9.12.69, 1.5.70, D1071H/B/S/476/9,12.
26. Shannon, vol. 2, p.85.
27. 'Long walk with Dufferin. He has seen the Land Bill and approves it generally.' Kimberley, *Journal*, 6.2.70, p.244.
28. Sir A. West, *Recollections* (1899), vol. 1, p.358.
29. Gladstone diary, 17.4.70. On impact of the 1870 Land Act, see Paul Bew, *Land and the National Question*, p.235; Foster, *Modern Ireland*, p.378.
30. Ponsonby to the Queen, 28.3.72, MIC 340.
31. Interestingly he made another attempt to drop the Dufferin name: Spencer among others successfully urging him to adopt the Earl of Dufferin (an 'excessively pretty and pleasant title') and use Clandeboye as a second title.
32. Kimberley refers to Gladstone's 'intention to offer Dufferin Ireland' (after Spencer's resignation?). As he had just arrived in Canada this is a reflection of Dufferin's new standing. Kimberley, *Journal*, 26.7.73, p.281.
33. Parry, p.183.

CHAPTER 12: FAMILY DEBTS

1. As a crude measure one should multiply the nineteenth-century figure by 100 to get an estimate of the present day value. 'Consumer Price Inflation Since 1750' (*Economic Trends* No. 604 (2004), pp. 38–46) by Jim O'Donoghue, Louise Goulding and Grahame Allen.
2. For a full analysis of Dufferin's finances, see Harrison, pp. 279–99.
3. Elizabeth Argyll to Dufferin, 15.11.62, MIC22/13.
4. Dufferin to Argyll, 7.5.74, D1071H/B/F.
5. In lieu of a £135,000 mortgage.

6. Cannadine, *The Decline and Fall of the British Aristocracy*, pp. 595–8.

7. Chedzoy, *A Scandalous Woman*, pp. 275–6; John Pope-Hennessy, *The Flight of Youth*, p.186. Alice Acland, *Caroline Norton* (1948), pp. 221–6.

8. Helen to Dufferin, 14.12.61, 22.11.63, Letter Books, iv, 32, 96. Caroline to Dufferin, 7.1.64, MIC 22/18.

9. Brian Masters, *The Dukes* (1988 ed.), pp. 69–73.

10. Helen to Dufferin, 30.12.65, Letter Books, iv, 193.

11. Elizabeth Argyll to Dufferin, 24.10.69, D1071H/B/C/88/44.

12. Helen to Caroline, 28 and 29.6.64, 8.7.64, Letter Books, iv, 114, 115, 118. Helen to Hariot, 26.10.63, Letter Books, iv, 89. Elizabeth Argyll to Dufferin, 17.12.63, MIC 22/18.

13. Delane to Dufferin, 16.11.71.

CHAPTER 13: CANADA: THE IMPERIAL FRONTIER

1. Marchioness of Dufferin and Ava, *My Canadian Journal, 1872–8* (1891), 14–19 June 1872; Dufferin to Elizabeth Argyll, 31.7.72, D1071/H/B/C/88. Marjory Harper, 'Rhetoric and Reality: British Migration to Canada, 1867–1967', in Buckner (ed.), *Canada and The British Empire* (2010), pp. 167–73.

2. *My Canadian Journal, 1872–8* (1891), 14–19 June 1872; Dufferin to Elizabeth Argyll, 31.7.72, D1071/H/B/C/88.

3. Dufferin to Lady Dartrey, 24.7.72, D1071H/B/D/78.

4. Dufferin to Elizabeth Argyll, 13.8.72, D1071/H/B/C/88/65.

5. Gladstone's 12.7.65 memo cited in Ged Martin, 'Canada from 1815', in *The Oxford History of the British Empire* (OHBE), vol. 3, p.525.

6. Geo Browne, Marquess of Sligo to Dufferin 16.9.72, D1071H/B/B/811/3; James Winter, *Robert Lowe* (Toronto, 1976). In 1869 Trollope has Phineas Finn declare that 'Not one man in a hundred cares whether Canadians prosper or fail to prosper.' However, they did care 'that Canada should not go to the States because, though they don't like the Canadians, they do hate the Americans'. Trollope, *Phineas Finn*, p.464.

7. P. B. Waite. *Macdonald, Life and World*, p.92.

8. Ged Martin, OHBE, vol. 3, p.528.

9. Ged Martin, OHBE, vol. 3, p.537.

10. Cain and Hopkins, *Innovation and Empire 1688–1914*, p.264; Cannadine, 'Imperial Canada: Old History, New Problems' in Colin Coates (ed.), *Imperial Canada 1867–1917* (Edinburgh 1997), pp. 1–19; Ged Martin 'Canada from 1815' in OHBE vol. 3, pp. 525, 535–7; see also OHBE, vol. 3, pp. 35, 44–5, 354.

11. John Darwin, *The Empire Project* (2009), pp. 144–9.

12. Waite, p.126.

13. Phillip Buckner, 'The Creation of the Dominion of Canada', in Phillip Buckner (ed.), *Canada and the British Empire* (2010), pp. 66–73.

14. Especially after Britain's failure in the 1871 Washington Treaty to protect the Canadian fishing industry from American competition.
15. Lyall, vol. 1, p.286. Girouard, *Age of Chivalry*, p.224.

CHAPTER 14: FRONTIER POLITICS

1. Dufferin to Elizabeth Argyll, 17.2.73, D1071/H/B/C/88/71, on the need to make the Governor General 'a personage again'. Barbara J. Messamore, *Canada's Governors General, 1847–1878* (2006), pp. 17–19.
2. Messamore, *Governors General*, p.28.
3. *My Canadian Journal*, 25.6.72. Dufferin to Lady Dartrey, 24.7.72, D1071H/B/D/78. Dufferin to Knatchbull-Hugenson, 15.3.73, D1071/H/B/K/661/9. Donald Creighton, *J. A. Macdonald: The Old Chieftain* (Toronto, 1955), p.2.
4. The Rothschilds were more interested in a rail link with the US.
5. *Globe*, 4 and 17.7.73. The Liberals (or 'Grits') were rooted in the agrarian-radical tradition of the pioneer farmers, especially of Ontario, and whose views were reflected in the *Globe*, the most influential national paper; whose editor indeed produced their first leader, George Brown.
6. Gwyn, *Nation Maker*, pp. 231–8.
7. *My Canadian Journal*, 30.7.73, 7.8.73. Dufferin to Kimberley, 5.8.73 D1071H/H2/1.
8. Dufferin to Kimberley, 15.8.73 D1071H/H2/1; Kimberley to Dufferin 12.6.73; 24.7.73. Messamore, pp. 161–5.
9. Harrison, p.364. Creighton, pp. 159–65; *My Canadian Journal*, 16.6.73. Gwyn, pp. 218–31. The baby was named Victoria at the Queen's instruction.
10. Messamore, pp. 162–5.
11. Dufferin to Delane, 26.9.73; 3.10.73, D1071/H/B/D/100; Dufferin to Elizabeth Argyll, 3.9.72, D1071/H/B/C88/67. Gwyn, pp. 245–7.
12. Creighton, p.166; Joseph Schull, *Edward Blake: The Man of the Other Way* (Toronto 1975).
13. Creighton, p.168.
14. Argyll to Dufferin, 18.8.73, D1071/H/B/C/95/65. Dufferin to Day 16.8.73 D1071H/H7.
15. *My Canadian Journal*, 5.9.73; Dufferin to Kimberley 26.9.73 D1071H/H2/1.
16. Dufferin to Argyll, 20.9.73, D1071/H/B/C/95/66. Kimberley to Dufferin, 8.10.73 D1071H/H2/1.
17. Dufferin to Queen, n.d [Nov (?), 1873], G. E. Buckle (ed.), *Letters of Queen Victoria 1862–78*, 2nd series, vol. 2 (1928), p.287.
18. Dufferin to Kimberley, 26.10.73, D1071H/H2/1. Gwyn, pp. 247–9. Messamore, pp. 169–72.
19. Creighton, p.168; Dufferin to Queen, n.d., Buckle, p.287.
20. Sir Charles Tupper, *Recollections of 60 years* (1914), pp. 156–7.
21. Dufferin to Kimberley, 26.10.73, D1071H/H1/1.
22. Dufferin to Kimberley, 6.11.73, D1071H/H2/1.

23. Waite, pp. 101–6.

24. Gwyn, pp. 250–5.

25. Although he did make a bizarre request for a closet 'no matter how dark or inconvenient' from which he might listen in secret. Messamore, p.172.

26. *My Canadian Journal*, 8.11.73

27. Kimberley to Dufferin, 29.10.73. Dufferin to Kimberley, 6.11.73 D1071H/H2/1.

28. Dufferin to Delane, 26.9.73; 3.10.73. D1071H/B/D/100; Dufferin to Kimberley 11.10.73. D1071H/H2/1.

29. Argyll to Dufferin, 12.11.73, D1071/H/B/C/95/67.

30. Dufferin to Kimberley, 6.1.73 D1071H/H2/1.

31. Dufferin to Delane, 20.11.73, D1071H/B/D/100.

32. Ponsonby to Kimberley, 6.10.73, 15.11.73, 1.12.73, in G. E. Buckle (ed.), *Letters of Queen Victoria*, 2nd series, vol. 2 (1928), pp. 285, 291–3. Queen to Dufferin, 12.12.74, MDACQ.

33. Argyll to Dufferin, 17.3.74, D1071/H/B/C/95/69. 'The vindication of Lord Dufferin is complete', *The Times*, 6.11.73.

34. Despite liking him 'very much', Dufferin felt Mackenzie to be 'small [minded] and narrow', which he attributed less to his 'long, bleak, severe, Scottish countenance' and almost entirely to the former stonemason not being a gentleman. Dufferin to Delane, 26.9.73, 3.10.73, D1071H/B/D/100. Dufferin to Argyll, 7.5.74, D1071/H/B/C/95/70. *Blake*, pp. 116–17, Creighton, p.189.

35. On becoming Colonial Secretary, following the Tories' victory in 1874, Carnarvon wrote to Dufferin to say 'how glad I am to have an old friend like yourself in Canada'. Defending Dufferin against criticism, Carnarvon wrote in his diary (18.9.74), 'I am naturally disposed to see his merits rather than any past defects'. Peter Gordon (ed.), *The Political Diaries of the 4th Earl of Carnarvon, 1857–1890*, Camden, 5th Series, vol. 35 (2009). On Liberal surprise at the election result, see Argyll to Dufferin, 17.3.74, D1071/H/B/C/95/69.

36. Harrison, pp. 392–5. Gwyn, pp. 265–8. Messamore, pp. 187–9.

37. Reproduced in Thompson, *Alexander Mackenzie*, p.224.

38. Dufferin to Carnarvon, De Kiewiet and Underhill (eds.), *Dufferin–Carnarvon Correspondence*. Blake, pp. 116–47; Lyall, p.247.

39. Messamore, pp. 180–9. Not only did Dufferin seek to acquire new responsibilities but he also because of them sought another £5,000 in salary from the Canadian government.

40. G. Hamilton, *The Days Before Yesterday*, pp. 238, 269. Tupper *Recollections*, p.135. *My Canadian Journal*, 16–22.8.76. Harrison, p.754.

41. *Blake*, pp. 173–5. Dufferin to Carnarvon, 8.10.76, 4.11.76, 14.11.76, 19.11.76; Carnarvon to Dufferin 13.12.76, De Kiewiet and Underhill (eds), *Dufferin–Carnarvon Correspondence* pp. 259–330. Messamore, pp. 198–208.

42. Messamore, pp. 209–13.

CHAPTER 15: REINVENTING BRITISH CANADA

1. Richard Gwyn, *Nation Maker. Sir John Macdonald: His Life and Times*, vol. 2 (2001), pp. 218–20. Lyall, p.260. In his speech, Dufferin referred to Canadian volunteers' willingness to serve militarily abroad in service of the Queen. Dufferin to Queen, 29.5.1878, VIC MAIN/P25/75.

2. *My Canadian Journal*, 9.8.72.

3. *My Canadian Journal*, 9.8.72.

4. Dufferin to Elizabeth Argyll, 3.9.72, D1071/H/B/C/88/67.

5. Lyall, pp. 200–1; *My Canadian Journal*, 23.9.72; Dufferin to Elizabeth Argyll, 29.11.72, D1071H/B/C/88/68. Kenneth Munro, 'The Crown and French Canada: The Role of the Governor General in the Making of the Crown Relevant, 1867–1917', in *Imperial Canada*, pp. 109–21.

6. Lyall, pp. 200–1. 'No governor general had ever reached out to the people in this way and the Dufferins did so as a couple'. Gwyn, *Nation Maker*, pp. 218–20.

7. Dufferin to Lady Dartrey, 29.11.72, D1071H/B/D/78.

8. Dufferin to 'Darling Nell', n.d., D1071 H/B/B110/28.

9. Dufferin to Elizabeth Argyll, 17.2.73, D1071/H/B/C/88/71.

10. *My Canadian Journal*, 17.11.72, 24–28.12.72, 8.1.73.

11. *World*, 17.4.78.

12. Cited in Wade A. Henry, 'Severing the Imperial Tie? Republicanism and the British Identity in English Canada, 1864–1917', in *Imperial Canada*, p.181.

13. Cannadine, *Ornamentalism*, p.34. Dufferin to Carnarvon cited in *Blake*, p.124.

14. *My Canadian Journal*, 23.1.73; ed. A. Houltain, *The Correspondence of Goldwin Smith*, p.86; Messamore in *Imperial Canada*, p.85.

15. *My Canadian Journal*, 6.3.72; Dufferin to Argyll, 15.3.73, D1071/H/B/C/95/63.

16. Symbolically by train through the US via Chicago to San Francisco, from whence they went by ship to Victoria.

17. Dufferin to Lady Dorothy Nevill, 1.10.77, cited in Lyall, p.258.

18. Dufferin to Carnarvon, 21.12.74 in De Kiewiet and Underhill (eds.), *Dufferin–Carnarvon Correspondence*, p.125.

19. 'Never was I so stared at as today', noted Hariot apprehensively in August 1873, having travelled to St John, New Brunswick ahead of her husband.

20. *My Canadian Journal*, 27.8.74, 3.9.74, 16.8.74. Interview with Mrs Crakanthorpe, 1936, City Archives, Vancouver, in Dufferin Archives, D1071/H/H14/27. *My Canadian Journal*, 45.9.76. Dufferin to the Queen, 11.9.1874, VIC MAIN/P24/105.

21. Philip Buckner, 'The Creation of the Dominion of Canada', in *Imperial Canada*, p.82.

22. *My Canadian Journal*, 7.9.74; Another factor is how few of the journalists seem to have short-hand.

23. *Lord Dufferin's Speeches and Addresses*, p.160. *My Canadian Journal*, 25.8.74.

24. *Lord Dufferin's Speeches and Addresses*, p.242.

25. 'Words cannot express', Dufferin declared in Toronto in 1874, 'what pride I feel as an Englishman in the loyalty of Canada to England. Nevertheless I should be the first to deplore this feeling if it rendered Canada disloyal to herself, if it either dwarfed or smothered Canadian patriotism or generated a sickly spirit of dependence. Such however is far from being the case.'

26. Dufferin to Carnarvon, 25.4.78, D1071H/H1/2. That said, Dufferin enjoyed being lionised by Longfellow, Lowell, Emerson and Wendell Holmes on his visits to New York and Boston. For Hariot, the moral threat was more conventional: Chicago was 'just a money making town'; the 'ladies' in San Francisco were 'fast'; while in Salt Lake City she got so 'irritable' to be in the vicinity of the polygamist Brigham Young that Dufferin had to decline a meeting with the Mormon leader. By contrast Canada was a moral sanctuary: like Ulster but bigger. *My Canadian Journal*, 15.8.74, 17–31.10.74, 6–8.8.76. Dufferin to Argyll, 2.10.76, D1071/H/B/C/95/74.

27. M. Bence-Jones, 'The Building Dreams of a Viceroy', part 2, *Country Life*, 8.10.1970, pp. 900–1.

28. Dufferin to Mme d'Harcourt, 17.8.72, D1071/H/ BH/167/1.

29. Lady D. Nevill, *Reminiscences* (1906). p.150; W. O. Buchanan to Dufferin, 1878–81, D1071H/B/B/864/1–3.

30. Dufferin to Argyll, 25.4.74, cited in Lyall, pp. 214–16. As he explained to his successor, he saw his role as 'consolidating the various elements of which the Canadian Community is composed as well as towards creating a more intimate union between the Colony and the Mother Country'. J. A. Mangan (ed.), *The Cultural Bond: Sport, Empire and Society*, pp. 162–3.

31. Robert Cassels to Dufferin, 13.2.77, D1071H/B/C/212/1. Dufferin, one of 'the most influential promoters of a Canadian national art', promoted centralised cultural institutions: 'I believe the cultivation of art to be a most essential element in our national life' he declared on becoming official patron of the Ontario Society for the Arts. Jonathan F. W. Vane, *A History of Canadian Culture* (2009), p.153.

32. Gerald Redmond, 'Viceregal Patronage: The Governor Generals of Canada and Sport in the Dominion, 1867–1909', in J. A. Mangan (ed.), *The Cultural Bond: Sport, Empire and Society*, pp. 154–77. *My Canadian Journal*, 10.10.72; DD 27.6.76.

33. OHBE, vol. 3, pp. 46–8.

34. 'The whole of Canada has been made very indignant by an article in *The Times*'. Dufferin to Argyll, 27.11.72, D1071/H/B/C/95/62. The assertion that the British connection 'damps the ardour of Canadian Nationality is a pure invention'. Dufferin to Tennyson, 25.2.73. D1071H/B/T/101/6-7. Dufferin to Delane, 7.1.76, D1071H/B/D/100.

35. De Kiewiet and Underhill (eds.), *Dufferin–Carnarvon Correspondence* (Toronto, 1955), pp. xxvii–xxviii. Patrick Dunae, *Gentlemen Emigrants: From the British Public Schools to the Canadian Frontier* (Vancouver, 1981), pp. 67–79.

CHAPTER 16: THE MAKING OF A CELEBRITY

1. *My Canadian Journal*, 24.5.78. Colin M. Coates, 'French Canadians' Ambivalence to the British Empire', in Philip Buckner (ed.), Canada and the British Empire (2008), p.192.
2. Richard Gwyn, *Nation Maker. Sir John Macdonald: His Life and Times*, vol. 2 (2001), pp. 218–20.
3. John Darwin, *The Empire Project*, p.149.
4. Philip Buckner, 'The Creation of the Dominion of Canada', in *Canada and the British Empire*, pp. 72–3, 84.
5. *My Canadian Journal*, 8.2.78, 17.5.78, 24.5.78. De Kiewiet and Underhill (eds.), *Dufferin–Carnarvon Correspondence*, pp. xxv–xxvi.
6. Not strictly true: the Marquess of Lorne was *married* to royalty, his wife being Princess Louise, daughter of Queen Victoria.
7. De Kiewiet and Underhill (eds.), *Dufferin–Carnarvon Correspondence*, pp. xxvii–xxviii; Toronto speech, 12.1.77.
8. De Kiewiet and Underhill (eds.), *Dufferin–Carnarvon Correspondence*, pp. xxvii–xxviii.
9. Smith to Gladstone, 23.11.78 in A. Houltain (ed.), n.d., (London), *The Correspondence of Goldwin Smith*, pp. 70–2; 22.1.80, p.86, cited in Messamore, p.85; *Montreal Spectator*, 5.10.78; Cannadine, *Ornamentalism*, pp. 29–34; Wade Henry, 'Severing the Imperial Tie?': Republicanism and the British Identity in English Canada', in *Imperial Canada*, p.181.
10. Toronto speech, 2.9.74, *Lord Dufferin's Speeches and Addresses*.
11. De Kiewiet and Underhill (eds.), *Dufferin–Carnarvon Correspondence* pp. xxvii–xxviii; OHBE, vol. 3, pp. 46–8. Granville to Dufferin, 12.12.77, D1071H/B/G/281/9; Lyall, p.263. Carl Berger, *The Sense of Power: Studies in the Ideas of Canadian Imperialism, 1867–1914* (Toronto, 1970), pp. 89–108. Brian W. Hodgins, 'The Attitudes of the Canadian Founders toward Britain and the British Connection: A Personal Re-examination', in Coates, *Imperial Canada*, p.37.
12. 'Viceroys of Canada', Dufferin once protested to an audience in Montreal, 'are but fleeting shadows and evanescent apparitions that haunt your history, but scarcely contribute a line to its pages'. Montreal, 14.2.78, *Lord Dufferin's Speeches and Addresses*, p.254.
13. De Kiewiet and Underhill (eds.), *Dufferin–Carnarvon Correspondence*, pp. xxvii–xxviii.
14. De Kiewiet and Underhill (eds.), *Dufferin–Carnarvon Correspondence*, pp. xxv–xxvi.
15. Professor Byers, *Address to Queen's College, Belfast* (Belfast 1906), p.26.
16. *Globe*, 13.2.02; Montreal speech, 14.2.78, *Lord Dufferin's Speeches and Addresses*.
17. Byers, pp. 22–6; W. H. Hurlbert to Dufferin, 27.1.77, 20.7.77, 27.10.77, 8.3.78, D1071H/B/H/703; De Kiewiet and Underhill (eds.), *Dufferin–Carnarvon Correspondence*, p.xxvi.
18. Gwyn, p.218.
19. To this day, for example, there is Dufferin County in Ontario and a street and a subway station named after him in Toronto. His statue still stands outside the provincial legislature in Manitoba.

20. John Devereux to Dufferin, D1071H/B/D/133/1; Dufferin to Elizabeth Argyll, 18.3.76, D1071 H/B/C/88/83.

21. William Leggo to Dufferin, 13.4.78, 21.6.78, 25.6.78, 12.7.78, 4.12.78, D1071/H/B/L/207/4, 13, 15–16, 29. Mackenzie to Dufferin, 11.2.79, D1071H/B/M/212.

22. Dufferin to Tennyson, 25.2.73, D1071H/B/T/101/6–7; Tennyson, *Idylls of the King* (1872). Dufferin to Argyll, 27.11.72, D1071H/B/C/95/62. Lyall, pp. 262–3.

23. Lyall, p.231.

24. *Spectator*, 26.9.74; Lyall, pp. 231–2.

25. *World*, 17.4.78; famously Gladstone was to commandeer Canada for his own political purposes, declaring that 'Canada didn't get home rule because she was loyal and friendly, but she has become loyal and friendly because she has home rule', a sentiment Dufferin deplored.

26. Colonel H. Fletcher to Dufferin, 'December 1875', 8.7.76, 14–15.10.76, 24.9.78, 9.1.79, D1071H/B/F/196/23–6, 35, 38–9, 53–4.

27. Brodrick to Dufferin, 15.11.73, 28.12.73, 30.9.74, D1071H/B/B/756/13, 15, 18.

28. Granville to Dufferin, 23.5.77, D1071H/B/9/289/9; Sir E. R. Knatchbull-Hugessen to Dufferin, 30.10.78, D1071/H/B/H/661.

29. Hugh Childers to Dufferin, 5.11.78, D1071H/B/C/335/25.

30. Queen to Dufferin, 24.2.77, MDACQ; Cairns to Dufferin, 22.6.78, D1071H/B/C/21/8.

31. G. E. Buckle (ed.), *Disraeli*, vol. 5, pp. 434–7; *World*, 17.4.78; John Bright *Diary*, p.228 (26.11–1.12.78); on the limited involvement of the aristocracy in the British Empire, see Porter, *Absent-Minded Imperialists*.

CHAPTER 17: 'THE MAN FOR HIGH LATITUDES'

1. Elizabeth Argyll to Dufferin, 31.5.73, D1071H/B/C/88/73.

2. A tone echoed by the Queen who now described Caroline as 'one of the most gifted as well as one of the handsomest of women, and who had many fine qualities, just when her troubled and stormy life seemed to have entered a safe and happy haven!' Queen Victoria to Dufferin, 23.8.77, MDACQ. She had not lived to see the Married Women's Property Act (1882) for which cause she had campaigned tirelessly and suffered much. But her incessant pamphleteering did contribute to the Infant Custody Act (1839), the Matrimonial Causes Act (1857) an the Married Woman's Property Act (1870). Atkinson, *Conversation*, p.423.

3. Duke of Argyll to Dufferin, 27.5.78, D1071/H/B/C/95/78.

4. Constance Grosvenor to Dufferin, 10.2.79 and 5.2.80, D1071/H/B/G/460/5,6. DD, 10.1.80, 6.3.80, 26.3.80. But see also the 1894 diary where he recounts the whole tale. DD, 30.3.95.

5. Indeed some Whig hostesses, such as Lady Frances Waldegrave positively encouraged Disraeli. Hewitt, *Strawberry Fair* (1956), p.259. 'It is good for England that Lord Dufferin should go to charm the Russians. But from a party point of view I regret

it. We shall probably turn him into a Tory. It is clever of Dizzy to appoint him.' Maurice Brett (ed.), *Journals and Letters of Viscount Esher*, vol. 1, p.57.

6. Salisbury to Queen Victoria, 27.1.79. T. G. Otte, *The Foreign Office Mind: The Making of British Foreign Policy 1865–1914*, pp. 179–80.

7. Somerset to Dufferin, 21 and 26.1.79, D1071H/J1/1–2. Initially Somerset had been sceptical, urging only to accept India ('you are certain of the governorship of India'). Somerset to Dufferin, 19.11.78, D1071H/B/S/204/18.

8. Granville to Gladstone 2.2.79; Gladstone to Granville, 3.2.79, in Agatha Ramm (ed.), *The Political Correspondence of Mr Gladstone and Lord Granville, 1876–86* (1962), vol. 1, pp. 144–5. More disturbing was Gladstone's observation: 'I don't know why Dufferin should consider himself to be under any sort of obligation to me.'

9. Lyall, *Dufferin*, pp. 264–5. Nicolson, *Helen's Tower*, p.165.

10. Lyall, p.264.

11. Somerset to Dufferin, 21,26.1.79, D1071H/J1/1–2.

12. Dufferin to Argyll, 16–28.3.79, D1071/H/B/C/95/79.

13. Salisbury to Dufferin, 31.1.79, D1071H/J1/1/13. Somerset to Dufferin, 26/1/79, D1071/H/J1/1. Somerset's argument to Dufferin in favour of accepting Disraeli's offer included these two points. Firstly, 'there is strictly no diplomatic profession in this country'. Secondly, the policy required was essentially that of the Liberals: 'namely peace with Russia, tranquillity for Europe, security for India'. Otte, p.84.

14. *Esher Journals*, 8.6.79, p.61.

15. Dufferin to Argyll, 16–28.3.79, D1071/H/B/C/95/79.

16. Disraeli to the Queen, 11.3.79, G. E. Buckle (ed.), *Life of Disraeli* (1920).

17. Lady Gwendolen Cecil, *The Life of Lord Salisbury* (1921), vol. 2, p.346. Esher, *Journals*, 14.2.79, p.68. As the press unkindly put it, 'to get a Dufferin, they had to get a duffer out'.

18. Kennedy, 'Russia, 1879–81', pp. 1–2, Dufferin Archive, DA565.D8/2.

19. Gower, *My Reminiscences*, p.506. Kennedy, 'Russia, 1879–81'. As ever the Dufferins struggled to make ends meet. Hariot was startled to find Russians paying 12,000 roubles a year for English tutors ('and to think we find Eton expensive at £300'). Appearances didn't come cheap either. Hence, on discovery that the Russian court was in mourning, 'it is vexatious, when one has ruined oneself in coloured gowns to let one's gay feathers grow old fashioned in a box'. Hariot Dufferin, *My Russian and Turkish Journals* (1916), pp. 6, 34.

20. Dufferin to the Queen, 11.2.1880, MIC 340.

21. Kennedy, 'Russia, 1879–1881'.

22. Hastings Doyle to Dufferin, 21.9.79, D1071/H/B/D/223/15. RA VIC/ADDA36/1777, Sir H. Ponsonby to Lady M. Ponsonby, 16 June 1880.

23. Kennedy, 'Russia, 1879–81'.

24. Queen to Dufferin, 6.4.1880, MDACQ.

25. Disraeli to the Queen, 11.3.79, in G. E. Buckle, *Life of Disraeli*, vol. 6 (1920). Dufferin to Argyll, 14–28.3.79, D1071/H/B/C/15/79. Quoted also in Lyall, pp. 270–1.

26. Andrew Roberts, *Salisbury*, pp. 231–2.

27. Disraeli to Lady Bradford, 22.8.79, Zetland, p.233.

28. Lady G. Cecil, ii, p.337. Roberts, *Salisbury*, p.224.

29. Russia's drive for expansion appeared almost 'compulsive'; indeed since 1683 the Russian empire had grown on average by up to 55 square miles *per day*. Norman Davies, *Europe: A History* (Oxford, 1996), p.869.

30. Roberts, pp. 220–4

31. Roberts, pp. 214–17.

32. Disraeli to Lady Bradford, 22.8.79, in Marquis of Zetland (ed.), *Letters of Disraeli to Lady Bradford and Lady Chesterfield* (1929), p.207.

33. Roberts, pp. 232–6.

34. 'What induced him to pitch his tent in such a God forsaken district of Pomerania, I cannot conceive.' Dufferin to Argyll, 6.1.80, D1071/H/B/C95/83. Lady G. Cecil, 23.12.79, ii, p.372. Nicolson, *Helen's Tower*, p.176.

35. Odo Russell to Dufferin, 26.12.79, in Lyall, p.280.

36. Bismarck to Dufferin, 20.1.80. in Lyall, p.281.

37. Lyall, pp. 274–5: 'Nothing could have been prettier', Dufferin reported, 'than to see the several batteries discover themselves among the woods in the far distance by their unexpected puffs of white smoke . . . The place was alive with scattered pelotons of tirailleurs.' The climax was a cavalry charge of 6,000–7,000 dragoons, 'their breast plates and helmets glittering in the sun . . . This last performance was really glorious.' But seemingly more opera than shock and awe: see *Letters to Lady Bradford and Lady Chesterfield*, pp. 233–4.

38. Kennedy, pp. 4, 12–14.

39. D. W. R. Bahlman (ed.), *The Diary of Sir Edward Walter Hamilton, 1880–1885*, vol. 1, 4.11.80.

40. Argyll to Dufferin, 13.1.80, D1071 H/B/C/95/84.

41. Kennedy p.19. Marquess of Sligo to Dufferin, 30.3.80, D1071H/B/B/811/8.

42. Dufferin to Argyll, 5.2.80, D1071H/B/C/95/85.

43. Dufferin to Lady Dartrey, 4.6.80, cited in Lyall, p.286.

44. The only other candidate was Kimberley who turned it down. Argyll explained that Ripon was appointed as 'a Cabinet man and a Catholic' for whom something had to be found. Shannon, ii, p.249. Argyll to Dufferin, 28.9.80, D1071H/B/C/95//88. Harrison, p.433.

45. Although it could still throw up some surprises, such as the ancient 'Prince Orloff Davidoff . . . who was educated in Edinburgh, had dined with Sir Walter Scott and Moore, and stayed with Miss Edgeworth.' *My Russian and Turkish Journals*, p.22.

46. The two bears presently there are more recent. The original bear had been severely provoked but local wisdom decreed that once the bear had discovered the taste of human blood it would need to be shot.

47. The Queen to Dufferin, 8.12.78, 6.4.80, MDACQ. See also RA VIC/MAIN/QVJ: 1878, 14 November. She herself would have been more astonished by a conversation in 1881 during which Dufferin asked Granville, 'Would it be so bad a thing for us if

Russia were at Constantinople?' Granville agreed that it would not, 'though I dare not say so'. Dufferin to Grant Duff, 12.1.96, D1071H/03/54.

48. Buckle, vol. 6, p.844. Dufferin to Granville, 17.8.80, cited in Lord Edmond Fitzmaurice, *Life of Granville* (1905).

CHAPTER 18: REVOLUTIONARY TIMES

1. Gregory to Dufferin, 'March 1881', D1071/H/B/G/398/1. 'The religious bitterness has become quite dreadful'. Dartrey to Dufferin, 14.12.82, D1071/H/D/78/126. All of which Dufferin relayed to the Queen. QVD, 22.9.80, 73, pp. 32–3; 26.11.80, 73, p.98.

2. Dufferin to Argyll, 6.1.80, D1071H/B/C/95/83. Dufferin to Argyll, 2.9.80, D1071H/B/C/95/89. By now he was claiming that his land sales were nothing to do with debts but astute asset management: 'I foresaw that no English government would have the courage, the virtue or the good sense to withstand the gathering agrarian agitation.' Dufferin to Lansdowne, 4.7.80, D1071H/B/F175/7.

3. So desperate in fact that, when delayed in Russia by Hariot falling ill, after ten days he could wait no longer and left her to make her own way back. Paul Bew, *Ireland: The Politics of Enmity, 1789–2006* (2007), pp. 325–6.

4. Hamilton, *Diary*, 4.11.80.

5. Granville to Gladstone, 30.11.80, *Ramm*, vol. 2, p.225; McKnight, *50 Years of Ulster*, p.261.

6. Harrison, pp. 426–7. 'He is against the expropriation of the landlords covert or open.' Hamilton, *Diary*, 12–15.12.80, pp. 88–9. Shannon, *Gladstone*, vol. 2, p.270.

7. Gladstone to Granville, 30.12.80, MIC 331.

8. Dufferin to Gladstone, 24.12.80, MIC 331: Gladstone was 'most reassuring in every way [over Ireland] and I hope your ingenuity may contrive for us some final settlement'.

9. Shannon, vol. 2, p.254. 'Very bitter attack . . . in the *Pall Mall* . . . I knew I should have to stand my shot.' Dufferin to Brin, 25.2.81, D1071H/B/S/251B/5. Harrison, p.414.

10. Argyll to Dufferin, 11.2.81, D1071H/B/C/95/103-4 and MIC 320.

11. Dufferin to Gladstone, 7.12.80, 22.2.81, 10.3.81, MIC 331.

12. Duke of Somerset, *Letters*, pp. 514, 518. In fact the coterie around Gladstone were remarkable in their sensitivity to Dufferin's plight and as late as May Hamilton was enduring a 'long talk . . . with Dufferin. He can't swallow the Bill.' Hamilton, *Diary*, 4.5.81, p.137. Dufferin chose instead to take comfort from the fact that Gladstone's 'disapproval [of his pamphlet] had been less than I had expected'. Dufferin to Argyll, 7.4.81, D1071H/B/C/95/105-6.

13. Argyll to Dufferin, 7.4.81, D1071H/B/C/95/105-6. Dowager Duchess of Argyll (ed.), *George Douglas, Eighth Duke of Argyll: Autobiography and Memoirs* (1925–7), p.381. Dufferin to Lansdowne, 8.1.81, D1071H/B/F/175/10.

14. Dufferin to Gregory, *c.*1881, in Brian Jenkins, *Sir William Gregory of Coole, A Biography of Anglo-Ireland,* (1986), p.282.

15. As Goschen recounted, 'belief in Gladstone became so strong towards the end that any expression of qualified feelings towards the Bill were considered a sin against the Holy Ghost.' And this despite: 'The stories of Gladstone's nocturnal conversations with the ladies who frequent the Haymarket . . . are more numerous . . . The most absurd part of it all is that it is all done under the surveillance and chaperonage, so to say, of the two policemen who never have him out of their sight! No-one suggests any *real* scandal but . . . it really looks like a species of insanity.' Dartrey to Dufferin, 8.3.82, D1071H/B/D/78/117.

16. Dufferin to Argyll, 25.7.82, D1071H/B/C/95/111; T. J. Spinner, *Goschen,* p.85. Dufferin's assessment of Gladstone said more about himself: 'an able honest man . . . essentially a middle class man and wanting in appreciation of of [sic] the importance of the external trifles of life'. RA VIC/ADDA36/1583, Sir H. Ponsonby to Lady M. Ponsonby, 13 November 1878.

17. Lyall, pp. 290–3. Kennedy, p.26.

18. Dufferin to the Queen, 19.2.80, MIC 340. 'What a state of things! What a life for the poor Emperor!' after a previous attempt. Queen to Dufferin, 3.3.80, Helen's Tower Library.

19. Lyall, p.292. Dufferin's telegram on the assassination 'gave us all a thrill of ineffable horror!' QVD, 13.3.1881, 74, p.111.

20. Dufferin to Lady Dorothy Nevill, 27.3.81, in R. Nevill (ed.), *The Reminiscences of Lady Dorothy Nevill* (1906), pp. 153–5.

21. Dufferin to Ponsonby, ii, *Letters,* p.332; Lyall, p.292; Kennedy, p.26. Jane Ridley, *Bertie* (2012), p.230. Dufferin to Queen, 31.3.1881, VIC/MAIN/H/43/121.

22. Hamilton *Diary,* 11.4.81, p.127; Granville to WEG, 11.4.81, no. 462, Ramm, pp. 255–6.

23. Lyall, p.293; see also Dufferin to Queen, 25.2.80, MIC 340, 'extraordinary' numbers of Jews among nihilist ranks – 'much hated in Russia'.

24. Draft article, 'Assassination of the Emperor Alexander of Russia', Nov. 1897, published in USA 28.9.99.

25. Dufferin to Argyll, 19.4.81, Argyll, *Autobiography,* pp. 380–1.

26. *My Russian and Turkish Journals,* pp 3–6.

27. Dilke to Dufferin, 3.9.81, D1071H/B/D/158.

CHAPTER 19: FINDING ONE'S ASSIETTE

1. H. Nicolson, *Portrait of a Diplomatist* (1930), pp. 22–4.

2. They married from the embassy on 20 April 1882 with Dufferin giving the bride away – but only after checking out the bridegroom's financial prospects and sounding out his views on Irish nationalists (eager to please Nicolson declared Dillon, Healy and Biggar were 'wild revolutionist[s] – the last humped back

and distorted, a veritable Quasimodo'). Nicolson to Dufferin, 19.3.82, 10.6.82, D1071H/B/B/756/1.

3. The three ambassadors were Nicolson, Edward Goschen and Hardinge. Also seconded to the embassy were Robert Kennedy who followed Dufferin from St Petersburg and Donald Mackenzie Wallace of *The Times*.

4. Lord Charles Hardinge of Penshurst, *Old Diplomacy*, pp. 13–22. Sir Edwin Pears, *Forty Years in Constantinople*, pp. 95–9.

5. Hardinge, pp. 12–14, 21; Pears, pp. 97–9.

6. DD, 16.10.82; HD, *My Russian and Turkish Journals*, pp. 229–30.

7. As ever the financing of such extravagance was 'reckless'. When to meet Dufferin's escalating debts Hardinge had, at Dufferin's instruction, duly found £500 of savings, he was horrified to discover a few days later that the ambassador spent a similar sum on jewellery for his wife. 'But did you not say that we had saved me £500?' Dufferin responded a little sheepishly.

8. Hardinge, pp. 13–14.

9. Nicolson, *Helen's Tower*, p.180.

10. Mansel, pp. 313–17.

11. Ibid.; Peter Mansfield, pp. 76–7.

12. Interestingly Dufferin's first impression was that while the Ottoman Empire was 'sicker than ever', 'yet it maybe so easily put right' (such were its resources – compared to which its debt was a 'mere fleabite'). Dufferin to Argyll, 6.8.81, D1071/H/B/C/95/108.

13. Mansfield, *History of the Middle East*, p.76

14. Hardinge, p.19. Even corruption didn't work with the annual retainer of £1,500 paid by the embassy to the assistant foreign minister being particularly ineffective.

15. On British loss of influence see Robinson and Gallagher, *Africa and the Victorians: The Official Mind of Imperialism* (1961), p.105.

16. Pears, pp. 87–8

17. Dufferin to Layard, 31.1.82, MIC320. Hamilton, *Diary*, 26.12.81, p.205. Shannon, vol. 2, p.266.

18. Especially in the Army where native promotion had been regularly blocked and indeed 'Urabi had not been promoted since 1863. Eugene Rogan, *The Arabs: A History* (2009), pp. 123–32.

19. Egyptian foreign debt rose from £3m to £91m (1863–1876). Mansel, *Levant*, p.114.

20. Donald Malcolm Reid, 'The 'Urabi Revolution and British Conquest', in M. Daly (ed.), *The Cambridge History of Egypt*, vol. 2, pp. 219–22. Peter Mansfield, *Britain and Egypt* (1971), p.7. John Darwin, *The Empire Project: The Rise and Fall of the British World System 1830–1970* (2009), pp. 69–75.

21. Thomas Pakenham, *Scramble for Africa*, p.127. Similarly Sir William Gregory, retired colonial administrator, to Gladstone, that 'Urabi was 'the purest and noblest oriental I have ever met'. Shannon, vol. 2, p.301. Rogan, *The Arabs*, pp. 123–32.

22. Lyall, pp. 309–10. DD, 2 and 12.11.81.

23. Robinson and Gallagher, *Africa and the Victorians*, p.95.

24. Mansfield, *Britain and Egypt*, p.33; E. Karsh and I. Karsh, *Empires in the Sand* (1999), p.55; W. S. Blunt, *A Secret History of the English Occupation of Egypt* (2nd ed., 1907), p.189.

25. The army was purged of many of its Turko-Circassian officers, fifty of whom were tortured in revenge. Rogan, *The Arabs*, p.128.

26. D. M. Reid, pp. 228–30. Mansfield, *Egypt*, p.94.

27. Karsh, p.54; Shannon, vol. 2, p.293.

28. And all for a sideshow: 'Here nobody cares much for anything except Ireland'. Philip Currie to Dufferin, 9.6.(1882), D1071 H/B/C/1774/23. Even when Gladstone did spare time for the Middle East, it was only to urge Dufferin to keep the pressure on the Sultan over the Armenians.

29. Hamilton, *Diary*, 'April 1882', p.256.

30. The June massacre saw far more Egyptian dead (over 250) than Europeans ('proof of Europeans' superior firepower'). Mansel, *Levant*, p.120.

31. D. M. Reid, pp. 231–2; Mansfield, *Britain and Egypt*, p.39.

32. But never Gladstone.

33. *The Economist*, 1.7.82 cited in Matthew, *Gladstone Diaries*, p.lxix. Compare with the initial verdict of *The Times* on 'Urabi's revolt: 'The army is the only native institution which Egypt now owns. All else has been invaded, controlled and transformed by Britain and France' (12.9.82). At a garden party at Marlborough House 'everyone was talking of these horrors, which seem to multiply upon us and (not unnaturally) we go on in the usual course marrying and giving in marriage and eating and drinking whilst the flood is arising around us.' Gordon, *Carnarvon Diaries*, 13.7.82, p.339.

34. Matthew, *Gladstone Diaries*, p.lxix; Shannon, vol. 2, pp. 300–1.

35. Gladstone's memorandum, 21.6.82, Ramm, no. 730, p.381. Robert T. Harrison, *Gladstone's Imperialism in Egypt* (1995), pp. 12–14.

36. 23.6.82, Shannon, vol. 2, p.302.

37. Or indeed the Queen, who early on instructed Dufferin (who was 'to represent her at the Conference') that 'Whatever is done, England must prevail in Egypt. She must be first and have her interests secured. We can never let anyone else have Egypt but ourselves; but we don't want to have it if we can help it. Germany wishes us to have it.' Queen to Dufferin, 3.1.82, MDACQ.

38. Granville to Hartington, 20.6.82, in Robinson and Gallagher, *Africa and the Victorians*, p.108.

39. Granville to Gladstone, 15.4.82; Gladstone to Granville, 16.4.82, Ramm, nos. 676 and 678, pp. 360–1.

40. Interestingly Lord Lyons reported back on 'Dufferin's misgivings [over] either controlling the Turks if they set foot in Egypt or of ever getting them out'. Lyons to Granville, 26.5.82, in Lord Newton, *Lord Lyons*, vol. 1 (1913), pp. 283–4. Gladstone to Granville, 30.5.82, Robinson and Gallagher, p.105.

41. Gladstone to Granville, 21.6.82, 1.7.82, Ramm, pp. 381–3.

42. DD, 10–12.6.82.

43. Lyall, p.312. Mansel, pp. 320–5, 338. For all his initial difficulties, Dufferin was quite

pleased at the make-up of the conference, knowing many of the delegates well. Dufferin to Queen, 27.6.1882, VIC MAIN/O/13/48.

44. Granville to Gladstone, 26.6.82, Ramm, no. 732, p.381; E. Karsh and I. Karsh, *Empires in the Sand* (1999), pp. 57–9. 25.6.82, Queen Victoria's Journal, in Buckle (ed.), *Letters*, iii, pp. 302–3.

45. Hamilton diary, 2.7.82, 7.7.82, p.278. Lyons to Granville, 20.6.82, Newton, vol. 1, pp. 286–7. Gladstone to Granville, 27.6.82, 1.7.82, Ramm, pp. 382–3. Granville to Spencer, 26.6.82, in Robinson and Gallagher, *Africa and the Victorians*, pp. 105, 109.

46. Harrison, p.17.

47. Mansel suggests that Seymour's aggressive stance was in part fuelled by the murder of his manservant in the June riots. *Levant*, p.120.

48. Mansfield, *Britain and Egypt*, pp. 42–3; Harrison, pp. 11–17, 67–114.

49. Chamberlain to Dilke: 'We have got the Grand Old Man into a corner now and he must fight.' Cited in Longford, *Pilgrimage of Passion*, p.185.

50. Gladstone to Granville, 5.7.82, *Ramm*, p.385; Hamilton, *Diary*, 7.7.82, p.299; Matthew, *Gladstone Diaries*, pp. lxx–lxxi; Shannon, vol. 2, p.303; Roy Jenkins, *Gladstone*, p.504. Mansfield, *Britain and Egypt*, p.44; *Modern Egypt*, p.94.

51. Mansel, *Levant*, pp. 122–3. Virtually all of these were Egyptians, as by 9 July most of the foreigners had sought refuge on the ships.

52. Harrison, pp. 17–24.

53. Lyall, pp. 313–14. Granville to Gladstone, 16.7.82, Ramm, no. 766, p.397. DD, 10, 15, 16, 20.7.82. Mansfield, *Britain and Egypt*, pp. 45–6.

54. Hamilton, *Diary*, 18.7.82, p.309. Albert Hourani, *A History of the Arab Peoples* (1991), p.238. Lyall, p.314. Karsh, pp. 60–2. Pears, pp. 89, 92–3.

55. Gladstone to Granville, 14, 16.7.82, pp. 396–7. Karsh, p.61.

56. Robinson and Gallagher, *Africa and the Victorians*, p.116.

57. Harrison, p.119.

58. Gladstone to Granville, 27.6.82, Ramm, p.382.

59. Shannon, *Gladstone*, vol. 2, p.304. For all the rhetoric of Britain acting on behalf of Europe, Russia's attempt to reopen discussions on the military convention were firmly rebuffed as only a concern for Britain. QVD, 14–16.8.1882, 77, pp. 85–90.

CHAPTER 20: 'A MASTER OF HIS PROFESSION'

1. Thus Gladstone's insistence to the House that there was 'not the smallest rag or shard of evidence to support' the claim that the 'military party was the popular party . . . struggling for the liberties of Egypt'. Harrison, pp. 109–14. Mansfield, *Britain and Egypt*, pp. 35–6.

2. Salisbury to Sir Henry Elliot, 30.12.79, in Lady G. Cecil, *Salisbury*, vol. 2, p.359. Argyll to Dufferin, 8.6.82, D 1071/H/B/C/95/110. 'I have no views at all' on the Egyptian crisis, declared the young Lord Rosebery when confronted in Downing Street by Blunt, 'but those of a bondholder'; a view he later claimed, after Blunt had

leaked it, to be 'a joke'. Elizabeth Longford, *A Pilgrimage of Passion* (1979), p.180. Leo McKinstry, *Rosebery* (2005), p.103. One for whom it wasn't a joke was Argyll's third son, Lord Walter Campbell, who wrote to Dufferin asking for inside information about the financial situation in Egypt (June/July 1882) lest the stock market panic ruined him. Campbell to Dufferin, D1071H/B/C/114/1–9. Similar pressure came from foreign bondholders. Edward Bouverie (Chairman of the Corporation of Foreign Bondholders) to Dufferin, D1071H/B/B/618/3.

3. Mansel, *Levant*, p.117.
4. My italics. Matthew, *Gladstone Diaries*, pp. lxix, lxxi–xxii. Roy Jenkins, *Gladstone*, pp. 507–8. Mansfield, *Britain and Egypt*, p.8. Niall Ferguson, *Empire* (2003), pp. 283–4. *My Russian and Turkish Journals*, pp. 215–19. Shannon, vol. 2, pp. 303–4.
5. Cromer, *Modern Egypt*, vol. 1, pp. 310–22.
6. Nicolson, *Portrait of a Diplomatist*, p.29. Hamilton, *Diary*, 21.8.82, 25.8.82, p.322.
7. Stephen Gwynn and G. M. Tuckwell, *The Life of Sir Charles W. Dilke* (1917), vol. 1, pp. 474–5.
8. Intriguingly by 24.8.82 the embassy received intelligence of a plot by Turkish 'police' to assassinate Dufferin at Therapia. D1071H/K2/A4.
9. Peter Gordon (ed.), *The Red Earl: The Papers of the 5th Earl of Spencer, 1835–1910*, p.219.
10. DD, 18.8.82. Hamilton, *Diary*, 21.8.82, 27.8.82, pp. 322, 326. Granville to Gladstone, 21.8.82, Ramm, no. 83 and fn 4, pp. 410–11.
11. Hamilton, *Diary*, 29, 31.8.82, 1.9.82, pp. 326–30.
12. Hamilton, *Diary*, 2,7,10.9.82, pp. 334–6. Gladstone to Granville, 7.9.82, Ramm, no. 813, p.416. Lyall, p.315.
13. Nicolson, *Portrait of a Diplomatist*, pp. 31–2. Dufferin to Lady Dartrey, 23.9.82 in Lyall, p.321.
14. Lyall, p.317.
15. Donald Mackenzie Wallace, 'Egypt and the Egyptian Question', pp. 99–100, cited in Lyall, pp. 318–19.
16. Shannon, vol. 2, p.265.
17. Hamilton, *Diary*, 29.8.82, p.327.
18. Dufferin to Granville, 19.9.82, in Lyall, p.319. Nicolson, *Portrait of a Diplomatist*, p.30.
19. Dufferin to Lady Dartrey, 23.9.82, in Lyall, pp. 320–2. Argyll to Dufferin, 1.8.82, D1071/H/B/C/95/112.
20. Not that he was incommunicado on the Bosphorous and indeed he did break off his holiday at the summons from the Sultan. DD, 1–6.9.82.
21. RA VIC/ADDA36/2097, 2099, Sir H. Ponsonby to Lady M. Ponsonby, 9 and 11 September 1882. 'Granville telegraphed Lord Dufferin to procrastinate.' RA VIC/MAIN/QVJ: 1882, 11 September.
22. Cromer, *Modern Egypt* (1908), vol. 1, p.321.
23. 'I got more credit than I deserved for it was the stupidity of the Turks and not my subtlety that brought about the desirable diplomatic results'. Dufferin to Brin, [28.10?]1882, D1071H/B/S/251B/6.

24. Lyall, p.320.

25. Ferguson, *Empire*, p.235.

26. Lyall, p.319.

27. Harrison, p.533. Also in Nicolson, *Helen's Tower*, p.183.

28. See cartoon in the *World*, 'Christmas number 1882', Dufferin's Press Cuttings volume, Helen's Tower Library.

29. Dufferin to Lady Dartrey, 23.9.82, in Lyall, p.320.

30. Dufferin to Granville, 19.9.82, in Lyall, p.319.

31. Hamilton, *Diary*, 25.8.82, p.324. Matthew, *Gladstone Diaries*, p.lxxiii.

32. Granville to Gladstone, 1.10.82; Ponsonby to Dufferin, 9.11.82, Buckle (ed.), *Letters*, vol. 2 (1928), p.357; Dufferin to Queen, 21.11.82, Buckle, *Letters*, vol. 2, p.363. To Dufferin's further embarrassment the Queen learnt of his refusal. David Cannadine, *Ornamentalism* (2001), p.95. He chose to value 'Your Majesty's friendship and approbation more than any honour'. RA VIC MAIN/O18/84a, Lord Dufferin to Queen Victoria, 30 November 1882. RA VIC/MAIN/QVJ: 1882, 30 November.

CHAPTER 21: STATECRAFT AND THE ART OF CASTING A VEIL

1. *My Russian and Turkish Journals*, pp. 221–31. Lyall, p.324.

2. Shannon, vol. 2, pp. 305–6; Gladstone to Granville, 22.9.82, Ramm, no. 835, p.429. As Hartington later reminisced: '[Gladstone's] belief, or rather his self-justification, at the time, was that his Government were merely repressing a military tyranny "incompatible with the growth and existence of freedom".' Cited in Harrison, p.138.

3. They particularly disagreed over Dufferin. Gladstone thought he would be 'capital' but Granville, with an eye to Foreign Office morale again resisted; and together with Wolseley persuaded the Queen to propose Mallet (the existing Representative in Cairo). Mallet, however, insisted on Dufferin! Sir Edward Mallet, *Shifting Scenes* (1901), p.77. Gwynn and Tuckwell, *Dilke*, vol. 1, pp. 548–9. Gladstone to Granville, 16 and 22.9.82; Granville to Gladstone, 1.10.82, Ramm, nos 826, 835, 850, pp. 421, 428, 436.

4. *Daily Telegraph*, 2.11.82; *The Times*, 3.11.82. *Punch*, 11.11.82. Dufferin's Egyptian Press cutting album.

5. Mallet, *Shifting Sands*, p.77.

6. The Queen to Dufferin, 9.11.82, MDACQ.

7. 'We are in a great "fix" about Arabi. The trial has become a farce. The wisest thing to do in my opinion is simply to exile him, dropping the trial . . . Dufferin is our "deus ex Machina" and we must hope he may drag the coach out of the rut.' Angus Hawkins and John Powell (ed.), *The Journal of John Wodehouse, 1st Earl of Kimberley* (for 1862–1902), Camden, 5th Series, 9 (1997), pp. 333, 20.11.82.

8. Granville to Gladstone, 15.11.82; Gladstone to Granville, 19.11.82, Ramm, nos. 877, 885, pp. 452–5. Dufferin to Granville, 27.12.82. Elizabeth Longford, *The Pilgrimage of Passion*, pp. 187–9.

9. Hamilton, *Diary*, 4,10.12.82, pp. 370, 373. Buckle, *Letters*, pp. 218–19. Queen to Granville, in Ramm, p.465. Lyall, p.330, on Gregory's continued critique of Dufferin for failing to exonerate 'Urabi. Blunt, *Secret History of the English Occupation of Egypt* (2nd ed.; 1st ed., 1895), pp. 465, 473–4. 'Urabi was allowed to return to Egypt in 1901 and died of cancer in 1911. Harrison, pp. 138–43.

10. To the surprise of critics such as Blunt and Granville who had questioned Dufferin's appetite for the hard work of reconstruction. Blunt, *Secret History*, p.460.

11. Ridley, *Bertie*, p.210.

12. Dufferin to Queen, 21.11.82, 12.12.82, Buckle, *Letters*, vol. 3, pp. 362–3, 375. Wood's sister would later rise to prominence as Mrs O'Shea. Mansfield, *Britain and Egypt*, pp. 84, 110, 123–8.

13. Mansfield, *Britain and Egypt*, p.56.

14. Kenneth Rose, *Superior Person* (1969), p.84. Nicolson, *Portrait of a Diplomatist*, p.35.

15. Dufferin to Dilke, nd, 12.12.82, MIC 342. Gladstone to Granville, 8.12.82, Ramm, i, p.465.

16. Granville to Gladstone, 3.1.83, Ramm, ii, no. 948, p.3. Matthew, *Gladstone Diaries*, 15.11.83.

17. All the quotations from the report are drawn from Dufferin's State paper: C.3529PP (1883) LXXXIII. See also Lyall, pp. 331–41. Mansfield, *Britain and Egypt*, pp. 56–8.

18. Cromer, *Modern Egypt*, vol. 2, p.275. Dufferin to Grant Duff, 12.1.96, D1071H/03/5.

19. Sheldon Amos, 'The New Egyptian Constitution', *Contemporary Review*, xliii (June 1883), pp. 909–22. Interestingly Dufferin thought the educational opportunity existed also for the Europeans who through greater interaction with Egyptians in administration 'might obtain an insight into the inner mind and less obvious wants of the native population'. Cromer, vol. 2, p.275.

20. Dufferin to Granville, 25.2.83, Ramm, ii, p.37. Dufferin to the Queen, 23.1.83, Buckle, *Letters*, vol. 3, p.403.

21. And there was the additional stress of working alone, with his wife and her sister in Greece recuperating from typhoid. The Queen thought Dufferin 'much aged'. RA VIC/MAIN/QVJ: 1883, 29 June.

22. Milner, *England in Egypt*, cited Lyall, p.336.

23. Nicolson, *Helen's Tower*, p.185.

24. 'I had a very multifarious audience to address: France, Europe, the Sultan, the Egyptians, the people who wanted to take Egypt altogether, those who wished to let her "stew", my own Government, the Radicals, and lastly the British "Lion".' Dufferin to Brin, 6.4.83, D1071H/B/S/251B/8.

25. DD, 7, 8, 20.1.83. Blunt, pp. 460, 465. Granville to Gladstone, 9.2.83, Ramm, vol. 2, p.22. Interestingly Wallace was surprised and embarrassed by the leak. Apologising to Dufferin he promised to investigate the source, which suggests that Dufferin was working alone in feeding (or talking too indiscreetly to) Bell; much as he had in 1878 with his Canadian biographers. Wallace to Dufferin, 9.2.83, cited in Harrison pp. 527–8.

26. Lyall, p.337. Cromer, p.345.

27. *The Times*, 20.3.83. *Saturday Review*, 24.3.83.

28. *Pall Mall Gazette*, 21, 28.3.83. *Spectator*, 24.3.83. Mansfield, *Britain and Egypt*, p.58.

29. *Standard*, 20.3.83. *Globe*, 20.3.83. *The Times*, 20.3.83.

30. *St James's Gazette*, 24.3.83. *Globe*, 20.3.83. *Saturday Review*, 24.3.83. *Daily News*, 20.3.83.

31. Dufferin to Granville, 28.3.83, cited in Lyall, pp. 337–8. *The Times*, 13.4.83. Hamilton *Diary*, p.415. *Observer*, 1,15.4.83. *The Economist*, 7.4.83.

32. Dufferin to Amos, 4.7.84, T3282/1.

33. *The Times*, 24.7.83, 8–30.8.83, 9.11.83. Dufferin to Gladstone, 5.8.83, 1.9.83, MIC 331.

34. 'Fortunately, as far as my credit is concerned, I put on record before I left Egypt a strong opinion against the expedition.' Dufferin to Lansdowne, 28.11.83, D1071H/B/F/175/13. Yet Hicks viewed him as a supporter and in December 1883 Dufferin was still lamenting the loss of Khartoum ('an outpost of civilisation as well as of Egypt') and the following spring would find him writing encouraging letters to Gordon who, having gone beyond his brief and regained the town, was now an increasingly beleaguered correspondent ('we are in a pickle here'). Lyall, pp. 342–7.

35. The best Gladstone achieved was their withdrawal from Cairo; all in all, British governments made seventy-two public commitments to evacuate her troops in the seventy-four years of occupation.

36. Hamilton, *Diary*, 29.10.82, vol. 1, p.352; 11.11.83, 29.12.83, vol. 2, pp. 503, 533. Charles Chevenix-Trench, *Charley Gordon* (1978), p.193. Charles Whibley, *Lord John Manners and his Friends*, vol. 2, pp. 214–15. Samuel White Baker, 'Egypt's Proper Frontier', *Nineteenth Century* (July 1884), Dufferin to Queen, 13.12.83, Buckle, *Letters*, vol. 3, p.462.

37. Mansfield, *Britain and Egypt*, p.128.

38. Mansfield, *Britain and Egypt*, pp. 100–5. Dufferin to Amos, 4.7.83, T3282/1. On the successful exclusion of the French, see Lyons to Granville, 15.5.83, Newton, vol. 1, p.88. *Saturday Review*, 7.4.83. That said, historians taking the report at face value and in the light of the autocratic regime that emerged under Baring, dismiss 'facile constitutional schemes (like Dufferin's report of 1883)' as being at best before their time. Darwin, *Empire Project*, pp. 74–5. Robinson and Gallagher, *Africa and the Victorians*, p.280.

39. Amos, 'The new Egyptian Constitution'; D. M. Wallace, *Egypt and the Egyptian Question* (1883).

40. *Vanity Fair: Foreign Office, Diplomatic, and Consular Sketches* (1883).

41. Count Paul Vasili, *The World of London* (1885), pp. 170–2.

42. *The Times*, 21.3.83.

43. *The Times*, 13.7.83. Such ideas would be popularised six months later by the coming man of Liberal politics, Lord Rosebery, when he described the British Empire as 'a Commonwealth of Nations'. McKinstry, pp. 121–4.

44. John M. Mackenzie (ed.), *Imperialism and Popular Culture* (1986). Bernard Porter, *The*

Absent-Minded Imperialists (2004). Andrew Thompson, *The Empire Strikes Back* (2005). McKinstry, pp. 122–4.

45. Cairns to Dufferin, nd, D1071/H/B/C/21/9.

CHAPTER 22: AN INDIAN INHERITANCE

1. Argyll to Dufferin, nd, 'January' 1872, D1071H/B/C/95; Harrison, pp. 458–70.
2. Angus Hawkins, John Powell, *The Journal of John Wodehouse, 1st Earl of Kimberley (1862–1902)*, Camden, 5th Series, vol. 9 (1997), pp. 345, 497, 237–4. Lady Spencer to Lord Spencer, 11.9.84, Peter Gordon (ed.), *The Red Earl: The Papers of the 5th Earl of Spencer, 1835 to 1910* (1981), vol. 1, pp. 234–7.
3. Hamilton, *Diary*, 11.9.84, p.681. Kimberley, *Journal*, p.18. *Morning Post*, 11.9.84; *The Times*, 11.9.84; *Liverpool Daily Post*, 11.9.84. *Daily News*, 11.9.84; *Weekly Dispatch*, *People*, 14.9.84; *Pall Mall Gazette*, 11.9.84. Roy Foster, *Lord Randolph Churchill* (1981), p.179.
4. *Punch*, 20.9.84; *Evening News*, 11.9.84. With his public standing so high, Dufferin's binding of these press cuttings reflected understandable pride; but the entitling of the cutting from the *Weekly Dispatch* – 'the Ignoble Exception' – reaffirmed his vulnerability, even at the height of his popularity, to any slight.
5. Hardinge to Dufferin, 15.9.84, MIC 22/11. His 'unusually swarthy complexion, sensuous lips, the heavy lidded eyes . . . a monocle, which would leap engagingly from his face when he greeted someone', Mark Bence-Jones, *The Viceroys of India* (1982), p.131. Charles Allen, *Kipling Sahib* (London, 2007), p.185.
6. Often when seemingly indiscreet, he was drawing out information or testing the ground. Yet he was also constantly anxious about security: hence the frequent PS in his correspondence to burn his letters (while of course keeping a copy for himself). Harrison, p.525.
7. At a shooting party in Scotland in 1884, Rosebery, a genuine celebrity in his own right, declared that he 'placed Lord Dufferin . . . among the first rank of conversationalists'.
8. Hamilton, *Diary*, 16.9.84, p.683. Harrison, p.531. Lord Frederick Hamilton, *The Vanished Pomps of Yesterday* (London, 1950), p.380.
9. Hariot, Lady Dufferin, *Our Viceregal Life*, vol. 1, pp. 6–10. Dufferin to Lady Dartrey, 13.1.85, in Lyall, pp. 360–1.
10. Ibid.
11. Ibid.
12. *Our Viceregal Life*, vol. 1, pp. 12–13. DD, 15.12.84. And all the more so for receiving that night a telegram with the news that after a long illness the Duchess of Somerset – the last of the Sheridan beauties – had died.
13. Niall Ferguson, *Empire* (pb ed 2004), pp. 197–8, 210. David Gilmour, *The Ruling Caste* (2005), pp. 252–61. Darwin, *After Tamerlane: The Global History of Empire* (2007), pp. 348–9.

14. Lawrence James, *Raj: The Making and Unmaking of British India*, p.343.

15. For all that, by the end of the nineteenth century, and most overtly with Curzon, the British came to see them 'not as relics but as rulers; not as puppets but as living factors in the administration'. Gilmour, *Ruling Caste*, pp. 176–7, 189–90. James, *Raj*, pp. 333–9.

16. Gilmour, *Ruling Caste*, pp. 195–6.

17. Indians were eligible for the ICS but the curriculum, the holding of exams in London and lower age limit of nineteen, combined, as was intended, to keep them out. By 1900 out of 1,021 members of the ICS, only 33 were Indian. All of which made a mockery of the 1858 Declaration's promise of 'perfect equality . . . so far as all appointments were concerned, between Europeans and Natives'. R. J. Moore, 'Imperial India, 1858–1914' in *The Oxford History of the British Empire*, ed. Andrew Porter, pp. 429–32.

18. Harrison, pp. 481–516. Gilmour, *Ruling Caste*, pp. 132–4. Niall Ferguson, *Empire* (pb ed 2004), pp. 198–205.

19. As Grant Duff (Governor of Madras) explained in a memorandum for Dufferin on his arrival: 'One school says "You are only here to educate the natives to govern themselves. That done, you only have to go about your business." The other school says "No man knows the secret of the future; but for practical purposes you must act as if Great Britain were to govern India for all time, doing nothing which in your judgement has any tendency to undermine the foundations of British power."' Gilmour, *Ruling Caste*, pp. 22–8; H. G. Wells *The New Machiavelli* (1912), p.356.

CHAPTER 23: GOVERNING INDIA

1. John Darwin, *The Empire Project* (2009), p.85. But note Kimberley's alternative, if a shade defensive, perspective: 'Cabinet Minister is higher employment than the Viceroy, and though it looks such a fine thing to govern 130 millions of Indians, it is a much finer thing to govern 32 millions of Englishmen with the general control of the whole of our vast Empire, India included.' Kimberley, *Journal*, p.265.

2. Kipling, 'One Viceroy Resigns'. Allen, p.185. Gilmour, *Recessional*, p.76. Kipling famously derided Dufferin's Councillors in 1885 as men who after death would transmigrate into 'the bodies of the great grey Langurs'. Later in 1888 he described them in Simla as 'very like apes' with their 'grey, hairy monkeyish faces'. Yet Curzon felt his Council was 'far less able' than Dufferin's eleven years earlier. Gilmour, *Curzon*, p.154. Gilmour, *Ruling Caste*, pp. 100, 213, 234, 239, 246, 264.

3. DD, 22.1.86. *Our Viceregal Life*, 2.3.85, vol. 1, p.73.

4. Oddly (for historic reasons) the Secretary of State appointed the governors of Madras and Bombay along with the chief justice and the non-civilian members of the Viceroy's Council (the heads of the financial, legal and military departments). In practice on such matters with both viceroy and Secretary of State able to exercise a

veto, such posts were resolved amicably. And, through careful handling of the India Office (whose Permanent Undersecretary, Arthur Godley, 1883–1909, never visited India), Dufferin largely retained control of patronage and made full use of it to assert his authority. Gilmour, *Ruling Caste*, pp. 218, 234–6.

5. Gilmour, *Ruling Caste*, p.238. A. N. Wilson, *The Victorians* (2002), pp. 473–4.

6. Briton Martin, 'The Viceroyalty of Lord Dufferin', *History Today*, x, 12 (December 1960), p.61. Gilmour, *Ruling Caste*, pp. 202–6.

7. 'It is a great pity that Griffin's considerable abilities', he wrote to Cross, 'should be marred by this [his private life] and other faults, but his vanity and egotism, and his cynical indifference to "les convenances", have spoiled an otherwise valuable public servant.' Gilmour, *Ruling Caste*, pp. 218, 234–6. Dufferin to the Queen, 31.3.87, MDACQ.

8. However, after forty years theirs was a more intimate relationship. She would write of 'the relief to unburden her poor heart' to him and even with him in India. The Queen regularly consulted him on diplomatic questions outside his Indian brief, sharing confidential correspondence from Berlin as well as personal matters such as concerns over her children and her 'loneliness', which only Dufferin 'truly felt'. In return she could be a powerful shield against critical politicians. The Queen to Dufferin, 24.10.84, 11.11.84, 28.5.85, MDACQ. RA VIC/MAIN/QVJ: 1883, 24 October.

9. Gilmour, *Ruling Caste*, p.214. James, *Raj*, pp. 312–21. Lyall, pp. 406–7.

10. Gilmour, *The Long Recessional*, p.32. Lyall, p.361. Martin, *History Today*, x, p.824. *Our Viceregal Life*, 12.3.85, vol. 1, p.80; 17.3.85, vol. 1, p.84; 17.11.86; vol. 2, p.67; 17.1.87; vol. 2, p.108.

11. 'His speech is slow and rather hesitating, and he writes little, having not been trained to office work, but he very quick in seizing points of a subject; a man with more training in dealing with men than in dealing with papers.' P. Sykes, *Sir Mortimer Durand* (1926), p.152.

12. Briton Martin, 'The Viceroyalty of Lord Dufferin', *History Today*, x, 12 (December 1960), p.821.

13. *Our Viceregal Life*, 16.12.84, vol. 1, p.15; vol. 2, 14.12.86; p.98.

14. Viscount Mersey, *The Viceroys and Governor Generals of India* (1949), p.103.

15. Andrew Lycett, *Kipling* (1999), p.162.

16. Martin, *History Today*, x, p.824. Martin, *History Today*, xi, 1 (January 1961), p.56.

17. Martin, *History Today*, x, pp. 823–4.

18. Briton Martin, *New India 1885* (Los Angeles, 1969), pp. 22–4. Hon J. Gibbs to Dufferin, 4.2.84, MIC 22/46. Fergusson to Dufferin, 22.12.84, MIC 22/46.

19. Harrison, pp. 550–8. Dufferin to Kimberley, 15.12.84, D1071H/M1/4.

20. Dufferin to Queen, 30.12.84, D1071H/M1/1. Dufferin to Kimberley, 15.12.84. Dufferin to Sir James Fitzjames Stephen, 28.7.85, MIC22/43.

21. Dufferin to Stephen, 20.7.85, MIC 22/43.

22. Ilbert Diary, 15.12.84, Ilbert papers, India Office, Eur.Ms.D.594/4.

23. Penny and Roger Beaumont, *Imperial Divas: The Vicereines of India* (2010), p.173.

Dufferin to Kimberley, 15.12.84, D1071H/M1/4. *Our Viceregal Life*, vol. 1, pp. 18–22. Allen, p.176.

24. As he confided to the Queen, with 'the excitement' already 'toning down', his 'aim' would be 'to keep very quiet, and to pursue as commonplace and unsensational a policy as possible'. See also Dufferin to Stephen, 20.7.84, MIC 22/43.

25. Harrison, pp. 558–62. *Our Viceregal Life*, 27.2.85; vol. 1, p.70. Dufferin to Argyll, 23.3.85, D1071H/B/C/95. Lyall, pp. 364–6. Martin, *New India*, pp. 32–8. James, *Raj*, p.314. Dufferin to the Queen, 16.2.85, MDACQ.

26. Ferguson, *Empire*, pp. 197–203.

27. A quarter of Lancashire's exports went to India alone (for much of this paragraph see Darwin, *Empire Project*, Ch 5; pp. 282–4). Mackenzie Wallace, *The Viceroyalty of the Marquess of Dufferin and Ava* (Calcutta, 1888), p.352.

28. Wallace, *Viceroyalty*, pp. 367–70. Dufferin's promotion of 'canal colonies' and other irrigation schemes was 'crucial'. Patrick O'Leary, *Servants of Empire: The Irish in the Punjab 1881–1921* (2011), p.149.

CHAPTER 24: PLAYING THE GREAT GAME

1. Darwin, *Empire Project*, p.185.

2. James, *Raj*, pp. 364–9. Russia played on such fears in the 1870s and 1880s and in 1885 Britain laid plans for extra troops to be sent out to bolster internal security in such an eventuality (the 1901 plan estimated that an additional 121,000 troops would be needed on top of the defence force).

3. Roberts to Dufferin, 23.8.84. Dufferin to Argyll, 23.3.88, D1071H/B/C/95/114. James, *Raj*, p.379.

4. The Queen to Dufferin, 6.3.85, MDACQ.

5. By comparison, Dufferin estimated that he had 20,000 troops at Rawalpindi and could call on a further 15,000 European troops and 35,000–40,000 Indian troops. The remainder would be required to maintain internal order. Dufferin to the Queen, 10.3.85, MDACQ. Even though it was '500 miles from our frontier' the Russian occupation of the Afghan base at Herat would be 'a shock to our prestige in India, which is a very real factor here, whatever it may be elsewhere'. Dufferin to Argyll, 23.3.85, D1071H/B/C/95/114.

6. Dufferin to Kimberley, 23.3.85, 13.4.85, D1071H/M1/4; also Wallace, *Viceroyalty*, pp. 209–10. Dufferin to Kimberley, 24.2.85, D1071H/M1/4.

7. Dufferin to Argyll, 23.3.85, D1071H/B/C/95/114. Wallace, *Viceroyalty*, pp. 214–18. Kimberley recorded that the cabinet settled its answer on the Herat expedition in light of Dufferin's telegram on 24.3.85. Kimberley, *Journal*, p.353.

8. 'His great fear', Dufferin later reported, was that he should be treated more as 'a feudatory than an independent ruler'. Martin, *New India*, pp. 91–6; Lyall, pp. 370–84.

9. Wallace, *Viceroyalty*, pp 221–2. Mark Bence-Jones, *The Viceroys of India* (1982), p.139.

10. Witnessed by Kipling as a young cub reporter with the *Civil and Military Gazette* and later adapted for his short story 'Servants of the Queen' and again more famously in his poem 'Boots'. Charles Allen, *Kipling Sahib* (London 2007), pp. 180–5.

11. Wallace, *Viceroyalty*, p.224.

12. Wallace, *Viceroyalty*, p.225.

13. Hamilton, *Diary*, pp. 828–31, 837. Kimberley, *Journal*, p.353.

14. Hamilton, *Diary*, p.837. Martin, *New India*, pp. 95–6.

15. Wallace, *Viceroyalty*, pp. 226–7. Hamilton, *Diary*, 1–4.5.85, p.854. Lyall, pp. 376–84. Dufferin to the Queen, 27.4.85; the Queen to Dufferin, 28.5.85, MDACQ.

16. *Our Viceregal Life*, vol. 1, pp. 126–8.

17. Roberts, pp. 339–42. Dufferin over Zulficar sided with the Tories as it had been part of the Penjdeh compromise with the Amir. Dufferin to the Queen, 19.6.85, MDACQ.

18. Indeed he had admitted as much to Dufferin years before. 'The pushing of France into Tunis, of Austria southwards, and of Russia towards India, is exactly in accordance with what Bismarck told me would be his policy when I saw him on my passage through Berlin to St Petersburg in 1879', wrote Dufferin six years later, 'and I have never ceased to deplore that we in England should have taken so little account of his power of making matters unpleasant for us whenever he chooses.' Kimberley to Dufferin, 25.3.85, Harrison, p.565. Kimberley to Dufferin, 10.4.85. Dufferin to Sir James Fitzjames Stephen, 28.7.85, MIC 22/43.

19. Roberts, *Salisbury*, p.341. James, *Raj*, p.381. Peter Hopkirk, *The Great Game*, p.429. 'Our real function, I imagine, will be to retain a considerable proportion of Russian troops on this side of Asia, while you attack her in Europe.' Dufferin telegraph to India Office, April 1885, VIC MAIN/H45/26.

CHAPTER 25: TIGER SHOOTING WITH CHURCHILL

1. How it must have grated on Dufferin to read Churchill's take on the philandering egotist: 'One of the most attractive, cultivated persons I ever had the good fortune to become intimate with; if all Indian officials resemble him, I imagine your Excellency's government will be well supported.' R. F. Foster, *Lord Randolph Churchill* (1981), pp. 167–73.

2. Churchill to Dufferin, 26.6.85, cited in Lyall, p.384.

3. Dufferin to Godley, 12.8.85, Foster, *Churchill*, p.187. 3.7.85; Martin, *New India*, p.138.

4. It was not all intimidation. In his handling of the India Council he was uncharacteristically humble, admitting after his first meeting that he felt 'like an Eton boy presiding at a meeting of the Masters'. A. Kaminsky, *The India Office* (1986), p.67.

5. Kaminsky, p.149. On Churchill's death, he would write that he was always struck most by 'the receptivity of his mind'. While most people immediately weary of new ideas, he was quite the reverse. Dufferin to T. H. J. Escott, 19.3.95, D1071 H/NI/34.

6. In fact from July 1885 Lytton was advising Roberts directly on military policy and consulting Churchill on Indian finance.

7. Foster, *Churchill*, pp. 184–8. The Queen to Dufferin, 12.10.85, 29.10.85; Dufferin to the Queen, 17.10.85, MDACQ.

8. Foster, *Churchill*, pp. 186–8.

9. *Our Viceregal Life*, vol. 1, pp. 322–6.

10. Wallace, *Viceroyalty*, p.288. A. T. Q. Stewart, *The Pagoda War*, pp. 61–4. Thant Myint-U, *The Making of Modern Burma* (Cambridge, 2001), pp. 154–86.

11. Foster, *Churchill*, pp. 206–13. Martin, *History Today*, x, p.829. Stewart, *Pagoda War*, p.72.

12. Myint-U, p.191. Stewart, *Pagoda War*, pp. 111–17.

13. Myint-U, p.190.

14. Foster, *Churchill*, p.209. Dufferin to Churchill, 28.12.85, D1071H/M1/4. Stewart, *Pagoda War*, p.115.

15. Wallace, *Viceroyalty*, pp. 292–3. Harrison, pp. 577–81.

16. Dufferin to Kimberley, 12.1.85 in D1071H/M1/4; Stewart, *Pagoda War*, p.70.

17. Dufferin to Churchill, 19.10.85, D1071H/M1/4.

18. Interestingly he did not mention France in his explanation to the Queen. Instead, perhaps reflecting his recipient, he simply portrayed the war as an opportunity to establish 'once and for all our ascendancy along the whole line of the Irrawaddy valley'. Dufferin to the Queen, 18.11.85, MDACQ.

19. Dufferin to Grant Duff, the Governor of Madras, 22.10.85, Stewart, *Pagoda War*, p.75.

20. *Our Viceregal Life*, vol. 2, p.192.

21. Martin, *New India 1885* (Los Angeles, 1969), pp. 245, 252–3.

22. Dufferin to Ponsonby, 22.11.85, Buckle (ed.), *Letters*, vol. 2, p.354.

23. Wallace, *Viceroyalty*, pp. 301–2.

24. Stewart, *Pagoda War*, pp. 110, 116. Wallace, *Viceroyalty*, p.302. Dufferin to Kimberley, 14.2.86, D1071H/M/5.

25. Dufferin to Kimberley, 14.2.86, D1071H/M1/5.

26. Stewart, *Pagoda War*, p.93.

27. Queen to Dufferin, 1.1.86, D1071H/B/V/102-103. 'The Queen-Empress hopes the Viceroy will not think her greedy when she asks if some of the Burman jewels will be sent to her.'

28. Even before the Afghan crisis blew up, Colvin had warned him in February 1885 that there would be a £700,000 deficit on ordinary expenditure. Later he put the additional military cost at £2.5m. Wallace, *Vice-royalty*, pp. 241–5. Ilbert papers, Eur. Ms. D594/7, ff.32–7. Dufferin to Churchill, 3.7.85, D1071H/M1/4.

29. Martin, *New India*, pp. 84, 98, 140. Hamilton, *Diary*, 1.5.85, 3.6.85, pp. 854, 874. Lyall, p.390. 'Offensive operations against Russia on the Oxus, or in Central Asia, from a base in India, are in my opinion, the dream of a madman, whose head is filled with military theories from the time of Xerxes or Alexander the Great.' Sir Garnet Wolseley. James, *Raj*, pp. 385–6.

30. Wallace, *Viceroyalty*, p.260.

31. 'Pray beware of the spying Russian Military Attaché', warned the Queen. The Queen to Dufferin, 15.12.85. Putting a brave face on the weather, the viceroy reported that the soldiers being 'up to the knee in mud . . . it brought out in stronger relief the endurance, discipline and good drill of Your Majesty's troops'. Dufferin to the Queen, 24.1.86, MDACQ.

32. Dufferin to [F.T.?] Blackwood, 7.12.97, MIC 326.

33. Other defence measures included the fortification of the ports at Bombay, Calcutta, Madras, Kurrachee, and Rangoon. Dufferin to the Queen, 19.8.87, 21.10.87, MDACQ.

34. This was a major commitment, costing initially £1m, which inevitably had a significant and permanent impact on Indian finances (although after Dufferin had left office).

35. Dufferin to Cross, 20.10.88, D107H/M1/7 for summary of a five-stage defensive strategy. Wallace, *Viceroyalty*, pp. 248–54.

36. Salisbury to Dufferin 14.9.87; Dufferin to Salisbury, 5.2.88, MIC 22/44.

37. Harrison, p.570. On the return of the Tories Sir Richard Cross succeeded Churchill as Secretary of State.

CHAPTER 26: THE MILITARY CONSEQUENCES OF LORD RANDOLPH CHURCHILL

1. Stewart, *Pagoda War*, pp. 132–9; *Our Viceregal Life*, vol. 1, pp. 292–336. Dufferin to Lady Dartrey, 14.3.86. Lyall, pp. 402–3. Yet even in this lost world the modern could intervene: by a pagoda in Rangoon 'we saw a game of football going on, which was remarkably pretty and lively. The ball is made of wickerwork, and must not be touched by the arm or the hand during the game. One man begins and plays ball with it, catching it on his knee, foot or shoulder, and then suddenly throws it to another, who keeps it up as long as he can, or until it pleases him to send it further.'

2. Stewart, *Pagoda War*, pp. 18–20, 134.

3. DD, 12.2.86. Wallace, *Viceroyalty*, p.311. Dufferin to Kimberley, 14.2.86, D1071H/M1/5.

4. 'You are the first person in an official position who has told me that,' Dufferin exclaimed to White. Stewart, *Pagoda War*, p.139.

5. Wallace, *Viceroyalty*, p.312. Myint-U, pp. 194–6. *Our Viceregal Life*, 18.2.85; vol. 1, p.326.

6. In July at the Chefoo Convention China accepted the British in Burma if Dufferin would block a British mission to Tibet – which he did with alacrity.

7. Wallace, *Viceroyalty*, p.312. Myint-U, pp. 198–207.

8. James, *Raj*, pp. 412–14. DD, 26.3.86.

9. Stewart, *Pagoda War*, p.125.

10. 'I fear that these untoward circumstances will strengthen the hands of those who may be disposed to criticize our conquest of the country.' Dufferin to Churchill, 26.1.86. Dufferin to the Queen, 5.3.86, MDACQ. Dufferin to Brin, 13.3.85, D1071H/B/251B/11.

11. Dufferin to Kimberley, 26.2.86, D1071H/M1/5.

12. Dufferin to Kimberley, 11.6.86, D1071H/M1/5.

13. Stewart, *Pagoda War*, pp. 140–1, 165–6.

14. Ibid., p.176.

15. Dufferin to Cross, 27.9.86, cited in Stewart, p.171.

16. Even the Queen wavered, calling for more troops, only to be reminded by Dufferin that there were already 'a greater number than your Majesty sent to Crimea': Dufferin to the Queen, 8.9.86, MDACQ.

17. Ibid., Dufferin to the Queen, 17.8.86.

18. Stewart, *Pagoda War*, pp. 170–81. Dufferin to Goschen, August 1886, in Lyall, p.407. James, *Raj*, pp. 411–12. This was not the end of the matter and indeed in the same month Henry Cotton, a judge in the ICS and sympathetic to Indian nationalism, when writing in the *Civil and Military Gazette*, even compared Burmese resistance to 'Hereward of old in the Fens of Lincolnshire' holding out against a foreign invader.

19. 28–29.1.87; Gilmour, *Ruling Caste*, pp. 248, 286. Dufferin to Helen, 27.5.87, Helen's Tower Library.

20. Myint-U, p.201.

21. Stewart, *Pagoda War*, pp. 183–4.

22. Thant Myint-U, *The River of Lost Footsteps* (London, 2007). Terence Blackburn, *Executions by the Half-Dozen: The Pacification of Burma* (New Delhi, 2008). M. S. Ali, 'The Beginnings of British Rule in Upper Burma: A Study of British Policy and Burmese Reaction, 1885–1890', unpublished PhD thesis, University of London, 1976. Maung Htin Aung, *Lord Randolph Churchill and the Dancing Peacock: British Conquest of Burma 1885* (New Delhi, 1990). Kwasi Kwarteng, *Ghosts of Empire* (2011), pp. 188–208.

23. Cross to Dufferin, October 1885; Martin, *New India*, p.247.

24. Dufferin to Cross, 25.10.86, Stewart, *Pagoda War*, p.171.

25. Viscount Bangor to Dufferin, 1887, D1071H/B/W/106.

26. Gilmour, *Ruling Caste*, pp. 218, 239.

27. Nicolson, *Helen's Tower*, p.208. Lyall, pp. 415, 462; DD 19.10.88. So sensitive to ridicule was he that he asked Salisbury 'if it might be intimated that [the choice of title] is in obedience to the Queen's command'. When Dufferin's first choice of Quebec was turned down by the Queen, it was remarkably the third time that Dufferin had met with embarrassment over his choice of a title.

CHAPTER 27: A VERY PUBLIC PRIVATE LIFE

1. The most 'English' was Ootacamund – Ooty – which at best looked like Australia but, on the principle that wishing is believing, was declared by Lytton to be 'a combination of Herfordshire lanes, Devonshire downs, Westmorland lakes and Scottish trout streams'. Gilmour, *Ruling Caste*, p.227.
2. Dufferin to Dartrey, 15.5.85, in Lyall, pp. 385–6.
3. In Simla during 1887 they hosted 12 big dinners and 29 smaller ones, 3 full balls, 6 dances, 2 garden parties and 54 other functions.
4. *Our Viceregal Life*, vol. 2, pp. 41–6. Gilmour, *Ruling Caste*, pp. 269–73. Allen, pp. 184–5, 188, 229. DD, 21.7.86.
5. Allen, pp. 188–92. *Our Viceregal Life*, vol. 2, p.38.
6. And having 'never lived in such a small house before', she made it quite plain to the Queen that the residence was 'a little common' for Her Majesty's representative. Penny and Roger Beaumont, *Imperial Divas: The Vicereine of India* (2010), p.58.
7. With obvious parallels with the Government House they adapted out of the guard-room in Quebec with its spectacular view from the terrace.
8. Dufferin's 'long cherished dream of building a romantic country house somewhere'. Jan Morris with Simon Winchester, *Stones of Empire: The Buildings of the Raj* (2005 edition), pp. 74–5.
9. Dufferin to Nelly, 15.7.87. Helen's Tower Library. DD, 7.9.85, 4.5.86, 18.5.86, 10.5.87, 7.6.87, 10.7.87, 3.9.87, 14.4.88, 16.4.88; moved in, 23.7.88. Bence-Jones, *Viceroys of India*, p.143. Gilmour, *Ruling Caste*, p.225. *Our Viceregal Life*, vol. 1, pp. 130–5. Harrison, p.807 fn 420.
10. As it was, the innovation caused consternation among Simla ladies, who found it less forgiving than candlelight on their older dresses.
11. Dufferin to Nelly, 2.9.87, 9.10.87, Helen's Tower Library. 'The romance of it is true', Jan Morris, *Stones of Empire*, pp. 74–5; Bence-Jones, *Viceroys*, p.143. *Our Viceregal Life*, vol. 2, pp. 288–96. Beaumont, p.61. Dufferin to Ilbert, 26.7.88. in Gilmour, *Ruling Caste*, p.225. David Gilmour, *Curzon*, p.147. See also Lansdowne's tongue in cheek praise for 'your beautiful chateau' at Simla. Lansdowne to Dufferin, 5.5.89, D1071H/B/F/175/19.
12. *Our Viceregal Life*, 10.2.85, vol. 1, p.8
13. Dufferin to Nelly, 20–29.3.87, Helen's Tower Library.
14. 'There were 83 to dinner and 32 servants (I counted) and 250 afterwards', recorded Lady Gregory, plainly thrilled by the spectacle. Mary Lou Kohfeldt, *Lady Gregory* (1985), pp. 75–6.
15. Less appealing was Rosebery's treatment of his wife who 'bores him to death and it shows which is not nice. When she says something particularly silly, he has a way of putting a stony glance into his bright blue eyes which is quite appalling, the pupils dwindling to the size of a pin's head.' Dufferin to Nelly, 25.1.87, 8.3.87, Helen's

Tower Library; for all this he was devoted to her. Leo McKinstry, *Rosebery: Statesman in Turmoil* (pb ed. 2006), pp. 196–203. *Our Viceregal Life*, vol. 1, p.46.

16. Beaumont, p.42. Dufferin to Lady Dartrey, 13.1.85 in Lyall, pp. 360–1. Dufferin to Nelly 1.3.87, Helen's Tower Library. Bence-Jones, p.144. *Our Viceregal Life*, 28.1.85, 1.2.85, 22–25.10.86; vol. 2, p.56, 12.2.88. Robert Bernard Martin, *Tennyson: The Unquiet Heart* (1983), pp. 556–8. Christopher Ricks, *Tennyson*, pp. 277–8. Hariot's sister Gwendolyn died 'on her homeward journey' from India. The Queen to Dufferin, 8.9.85, MDACQ.

17. 'She acquired a dignity and a grace and a dress sense that quite made up for her nondescript looks', in the ungracious comment of one historian. Beaumont, p.171. Bence-Jones, p.132.

18. *Our Viceregal Life*, vol. 1, pp. 27–8.

19. *Our Viceregal Life*, vol. 1, pp. 15–17, 25, 273.

20. *Our Viceregal Life*, vol. 1, pp. 16, 24, 28–9; vol. 2, pp. 146–152.

CHAPTER 28: PARENTS AND LOVERS: AN INDIAN CHILDHOOD

1. Beaumont, pp. 48–9.

2. In order of birth, they were Archie (1863), Helen (1865), Terence (1866), Hermione (1869), Basil (1870), Victoria (1873), Freddie (1875).

3. *Our Viceregal Life*, 4.11.86, 8.12.86, 13.11.87; vol. 2, pp. 60, 95, 204–5.

4. Lyall, pp. 438 40

5. Dufferin to Nelly, 11.1.87, 25.1.87, 1.2.87, 27.5.87, Helen's Tower Library.

6. Melanie Oppenheimer, 'The "Imperial Girl": Lady Helen Munro Ferguson, The Imperial Women and her Imperial Childhood', in *Journal of Australian Studies*, vol. 34, no. 4 (December 2010), pp. 519–20. Dufferin to Nelly, 27.10.89, D1071 KG/5/2/2/28.

7. Nelly to Dufferin, 26.12.86, 17.3.87, Helen's Tower Library.

8. Dufferin to Nelly, 11.1.87, 5.8.87, Helen's Tower Library. More distasteful was the pressure of expectation he placed on his daughters. Hermione's figure, he reported to Helen, 'is not yet quite what it should be', and needs 'a little telescoping outwards'. His verdict of a 'Sweet face . . . very pretty bust' but waist 'thick' and legs 'short' would have done little to instil confidence in one destined never to marry.

9. DD, 15.9.87, 28.9.87, 18.6.88. Sir Benjamin Simpson to Dufferin, 1888–1900, D1071H/B/S/291/1–5.

10. Dufferin to Nelly, 14.7.87, 5.8.87, Helen's Tower Library.

11. Perhaps with good reason as the lady later pursued him to London, asking for 'one of our Simla chats'. Meta Bradley to Dufferin, 1.6.89, D1071H/B/B/683/1.

12. Dufferin to Nelly, 4.12.86, 11.1.87, 8.3.87, 14.3.87, 3.6.87. Nelly to Dufferin, 15.6.87, Helen's Tower Library.

13. *Our Viceregal Life*, 23.10.87; vol. 2, p.194.

14. And indeed, staying with her father's aunt, Lizzie Ward, her report could easily come from the pen of her namesake: 'All the people of Torquay are blind or deaf and I get quite mixed between them and shout at the blind and feel for the deaf.' Nelly to Dufferin, 15.12.86, Helen's Tower Library.

15. Dufferin to Nelly, 15.12.86, 27.1.87, 27.5.87, 3.10.87; Nelly to Dufferin, 27.1.87, Helen's Tower Library. Lyall, pp. 441–2.

16. Dufferin to Nelly, 2.5.87, 16.5.87, 1.7.87, Helen's Tower Library.

17. Nelly to Dufferin, 15.6.87, 6 and 8.9.87. Dufferin to Nelly, 26.9.87, Helen's Tower Library. Dufferin explained the lack of sailors due to homesickness caused by three chaperones going into mourning and then the death of her 'chief playfellow', Lady Houghton. Dufferin to the Queen, 1.7.87, 21.10.87, MDACQ.

18. Dufferin to Nelly, 10.11.86, 18.1.87, 27.5.87, Helen's Tower Library.

19. Nelly wasn't the only one to be so designated. In terms of looks, it was Hermione who most 'resembles my mother'. Dufferin to Brin, 16.10.82, D1071H/B/S/251B/12. Hence his disappointment when her figure did not match the face.

20. On Archie's lack of interest, see Anne de Courcy, *The Fishing Fleet* (2013). Hariot's shamrock diamond tiara is now on display in the Victoria and Albert Museum.

21. Allen, pp. 227, 238–9.

22. David Gilmour, *The Long Recessional* (2002), p.32. Allen, pp. 225, 257. Andrew Lycett, *Rudyard Kipling* (1999), p.257.

23. Dufferin to Nelly, 25.4.87. Nelly to Dufferin, 27.5.87, Helen's Tower Library. Lyall, p.438.

24. *Our Viceregal Life*, vol. 1, pp. 259–60.

25. Dufferin to Nelly, 25.4.87, Nelly to Dufferin, 27.5.87, Helen's Tower Library.

26. Nelly to Dufferin, 21.9.87, Helen's Tower Library.

CHAPTER 29: DUFFERIN'S INDIA

1. DD, 29.11.85; Lyall pp. 391–2; *Our Viceregal Life*, 26.11.85, i, pp. 254–5. Oddly the Taj Mahal evoked very different reactions. Architecturally, Dufferin condemned it as 'the outcome of a period of art on the verge of degeneration'; likening it to 'a ripe pear that you must get up in the middle of the night to eat before it has turned rotten at the core by morning'. Hariot, however, was transfixed and three years later she would return, without her husband, in pursuit of its 'soul'.

2. Gilmour, *Curzon*, p.183.

3. *Our Viceregal Life*, 24–7.11.86; vol. 2, pp. 76–84.

4. Dufferin to Nelly, 4.12.86, Helen's Tower Library.

5. *Our Viceregal Life*, vol. 2, pp. 200–3.

6. Dufferin to Sir George Bowen, 8.1.88, in Lyall, p.444. Dufferin to the Queen, 3.1.88, MDACQ.

7. *Our Viceregal Life*, vol. 2, pp. 326–7. What started the fire was never discovered.

8. There was a short detour to Lahore and later Dhaka (Eastern Bengal). Otherwise it was straight to Calcutta.

9. DD, 29.3.86, 9.4.86, 8–8.4.88. *Our Viceregal Life*, vol. 2, p.18, 6.4.86. Dufferin was keen to pay homage at the Black Hole of Calcutta and to seek out the native pensioners at Lucknow for tales of the siege. 'Some people say we should try to forget these misfortunes', recorded Hariot after a day at Cawnpore, 'and the experience of the Mutiny; but others consider that we cannot remember them too well, and that we should not let the people think that we have forgotten them.' *Our Viceregal Life*, 9.4.86, vol. 2, p.24. However, what really excited him were the deserted ruins of the ancient Mughal dynasties.

10. Harrison, p.612.

11. *Our Viceregal Life*, 6.4.86, vol. 2, p.16. Cannadine, *Ornamentalism*, pp. 44–51.

12. *Our Viceregal Life*, vol. 1, pp. 20–1; vol 1, p.241.

13. When Cross was 'a little startled' by the scale of the amnesty, the Viceroy dismissed such concern with a magisterial 'Quantities in India are always large'. Dufferin to the Queen, 28.2.87, MDACQ.

14. Dufferin to Cross, 11.3.87, in Lyall, pp. 433–4. *Our Viceregal Life*, 16–17.2.87, vol. 2, pp. 115–21.

15. *Our Viceregal Life*, 1.10.85, vol.1, p.187. DD, 29–30.8.87.

16. The Marquis and Marchioness of Aberdeen, *More Cracks with 'We Twa'* (1929), pp. 33–7.

17. The Queen to Dufferin, 20.7.87, MDACQ.

18. 'If we have with us the princes, we shall have with us the people', he had reassured the Queen in 1877. Cannadine, *Ornamentalism*, p.139.

19. The Queen to Dufferin, 16.7.86; 19.8.87, MDACQ.

20. Esher, *Letters*, vol. 2, p.355. Lyall, p.424.

21. Dufferin to Sir Harry Verney, 6.1.89, BL, OIOC, Eur. F 130/29A.

22. Harrison, pp. 584–5.

23. H. Spencer Williamson, *Thirty Five Years* (1933), p.136.

24. Dufferin to Kimberley, 3.2.85, D1071H/M1/4.

25. Harrison, pp. 586–7, 593–4.

26. Dufferin to Churchill, 17.7.85 in Harrison, p.806.

27. See Dufferin's Mansion House speech, 29.5.89, cited in Lyall, p.487.

28. *Our Viceregal Life*, 5.4.86, 21.2.87, vol. 2, pp. 14, 123–4. DD, 16.2.87.

29. Cecil Woodham-Smith, *Florence Nightingale* (1950), p.563. Jharna Gourlay, *Florence Nightingale and the Health of the Raj* (2003), pp. 165, 192–200. *A Report on the Conditions of the Lower Classes of Population in Bengal* (1888), otherwise known as the Dufferin Report.

30. DD, 27.3.88; *Our Viceregal Life*, vol. 2, p.275.

CHAPTER 30: HARIOT'S INDIANS

1. So impractical were some of the traditional costumes that the Maharajah Tukoji Holkar II struggled even to get out of his carriage, his six-year-old heir making it plain to Hariot that his red court petticoats were 'only put on to show me'.

2. *Our Viceregal Life*, 13–18.3.85, 6.4.85, vol. 1, p.108; 15.11.85, vol. 2, p.211. The original letter to Mother used 'barbarian', which was edited from the published version.

3. *Our Viceregal Life*, 9.10.85; 10.11.85, 17.11.85, 7.2.86, vol. 1, pp. 228, 238; 7.4.86, 1.12.86, 26.11.87, vol. 2, pp. 21, 91, 218–19. Deepali Dewan and Deborah Hutton, *Raja Deen Dayal* (2013), pp. 74–5, 217.

4. *Our Viceregal Life*, 9.8.85, 13.11.85, vol. 1, pp. 226, 232–3.

5. *Our Viceregal Life*, 2.3.85, vol. 1, p.74; 15.11.86, vol. 2, p.65; DD, 25.2–1.3.86. Allen, pp. 239–40. Kipling denounced too the resistance to widow remarriage (an inevitable consequence of young girls married off to much older men) which often led to their prostitution.

6. *Our Viceregal Life*, vol. 1, p.186. S. E. Lang, 'Maternal Mortality and the State in British India, 1840–1920', PhD thesis 2007, pp. 315–17.

7. Lang, pp. 318–19. Hariot's initial presumption had been to work with the missionaries and was caught out by the Queen's vehement insistence on their exclusion. Although Hariot deeply regretted it, she crucially never gave way on the principle and nor did she reveal the monarch's intervention.

8. *Our Viceregal Life*, 26.6.85, vol. 1, pp. 163–4. Lang, p.317.

9. *Our Viceregal Life*, 19.9.85, 12.11.86; vol. 2, pp. 63–4, 17.2.87. In 1885 a rupee = 1s 7d or 12.6 to the £1 sterling. For the modern inflation-adjusted sterling value multiply by 100.

10. Wallace, *Viceroyalty*, pp. i–vii.

11. Lang, pp. 350–6; Maneesha Lal, 'The Politics of Gender and Medicine in Colonial India: The Countess of Dufferin Fund 1885–1888', in *Bulletin of the History of Medicine*, 68 (1994); D. Arnold, *Science, Technology and Medicine in Colonial India* (Cambridge, 2000), pp. 88–90.

12. Lang, p.374. The problem was as much cultural as one of gender with the national education system heavily slanted to the arts, rather than science and medicine: thus Calcutta University produced 1,589 arts graduates and only 176 doctors (1857–82).

13. Dufferin to Ponsonby, 21.9.85, RA/VIC/1885/2411; Lang, p.322. 'For the Women' by Rudyard Kipling, *Civil and Military Gazette*, February 1887. It has the subtitle 'Ave Imperatrix, Moriturae Te Salutant!' ('Hail, Empress, the women about to die salute thee!').

14. Lang, pp. 323–4, 355–7, 399.

15. Churchill was not alone in urging his wife 'you ought to take it up warmly and publicly'. Lang, p.357.

16. Beaumont, *Imperial Divas*, p.291. *Our Viceregal Life*, 4.12.88, vol. 2, pp. 338–9.

17. Antoinette Burton, *Burdens of History: British Feminists, Indian Women and Imperial Culture, 1865–1915* (1994).

18. Dufferin to Terence, 20.12.88, D1071H/N1/34.

19. Kipling to Dufferin, 2.1.1902; D1071H/B/K/150/4; Lang, p.361.

20. Lucy Moore, *Maharanis* (2004), pp. 69–71. *Our Viceregal Life*, 12.3.88, vol. 2, pp. 265–7.

21. Amanda Andrews, 'The Great Ornamentals: The New Vice-regal Women and their Imperial Work, 1884–1914', PhD thesis, University of Western Sydney, 2004, p.2;

cited in Melanie Oppenheimer, 'The "Imperial Girl": Lady Helen Munro Ferguson, the Imperial Women and her Imperial Childhood', in *Journal of Australian Studies*, vol. 34, no 4 (December 2010), p.516. See also Val McLeish, 'Imperial Footprints: Lady Aberdeen and Lady Dufferin in Ireland, Canada, and India, 1871–1914', PhD thesis, University of London, 2002.

22. Melanie Oppenheimer, p.521; see also her '"The Best PM for the Empire in War?" Lady Helen Munro Ferguson and the Australian Red Cross Society, 1914–1920', in *Australian Historical Studies*, vol. 33, no. 119 (2002), pp. 108–24.

23. Melanie Oppenheimer, '"Hidden Under Many Bushels": Lady Victoria Plunket and the New Zealand Society for the Health of Women and Children', *New Zealand Journal of History*, vol. 39, no. 1 (2005), pp. 22–38.

CHAPTER 31: FACE TO FACE WITH THE NEW INDIA

1. Dufferin to Kimberley, 17.5.86, Martin p.316. DD, 20.8.87.

2. Martin, pp. 248–51, 277. For these tax rises the Finance Minister, Colvin, was pilloried by Kipling in 'The Rupaiyat of Omar Kal'vin'.

3. Harrison, p.590. Dufferin to Kimberley, 29.5.85; Dufferin to Churchill, 10.7.85; 7.8.85, D1071H/M1/4.

4. Martin, *New India*, Ch. 5.

5. Congress in the 1880s did make great efforts to promote a secular approach and be rhetorically inclusive. Indeed 1888 would see a Muslim president.

6. Darwin, *Empire Project*, pp. 186, 193.

7. Hume was also a renowned ornithologist: dubbed the 'Pope of Ornithology', with 82,000 eggs worth £20,000 which he left to the Natural History Museum. Martin, *New India*, pp. 60–7.

8. DD, 23, 25–6.2.87, 7.2.87, 31.10.87.

9. Martin, *New India*, pp. 223–40. Dufferin spoke on an impending commission on access to the civil service: 'almost the first time since he came to India that Dufferin has let himself speak out'. *Our Viceregal Life*, 19.11.86, vol. 2, p.70.

10. Dufferin to Cross, 18.1.87 in Lyall, p.424; *Our Viceregal Life*, vol. 2, pp. 69–70.

11. James, *Raj*, p.347; Gilmour, *Ruling Caste*, pp. 54–5. This does need qualifying as even non-Irish made the connection: Colvin to Dufferin, 25.4.88, deeply anxious about 'sans cullotte [sic] Young India', and claimed Congress were trying to 'establish a League in India, not unlike that recently suppressed in Ireland. But its roots lay not in Ireland or India but in revolutionary France. C. Bayly, 'Ireland, India and Empire 1780–1914', in *Transactions of the Royal Historical Society* (2000), pp. 390–7.

12. The Irishness of India was reinforced from a different perspective by the fact that in 1886 there were as many as five Irishmen on the Viceroy's Council. See Bayly above. O'Leary, *Servants of the Empire: The Irish in the Punjab 1881–1921*.

13. Dufferin to Reay, 17.5.85, MIC 22/46. Harrison, pp. 598–600; W. C. Bonnerjee (ed.), *Indian Politics* (Madras, 1898).

14. Martin, *New India*, p.319. Dufferin to the Queen, 10.6.86, 8.7.86. By 1.7.87 he admitted to the Queen to being 'glad' that the Liberal Unionists were gaining strength. MDACQ. Dufferin to Nelly, 1.2.87; Nelly to Dufferin, 27.10.87. Helen's Tower Library. Blunt, his bête noir in Egypt, had now taken up the cause of Irish Home Rule.

15. Dufferin to Maine, 9.5.86, MIC 22/43.

16. Dufferin to Kimberley, 21.3.86, D1071H/M1/5.

17. Lyall, pp. 425–33.

18. Dufferin to Kimberley, 21.3.86, D1071H/M1/5.

19. Even 'the most extravagant Bengalee Baboo that ever "slung ink"' was not a separatist, Dufferin assured the Queen, 31.3.87, MDACQ.

20. Harrison, pp. 603–5. Martin, *New India*, pp. 47–50.

CHAPTER 32: COUNTER-ATTACK

1. Dufferin to Cross, 4.1.87, 3.12.88, in Martin, *New India*, pp. 325–6. In similarly dismissive vein he reported back on the second Congress in Calcutta as: 'very childish . . . rather of an Eton or Harrow Debating Society than even an Oxford or Cambridge Union'.

2. Martin, *New India*, p.326.

3. Harrison, p.620. Dufferin to the Queen, 21.10.87, MDACQ.

4. On 4.2.88 Salisbury telegrammed, offering Rome if Dufferin stayed until the end of the year. Dufferin retired largely on personal grounds. See next chapter.

5. 'The conduct of this little clique has been so outrageous, their influence so insignificant and their numbers so few'. Dufferin to the Queen, 26.3.88, MDACQ. Indeed if anything, the prospect of the end in sight rejuvenated Dufferin.

6. *Our Viceregal Life*, 13.2.88, vol. 2, p.254. DD, 17.2.88. Cross to Dufferin, 17.2.88. D1071H/M1/7.

7. Dufferin to Cross, 4.3.88, D1071H/M1/7.

8. Wallace, *Viceroyalty*, pp. 384–5. Dufferin claimed that 120 places were transferred.

9. Dufferin to Cross, 10.8.88. D1071H/M1/7. The 1880s saw 6 Indians recruited into the ICS; by the 1890s this had only increased by 34. By the time the reform was fully operational in 1910 only 6 per cent of the ICS was Indian. Gilmour, *Ruling Caste*, pp. 48–50.

10. Dufferin to Cross, 17.9.88. D1071H/M1/7. Harrison, p.806 fn 410 exposes Gopal's misunderstanding of the evidence to make this criticism.

11. Dufferin to G. Allen, 1.1.87, Harrison p.623. When Griffin made 'a very silly speech' doing just that, Dufferin could not have been more withering. Dufferin to the Queen, 3.1.88, MDACQ. Dufferin knew full well the dangers, drawing parallels with Ireland: typically the religious riots in Delhi he described as being 'almost

as difficult to manage as... Belfast['s]'. Dufferin to the Queen, 16.10.86, MDACQ.

12. Colvin to Hume, 8.10.88, D1071H/M15/2.
13. Dufferin to Cross, 17.8.88. A similar line was adopted to the Queen, 10.8.88, MDACQ.
14. Harrison, p.619.
15. MacDonnell, Chesney, Aitchison, together with a financial official, J. Westland.
16. Dufferin to Russell, 5.11.88, in Lyall, p.465.
17. Wallace, *Viceroyalty*, p.399.
18. Interestingly Salisbury had suspected from the outset what Dufferin was up to: 'I hope Dufferin is not going to try any rash experiments at "Liberalising" the Provincial Councils. His experiment in Egypt should have sufficed him.' Salisbury to Cross, 28.9.88, cited in Lady G. Cecil, *Life of Lord Salisbury*, p.194.
19. Wallace, *Viceroyalty*, pp. 387–402 for Dufferin's covering minute.
20. Lady G. Cecil, *Life of Lord Salisbury*, p.196. Under the guise of an apology, Lansdowne implied the likely source: 'How it [the *Bengalee*] obtained a copy [of Dufferin's Minute on the Legislative Councils] I do not know. The publication did not take place until after Wallace had left, and we have no clue.' Lansdowne to Dufferin, 5.5.89, D1071H/B/F/175/19.
21. Dufferin to Cross, 3.12.88, in Harrison, p.617.
22. Cross to Dufferin, 21.12.88, D1071H/B/C/732/4. Dufferin to Cross, 6.1.89, D1071H/N1/34. Roberts, *Salisbury*, pp. 507–8.
23. Harrison, pp. 605–22.
24. A recent census had identified 106 different Indian languages.
25. Dufferin to Kimberley, 26.4.86, D1071H/M1/5. Harrison, pp. 605, 621, 805. Hume's choice of retaliation was instructive: spreading the rumour that the viceroy had been in consultation with leading Indians regarding the stage-management of his departure celebrations to make sure they measured up to Ripon's triumphal return. Whether or not this allegation was true, Dufferin would certainly have been 'touchy' over his finale.
26. An alternative view suggests that he was setting out his unionist credentials before returning to the UK by denouncing the 'Home Rule party in India'; see T. G. Fraser, 'Ireland and India', in Keith Jeffrey (ed.), *Aspects of Ireland and the British Empire* (Manchester, 1996), pp. 86–7.
27. See Harrison, pp. 621–2.

CHAPTER 33: CONCLUSION: KIPLING'S VICEROY?

1. Lord Newton, *Lord Lansdowne*, p.58.
2. An earlier draft in the *Pioneer*, 10.11.88, written in prose form and titled 'A Free Hand' was even sharper, portraying Dufferin telling Lansdowne: 'You stand on the

threshold of new experiences – most of which will distress you and a few amuse. You are at the centre of a gigantic practical Joke. Strive to enter the spirit of it and jest temperately.' Cited in Lewis Wurgaft, *The Imperial Imagination* (1983), p.129.

3. Lyall, p.446.
4. When this was published by Lyall, John Morley asked Lansdowne to confirm that much of the work was 'tiresome and monotonous'; as for Lytton, he was 'undisguisedly bored to death'. Morley, *Recollections* (1917), vol. 2, p.190.
5. Similarly as he retired he would write to Cross: 'When I consider the many dangers we have run, and the innumerable mischances which might have overtaken us, even without any fault of our own, I am truly grateful to be able to escape out of India under these tolerable conditions, and without any deep scratches on my credit and reputation.' Lyall, pp. 435–6, 443, 451.
6. Lyall, p.443.
7. Dufferin to Sir William Gregory, October 1887, Lyall, p.447.
8. Dufferin to the Queen, 7.2.88, MDACQ. As early as May 1887 he was talking of leaving India by 'end of the present year' and imagined 'that the Court of Rome is a very pleasant one to be accredited to'. RA VIC MAIN/N/44/21, Lord Dufferin to Albert, Prince of Wales, 5.5.87.
9. DD, 24.5.86. Interestingly Dilke, in his memoirs, remembers meeting Dufferin at the Duchess of Manchester's as he prepared to embark for India. There the new viceroy 'shone but his health and spirits were now beginning to decline'. If he was showing his age in 1884, by 1888 he was feeling it too. Gwynn and Tuckwell, *Dilke*, vol. 2, p.72.
10. 'Much surprised' at Dufferin's resignation and hearing that the reasons for 'this strange step are pecuniary. If this is true, it is a rather pitiful affair from every point of view.' Kimberley, *Journal*, 9.2.88, p.380.
11. Dufferin to James Stephen, 28.7.86. Lyall, pp. 415, 462; DD, 19.10.88.
12. Longford, *Passion*, p.206.
13. George Hamilton to Curzon, 17.5.1900, Foster, *Churchill*, p.213.
14. Churchill to Dufferin, 28.8.85, Lyall, pp. 388–89.
15. Giles St Aubyn, *Queen Victoria* (1991), p.501. D1071H/B/V/102-5.
16. Mark Bence-Jones, *The Viceroys of India* (1982), pp. 131–49.
17. Mary Lou Kohfeldt, *Lady Gregory* (1985), pp. 75–6. Gilmour, *Curzon*, p.210.
18. Harrison, pp. 511, 581.
19. Dufferin to Cross, 3.12.88, in Lyall, pp. 463–4, 471–3. Bence-Jones, *Viceroys*, p.133.
20. Churchill to Roberts, 22.6.94, in Martin, *New India*, p.157. 'Dufferin knew better than most how the shifts of mood in Westminster could subvert the oligarchies of the Empire.' John Darwin, *The Empire Project*, p.200.
21. Churchill to Roberts, 9.9.88, in Foster, *Churchill*, p.188. Compare: 'the period of your Viceroyalty was a time of recovery and of reform for India, mainly owing to the wonderful manner in which your Excellency grasped and treated many Indian problems', Churchill to Dufferin, 24.7.90, D1071H/B/C/364/1. Bence-Jones, *Viceroys*, p.133.

22. Lyall, p.434. Bence-Jones, *Viceroys*, p.134.

23. Bence-Jones, *Viceroys*, p.135.

24. Ironically it had been MacDonnell who would brief the paper. Dufferin to Wallace, 17.1.89; Dufferin to J. Luard Pattison, 23 and 27.1.89; Dufferin to Lyall, 27.1.89; Dufferin to Crosthwaite, 27.3.89, D1071H/N1/34. Sir Donald Mackenzie Wallace, *The Viceroyalty of the Marquess of Dufferin and Ava: A Brief Account of Lord Dufferin's Indian Administration* (Calcutta, 1888). In February 1890 Hariot's latest publication of her journal sold over 4,000. Lyall to Dufferin, 21.2.90, D1071H/B/L/462/3.

25. Dufferin to General Sir George Chesney, 8.12.88, D1071H/B/C/324. 'But for the interest you have taken in the defences . . . it might have been years before we reached our present advanced state', Roberts to Dufferin, 9.2.88, D1071 H/B/234/3.

26. Dufferin to Salisbury, 5.2.88, in Lyall, pp. 448–50.

27. That said, enthusiasm (as opposed to significant action) for the Forward School would wax and wane periodically through to 1919.

28. Lyall, pp. 465–71.

29. Martin, 'The Viceroyalty of Lord Dufferin', *History Today*, vol. 11, p.64. But compare: 'Dr Gopal['s] . . . venomous verdict . . . seeks not to understand Dufferin but to discredit him'. R. J. Moore, 'Review of British Policy in India, 1858–1905, by S. Gopal', in *English Historial Review*, vol. 82, no. 325 (October 1967), pp. 804–7.

30. Martin, *New India*; 'The Viceroyalty of Lord Dufferin', *History Today*, vol. 11, p.60.

31. Martin, *New India*, p.46. John Darwin, *After Tamerlane* (2008), pp. 392–3.

32. Darwin, *Empire Project*, pp. 201, 291.

33. He never lost sight of the fact that 'India is an integral . . . and one of the most important portions of the mighty British Empire', Wallace, *Viceroyalty*, p.392.

34. By contrast his verdict after seeing Dufferin first hand was altogether more complimentary. Gilmour, *Curzon*, p.68.

35. Moore, 'Imperial India, 1858–1914', pp. 434–7. Lord Curzon, *British Government in India*, vol. 2, pp. 245–9.

36. Bence-Jones, *Viceroys*, p.132.

37. DD, 4.1.97.

38. DD, 10.12.88; *Our Viceregal Life*, vol. 2, pp. 341–3; Lyall, p.474

39. Martin, 'The Viceroyalty of Lord Dufferin', *History Today*, vol. 11, p.64. Paid by public subscription of R60,000 (*Our Viceregal Life*, vol. 2, p.273).

40. Stewart, *Pagoda War*, p.185. 'Of all his revelations and reminiscences, the one sentence that stays with me is: "and so, you see, there can be no room" (or was it allowance?) "for good intentions in one's work."'

41. Angus Hawkins and John Powell, *The Journal of John Wodehouse, 1st Earl of Kimberley (1862–1902)*, Camden, 5th Series, vol. 9 (1997), pp. 265–6.

CHAPTER 34: ROMAN HOLIDAY

1. So exhausted was he that he soon fell ill and in July 1889 was granted four months' leave to recover.
2. Nicolson, *Helen's Tower*, p.213.
3. Lyall, *Dufferin*, p.478. Nicolson, *Helen's Tower*, p.213.
4. Dufferin to Queen Victoria, 12.12.90, D1071H/N1/34. Dalby-Gatt to Hariot, 18.4.90, D1071H/B/D/60/1; Rev. John Gaston to Dufferin, (Feb?) 1892, D1071H/B/G/54/1–3.
5. Baring to Dufferin, 8.8.90, 6.12.90, D1071H/B/B/106. Salisbury to Dufferin, 16.1.91, D1071H/N1/1a. Dufferin to Lansdowne, 1.1.91, D1071H/N1/4. Lyall, p.495. Bismarck in conversation with Dufferin in 1879 'described the Italians as "mere pickpockets"'.
6. Dufferin to Spencer, 19.2.90, Harrison, p.300. NB Salisbury had arranged for Dufferin a generous salary of £7,000 p.a. plus a fitting out allowance of £1,700. Salisbury to Dufferin, 20.12.88, D1071/H/B/C/250/22D. DD, 21.11.89, 10.1.90.
7. Dufferin to Nelly, 10.3.90, in Lyall, pp. 499–500. Dufferin to Gawn Hamilton, 26.12.91; Dufferin to Nelly, 27.9.90, Lyall, pp. 504–5.
8. Lyall, *Dufferin*, pp. 505–6.
9. Charles Beresford, *Memoirs of Lord Charles Beresford* (1914), vol. 2, p.374; DD, 14.8.90.
10. DD, 26.10.90; Antonio Esposito to Dufferin, 1890–9, D1071 H/B/E/105/1–5.
11. Young, high-spirited and boat mad, as fate would have it, she was to die two years later of blood poisoning. Eustace Neville-Rolfe, 8 and 13.4.92, D1071H/B/N/59/7,15.
12. DD, 19.3.91.
13. DD, 2–6.1.90; 10.3.90. Elizabeth Longford, *Darling Loosy* (1991), pp. 54, 60–1. Lorne to Dufferin, n.d., D1071/H/B/C/104/44. Among the more lurid assertions was that a winch was required to lift the 'substantial' Boehm 'from his royal lover'. The statue from which the bust was taken was already in situ in Calcutta. QVD, 13.12.90, 92, p.179.
14. Advice she did in the end take but some three years later, marrying Herbert Asquith, by then the coming man in the Liberal Party and future prime minister. Margot Asquith to Dufferin, 4.7.91, 28.7.91, 11.7.96, D1071H/B/A/292/1, 3, 10, 12. Margot Asquith, *Places and Persons* (1925), pp. 20–1.
15. *Diary of Gathorne Hardy*, 6.11.90, p.812. Horace Hutchinson (ed.), *Private Diaries of Sir Algernon West* (1922), p.24. West was Gladstone's Private Secretary. Dufferin to Mackenzie-Wallace, 7.12.91, D1071H/N1/17.
16. Lyall, pp. 511–13, 520–1; Nicolson, *Helen's Tower*, p.226; DD, 16.7.91.
17. Lyall, pp. 514–15.

CHAPTER 35: THE GREAT PRIZE

1. Dufferin to Salisbury, 10.12.91, Lyall, p.514; Egremont, *Balfour*, p.100.
2. For a description of the embassy under the Dufferins see 'The British Embassy in Paris' by Mary Spencer-Warren, in the *Strand Magazine*, vol. 7 (1894), pp. 289–300; Nicolson, *Helen's Tower*, pp. 1–22 and 33.
3. 'I believe that if one was a *very* rich person, this would be the nicest of all appointments . . . [but their being] under less wealthy circumstances puts the drop of anxiety into the cup which destroys its taste somewhat!', she confessed to her niece. Hariot to Ulrica Thynne, 11.4.(92), D1071J/B/6.
4. Dufferin to Munro Ferguson, 18.12.91, Helen's Tower Library. DD, 25.3.95. de Coubertin to Dufferin, 1892–8, D1071H/B/D/624/1–4
5. DD 27.3.95; Salisbury to Dufferin, 16.4.95, D1071/H/B/C/250/35.
6. Hardinge, pp. 55–6. Kwasi Kwarteng, *Ghosts of Empire* (2011), p.159. Russell to Dufferin, 11.9.94, D1071H/B/R/430/2. Russell was the grandson of Dufferin's patron, Lord John Russell.
7. Dufferin to Nelly, 13.4.92, Helen's Tower Library. DD, 19.8.92; 24.10.92; 6.1.93; 25.2.95. Mabel Sheible to Dufferin, '1892', D1071/B/B/S/237/1–2.
8. Nicolson, *Helen's Tower*, pp. 89–90.
9. Paul Heuzé, *Do the Dead Live?* (1923). Melvin Harris, *Investigating the Unexplained* (2003).
10. P. Armytage, *By the Clock of St James's* (1927), pp. 337–8.
11. Dufferin to Waddington, 18.12.91, D1071H/N/23; Dufferin to Mme d'Harcourt, 21.12.91, D1071H/B/D/25.
12. Nicolson, *Helen's Tower*, pp. 227–9.
13. Such views were commonplace even among the more francophile in the Foreign Office. Thus Sir Thomas Sanderson shared with Dufferin his view that 'The French are a curious people. Everybody I think likes them but nationally they are on the worst of terms with all their neighbours . . . [while] they are in constant admiration of their dignity, correction and [the] benevolence of their attitude.' Sanderson to Dufferin, 9.4.95, D1071 H/B/S/62/107. Dufferin to Queen Victoria, 4.1.93, D1071H/03/5; 26.4.96, D1071H/03/62. Dufferin to Lansdowne, 3.12.92, D1071H/03/3.
14. Lyall, p.521. Dufferin to HRH Princess Louise, 1.2.94, D1071H/03/22.
15. Dufferin to Queen Victoria, 26.10.93, D1071H/03/20; *Le Petit Journal*, 12.6.92; Nicolson, *Helen's Tower*, p.230; DD, 2–6.8.92.
16. Dufferin was acutely sensitive to such measures of his popularity. Hence his relief when beautiful weather four months later saw 1,200 attend the embassy summer garden party, including 'the whole society of Paris'. Dufferin to Rosebery D1071H/05/1–2; 4, 5, 13.9.92; Dufferin to Nelly, Feb 1893, in Lyall, pp. 522–5; DD 22.2.93; 7.6.93. Princess Berthe de Wagram to Dufferin, 1893–1900, D1071H/B/D/15.

17. Winning corrections and apologies from the *Daily Telegraph*, the *Illustrated London News*, the *Daily Graphic* and *the Anglo-American Annual*, as well as numerous French journalists. DD, 24.3.92. Edwin Arnold to Dufferin, 5.3.92, D1071H/B/A/262B/1; Harold Cox, 1896, D1071H/B/C/660/1-4, editor of the *Illustrated London News* to Dufferin, 1893, D1071H/B/I/6/1; G. G. Drewett to Dufferin, 16.5.92, 13.10.96, D1071 H/B/D/236/1-2; Richard L. Hobart to Dufferin, 1890–92, D1071H/B/H/505/1-2.

18. Blunt, *My Diaries*, 16.7.93, 2.8.93, pp. 138–9. Needless to say, Blunt shamelessly invited himself to stay at Dufferin's embassies in Rome and Paris.

19. Leo McKinstry, *Rosebery: Statesman in Turmoil* (2005; pb edition 2006), pp. 261–3; G. Martel, *Rosebery and the Failure of Foreign Policy* (1986), pp. 128–34.

20. DD, 1.8.93; McKinstry, *Rosebery*, pp. 261–3.

21. Dufferin to Munro Ferguson, 15.7.94, 16.3.96, Helen's Tower Library.

22. Bernard Allen, *Sir Robert Morant* (1934), pp. 80–1.

23. Sir Philip Currie at the Foreign Office congratulated Dufferin on his 'brilliant speech . . . just what was wanted to turn the tide of animosity against England (which has, I think, been flowing with less violence of late)'. Currie to Dufferin, 11.3.(94?), D1071 H/B/C/774/58. DD, 7.2.94. Dufferin to Casimir-Perrier, 5.5.94, D1071H/03/28; Lyall, p.531.

24. Currie to Dufferin, 25.6.(93?), D1071H/B/C/774/45. DD, 6.10.96; Dufferin to Munro Ferguson, 16.3.96, Helen's Tower Library.

25. Lyall, pp. 525–6, 549–50. Reinforcing this view was the survival of 'that scoundrel of a Sultan . . . exterminating the Armenians at his leisure. It is sad to think how slowly grind the mills of the gods; but his time will come.' Dufferin to Munro Ferguson, 10.1.96, Helen's Tower Library.

26. Matters being further exacerbated by 'the Dunraven business' – a public row over accusations of cheating in the America's Cup – the vulgarity of which Dufferin deplored. RA VIC/MAIN/J/90/21, Lord Dufferin to Queen Victoria, 1.1.96, cited in K. Bourne, *Britain and the Balance of Power in North America* (1967), pp. 339–40. Dufferin to Munro Ferguson, 21.12.95, Helen's Tower Library. Dufferin to Grant Duff, 12.1.96, 17.3.96; D1071H/03/54, 58.

27. Dufferin to Gregory, 20.12.90, D1071H/N1/1 D-N; 20.3.93, D1071H/03/6.

28. Barrington to Dufferin, 20.12.95, D1072H/B/B/148/2. Lyall repeated this to Lady Dufferin, 21.12.95, clearly to ensure that the message got through: 'take the greatest care to do nothing'. D1071H/B/L/462/59.

29. West, 3.3.93, *Diaries*, p.146.

30. But he never hid, unlike his successor, who some French criticised for 'shunning society'. Princesse Berthe de Wagram to Dufferin, 1893–1900, D1071H/B/D/15/1–21.

31. Dufferin to Lord Arthur Russell, 24.12.90, D1071H/N1/21. DD, 3.2.96, 5.3.96.

32. But at least he was a gentleman, and with thirty-five sittings, Dufferin was rewarded with a 'wonderfully good likeness' which he had copied for Clandeboye. (By Mr Durangel, 20.2.96; who was then asked to copy a picture of the three sisters:

Helen, Georgy, Caroline.) Dufferin to Nelly, 16.11.95, Helen's Tower Library. DD, 12.11.95.

33. Dufferin to Nelly, 29.12.95, Helen's Tower Library. DD, 19.6.94, 23.12.95. Dufferin to Lord Powerscourt, 1.12.90, D1071H/N1/7. Robert Kee, *The Laurel and the Ivy* (1994), p.548.

34. Dufferin to Hariot, 26.1.89, in Lyall, p.478. Margot Asquith 19.11.91, *Places and Persons* (1925), pp. 20–1.

35. DD, 28.3.94, 10.4.94, 19.4.94, 4.2.95. Dufferin to Nelly, 4.8.1893, Helen's Tower Library.

36. 'He had a fine nature in many ways, poor fellow [but] fell into the depths of degradation at last, owing to his weakness about women.' Duferin to Argyll, 23.9.92, D1071H/B/C/95/124.

37. DD, 18.3.94. Lyall, pp. 457, 537–8; Dufferin to Lady Mount Temple, 3.4.95, D1071H/03/44; DD, 30.3.95; Dufferin to Nelly, in Lyall, p.539. Before Lady Jocelyn died she had confided to a friend: 'I have only known two men in my life thoroughly immersed in the world and quite unspoilt by it – my brother William and Lord Dufferin.'

38. DD, 3.6.96.

39. 'The cynosure of all the cultured world', Vere Viscountess Galway, *The Creed of Love and Other Poems* (1895), pp. 55–6; Duke of Argyll, 'To The Marquis of Dufferin and Ava', October 1896, Helen's Tower Library.

CHAPTER 36: MAKING SHERIDANS

1. Dufferin, Draft memoir, 15.7.94, D1071H/W1/27.

2. As it was, Sheridan's plays were highly political both in motive and nuance. See Fintan O'Toole, *A Traitor's Kiss* (pb edition 1998), p.151.

3. Historians, instead, point to his rivalry with Burke, or his closeness to the Prince of Wales (whose friendship could be both a source of influence and an obstacle to power). Nor could there be any escaping from his attachment to political causes such as Reform and Ireland that would leave him in the 1790s on the wrong side of history. See A. Norman Jeffares, 'Richard Brinsley Sheridan', in DNB; Linda Kelly, *Richard Brinsley Sheridan: A Life* (1997); Fintan O'Toole, *A Traitor's Kiss: The Life of Richard Brinsley Sheridan* (1997); Madeline Bingham, *Sheridan: The Track of a Comet* (1972).

4. Maud, Lady Leconfield and John Gore (eds.), *Three Howard Sisters* (1955), p.161, n.1.

5. Dufferin to Rosebery, 15.10.93, MIC 326. Harold and Ruth were products of Ferdy's long, secret liaison with Rosa Swann. The daughter of a Suffolk bricklayer, she was the pretty, sultry girl he had disguised as a boy in the Garibaldi campaign.

6. In fact, convinced that her husband would leave the children nothing, for many years Georgy had been squirrelling away most of the housekeeping money, firmly asserting the virtues of her 'ragout of guinea-pig'. Brian Masters, *The Dukes*, pp. 69–77.

7. Peter Gordon (ed.), *The Political Diaries of the Fourth Earl of Carnarvon, 1857–1890*, Camden, 5th Series, vol. 35 (2009), p.401 (2.10.85). His source was Lord Randolph Churchill, and seemed to depend wholly on Dufferin's manner and complexion.

8. Aunts Gwen and Ulrica were Georgy's children and so actually Nelly's second cousins.

9. Nelly to Dufferin, 5.1.87, 24.2.87, 12.5.87, 2.6.87, 8.8.87. Dufferin to Nelly, 12.8.87. Helen's Tower Library.

10. *Edinburgh Review* (January 1895). Sir Robert Meade (Sidney Herbert's nephew) wrote in support to *The Times* – Meade's aunt insisting that her husband and Caroline were not lovers on the grounds that she would have known.

11. Dufferin did consider publishing a biography of Caroline, D1071/H/B/M/36/1–2. In fact most editors accepted his arguments and wrote apologies. E. T. Cook to Dufferin, 6, 12.11.94, D1071H/B/C/561/12. The affair with Herbert was widely known though it ended with his marriage. It is very unlikely that Caroline sold secrets but she was quite capable of blurting out private information to impress. Melbourne had suffered before as a consequence. Alan Chedzoy, *A Scandalous Woman* (1992), pp. 212–17, 291–3. D1071F/E5/8, 5.12.96.

12. DD, 7.7.96; W. S. Blunt, *My Diaries* (1920), vol. 2, p.17; Lyall, p.517; 'A Sketch of My Mother' in Dufferin (ed.), *Songs, Poems and Verses by Helen, Lady Dufferin (Countess of Gifford)* (1894), pp. 69–71.

13. Lyall, pp. 500–1; 'Sketch', p.54. 'I do not remember a day which made a greater impression on me than that which I spent in wandering about the deserted and . . . unaltered rooms and courtyards of this old castle, where perhaps my mother passed some of the happiest moments of her life . . . her new found treasure in her arms.' DD, 8.3.92.

14. 'Sketch', pp. 57, 74–5.

15. She was actually more concerned in her consultation with the doctors over whether Gifford would be able to consummate the marriage, such was her dread of childbirth, despite being now in her fifties.

16. 'Sketch', pp. 90–4. The Giffords married on 13 Oct 1862; Dufferin on 23 Oct 1862.

17. 'Sketch', pp. 3, 56, 76, 101.

18. Nicolson, *Helen's Tower*, pp. 50–1.

19. Dufferin to Nelly, n.d., Lyall, pp. 529–30; 'Sketch', pp. 1–37; Nicolson, *Helen's Tower*, p.247.

20. 'If a claim to good birth is dependent upon ancient descent and feudal distinction, Sheridan was as well born as Pitt, Fox, North or any of the fine gentlemen with whom he associated.' 'Sketch', pp. 13, 21.

21. 'Sketch', p.102.

22. O'Toole, pp. 27, 49, 53, 64, 198.

23. Ibid, pp. 22, 174, 212–19, 250–4, 459. And his grandson, Dufferin's Uncle Brinsley, actually served in the company in the 1820s which suggests that the family tradition was not all it was presumed.

24. DD, 15.3.94. His only regret was that his cousin Joseph Sheridan Le Fanu (author of *House by the Churchyard* and *Uncle Silas*, which was dedicated to the Countess of

Gifford) never wrote it but Caroline Norton had always put him off by saying that she would do it herself. Le Fanu did provide Dufferin with a ten-page history in 1864 on the Le Fanu–Sheridan connection. W. J. McCormick, *Sheridan Le Fanu and Victorian Ireland* (Oxford, 1980), pp. 206, 235.

25. Dufferin to Fraser Rae, 5.11.92, D1071H/03/2.
26. Dufferin to Fraser Rae, 21.3.95, D1071H/03/43.
27. As Dufferin explained to Augustine Birrell, Rae was 'a painstaking searcher after truth'. 'All the disparaging anecdotes and misrepresentations – all this rubbish had to be cleared away . . . before anything very entertaining could be written.' Dufferin to Birrell, 16.6.96, D1071H/03/65.
28. Dufferin to Gladstone, 4 and 9.5.96, MIC 331; *Nineteenth Century* (June 1896, pp. 1037–42). But O'Toole acknowledges that Sheridan did lots of committee work, *Traitor's Kiss*, pp. 200–1.
29. DD, 8.7.96; 5.9.98. Revealingly, when Rae uncovered some of her letters in possession of an American actor called Daley, Dufferin comments: 'Some of these letters ought to have been destroyed. It is unfortunate that they should be in the hands of an American' (DD, 22.10.94). *The Times*, 6.9.98; *Bath Chronicle and Weekly Gazette*, 8.9.98.
30. DD, 11.6.96. Durangel copied the three sisters; J. H. Anderson arranged the copying of Romney's portrait of Miss Linley. Anderson to Dufferin, 26.3.72, 2.4.72, D1071H/B/A/160/1–6. Nicolson, *Helen's Tower*, p.47; Dufferin bought a portrait of Sheridan in Willis rooms for £4 12s 0d supposedly by Shee, but Dufferin and later experts came to believe that it was by Opie as too vigorous for Shee. DD, 17.3.99. But this is not the Library picture. It is more likely to be the Sheridan portrait in Caroline Norton's drawing room (Chedzoy, *Scandalous Woman*, p.120). So possibly this portrait came to Clandeboye after her death.
31. Cruickshank, *The Country House Revealed*, pp. 207–11.
32. Cruickshank describes Clandeboye as 'his autobiography in mason and mortar'. It was even more so in its interior decoration. Cruickshank, *The Country House Revealed*, p.180.
33. F. J. Biggar, *Ulster Journal of Archaeology*, vol. 3 (April 1902), pp. 51–3.
34. Nicolson, *Helen's Tower*, p.42; Nancy Schoenberger, *Dangerous Muse*, (2001), p.14.
35. Nicolson, *Helen's Tower*, pp. 46–7.

CHAPTER 37: FUNDING SHERIDANS

1. Dufferin to Nelly, 10.7.92, in Lyall, p.519. DD, 28.9.94.
2. Cruickshank, *The Country House Revealed*, pp. 206–8.
3. Nicolson, *Helen's Tower*, pp. 248–9. DD, 10.9.97.
4. Dufferin to Terence and Basil Blackwood, 22.10.88, MIC 22/45. Dufferin to Nelly, 4.8.89, D1071H/N1/34. It is not clear whether they met when Rosebery came out to India in 1886 or when Nelly was visiting Tain with the Duchess of Sutherland in 1887. Dufferin to Queen Victoria, c.July 1889, Lyall, pp. 489–91.

5. On a later occasion he would write that 'your face . . . is always an unspeakable joy to me. I thought that your eyes never looked more beautiful than the evening I came away'. Dufferin to Nelly, 2.9.89, D1071H/N1/34. Dufferin to 'Nell', 16.11.95, Helen's Tower Library.

6. Dufferin to Nelly, 5.12.93, 13.5.94; Dufferin to Munro Ferguson, 8.6.94, Helen's Tower Library; DD, 5.7.99. It was felt that Victoria and Willie needed capital of £26,000, providing an income of £1,200 p.a. Dufferin could barely offer £1,000. The Plunkets' Guinness relations proved more forthcoming. RA, VIC/MAIN/F/40/44, Lord Dufferin to Queen Victoria, 8 May 1894.

7. In contrast to the Queen who had heard only good reports of 'Miss Davis': D1071H/B/V/106. Lady Gregory was more pragmatic. 'What is the use of getting a wife if you don't get a fortune along with her?'. Lady Augusta Gregory to Dufferin, 1892–99, D1071H/B/G/393/1-8. As it turned out, in the end Flora received a considerable inheritance from her father. Nicolson, *Helen's Tower*, p.25. Dufferin to Durand, 3.10.93, D1071H/03/14; Dufferin to Rosebery, 30.9.92, 15.10.93, MIC 326, the *Strand Magazine*, vol. 7 (1894), pp. 289–300, DD, 4.10.94. Dufferin to Lady Londonderry, 1.5.96, D2846/2/32/26.

8. Dufferin to Basil, 28.9.89, D1071H/N1/34. Lyall, pp. 506–7. Dufferin to Nelly, 16.11.95, Helen's Tower Library. Dufferin to Grant Duff, ND, D1071H/N1/30.

9. Including *The Bad Child's Book of Beasts* (1896), *More Beasts* (1897), *The Modern Traveller* (1898), *A Moral Alphabet* (1899), *Cautionary Tales for Children* (1907) and *More Peers* (1911). *The Modern Traveller* includes a caricature of his father.

10. Nicolson, *Helen's Tower*, p.237; Maurice Headlam, *Irish Reminiscences* (1947), p.56.

11. DD, 16.12.92; 19.11.94. Dufferin to 'Nell', 5.12.93, Helen's Tower Library. Eddie Marsh, *A Number of People* (1939), pp. 196–7. Dufferin to Hermione, 7.12.93, Blackwood papers, D1231/M/1/1–36; DD, 12.5.97. J. T. Brampton, Winchester to Dufferin (1891), who was glad that Freddie's departure will mean that he will lose touch with 'young D'Oyly Carte, who I have some reason not to think very well of'. D1071H/B/B/695/1–2.

12. 'Archie . . . as usual all sunshine', Ulrica Thynne to Dufferin, 11.1.(89?), D1071H/B/T/201/6.

13. DD, 13.6.91, 13.5.96, 11.7.96; Dufferin to 'my own darling little Nell', 13.4.92, 21.11.95, Helen's Tower Library; Dufferin to Lady Londonderry, 1.1.95, D2846/2/32/25; Nicolson, *Helen's Tower*, pp. 253–6. Mrs Vanderbilt to Dufferin, 6.11.(95?), inviting him to her daughter Consuelo's wedding. D1071H/B/V/14/1. Dufferin's attitude to homosexuality was noticeably tolerant for the times. When invited to dinner, Lord Ronald Gower and 'Bobsy' Meade would feel accepted enough to bring their lovers.

14. £1,000 in 1895 equates to £110,000 in 2014. As a crude measure one should multiply the nineteenth-century figure by 100 to get an estimate of the present-day value. 'Consumer Price Inflation Since 1750' (*Economic Trends* No. 604 (2004), pp. 38–46) by Jim O'Donoghue, Louise Goulding, and Grahame Allen.

15. DD, 30.4.98; Dufferin heard that the Land Courts ruled the Ulster Custom of

Tenant Right to be universal to Dufferin's land; a verdict Dufferin challenged and got overturned.

16. By 1896 25 per cent of the Peerage held directorships. John Darwin, *The Empire Project*, p.101.

17. Harrison, pp. 302–3. DD, 23.4.96; 29–30.7.97. Lord Grosvenor to Dufferin (1896), D1071H/B/G/464/1-7.

18. Thus in present-day figures he received an annual income of £300,000 and a signing-on fee of close to £1m.

19. David Kynaston, *The City of London: Golden Years 1890–1914* (1995), vol. 2, p.140. See also Richard Davenport-Hines in DNB and David McKie, *Guardian*, 2.2.2004.

20. DD, 21–22.9.97; 6.10.97; 8–9.1.98.

21. Kynaston, *The City*, p.140. Harrison, p.309. DD, 4.11.97, 27.1.98, 23.2.98, 24.5.99. Dufferin to Munro Ferguson, 24.7.99, Helen's Tower Library.

CHAPTER 38: DECLINE AND FALL

1. MacKnight, *Ulster as It Is* (1896), p.245. Dufferin to Stead, 1.1.91, D1071H/B/S/541; Dufferin to Rosebery, 20.1.91, D1071H/N1/10 and 16; Dufferin to Thomas MacKnight, 17.3.96, 22.3.96, D1071H/03/56, 59. Dufferin to Howe, 20.7.91, D1071H/N1/14. Dufferin to Gregory, 9.8.90 in Lyall, pp. 497–8. Andrew Gailey, *Ireland and the Death of Kindness* (1987), p.152. Patrick Maume, 'Burke in Belfast: Thomas MacKnight, Gladstone and Liberal Unionism', in D. G. Boyce and Alan O'Day (eds.), *Gladstone and Ireland: Politics, Religion and Nationality in the Victorian Age* (2010).

2. Alvin Jackson, 'Irish Unionists and Empire, 1880–1920: Classes and Masses', in Keith Jeffrey (ed.), *An Irish Empire*, pp. 123–48.

3. Thomas MacKnight, *Ulster as It Is*, pp. 242–6. Alvin Jackson, *The Ulster Party* (Oxford, 1989), pp. 226–8. McCarthy, *Five Years in Ireland* (1901), p.204.

4. W. S. Churchill, *My Early Life*, p.376.

5. Nicolson, *Helen's Tower*, pp. 248–51.

6. W. B. Stanford and R. B. McDowell, *Mahaffy* (1971), pp. 51–2; R. F. Foster, *W. B. Yeats: A Life*, vol 1, p.206. Lady Gregory to Dufferin, D1071 H/B/G/ 393/1–8. DD, 4–8.4.1900. QVD, 4.4.1900, 110, pp. 125–30.

7. Dufferin to Rosebery, 28.11.97; 11.12.97. MIC 326. 'He looks 1000 and is very deaf', noted one of the Queen's ladies-in-waiting after a dinner at Osborne. 'She [Hariot] seems to grow younger instead of older.' Marie Mallet, *Life with Queen Victoria*, Victor Mallet (ed.) (1968), p.132.

8. Lord Ronald Sutherland, 12.3.98, *Old Diaries*, p.331. At one such lunch (which included Cecil Rhodes, Sir Henry Irving, Lyall and Margot Asquith), their hostess persuaded the great actor to utter Richard III's famous speech ('Now is the winter of our discontent . . .') into a 'phonograph' and on playing it back Irving heard his voice for the first time.

9. DD, 9.5.98, 6.6.99.

10. At Gladstone's funeral, Dufferin thought Salisbury's eulogy too short; 'Walked through the crowds through Westminster Hall to see poor Mr Gladstone lying in state' (DD, 26.5.98). For all the political irritation they had remained friends.

11. Nicolson, *Helen's Tower*, p.258. Dufferin to 'Nell', 1.11.96, Helen's Tower Library.

12. 'Jameson's wild blow at Johannesburg [will cause] some temporary mischief.' Lyall to Dufferin, 6.1.96, D1071H/B/L/462/61.

13. DD, 24.10.99, 2.11.99, 16–17, 30.12.99.

14. DD, 12.1.1900, 17.1.1900. Betty Balfour to Hariot, 13.1.1900. Hariot to her mother, 20.3.1900, Helen's Tower Library. Ava's death a crushing blow'. RA VIC/ MAIN/P/16/29 Lord Dufferin to Queen Victoria, 13 January 1900.

15. DD, 1.7.1900, 25.9.1900; Dufferin to 'Nell', 27.9.1900, 29.3.1901, Helen's Tower Library.

16. DD, 27.12.1900, 29.12.1900.

17. Dufferin to Munro Ferguson, 30 December 1900, Helen's Tower Library.

18. *Critic*, 18.6.98.

19. Kynaston, *The City*, pp. 218–19.

20. Harrison, p.315; Kynaston, *The City*, pp. 173–4. DNB article by Richard Davenport-Hines.

21. DD, 16.2.98; 5.7.98; 28.9.98.

22. Kynaston, *The City*, pp. 173–4.

23. Kynaston, *The City*, pp. 180–1.

24. Harrison, p.313.

25. Kynaston, *The City*, pp. 216–18.

26. Dufferin to Sir Richard Garnett, in Lyall, pp. 556–7.

27. Dufferin to Pattisson, 22.1.1901, D1071A/K, cited in Harrison, p.316.

28. Dufferin to Spencer, 23.12.1901, Spencer papers; Dufferin to Munro Ferguson, 19.8.1901, Helen's Tower Library. Dufferin to Rosebery, 26.1.1901, MIC 326.

29. Lyall, p.561.

30. DD, 31.7.97.

31. Dufferin to Hermione Blackwood, 9.11.93, D1231/M/1.

32. Harry Furniss, *Some Victorian Men* (1924), pp. 92–4. Nicolson, *Helen's Tower*, p.279.

33. Harrison, pp. 312–13.

34. Lyall, p.556. Dufferin to Munro Ferguson, 31.7.1901, Helen's Tower Library.

35. David McKie, 'The Fall of Midas', *Guardian*, 2.2.2004.

CHAPTER 39: AT THE LAST

1. St John Ervine, *Craigavon* (1949), p.81. Kynaston, *The City*, p.218. R. Rodd, *Memories* (1925), p.5. Hardinge, p.81.

2. Dufferin to Nelly, 17.4.1901, Helen's Tower Library. DD, 7.2.1901, 2.5.1901, 19.6.1901. Still Dufferin's wealth at probate was £108,548 (17.3.1902). DNB.

3. The sudden death in April 1900 of his secretary, MacFerran, upon whose management of the estate Dufferin had relied for twenty years, was another blow; a measure of which was Dufferin's agreeing to MacFerran being the first to be actually buried at Campo Santo.
4. DD, 1–3.2.1901. Lyall, p.555.
5. J. H. Rivett-Carnac, *Many Memories* (1910), pp. 408–9. Giles St Aubyn, *Queen Victoria* (1991), p.599.
6. If this was a shock, it was as nothing to that awaiting their friends, the Gilmours, beside them on the quay and who, to Dufferin's horror, found their son brain-damaged and paralysed from a head wound.
7. DD, 9–11.3.1901.
8. Lyall, p.557.
9. DD, 4.11.99.
10. Dufferin to Salisbury, 9.2.1902, Nicolson, *Helen's Tower*, p.279.

CHAPTER 40: MYTHMAKING AND THE BIOGRAPHERS

1. W. S. Blunt, *My Diaries*, vol. 2, pp. 18–19.
2. He had earlier tried to get Dufferin to write his memoirs: 'This is the age of biographies and autobiographies'. Lyall to Dufferin, 21.10.96, D1071H/B/L/462/65.
3. Lyall to Lady Dufferin, 14.5.1904, 1.6.1904; although 19 and 24.8.1904, 7.10.1904 saw a stormy exchange over the biographers right of 'discretion'. D1071J/A/14. The particular issue was how far Hariot's health was the cause of Dufferin's early retirement from India.
4. Lyall to Lady Dufferin, 13,17.12.1904, agreeing to remove references to 'the financial catastrophe'. D1071J/A/14.
5. Lyall 'wished for some more glimpses into the domestic life' in vain. Lyall to Lady Dufferin, 19.10.1904, D1071J/A/14.
6. Devotees of Miss Plimsoll might read Harold Nicolson, *Some People* (1983 ed.), pp. 1–20.
7. Nicolson to Vita Sackville-West, in James Lees-Milne, *Harold Nicolson: A Biography*, vol. 2, 1930–1968 (1981), p.82.
8. Nicolson, *Helen's Tower*, pp. 51, 223–4.
9. Nicolson, *Helen's Tower*, pp. 245–7
10. One hundred and fifty years on, *High Latitudes* is still in print.
11. Nicolson, *Helen's Tower*, p.179.
12. Harrison, pp. 636–49.
13. R. F. Foster, *Lord Randolph Churchill*, p.186.
14. David Cannadine, *Aspects of Aristocracy* (1994), p.221. Parry, p.323.
15. DD, 19.4.96. Brodrick to Dufferin, 16.1.96, D1071H/B/B/756/69.
16. Lyall, pp. 522–5.
17. Douglas Hurd, *Choose Your Weapons* (2000), p.162.

18. Angus Hawkins and John Powell (ed.), *The Journal of John Wodehouse, 1st Earl of Kimberley* Camden, 5th Series (1999), vol. 9, p.18.

19. Dufferin to Nelly, 27.2.95, in Helen's Tower Library. Viscount Mersey, *The Viceroys and Governor Generals of India* (1949), p.103.

20. A. N. Wilson, *The Victorians*, pp. 461–2.

21. Argyll, *Autobiography and Memoirs*, p.461.

22. Frederic Mullally, *The Silver Salver: The Story of the Guinness Family* (1981), p.152.

23. Harrison, pp. 628–9.

24. *Punch*, 13.6.96.

25. By comparison to his gifts, 'his faults were trivial' and 'his life, until the griefs of 1900, was unusually happy; [while] he himself spread an unusual amount of happiness.' Richard Davenport-Hines in DNB.

26. Lyall, p.520.

27. Lord Derby's diary, 11.9.84 (cited in DNB), on Dufferin's appointment to India: 'Dufferin is popular everywhere, having pleasant manners, ready wit, considerable power as a speaker, and a fair share of Irish "blarney".'

28. 'Dufferin makes even the Queen's dinner lively. He told various stories last night to which we all listened and laughed – not that there is much in the stories themselves but in the manner he tells them.' RA VIC/ADDA/36/1584, Sir H. Ponsonby to Lady M. Ponsonby, 14 November 1878.

29. Lady St Helier, *Memories of Fifty Years* (1909), p.269.

30. Nicolson, *Helen's Tower*, p.103.

31. Lord Rossmore, *Things I Can Tell*, p.134. Lord Charles Beresford, *Memoirs* (1914), p.374.

EPILOGUE: IN THE SHADOWS OF ANCESTORS

1. Hariot to Mother, 18.3.1902. J/D 41 – Hariot's executor's papers.

2. In one of life's oddities Helen's Tower would prove the enduring symbol of Ulster's sacrifice in the First World War. Providing the last sight of their homeland for the 36th Ulster Division, doomed to be slaughtered on the Somme, it was replicated in their memory at Thiepval in 1921. Stamp, 'Helen's Tower', pp. 32–3.

3. There were numerous house sales, one of which in 1937 saw the statue of Amun sold.

4. Nancy Schoenberger, *Dangerous Muse: A Life of Caroline Blackwood* (2001), pp. 21–4.

5. Roy Strong, *Diaries 1967–1987*, pp. 10, 44. Schoenberger, *Dangerous Muse*, pp. 246–8.

6. Schoenberger, *Dangerous Muse*, p.14.

7. Lord Dufferin, 'Growing up at Clandeboye', *Clandeboye*, Ulster Architectural Heritage Society (1985).

8. John Witchell, 'Clandeboye – the fulfilment of a vision: the Irish estate that slept for a hundred years', Helen's Tower Library. For recent articles on Clandeboye, see Ptolemy Dean, 'Forgotten Genius', *Country Life*, 2.12.2009; John Goodall, 'An Imperial Adventure', *Country Life*, 9.12.2009.

Sources and Bibliography

Major Archives

This biography has largely drawn on the Dufferin and Blackwood Archives, a collection in the Public Record Office of Northern Ireland of over 96,000 documents and 850 volumes which date from the seventeenth century but predominantly relate to the career and family of the 1st Marquess. Thanks to the efforts of the late Dr Andrew Harrison, Dufferin's voluminous official correspondence has been complemented by the extensive microfilming of Dufferin material in other archives such as The National Archives (TNA), the British Library and the Royal Archives (RA). This has enabled virtually complete runs of all Dufferin's official correspondence. For his private correspondence there are numerous volumes covering his life up to the 1860s. For the period afterwards there is an archive of 40,000 loose letters from 12,000 correspondents which has only recently been catalogued after much painstaking work by the staff at the Public Record Office of Northern Ireland.

Other Archives

Blunt, Wilfrid Scawen (Fitzwilliam Museum, Cambridge)
Carnarvon, 4th Earl of (British Library and The National Archives)
Churchill, Lord Randolph (Churchill College, Cambridge)
Cross, 1st Viscount (British Library, Oriental and India Office)
Dilke, Sir Charles (British Library)
Fraser, Colonel A. J. (British Library)
Gladstone, W. E. (British Library)
Godley, Sir Arthur (British Library, Oriental and India Office)
Graham, Sir James (Cambridge University Library)
Granville, 2nd Earl of (The National Archives)
Ilbert, Sir Courtenay (British Library, Oriental and India Office)
Kimberley, 1st Earl of (Bodleian Library, Oxford and National Library of Scotland)
Lyall, Sir Alfred (British Library, Oriental and India Office)
Meade, R. H. (Public Record Office of Northern Ireland)

Northbrook, 1st Earl of (British Library, Oriental and India Office)
Rosebery, 5th Earl of (National Library of Scotland)
Royal Archives (Windsor Castle)
Russell, 1st Earl of (The National Archives)
Russell, Odo, 1st Baron Ampthill (The National Archives)
Salisbury, 3rd Marquess of (Hatfield House)
Somerset, 12th Duke of (Devon Record Office)

Published Works

Acland, Alice, *Caroline Norton* (1948)

Adburgham, Alison, *Silver Fork Society: Fashionable Life and Literature, 1814–40* (1983)

Allen, Bernard, *Sir Robert Morant* (1934)

Allen, Charles, *Kipling Sahib* (London 2007)

Amos, Sheldon, 'The New Egyptian Constitution', *Contemporary Review*, xliii (June 1883), pp. 909–22

Anon., *Journal of the Journey of His Excellency, The Governor General of Canada from Government House, Ottawa to British Columbia and Back* (1877)

Argyll, Dowager Duchess of (ed.), *George Douglas, Eighth Duke of Argyll: Autobiography and Memoirs* (1925–7)

Armytage, P., *By the Clock of St James's* (1927)

Arnold, D., *Science, Technology and Medicine in Colonial India* (Cambridge, 2000)

Askwith, Betty, *Piety and Wit: A Biography of Harriet, Countess Granville, 1785–1862* (1982)

Asquith, Margot, *An Autobiography*, 2 vols (1920, 1922)

——, *Places and Persons* (1925)

Atkinson, Diana, *The Criminal Conversation of Mrs Norton* (2012)

Aung, Maung Htin, *Lord Randolph Churchill and the Dancing Peacock: The British Conquest of Burma, 1885* (New Delhi, 1990)

Bahlman, D. W. R. (ed.), *The Diary of Sir Edward Walter Hamilton, 1880–1885* (1972)

Baker, Samuel White, 'Egypt's Proper Frontier', *Nineteenth Century* (July 1884)

Ballhatchet, Kenneth, *Race, Sex and Class under the Raj* (1980)

Bardon, Jonathan, *A History of Ulster* (1992)

Bayly, C., 'Ireland, India and Empire 1780–1914', in *Transactions of the Royal Historical Society* (2000), pp. 377–97

Beaumont, Penny and Rodger, *Imperial Divas: The Vicereines of India* (2010)

Bence-Jones, Mark, 'The Building Dreams of a Viceroy', 1, *Country Life* (1 October 1970), pp. 816–19

——, 'The Building Dreams of a Viceroy', 2, *Country Life* (8 October 1970), pp. 900–1

——, *The Viceroys of India* (1982)

Beresford, Lord Charles, *Memoirs* (1914)

Berger, Carl, *The Sense of Power: Studies in the ideas of Canadian Imperialism, 1867–1914* (Toronto, 1970)

Bew, Paul, *Ireland: The Politics of Enmity, 1789–2006* (2007)

——, *Land and the National Question, 1858–62* (1979)

Bingham, Madeline, *Sheridan: The Track of a Comet* (1972)

Black, Charles E. Drummond, *The Marquess of Dufferin and Ava: Diplomatist, Viceroy, Statesman* (1903)

Blackburn, Terence, *Executions by the Half-Dozen: The Pacification of Burma* (New Delhi, 2008)

Blake, Robert, *Disraeli* (1966)

Blunt, W. S., *A Secret History of the English Occupation of Egypt* (1895)

——, *My Diaries* (1919, 1920)

Bonham Carter, Mark (ed.), *The Autobiography of Margot Asquith* (1962)

Bonnerjee, W. C. (ed.), *Indian Politics* (Madras, 1898)

Bourne, K., *Britain and the Balance of Power in North America* (1967)

Bradford, Sarah, *Disraeli* (1983)

Brett, Maurice (ed.), *Journals and Letters of Viscount Esher* (1934)

Brodrick, G. C., *Memories and Impressions 1831–1900* (1900)

Buckle, G. E. (ed.), *Life of Disraeli* (1920)

——, *Letters of Queen Victoria 1862–78*, series 2, vol. 2 (1928)

Buckner, Phillip, 'The Creation of the Dominion of Canada', in Phillip Buckner (ed.), *Canada and the British Empire* (2010)

Burton, Antoinette, *Burdens of History: British Feminists, Indian Women and Imperial Culture, 1865–1915* (1994)

Byers, John, *Lord Dufferin as a Speaker* (1906)

Cain, P. J., 'Character, "Ordered Liberty" and the Mission to Civilise: British Moral Justification of Empire, 1870–1914', in *Journal of Imperial and Commonwealth History*, vol. 40, no. 4 (November 2012), pp. 557–78

Cain, P. J. and Hopkins, A. G., *Innovation and Empire 1688–1914* (1993)

Cannadine, David, 'The Context, Performance and Meaning of Ritual: The British Monarchy and the Invention of Tradition, 1820–1977', in E. Hobsbawn and T. Ranger (eds.), *The Invention of Tradition* (1983), pp. 101–64

——, *The Decline and Fall of the British Aristocracy* (1990)

——, *Aspects of Aristocracy* (1994)

——, 'Imperial Canada: Old History, New Problems' in Colin Coates (ed.), *Imperial Canada 1867–1917* (Edinburgh, 1997)

——, *Ornamentalism* (2001)

Carr, Peter, *Portavo* (Belfast, 2003)

Cavendish, Lady Frederick, *Diaries* (1928)

Cecil, Lady Gwendolen, *The Life of Lord Salisbury* (1921)

Chedzoy, Alan, *A Scandalous Woman: The Story of Caroline Norton* (1992)

Chevenix-Trench, Charles, *Charley Gordon* (1978)

Christiansen, Rupert, *Tales of the New Babylon* (1994)

Churchill, W. S., *My Early Life* (1930)

Coates, Colin M. (ed.), *Imperial Canada 1867–1917* (1997)

Creighton, Donald, *J. A. Macdonald: The Old Chieftain* (Toronto, 1955)

Crewe, Lord, *Rosebery* (1931)

Cromer, Lord, *Modern Egypt* (1908)

Crosthwaite, Sir C. E., *The Pacification of Burma* (1912)

Cruickshank, Dan, *The Country House Revealed* (2011)

Curtis, G. W. (ed.), *The Correspondence of J. L. Motley* (1889)

Curtis, L. P., *Apes and Angels* (1972)

——, 'Incumbered Wealth: Landed Indebtedness in Post Famine Ireland', *American History Review*, lxxxv (1980), pp. 332–67

Curzon, Lord, *British Government in India* (1925)

Darwin, John, *After Tamerlane: The Global History of Empire* (2007)

——, *The Empire Project* (2009)

Dasent, A. I., *John Delane, 1817–1879* (1908)

Davenport-Hines, Richard, 'Dufferin', in the *Oxford Dictionary of National Biography*

Davies, Norman, *Europe: A History* (Oxford, 1996)

de Courcy, Anne, *The Fishing Fleet* (2013)

De Kiewiet, C. W. and Underhill, F. H. (eds.), *Dufferin–Carnarvon Correspondence* (Toronto, 1955)

Denholm, Anthony, *Lord Ripon 1827–1909* (1982)

Dewan, Deepali and Hutton, Deborah, *Raja Deen Dayal* (2013)

Dixon, Hugh, *William Henry Lynn 1829–1915* (1978)

Dufferin and Ava, 5th Marquess of, 'Growing up at Clandeboye', in *Clandeboye* (Ulster Architectural Heritage Society, 1985)

Dufferin and Ava, Marchioness of, *My Canadian Journal, 1872–8* (1891)

——, *My Russian and Turkish Journals* (1916)

——, *Our Viceregal Life in India* (1889)

Dufferin, Helen, Lady, *Lispings from Low Latitudes* (1863)

Dufferin Lord (ed.), *Songs, Poems and Verses by Helen, Lady Dufferin (Countess of Gifford)* (1894)

Dufferin, Lord, 'A Last letter from High Latitudes', *Cornhill*, November 1898

——, *Mr Mill's Plan for the Pacification of Ireland Examined* (1868)

——, *Letters from High Latitudes* (1856)

Dufferin, Lord, and Boyle, G .F., *Narrative of a Journey from Oxford to Skibbereen* (Oxford, 1847)

Dunae, Patrick, *Gentlemen Emigrants: From the British Public Schools to the Canadian Frontier* (Vancouver, 1981)

Egremont, Max, *The Cousins* (1977)

——, *Balfour* (1980)

Ervine, St John, *Craigavon* (1949)

Faber, Richard, *Young England* (1987)

Ferguson, Niall, *Empire* (2003)

Fitzmaurice, Lord Edmond, *Life of Granville* (1905)

Fitzpatrick, David, *Irish Emigration 1801–1925* (Dublin, 1985)

Foster, R. F., *Lord Randolph Churchill* (1981)

——, *Modern Ireland* (1988)

——, *Paddy and Mr Punch* (1993)

——, *W. B. Yeats: A Life* (1997)

Fraser, T. G., 'Ireland and India', in Keith Jeffrey (ed.), *Aspects of Ireland and the British Empire* (Manchester, 1996)

Furniss, Harry, *Some Victorian Men* (1924)

Gailey, Andrew, *Ireland and the Death of Kindness* (1987)

Galway, Vere, Viscountess of, *The Creed of Love and Other Poems* (1895)

Gilley, Sheridan, *Newman and his Age* (1990)

Gilmour, David, *Curzon* (1994)

——, *The Long Recessional* (2002)

——, *The Ruling Caste* (2005)

Girouard, Mark, *The Return to Camelot: Chivalry and the English Gentleman* (Yale, 1981)

Gopal, Sarvepalli, *British Policy in India, 1858–1905* (1965)

Gordon, Peter (ed.), *The Red Earl: The Papers of the 5th Earl of Spencer, 1835–1910* (2009)

——, *The Political Diaries of the 4th Earl of Carnarvon, 1857–1890*, Camden, 5th Series, vol. 35 (2010)

Gore, John (ed.), *Creevey's Life and Times* (1934)

Gourlay, Jharna, *Florence Nightingale and the Health of the Raj* (2003)

Gower, Lord Ronald, *My Reminiscences* (1883)

——, *Old Diaries* (1902)

Greville, H. W., *Leaves from the Diary of Henry Greville* (1883–4)

Gunn, John (ed.), *Letters of Benjamin Disraeli* (1982)

Gwyn, Richard, *Nation Maker: Sir John Macdonald: His Life and Times*, vol. 2 (2001)

Gwynn, Stephen and Tuckwell, G. M., *The Life of Sir Charles W. Dilke* (1917)

Hamilton, Lord Frederick, *The Vanished Pomps of Yesterday* (1950)

Hamilton, Lord George, *The Days Before Yesterday* (1920)

Harcourt Williams, Robin, *The Salisbury–Balfour Correspondence, 1869–1892* (1988)

Hardinge, Sir Arthur, *The Life of Henry Howard Molyneux, 4th Earl of Carnarvon, 1831–1890* (1925)

Hardinge of Penshurst, Lord Charles, *Old Diplomacy* (1947)

Harper, Marjory, 'Rhetoric and Reality: British Migration to Canada, 1867–1967', in Buckner (ed.), *Canada and the British Empire* (2010), pp. 167–73

Harris, Melvin, *Investigating the Unexplained* (2003)

Harrison, Robert T., *Gladstone's Imperialism in Egypt* (1995)

Hawkins, Angus and Powell, John (ed.), *The Journal of John Wodehouse, 1st Earl of Kimberley (for 1862–1902)*, Camden, 5th Series, vol. 9 (1997)

Headlam, Maurice, *Irish Reminiscences* (1947)

Henry, Wade A., 'Severing the Imperial Tie? Republicanism and the British Identity in English Canada, 1864–1917', in Colin Coates (ed.), *Imperial Canada 1867–1917* (Edinburgh, 1997)

Heuzé, Paul, *Do the Dead Live?* (1923)

Hewitt, Osbert Wyndham, *Strawberry Fair* (1956)

Hilton, Boyd, *The Age of Atonement* (1988)

Hodgins, Brian W., 'The Attitudes of the Canadian Founders toward Britain and the British Connection: A Personal Re-examination', in Colin Coates (ed.), *Imperial Canada 1867–1917* (Edinburgh, 1997)

Hopkirk, Peter, *The Great Game* (1990)

Houghton, W. E., *The Victorian Frame of Mind, 1830–1870* (1957)

Houltain, Alfred (ed.), *The Correspondence of Goldwin Smith* (2010)

Hourani, Albert, *A History of the Arab Peoples* (1991)

Howard, George, Earl of Carlisle, *Extracts from the Journals kept by George Howard, Earl of Carlisle* (1871)

Hurd, Douglas, *Choose Your Weapons* (2000)

Hutchinson, Horace (ed.), *Private Diaries of Sir Algernon West* (1922)

Hyam, Ronald, *Empire and Sexuality* (1990)

Jackson, Alvin, 'Irish Unionists and Empire, 1880–1920: Classes and Masses', in Keith Jeffrey (ed.), *An Irish Empire?* (1996), pp. 123–48

——, *The Ulster Party* (Oxford, 1989)

James, Lawrence, *The Rise and Fall of the British Empire* (1994)

——, *Raj: The Making and Unmaking of British India* (1997)

Jeffares, A. Norman, 'Richard Brinsley Sheridan', in *Oxford Dictionary of National Biography*

Jenkins, Brian, *Sir William Gregory of Coole* (1986)

Jenkins, Roy, *Gladstone* (1995)

Johnson, Nancy E. (ed.), *Diary of Gathorne Hardy, Later Lord Cranbrook, 1866–1892* (1981)

Kaminsky, A., *The India Office* (1986)

Karsh, E. and Karsh, I., *Empires in the Sand* (1999)

Kee, Robert, *The Laurel and the Ivy* (1994)

Kelly, Linda, *Richard Brinsley Sheridan: A Life* (1997)

Kennedy, Paul, *The Rise and Fall of the Great Powers* (1988)

Kenny, Kevin (ed.), *Ireland and the British Empire* (2004)

Kipling, Rudyard, *Departmental Ditties and Other Verses* (1891)

Kissinger, Henry, *Diplomacy* (1994)

Kohfeldt, Mary Lou, *Lady Gregory* (1985)

Koss, Stephen, *The Rise and Fall of the Political Press* (1981, 1984)

Kwarteng, Kwasi, *Ghosts of Empire* (2011)

Kynaston, David, *The City of London: Golden Years 1890–1914* (1995)

Lal, Maneesha, 'The Politics of Gender and Medicine in Colonial India: The Countess of Dufferin Fund 1885–1888', *Bulletin of the History of Medicine*, 68 (1994)

Leconfield, Lady Maud and Gore, John (eds.), *Three Howard Sisters* (1955)

Lees-Milne, James, *Harold Nicolson: A Biography* (1981)

——, *The Enigmatic Edwardian* (1986)

Leggo, William, *The History of the Administration of the Right Honourable Frederick Temple, Earl of Dufferin, late Governor General of Canada* (1878)

Lewin, Thomas Herbert, *The Lewin Letters: A Selection from the Correspondence and Diaries of an English Family, 1756–1884* (1909)

Longford, Elizabeth, *A Pilgrimage of Passion* (1979)

——, *Darling Loosy* (1991)

Lyall, Sir Alfred, *The Life of Lord Dufferin* (1905)

Lycett, Andrew, *Rudyard Kipling* (1999)

McCarthy, Michael, *Five Years in Ireland* (1901)

McCormack, W. J., *Sheridan Le Fanu and Victorian Ireland* (1990)

Mackenzie, John M. (ed.), *Imperialism and Popular Culture* (1986)

McKie, David, 'The Fall of Midas', *Guardian* (2 February 2004)

McKinstry, Leo, *Rosebery: Statesman in Turmoil* (2005)

MacKnight, Thomas, *Ulster as It Is* (1896)

Mallet, Sir Edward, *Shifting Scenes* (1901)

Mallet, Marie, *Life with Queen Victoria* (1968)

Mallock, W. H., *Letters and Memoirs of Seymour, 12th Duke of Somerset* (1893)

Mangan, J. A. (ed.), *The Cultural Bond: Sport, Empire and Society* (2013)

Mansel, Philip, *Constantinople* (1995)

——, *Levant: Splendour and Catastrophe on the Mediterranean* (2010)

Mansergh, N., *The Irish Question 1840–1921* (1975)

Mansfield, Peter, *Britain and Egypt* (1971)

——, *History of the Middle East* (1991)

Marsh, Eddie, *A Number of People* (1939)

Marshal, P. J. (ed.), *The British Empire* (1996)

Martel, G., *Rosebery and the Failure of Foreign Policy* (1986)

Martin, Briton, 'The Viceroyalty of Lord Dufferin', part 1, *History Today*, x, 12 (December 1960); part 2, *History Today*, xi, 1 (January 1961)

——, *New India 1885* (Los Angeles 1969)

Martin, Ged, 'Canada from 1815', in Andrew Porter (ed.), *The Oxford History of the British Empire* (1999), vol. 3, pp. 522–45

Martin, Robert Bernard, *Tennyson: The Unquiet Heart* (1983)

Mason, P., *The English Gentleman: The Rise and Fall of an Ideal* (1982)

Masters, Brian, *The Dukes* (1988 ed.)

Matthew, H. C. G., *Gladstone Diaries* (1973–94)

——, *Gladstone, 1809–1898* (1999)

Maume, Patrick, 'Burke in Belfast: Thomas MacKnight, Gladstone and Liberal Unionism', in D. G. Boyce and Alan O'Day (eds.), *Gladstone and Ireland: Politics, Religion and Nationality in the Victorian Age* (2010)

Meredith, George, *Diana of the Crossways* (1885)

Mersey, Viscount, *The Viceroys and Governor Generals of India* (1949)

Messamore, Barbara J., 'British Imperialists and Canadian Nationalists', in Colin Coates (ed.), *Imperial Canada 1867–1917* (Edinburgh, 1997), pp. 78–108

——, *Canada's Governors General, 1847–1878* (2006)

Milner, Sir Alfred, *England in Egypt* (1893)

Milton, Henry (ed.), *Lord Dufferin's Speeches and Addresses* (1882)

Moneypenny, W. F. and Buckle, G. E., *The Life of Benjamin Disraeli, Earl of Beaconsfield*, 6 vols. (1910–20)

Moon, Sir Penderel, *The British Conquest and Dominion of India* (1989)

Moore, Lucy, *Maharanis* (2004)

Moore, R. J., 'Imperial India, 1858–1914', in Andrew Porter (ed.), *The Oxford History of the British Empire* (1999), vol. 3, pp. 429–32

——, *Liberalism and Indian Politics, 1872–1922* (1966)

Morley, John, *Recollections* (1917)

Morris, Jan, *O Canada!* (1990)

——, *Pax Britannica* (1968)

——, *Stones of Empire: The Buildings of the Raj* (1983)

Mullally, Frederic, *The Silver Salver: The Story of the Guinness Family* (1981)

Munro, Kenneth, 'The Crown and French Canada: The Role of the Governor General in the Making of the Crown Relevant, 1867–1917', in Colin Coates (ed.), *Imperial Canada* (Edinburgh, 1997), pp. 109–21

Myint-U, Thant, *The Making of Modern Burma* (Cambridge, 2001)

——, *The River of Lost Footsteps* (London 2007)

Nevill, R., (ed.), *The Reminiscences of Lady Dorothy Nevill* (1906)

Newton, Lord, *Lord Lyons* (1913)

Nicolson, Harold, *Helen's Tower* (1937)

——, *Portrait of a Diplomatist* (1930)

——, *Some People* (1926)

O'Donoghue, Jim, Goulding, Louise and Allen, Grahame, 'Consumer Price Inflation Since 1750', in *Economic Trends* No. 604 (2004), pp. 38–46

O'Leary, Patrick, *Servants of Empire: The Irish in the Punjab 1881–1921* (2011)

Oppenheimer, Melanie, '"Hidden Under Many Bushels": Lady Victoria Plunket and the New Zealand Society for the Health of Women and Children', in *New Zealand Journal of History*, 39, no. 1 (2005), pp. 22–38

——, '"The Best PM for the Empire in War?" Lady Helen Munro Ferguson and the Australian Red Cross Society, 1914–1920', in *Australian Historical Studies*, 33, no. 119 (2002), pp. 108–24

——, 'The "Imperial Girl": Lady Helen Munro Ferguson, the Imperial Woman and her Imperial Childhood', in *Journal of Australian Studies*, 34, no. 4 (December 2010), pp. 519–20

O'Toole, Fintan, *A Traitor's Kiss: The Life of Richard Brinsley Sheridan* (1997)

Otte, T. G., *The Foreign Office Mind: The Making of British Foreign Policy 1865–1914* (2011)

Otway, Sir Arthur (ed.), *The Autobiography and Journals of Admiral Lord Clarence Paget* (1896)

Pakenham, Thomas, *Scramble for Africa* (1991)

Parker, C. S., *The Life and Letters of Sir James Graham* (1907)

Parry, Jonathan, *Democracy and Religion* (1986)

——, *The Rise and Fall of Liberal Government in Victorian Britain* (1993)

Patterson, Henry, *Class Conflict and Sectarianism* (1980)

Pears, Sir Edwin, *Forty Years in Constantinople* (1916)

Ponsonby, Arthur, *Henry Ponsonby, Queen Victoria's Private Secretary: His Life from His Letters* (1943)

Pope-Hennessy, James, *Richard Monckton Milnes: The Years of Promise* (1949)

——, *The Flight of Youth* (1951)

Porter, Andrew (ed.), *The Oxford History of the British Empire: The Nineteenth Century* (1999)

Porter, Bernard, *The Absent-Minded Imperialists* (2004)

Rae, William Fraser, *Sheridan* (1896)

Ramm, Agatha (ed.), *The Political Correspondence of Mr Gladstone and Lord Granville, 1876–86* (1962)

Redmond, Gerald, 'Viceregal Patronage: The Governor Generals of Canada and Sport in the Dominion, 1867–1909', in J. A. Mangan (ed.), *The Cultural Bond: Sport, Empire and Society* (2011), pp. 154–77

Reid, Donald Malcolm, 'The 'Urabi Revolution and British Conquest', in M. Daly (ed.), *The Cambridge History of Egypt* (1998), vol. 2, pp. 219–22

Reeves, Henry (ed.), *Charles Greville: Memoirs* (1874)

Ricks, Christopher, *Tennyson* (1972)

Ridley, Jane, *Bertie: A Life of Edward VII* (2012)

Ridley, Jasper, *Palmerston* (1972)

Rivett-Carnac, J. H., *Many Memories* (1910)

Roberts, Andrew, *Salisbury* (1999)

Roberts, Field-Marshal Lord, *Forty-one Years in India* (1901 ed.)

Robinson, Ronald and Gallagher, John with Denny, Alice, *Africa and the Victorians: The Official Mind of Imperialism* (1961)

Rodd, R., *Memories* (1925)

Rogan, Eugene, *The Arabs: A History* (2009)

Rose, Kenneth, *Curzon: A Most Superior Person* (1969)

Rossmore, Lord, *Things I Can Tell* (1912)

Saab, Ann P., *Reluctant Icon: Gladstone, Bulgaria and the Working Classes* (1991)

Schoenberger, Nancy, *Dangerous Muse: A Life of Caroline Blackwood* (2001)

Schull, Joseph, *Edward Blake: The Man of the Other Way* (Toronto 1975)

Scott, Sir Walter, *Waverley* (1814)

Shannon, Richard, *Gladstone*, (1982; 1999)

St Aubyn, Giles, *Queen Victoria* (1991)

St Helier, Lady, *Memories of Fifty Years* (1909)

Stamp, Gavin, 'Helen's Tower', in Peter Rankin (ed.), *Clandeboye* (Ulster Architectural Heritage Society, 1985), pp. 29–33

Stanford, W. B. and McDowell, R. B., *Mahaffy* (1971)

Stewart, A. T. Q., *The Pagoda War* (1972)

Stewart, George, *Canada Under the Administration of the Earl of Dufferin* (1878)

Stockmar, Baron E. C. A., *Memoirs of Baron Stockmar* (1872)

Strong, Roy, *Diaries 1967–1987* (1997)

Sykes, P., *Sir Mortimer Durand* (1926)

Taylor, A. J. P., *The Struggle for Mastery in Europe* (1954)

Tennyson, Lord Alfred, *Idylls of the King* (1872)

Thompson, Andrew, *The Empire Strikes Back* (2005)

Thomson, Dale C., *Alexander Mackenzie: Clear Grit* (1960)

Trollope, Anthony, *Phineas Finn* (1869)

Tupper, Sir Charles, *Recollections of 60 Years* (1914)

Vane, Jonathan F. W., *A History of Canadian Culture* (2009)

Vasili, Count Paul, *The World of London* (1885)

Vaughan, W. E., *Landlords and Tenants in Ireland, 1848–1904* (Dublin 1984)

—— (ed.), *Ireland Under the Union* (1989)

Waite, P. B., *Macdonald: His Life and World* (1975)

Walder, D., *Nelson* (1978)

Walker, B. M., *Ulster Politics: The Formative Years 1868–86* (1989)

Wallace, Donald Mackenzie, *Egypt and the Egyptian Question* (1883)

——, *The Vice-royalty of the Marquess of Dufferin and Ava: A Brief Account of Lord Dufferin's Indian Administration* (Calcutta, 1888)

—— (ed.), *Speeches Delivered in India by the Marquess of Dufferin and Ava* (1890)

Walling, R. A. J. (ed.), *The Diaries of John Bright* (1930)

Wells, H. G., *The New Machiavelli* (1912)

West, Sir A., *Recollections* (1899)

Whibley, Charles, *Lord John Manners and his Friends* (1925)

Wiebe, M. G. (ed.), *Letters of Benjamin Disraeli* (1987)

Williamson, H. Spencer, *Thirty Five Years* (1933)

Wilson, A. N., *The Victorians* (2002)

Winter, James, *Robert Lowe* (Toronto, 1976)

Woodham-Smith, Cecil, *Florence Nightingale* (1950)

Woodruff, Philip, *The Men Who Ruled India* (1963)

Wurgaft, Lewis, *The Imperial Imagination* (1983)

Zachs, Fruma, ' "Novice" or "Heaven-born Diplomat"? Lord Dufferin's plan for a "Province of Syria": Beirut 1860–61', *Middle Eastern Studies*, vol. 36, no. 3 (July 2000), pp. 160–76

Zetland, Marquis of (ed.), *Letters of Disraeli to Lady Bradford and Lady Chesterfield* (1929)

Ziegler, Philip, *Melbourne* (1976)

Unpublished Works

Bowe, Patrick, 'James Fraser and Clandeboye', unpublished paper, Helen's Tower Library

Harrison, Andrew, 'The First Marquess of Dufferin and Ava: Whig, Ulster Landlord and Imperialist', PhD thesis, New University of Ulster, 1983

Lang, S. E., 'Maternal Mortality and the State in British India, 1840–1920', PhD thesis, Anglia Ruskin University, 2007

McLeish, Val, 'Imperial Footprints: Lady Aberdeen and Lady Dufferin in Ireland, Canada, and India, 1871–1914', PhD thesis, University of London, 2002

Witchell, John, 'Clandeboye – the fulfillment of a vision: the Irish estate that slept for a hundred years', unpublished paper, Helen's Tower Library

Contemporary Newspapers and Magazines

Anglo-American Annual, The
Bath Chronicle and Weekly Gazette
Belfast Newsletter
Critic, The
Daily Graphic, The
Daily News
Daily Telegraph
Downpatrick Recorder
Economist, The
Edinburgh Review
Evening News
Figaro, Le
Globe, The
Illustrated London News, The
Liverpool Daily Post
Morning Post
Nineteenth Century
Observer, The
Pall Mall Gazette
Petit Journal, Le
Punch
St James Gazette
Saturday Review, The
Spectator, The
Standard, The
Strand Magazine, The
Times, The
Vanity Fair: Foreign Office, Diplomatic, and Consular Sketches (1883)
Weekly Dispatch
World, The

Index

NOTE: Titles and ranks are generally the highest mentioned in the text. FD refers to Frederick, 1st Marquess of Dufferin and Ava.

Dufferin and Ava, 1st Marquess of *(cont'd)*
185–93; recommends amnesty for 'Urabi, 186;
appointed GCB, 195; appointed Viceroy of
India, 195, 197, 199–200; arrival in India,
200–1; and colonial policy, 200; dispute with
Griffin, 207; role and management in India,
207–11; delegates duties in India, 209, 292;
supposed indolence, 209, 292; and Afghan
War, 217–18; negotiates with Amir of
Afghanistan, 218–22; relations with Randolph
Churchill, 223–5, 231–2; doubts on
annexation of Burma, 227–30; and British
victory in Burma, 230; defence policy on
North-West Frontier, 231–2; disbelieves
Russian intent to invade India, 231; visits
Burma, 233–5; demands end to executions in
Burma, 237; and controversy over administration of Burma, 238–9; accepts honour for
achievements in Burma, 241; effect of Burma
campaign on, 241; hostility to Moylan, 241;
progresses and travels in India, 242, 257–9; life
and house in Simla, 243–5; social relations
and sports in India, 246–7; separation from
Hariot in India, 250; fondness for children,
251–3; affection for daughter Nelly, 252–5;
operation on hands, 252; marriage relations,
253, 319; gives poems to Kipling, 256; courts
Indian princes, 260; and Indian social
differences, 261–2; racial/social attitudes,
262–3; and reform in India, 264; praises
Hariot's work in India, 271; raises taxes in
India, 274; attitude to Indian nationalist
movement, 276–86, 289, 296; retires as
Viceroy, 281, 290–1, 297; elevated to
marquessate, 284; posted to Rome as
Ambassador, 284–5, 290, 301; portrayed by
Kipling, 288–9; achievements and disappoint-
ments in India, 289–98; vanity and love of
ceremony, 261, 292; demands of social round
in India, 294; greets Lansdowne as new
Viceroy, 297; leaves India, 297–8; activities in
Italy, 302; buys pictures, 302; resumes sailing,
302–3; Boehm bust of, 303; appointed
Warden of Cinque Ports, 304; as Ambassador
to Paris, 305–11, 314; elected Rector of St
Andrews University, 305; life and entertainments in Paris, 307–8; recounts personal
gothic experience, 307–8; French hostility to,
308–9, 313; on changes in diplomatic world,
311–12; despatch denouncing French press,
313; physical decline and deafness, 314, 333,

342–3; rumoured paternity, 316–17;
denounces Percy Fitzgerald's *Lives of the
Sheridans*, 317; reclaims Sheridans' history and
reputation, 319–23, 325; and daughter Nelly's
marriage, 327–8; careers and fortunes of
children, 328–9; grandchildren, 328;
retirement pension and City earnings, 329–31;
celebrity and honours in Ireland, 332–4;
embraces Ulster Unionism, 332; and London
and Globe crash, 335–9, 341; and son Archie's
death, 335; financial losses, 340–1; installed as
Lord Rector of Edinburgh University, 343;
stomach cancer and death, 343–4; biographies
and posthumous reputation, 345; literary
qualities, 346–7; sense of insecurity, 350;
sociability and kindliness, 351, 353; burial, 354
Dufferin and Ava, Hariot, Marchioness of *(née
Hamilton; 'Lal')*: FD courts and marries,
94–7; children and pregnancies, 100, 102–3,
140; social life, 100–1; marriage relations,
101–2, 253, 319; depression, 102–3, 107; on
FD's influence on Gladstone, 107; journal in
Canada, 121; regard for Sir John Macdonald,
127; witnesses Macdonald's defiance in
Canadian parliament, 131–2; deputises for FD
in Canadian west, 135; social role in Canada,
137–41; on Canadian lack of identity, 143; on
Queen's birthday celebrations in Montreal,
146; on Canadian biographies of FD, 150;
with FD in Russia, 155–6; life in Constantinople, 169; theatricals, 182; arrival in India,
201; on FD's work load in India, 208; and
ceremony in India, 212; on FD's ultimatum
to Thibaw, 229; in Burma, 234–5; life in
Simla, 243–5; and social life in India, 245,
248–9, 264, 265–7; fondness for Beresford,
247; style, 248–9; family in India, 249–51;
relations with daughter Nelly, 252;
disapproves of banter, 253; attitude to Trix
Kipling, 255; scorn for Kipling, 256; in
Hyderabad, 258; on India as Scott country,
259–60; on FD's dressing up, 261; photography, 266–7; learns Hindustani, 267; and
welfare of women in India, 267–73;
fundraising capabilities, 268–9; writings, 273;
suffers from Indian climate, 290; success of
hospitals in India, 295; leaves Rome for
London, 301; Margot Tennant excludes from
parties, 304; at Paris Embassy, 306; FD
returns present of *The Decameron*, 313;
portrait, 323; on death of son Archie in Boer